Software Development Patterns and Antipatterns

Software Development Patterns and Antipatterns

Capers Jones

CRC Press
Taylor & Francis Group
Boca Raton London New York

CRC Press is an imprint of the
Taylor & Francis Group, an **informa** business

AN AUERBACH BOOK

First edition published 2022
by CRC Press
6000 Broken Sound Parkway NW, Suite 300, Boca Raton, FL 33487-2742

and by CRC Press
2 Park Square, Milton Park, Abingdon, Oxon, OX14 4RN

ISBN: 978-1-032-02912-2 (hbk)
ISBN: 978-1-032-01722-8 (pbk)
ISBN: 978-1-003-19312-8 (ebk)

DOI: 10.1201/9781003193128

Typeset in Garamond
by SPi Technologies India Pvt Ltd (Straive)

Contents

Appreciation and Acknowledgments

This is my 22nd book. As always thanks to my wife Eileen for supporting my book writing over many years.

This book is dedicated to Watts Humphrey who was a pioneer in software quality control and effective development patterns. Watts worked at IBM and then helped create the software assessment program and the capability maturity model (CMMI) for the Software Engineering Institute (SEI). Watts was an industry leader in moving organizations from harmful patterns to effective patterns.

Thanks also to the faculty of the University of Florida and to my colleagues at IBM.

Preface

This book is divided into two sections. The first section discusses harmful patterns and practices that tend to cause schedule delays, cost overruns, and poor quality. The observations and data about these harmful patterns came from consulting studies and benchmarks carried out for clients of Namcook Analytics LLC who wanted to improve their software development practices and patterns.

The second section of the book shows optimal patterns that have proven to be successful for large systems. The successful patterns originated in companies and organizations that build large mission-critical software systems such as IBM, AT&T, ITT, Nippon Electric, NASA, and the Internal Revenue Service (IRS).

Software has been a troubling topic since it first started. There are seven chronic problems that have plagued software from the beginning:

1. Incomplete and ambiguous user requirements that grow by >2% per month.
2. Major cost and schedule overruns for large applications >35% higher than planned.
3. Low defect removal efficiency (DRE) <85% on large systems.
4. Cancelled projects that are not completed: >30% above 10,000 function points.
5. Poor quality and low reliability after the software is delivered: >5 bugs per FP.
6. Breach of contract litigation against software outsource vendors.
7. Expensive maintenance and enhancement costs after delivery.

These are endemic problems for software executives, software engineers, and software customers but they are not insurmountable. There are technical solutions for all seven. The solutions involve moving from harmful patterns of software development to effective patterns of software development.

Harmful patterns include carelessness in gathering requirements, failure to use design and code inspections for critical features, and failure to monitor progress against accumulated costs.

The first beneficial pattern is to match the features of new applications against libraries of existing software applications to ensure that all needed requirements will be included.

The second beneficial pattern is to select the optimum kinds of tools, methodologies, and programming languages for the new application to ensure optimal development.

The third beneficial pattern is to identify and select as many standard reusable components as possible. Custom manual software development is intrinsically slow and error prone, and using standard reusable components provides the best overall results.

The fourth beneficial pattern is to measure defect removal efficiency (DRE) and use methods such as static analysis and inspections that can increase DRE above 99%.

The fifth beneficial pattern is to carefully monitor progress and accumulated costs during development to ensure that the project will in fact be delivered on time and within budget. The measures will include function points completed to date, function points remaining, and growth of function points due to new requirements added during development.

Early and accurate measurements of accumulated costs and progress against planned checkpoints can eliminate the expensive cancellations of large applications before they are completed. It is interesting that the average accumulated cost at the day of cancellation is usually 20% higher than the budgeted cost for the entire application. Cancelled projects have zero value and cause CEOs to regard software teams as incompetent and undependable.

Biography

Capers Jones held both managerial and research positions at IBM. He managed a software quality assurance team at IBM in San Jose, California. As a software researcher, he designed IBM's first software cost-estimating tool in 1973 with Dr. Charles Turk. He received an IBM outstanding contribution award for improving quality of several IBM products. He has represented IBM as a speaker at major external software conferences. He has frequent contact with key IBM clients discussing on the topics of software quality, productivity and quality measurement, and software process improvement.

Capers Jones is currently VP and CTO of Namcook Analytics, LLC which is a leading vendor for developing software estimation tools. Namcook Analytics is also an international software consulting company with clients in 27 countries. He has also been a keynote speaker at major software conferences in the United States, Canada, Europe, South Korea, Singapore, Malaysia, and Japan. He was named software engineering advisor to governments of South Korea and Malaysia in 2011. Prior to founding Namcook Analytics, Capers Jones was Assistant Director of Software Engineering at the ITT Technology Center in Stratford, CT. He was tasked with helping to introduce state-of-the-art tools and methods to the 75 major companies owned by ITT that produced software. Some of the ITT companies included Hartford Insurance, Sheraton Hotels, Johnson Controls, Continental Baking, and more than 25 telecommunication companies in the United States and abroad.

WORST-CASE PATTERNS OF SOFTWARE DEVELOPMENT

This section of the book examines common software development problems that have been observed in many companies and government agencies. The data comes from consulting studies, breach of contract lawsuits, and the literature on major software failures.

It is an unfortunate fact of life that harmful development patterns are still more common than optimal development patterns. Even today a majority of large software applications run late, exceed their planned budgets, and have quality problems after release. Look at the reviews of Microsoft Windows updates to see how troublesome large systems are.

This section considers the factors involved with cost overruns, schedule delays, canceled projects, poor quality, and expensive maintenance after deployment.

DOI: 10.1201/9781003193128-1

Chapter 1

Challenges of Software Project Management

Project management in every industry is a challenging occupation. But the challenges and hazards of software project management are greater than those of most other industries. This fact is proven by the large number of software project cancellations and the high frequency of software project cost and schedule overruns. Software projects run late and exceed their budgets more than any other modern industry except for defense projects.

Academic training for software project managers is still not very good even today. Some technology companies have recognized the challenges of software project management and created effective in-house training for new software project managers. These companies with effective software project management training include IBM and a number of telecom companies such as AT&T, ITT, Motorola, Siemens, and GTE. Some other technology companies such as Google, Microsoft, and Apple also have effective software project management training. Many of the companies with good software management training build complex physical devices run by software. Most are also more than 75 years old and have had software measurement programs for more than 50 years.

A few companies even offer market effective software project management training. One of these is a subsidiary of Computer Aid Inc. called the Information Technology Metrics and Productivity Institute (ITMPI). The non-profit Project Management Institute (PMI) also offers effective training for software project managers.

Several years ago, a survey of engineering technology company CEOs (computers, Telecom, electronics, medical devices, autos, and aircraft) found that they regarded their software organizations as the least professional of any of the corporate engineering organizations. This was due to the fact that software projects had higher cancellation rates, longer schedule delays, and higher cost overruns than any of the other engineering organizations.

Lyman Hamilton, a former Chairman of the ITT Corporation, gave an internal speech to ITT executives in which he mentioned that newly hired software engineers just out of college needed about 3 years of internal training before being entrusted with critical projects. Other kinds of engineers such as mechanical and electrical engineers only needed about 12 months of internal training.

Hamilton was troubled by several major software failures of projects that were terminated without being completed. He was also troubled by the dissatisfaction expressed by customers in the quality of the software the corporation produced. He was further dissatisfied by the inability of internal software executives to explain why the problems occurred and what might be done to eliminate them.

It is interesting that the failing projects were all large systems in the 10,000 function point size range. Failures in this range are common, and managerial problems are usually a key factor.

Problems, failures, and litigation are directly proportional to the overall size of software applications measured using function point metrics. Table 1.1 shows the approximate distribution of software project results circa 2020.

As can be seen from Table 1.1, large software projects are distressingly troublesome and have frequent total failures, also a high risk of litigation. Poor project management is a key contributing factor.

Some leading companies have recognized the difficulty of successful software project management and taken active steps to improve the situation. Some of these companies include IBM, AT&T, ITT, Motorola, GTE, and Siemens. Google, Apple, and Microsoft have also attempted to improve software management although Microsoft has perhaps been too rigid in some management topics such as employee appraisals.

The companies that are most proactive in software project management tend to build complex engineered products such as computers, medical devices, aircraft controls, and switching systems that depend upon software to operate. The companies also tend to be mature companies founded over 75 years ago and having effective software measurement programs that are more than 40 years old. Most were early adapters of function point metrics and also early adapters of parametric software estimation tools.

Table 1.1 Normal Software Results Based on Application Size Circa 2020

Note: Costs Are Based on $10,000 per Month

Size in Function Points	Schedule in Calendar Months	Total Staffing	Productivity in Function Points per Staff Month	Cost in U.S. Dollars	Odds of Project Failure	Odds of Outsource Litigation
1	0.02	1	50.00	$200	0.10%	0.00%
10	0.40	1	25.00	$4,000	1.00%	0.01%
100	3.50	2	14.29	$70,000	2.50%	0.25%
1,000	15.00	6	11.11	$900,000	11.00%	1.20%
10,000	35.00	50	5.71	$17,500,000	31.00%	7.50%
100,000	60.00	575	2.90	$345,000,000	47.50%	23.00%

The software benchmarks studies carried out by Namcook Analytics LLC often show a significant number of serious software project management problems and issues. Table 1.2 summarizes 41 problems noted in a benchmark study for a Fortune 500 technology corporation.

Fifteen of the 41 problems or about 36.5% were software project management problems. This distribution is not uncommon.

The author of this book has been an expert witness in litigation for software projects that either failed without being delivered or operated so poorly after delivery that the clients sued the vendors. It is interesting that project management problems were key factors in every lawsuit. Inaccurate estimation, poor tracking of progress, and poor quality control are endemic problems of the software industry and far too common even in 2020. These problems have been part of every breach of contract case where the author of this book worked as an expert witness.

Table 1.2 Corporate Software Risk Factors Found by a Corporate Benchmark Study

1	Project management: no formal training for new managers
2	Project management: no annual benchmark studies
3	Project management: no annual training in state of the art methods
4	Project management: no training in software cost estimating
5	Project management: no training in software quality estimating
6	Project management: no training in software risk analysis
7	Project management: no training in cyber-attack deterrence
8	Project management: no training in function point metrics
9	Project management: no training in schedule planning
10	Project management: lack of accurate productivity measurements
11	Project management: lack of accurate quality metrics
12	Project management: incomplete milestone and progress tracking
13	Project management: historical data "leaks" by over 50%
14	Project management: managers continue to use inaccurate manual estimates
15	Project management: no widespread use of accurate parametric estimation
16	Quality control: no use of requirements models or QFD
17	Quality control: no use of automated proofs for critical features

Table 1.2 (Continued)

18	Quality control: no use of cyber-attack inspections
19	Quality control: no use of formal design inspections
20	Quality control: no use of formal code inspections
21	Quality control: no use of static analysis tools
22	Quality control: no use of mathematical test case design (cause-effect graphs)
23	Quality control: no use of test coverage tools
24	Quality control: defect potentials about 4.75 bugs per function point
25	Quality control: defect removal efficiency (DRE) below 90.00%
26	Maintenance: no use of complexity analysis or cyclomatic complexity
27	Maintenance: no use of renovation tools or work benches
28	Maintenance: no use of code restructuring tools
29	Maintenance: inconsistent use of defect tracking tools
30	Maintenance: no use of inspections on enhancements
31	No reuse program: requirements
32	No reuse program: design
33	No formal reuse program: source code
34	No reuse program: test materials
35	No reuse program: documentation
36	No reuse program: project plans
37	No formal corporate reuse library
38	No corporate contracts with third party reuse companies
39	Office space: small open offices; high noise levels, many interruptions
40	Insufficient meeting/breakout space for team meetings; no large meetings
41	Inadequate corporate responses to 2020 COVID virus

Improving Software Project Management Tools and Training

From consulting and benchmark studies carried out among top-tier technology corporations, they all have taken effective steps to improve and professionalize software project management. Some of these include at least 11 steps (Table 1.3).

Table 1.3 Eleven Steps to Effective Software Project Management

1	Formal internal training for new project managers (10 days)
2	Annual training for project managers and technical staff (5 days)
3	Guest lectures from top software professionals (3 days)
4	Acquisition and use of parametric estimation tools
5	Acquisition and use of effective progress and milestone tracking tools
6	Use of formal project offices for applications >5,000 function points
7	Use of and measurement of effective quality control methods
8	Elimination of bad software metrics and adoption of effective metrics
9	Commissioning annual software benchmark studies
10	Formal "best practice" analysis of tools, methods, reuse, and quality
11	Effective use of Zoom and remote work in response to COVID virus

Let us now consider each of these 11 steps in sequence.

Initial Education for New Project Managers

In many technology companies, project managers are often selected from the ranks of technical software engineering personnel. If this is so, they usually had close to zero management training at the university level. IBM recognized this as a problem back in the 1950s and introduced an effective training program for newly hired or newly appointed project managers.

This training is given to all project managers, but this report only covers software training topics. Since new project management training lasts for 10 days, there were 10 topics covered (Table 1.4).

Eight of the 10 topics are technical and deal with actual project issues such as cyber-attacks and risks. Two of the 10 topics deal with human resources and appraisals, which are of course a critical part of any manager's job.

Microsoft has received criticism for their appraisal system, which uses mathematical curves and requires that only a certain percentage of employees can be appraised as "excellent." The problem with this is that technology companies such as Microsoft tend to have more excellent employees than ordinary companies do, so this curve tended to cause voluntary attrition among capable employees who ended up on the wrong side of the "excellent" barrier.

Table 1.4   New Software Project Manager Curriculum

	Project Management Courses	Days	Value
1	Software milestone tracking	1	10
2	Sizing key software deliverables	1	10
3	Software project planning	1	10
4	Cyber-attack defenses	1	10
5	Software risk management	1	10
6	Software cost estimating: automated	1	10
7	Measurement and metrics of software	1	10
8	Software quality and defect estimating	1	10
9	Human resource policies	1	9
10	Appraisals and employee relations	1	9

Continuing Education for Software Project Managers

A study of software education methods carried out by Namcook Analytics LLC found that in-house education in major companies such as IBM and AT&T was superior to academic or university training for software project managers.

IBM and AT&T both employed more than 100 education personnel. These educators taught in-house courses to software and other personnel, and also taught customer courses to clients. The education groups operated initially as cost centers with no charges for in-house or customer training. More recently, they have tended to switch to profit-center operations and do charge for training, at least for some customer training.

Quite a few technology companies have at least 10 days of training for new managers and about a week of training each year for both managers and technical staff. When Capers Jones was a new manager at IBM, he took this 10-day training series and later taught some of the IBM project management courses on estimation, measurements, quality control, and software risk analysis.

Table 1.5 shows the rankings of 15 channels of software project management education in order of effectiveness.

A composite software project management curriculum derived from technology companies such as IBM, AT&T, ITT, Microsoft, and Apple is shown in Table 1.6.

Table 1.5 Ranking Software Management Education Channels

1	In-house education in technology companies
2	Commercial education by professional educators
3	University education – graduate
4	University education – undergraduate
5	In-house education in non-technology companies
6	Mentoring by experienced managers
7	On-the-job training
8	Non-profit education (IEEE, PMI, IFPUG, etc.)
9	Vendor education (management tools)
10	Self-study from work books
11	Self-study from CD-ROMs or DVDs
12	Live conferences with seminars and tutorials
13	On-line education via the Internet and World Wide Web
14	Project management books
15	Project management journals

Needless to say this curriculum would be spread over a multi-year period. It is merely a combination of the kinds of software project management courses available in modern technology companies.

Guest Lectures from Visiting Experts (Remotely via Zoom or Other Tools)

Over and above software classroom training, some technology companies have occasional internal seminars for all personnel which feature industry experts and famous software researchers. IBM, AT&T, and ITT had large seminars twice a year. One seminar was open only to employees and discussed some proprietary or confidential information such as new products and market expansion. The second large seminar was intended to demonstrate technical excellence to clients and customers, who were also invited to participate.

Among the well-known experts invited to companies such as AT&T, IBM, Siemens, and ITT were Al Albrecht (inventor of function points), Dr. Barry Boehm (inventor of COCOMO), Dr. Fred Brooks (author of *The Mythical Man-Month*), Watts Humphrey (creator of the SEI CMMI),

Table 1.6   Software Project Management Curriculum

	Project Management Courses	*Days*	*Value*
1	Software milestone tracking	1.00	10.00
2	Early sizing before requirements	1.00	10.00
3	Sizing key deliverables	1.00	10.00
4	Controlling creeping requirements	1.00	10.00
5	Software project planning	2.00	10.00
6	Cyber-attack defenses	2.00	10.00
7	Cyber-attack recovery	1.00	10.00
8	Software outsourcing pros and cons	1.00	10.00
9	Optimizing multi-country teams	1.00	10.00
10	Best practices in project management	1.00	10.00
11	Software risk management	1.00	10.00
12	Software cost estimating: automated	2.00	10.00
13	Software high-security architecture	1.00	10.00
14	Benchmark sources: ISBSG, Namcook, etc.	1.00	10.00
15	Measurement and metrics of software	2.00	10.00
16	Software quality and defect estimating	1.00	10.00
17	Software defect tracking	1.00	9.75
18	Software benchmark overview	1.00	9.75
19	Function point analysis: high speed	1.00	9.75
20	Human resource policies	1.00	9.60
21	Software change control	1.00	9.50
22	Principles of software reuse	1.00	9.40
23	Appraisals and employee relations	1.00	9.00
24	Software cost tracking	1.00	9.00
25	Software maintenance & enhancement	1.00	9.00
26	Methodologies: agile, RUP, TSP, others	1.00	9.00
27	The capability maturity model (CMMI)	2.00	9.00
28	Overview of management tools	1.00	9.00
29	Testing for project managers	2.00	8.75

(Continued)

Table 1.6   (Continued)

	Project Management Courses	Days	Value
30	Static analysis for project managers	0.50	8.75
31	Inspections for project managers	0.50	8.75
32	Project management body of knowledge	1.50	8.70
33	Software metrics for project managers	1.00	8.50
34	Software cost estimating: manual	1.00	8.00
35	Tools: cost accounting	1.00	8.00
36	Tools: project management	1.00	8.00
37	Tools: human resources	1.00	8.00
38	Tools: cost and quality estimation	1.00	8.00
39	Function points for project managers	0.50	8.00
40	ISO Standards for functional measures	1.00	8.00
41	Principles of agile for managers	1.00	7.75
42	Principles of RUP for managers	1.00	7.75
43	Principles of TSP/PSP for managers	1.00	7.75
44	Principles of DevOps for managers	1.00	7.75
45	Principles of containers for managers	1.00	7.75
46	Earned value measurement (EVM)	1.00	6.75
47	Principles of balanced scorecards	1.00	6.50
48	Six-Sigma for project managers	2.00	6.00
49	Six-Sigma: green belt	3.00	6.00
50	Six-Sigma: black belt	3.00	6.00
Total		60.00	8.82

Dr. Larry Putnam (inventor of SLIM), Dr. Jerry Weinberg (author of The Psychology of Computer Programming), Bill Gates of Microsoft, Donald Knuth (pioneer of computer algorithms), Admiral Grace Hopper of the Navy (inventor of COBOL), Ken Thompson (co-developer of UNIX), Linus Torvalds (developer of Linux), and many more.

Usually these events lasted for about half a day of technical topics, and then had either a lunch or a reception for the guests based on whether it was a morning event or an afternoon event. At the reception or lunch, the audience could meet and chat informally with the visiting experts.

Because the guest experts were world famous, these corporate seminars were attended by top software executives as well as software engineers and technical staff. This was a good method for bringing together all levels of a company to focus on critical software issues.

Having attended a number of these, they were usually very enjoyable and it was good to meet famous software researchers such as Admiral Grace Hopper face to face.

Needless to say this kind of event usually takes place in fairly large companies since they are expensive. However these seminars were also valuable and benefitted both the executives and technical staffs of IBM, ITT, AT&T, Microsoft, and other companies that have them.

Acquisition and Use of Software Parametric Estimation Tools

IBM discovered in the early 1970s that manual software cost estimates became increasingly optimistic and inaccurate as the application size increased from below 100 function points to more than 10,000 function points. Since applications grew rapidly in this era, IBM commissioned Capers Jones and Dr. Charles Turk to build its first parametric estimation tool in 1973. ITT did the same in 1979 and AT&T commissioned a custom parametric estimation tool for its electronic switching systems in 1983.

The technology and telecom sectors have been pioneers in the development and usage of parametric estimation tools.

Software has achieved a bad reputation as a troubling technology. Large software projects have tended to have a very high frequency of schedule over-runs, cost overruns, quality problems, and outright cancellations of large systems. While this bad reputation is often deserved, it is important to note that some large software projects are finished on time, stay within their budgets, and operate successfully when deployed.

The successful software projects differ in many respects from the failures and disasters. One important difference is how the successful projects arrived at their schedule, cost, resource, and quality estimates in the first place.

It often happens that projects exceeding their planned schedules or cost estimates did not use state of the art methods for determining either their schedules or their costs. Although the project is cited for overruns, the root problem is inadequate planning and estimation.

From large-scale studies first published in *Software Engineering Best Practices* (Jones 2010) and *The Economics of Software Quality* (Jones & Bonsignour 2011) usage of automated parametric estimating tools, automated project scheduling tools, and automated defect and quality estimating tools (all of these are combined in some tools such as

Software Risk Master (SRM)) are strongly correlated with successful outcomes.

Conversely, software project failures tended to use casual and manual methods of arriving at initial estimates. Indeed, for many software failures, there was no formal estimation at all. Analyzing 15 breach of contract lawsuits for failure, delays, and poor quality witnessed all of the projects were larger than 10,000 function points and all used manual estimating methods.

The first software parametric cost estimation tools were created by researchers who were employed by large enterprises that built large and complex software systems: IBM, Hughes, RCA, TRW, and the U.S. Air Force were the organizations whose research led to the development of commercial parametric cost estimating tools.

Some of the estimating pioneers who developed the first parametric estimating tools include in alphabetical order: Dr. Barry Boehm (TRW), Frank Freiman (RCA), Dan Galorath (SEER), Capers Jones (IBM), Dr. Larry Putnam (Air Force), and Dr. Howard Rubin (academic-SUNY).

In 1973, the author of this book and his colleague Dr. Charles Turk at IBM San Jose built IBM's first automated parametric estimation tool for systems software. This tool was called the "Interactive Productivity and Quality" (IPQ) tool. This internal IBM tool was proprietary and not put on the commercial market since it gave IBM competitive advantages. This tool was developed at IBM's San Jose complex and soon had over 200 IBM users at over 20 locations around the world.

Today in 2021, most technology and telecom companies use parametric estimation tools. These are normally used by project offices or by special estimating teams that provide estimates as a service to specific projects.

Some of the major parametric estimation tools today include in alphabetical order:

1. Constructive Cost Model (COCOMO)
2. CostXpert
3. ExcelerPlan
4. KnowledgePlan
5. SEER
6. SLIM
7. Software Risk Master (SRM)
8. True Price

These commercial parametric estimation tools are widely used by technology companies, defense contractors, and other large corporations. They are fairly expensive of over $5,000 per seat for most.

However, there is also the constructive cost model (COCOMO) developed by Dr. Barry Boehm. This estimating tool is free. Because COCOMO is free, it is widely used by universities and small companies that cannot afford the more expensive commercial estimation tools, but COCOMO does not have wide usage among U.S. technology companies which need more detailed estimates provided by commercial parametric tools.

For example the major features of the Software Risk Master (SRM) commercial software estimation tool include:

- Sizing logic for specifications, source code, and test cases.
- Sizing logic for function points and lines of code (LOC).
- Sizing logic for story points and use-case points.
- Sizing logic for requirements creep during development and post release.
- Activity = level estimation for requirements, design, code, testing, etc.
- Sophisticated quality estimates that predict defects and DRE.
- Support for 60 development methods such as agile, containers, DevOps, TSP, spiral, etc.
- Support for development, user costs, and three years of maintenance.
- Support for IFPUG function point metrics.
- Support for the new SNAP point metric for non-functional requirements.
- Support for other function point metrics such as COSMIC, NESMA, FISMA, etc.
- Support for older lines of code (LOC) metrics (both physical and logical).
- Support for modern topics such as cyber-defenses and cyber-attack recovery.
- Support for proprietary metrics such as feature points and object points.
- Support for software reusability of various artifacts.
- Support for 84 modern languages such as Java, Ruby, mySQL, and others.
- Support for systems applications such as operating systems and telecom.
- Support for IT applications such as finance and insurance.
- Support for web-based applications.
- Support for cloud applications.
- Support for ERP deployment and customization.
- Support for including commercial off the shelf software (COTS).
- Support for software portfolio analysis.

SRM also supports many advanced functions:

- Quality and reliability estimation.
- Numbers of test cases needed and test coverage.
- Litigation costs for breach of contract.
- Cyber-attack costs and recovery costs.
- ERP deployment and modification.
- Portfolio sizing and annual portfolio maintenance.
- Risk and value analysis.
- Measurement modes for collecting historical data.
- Cost and time to complete estimates mixing historical data with projected data.
- Support for software process assessments.
- Support for results from the five levels of the SEI CMMI.
- Special estimates such as the odds and costs of outsource litigation.
- Special estimates such as venture funding for software startups.

Other commercial software parametric estimation tools have similar features. The U.S. Air Force used to perform annual trials of commercial parametric estimation tools. All of the major parametric tools were within about 10% of one another, and all were significantly more accurate than manual estimates for large projects above 1,000 function points in size. Manual estimates were often optimistic on cost and schedules by more than 50% above 1,000 function points. Parametric estimation tools are almost never optimistic and usually come within 10% of actual results.

Of course another industry problem is that most companies do not have accurate results. Among the author's clients, the average accuracy of software project historical data is only 37%. The most common "leaks" from project historical data include business analysts, project managers, software quality assurance, technical writers, project office personnel, configuration control, and integration specialists. Measuring only developers and test personnel such as "design, code, and unit test" or DCUT is common but fundamentally inaccurate and inadequate for economic or quality analysis.

One new problem for software estimation was the arrival of the corona virus in March of 2020. This virus led to closure of many software office locations and a switch to working from home using computers for status meetings and progress discussions. The virus will no doubt have a major negative impact on software productivity rates and probably a negative impact on software quality. However, as of late 2020, there were very little quantitative data available because many large projects started in 2020 were not finished so their productivity and quality can't be measured until 2021 or later.

Acquisition and Use of Progress and Milestone Tracking Tools

In addition to parametric estimation tools, there are also many commercial project management tools. The phrase "project management tools" has been applied to a large family of tools whose primary purpose is sophisticated scheduling for projects with hundreds or even thousands of overlapping and partially interdependent tasks and large teams in the hundreds. These tools are able to drop down to very detailed task levels and can even handle the schedules of individual workers. Microsoft Project and Artemis Views are two samples of project management tools. The new automated project office (APO) tool of Computer Aid is a modern project management tool only recently put on the market. There are also open-source project management and tracking tools such as JIRA.

However, the family of project management tools are for general purpose in nature and do not include specialized software sizing and estimating capabilities as do the software cost estimating tools. Neither do these general project management tools deal with quality issues such as DRE. Project management tools are useful, but software requires additional capabilities to be under full management control.

Project management tools are an automated form of several management aids developed by the Navy for controlling large and complex weapons systems: the "program evaluation and review technique" (PERT), critical path analysis, resource leveling, and the classic Gantt charts. Project management tools used for defense projects also support earned-value analysis (EVA) although this is seldom used in the civilian sectors.

Project management tools have no built-in expertise regarding software, as do software cost estimating tools. For example, if you wish to explore the quality and cost impact of an object-oriented programming language such as Objective C, a standard project management tool is not the right choice.

By contrast, many software cost estimating tools have built-in tables of programming languages and will automatically adjust the estimate based on which language is selected for the application. Project management tools and software cost estimating tools provide different but complementary functions. Most software cost estimating tools interface directly with common project management tools such as Microsoft Project.

Project Management Tools	Software Cost Estimating Tools
Work-breakdown structures	Sizing logic for function points, code, etc.
Activity-based cost analysis	Quality estimates

(Continued)

Project Management Tools	Software Cost Estimating Tools
Earned-value calculations	Integral risk estimates
Effort by staff members	Staffing predictions (testers, programmers, etc.)
Cost accumulation	Cost estimating

Both kinds of tools are useful for large and complex software projects and are generally used concurrently by project office personnel. An average software project using both parametric estimation tools and project management tools would be a significant project of over 1,000 function points in size. Small projects below 100 function points are often estimated informally and use only normal corporate cost accounting tools rather than sophisticated project management tools.

The Use of Formal Project Offices (PMOs) for Applications >1,000 Function Points

When software started, most applications were small and below 100 function points in size. During the late 1960s and early 1970s, software applications such as operating systems and telephone switching systems grew above 10,000 function points.

These larger applications had development teams that often topped 100 workers and they had over a dozen managers, including some 2nd and 3rd line managers.

Due to the poor training of most software managers in topics such as sizing, planning, estimating, and measurement, it soon became obvious that expert help was needed for these critical tasks.

The project office concept is much older than software and appeared in the late 1800s for manufacturing and even for agriculture and commodity training. Many industries used project offices before software became important in the 1950s. IBM was a pioneer in the creation and effective use of software project offices in the late 1960s.

There are a number of levels and kinds of project offices, but for this report, the main emphasis is on specific software projects that are fairly large and complex such as 10,000 function points in size.

For these large systems, the main roles played by the software project office are the following:

1. Identifying important standards for the project such as ISO or OMG standards.
2. Identifying important corporate standards such as the IBM standards for software quality.

3. Identifying and monitoring government mandates such as FAA, FDA, or Sarbanes-Oxley.
4. Early sizing of project deliverables using one or more parametric estimation tools.
5. Early prediction of schedules, costs, and staffing using one or more parametric estimation tools.
6. Early prediction of requirements creep.
7. Early prediction of defect potentials and DRE.
8. Establishing project cost and milestone tracking guidelines for all personnel.
9. Continuous monitoring of progress, accumulated costs, and schedule adherence.
10. Continuous monitoring of planned vs. actual DRE.

Project offices are a useful and valuable software structure. They usually contain from 3 to more than 10 people based on the size of the project being controlled. Among the kinds of personnel employed in software project, offices are estimating specialists, metric specialists such as certified function point counters, quality control specialists, and standards specialists.

Project offices usually have several parametric estimation tools available and also both general and specialized project tracking tools. Shown in Table 1.7 are samples of some of the kinds of tools and information that a project office might utilize in a technology company for a major software application

As can be seen, software project offices add knowledge and rigor to topics where ordinary project managers may not be fully trained or highly experienced.

Use and Measurement of Effective Quality Control Methods

The #1 cost driver for the software industry for more than 50 years has been "the cost of finding and fixing bugs." Since bug repairs are the top cost driver, it is impossible to have an accurate cost estimate without including quality costs. It is also impossible to have an accurate cost estimate, or to finish a project on time, unless it uses state of the art quality control methods.

The #1 reason for software schedule delays and cost overruns for more than 50 years has been excessive defects present when testing starts, which stretches out the planned test duration by over 100% and also raises planned development costs. Without excellent quality control, software projects will always run late, exceed their budgets, and be at risk of cancellation if excessive costs make the ROI a negative value.

Table 1.7 Tools for Software Projects

	Tasks	Tools Utilized
1	Architecture	QEMU
2	Automated test	HP QuickTest Professional
3	Benchmarks	ISBSG, Namcook SRM, Davids, Q/P Management
4	Coding	Eclipse, Slickedit
5	Configuration	Perforce
6	Cost estimate	Software Risk Master (SRM), SLIM, SEER, COCOMO
7	Cost tracking	Automated project office (APO), Microsoft Project
8	Cyclomatic	BattleMap
9	Debugging	GHS probe
10	Defect tracking	Bugzilla
11	Design	Projects Unlimited, Visio
12	Earned value	DelTek Cobra
13	ERP	Microsoft Dynamics
14	Function points 1	Software Risk Master (SRM)
15	Function points 2	Function point workbench
16	Function points 3	CAST automated function points
17	Graphics design	Visio
18	Inspections	SlickEdit
19	Integration	Apache Camel
20	ISO tools	ISOXpress
21	Maintenance	Mpulse
22	Manual test	DevTest
23	Milestone track	KIDASA Softare Milestone Professional
24	Progress track	Jira, Automated Project Office (APO)
25	Project mgt.	Automated project office (APO)
26	Quality estimate	Software Risk Master (SRM)
27	Requirements	Rational Doors
28	Risk analysis	Software Risk Master (SRM)
29	Source code size 1	Software Risk Master (SRM)
30	Source code size 2	Unified code counter (UCC)

Table 1.7 (Continued)

	Tasks	*Tools Utilized*
31	SQA	NASA Goddard ARM tool
32	Static analysis	OptimMyth Kiuwin, Coverity, Klocwork
33	Support	Zendesk
34	Test coverage	Software Verify suite
35	Test library	DevTest
36	Value analysis	Excel and Value Stream Tracking

ISO and Other Standards Used for Project	
IEEE 610.12-1990	Software engineering terminology
IEEE 730-1999	Software assurance
IEEE 12207	Software process tree
ISO/IEC 9001	Software quality
ISO/IEC 9003	Software quality
ISO/IEC 12207	Software engineering
ISO/IEC 25010	Software quality
ISO/IEC 29119	Software testing
ISO/IEC 27034	Software security
ISO/IEC 20926	Function point counting
OMG Corba	Common Object Request Broker Architecture
OMG Models	Meta models for software
OMG funct. pts.	Automated function points (legacy applications)
UNICODE	Globalization and internationalization

Professional Certifications Used on Project	
Certification used for project = 1	
Certification not used for project = 0	

(*Continued*)

Table 1.7 (Continued)

Professional Certifications Used on Project	
Note: Some team members have multiple certifications.	
Certification – Apple	0
Certification – Computer Aid Inc.	0
Certification – Computer Associates	0
Certification – FAA	0
Certification – FDA	0
Certification – Hewlett Packard	0
Certification – IBM	1
Certification – Microsoft	1
Certification – Oracle	0
Certification – PMI	1
Certification – QAI	0
Certification – Red Hat	0
Certification – RSBC	0
Certification – SAP	0
Certification – Sarbanes-Oxley	0
Certification – SEI	0
Certification – Sun	0
Certification – Symantec	0
Certification – TickIT	0
Certification of computing professionals	0
Certified configuration management specialist	1
Certified function point analyst	1
Certified project managers	1
Certified requirements engineers	0
Certified scrum master	1
Certified secure software lifecycle professional	0
Certified security engineer	0

Table 1.7   (Continued)

Professional Certifications Used on Project	
Certified SEI appraiser	1
Certified software architect	0
Certified software business analyst	1
Certified software development professional	0
Certified software engineers	0
Certified software quality assurance	1
Certified test managers	0
Certified testers	1
Certified webmaster	1
Certified software auditor	1
Total	13

It is alarming that in several lawsuits where Capers Jones has been an expert witness, depositions showed that project managers deliberately cut back on pre-test removal such as inspections and truncated testing early "in order to meet schedules." From the fact that the projects were late and over budget, cutting back on quality control raised costs and lengthened schedules, but the project managers did not know that this would happen.

Table 1.8 shows the 16 major cost drivers for software projects in 2021. The cost drivers highlighted in red are attributable to poor software quality.

Table 1.8 illustrates an important but poorly understood economic fact about the software industry. Four of the 16 major cost drivers can be attributed specifically to poor quality. The poor quality of software is a professional embarrassment and a major drag on the economy of the software industry and for that matter a drag on the entire U.S. and global economies.

Poor quality is also a key reason for cost driver #2. A common reason for cancelled software projects is because quality is so bad that schedule slippage and cost overruns turned the project return on investment (ROI) from positive to negative.

Note the alarming location of successful cyber-attacks is in 6th place (and rising) on the cost-driver list. Since security flaws are another form of poor quality, it is obvious that high quality is needed to deter successful cyber-attacks.

Table 1.8   U.S. Software Costs in Rank Order

1	The cost of finding and fixing bugs
2	The cost of cancelled projects
3	The cost of producing English words
4	The cost of programming or code development
5	The cost of requirements changes
6	The cost of successful cyber-attacks
7	The cost of customer support
8	The cost of meetings and communication
9	The cost of project management
10	The cost of renovation and migration
11	The cost of innovation and new kinds of software
12	The cost of litigation for failures and disasters
13	The cost of training and learning
14	The cost of avoiding security flaws
15	The cost of assembling reusable components
16	The cost of working from home due to the virus

Note: No one yet knows the exact cost estimation of the impact of corona virus on software projects. No doubt productivity will drop and quality may also, but it is premature without actual data.

Poor quality is also a key factor in cost driver #12 or litigation for breach of contract. The author of this book has worked as an expert witness in 15 lawsuits. Poor software quality is an endemic problem with breach of contract litigation. In one case against a major ERP company, the litigation was filed by the company's own shareholders who asserted that the ERP package quality was so bad that it was lowering stock values!

If you can't measure a problem, then you can't fix the problem either. Software quality has been essentially unmeasured and therefore unfixed for 50 years. A very useful quality metric developed by IBM around 1970 is that of "defect potentials."

Software defect potentials are the sum total of bugs found in requirements, architecture, design, code, and other sources of error. The approximate U.S. average for defect potentials is shown in Table 1.9 using IFPUG function points version 4.3.

Table 1.9 Average Software Defect Potentials circa 2020 for the United States

• Requirements	0.70 defects per function point
• Architecture	0.10 defects per function point
• Design	0.95 defects per function point
• Code	1.15 defects per function point
• Security code flaws	0.25 defects per function point
• Documents	0.45 defects per function point
• Bad fixes	0.65 defects per function point
Total	**4.25 defects per function point**

Note that the phrase "bad fix" refers to new bugs accidentally introduced in bug repairs for older bugs. The current U.S. average for bad-fix injections is about 7%, i.e. 7% of all bug repairs contain new bugs. For modules that are high in cyclomatic complexity and for "error prone modules," bad-fix injections can top 75%. For applications with low cyclomatic complexity, bad fixes can drop below 0.5%.

Defect potentials are of necessity, measured using function point metrics. The older "lines of code" metric cannot show requirements, architecture, and design defects not any other defect outside the code itself. As of today, function points were the most widely used software metric in the world. There are more benchmarks using function point metrics than all other metrics put together.

Successful and effective software quality control requires the following 15 technical factors:

1. Quality estimation before starting project using parametric estimation tools.
2. Accurate defect tracking from requirements through post-release maintenance.
3. Effective defect prevention such as requirements models and automated proofs.
4. Effective pre-test defect removal such as inspections and static analysis.
5. Effective mathematical test case design using cause-effect graphs or design of experiments.
6. Effective cyber-attack prevention methods such as security inspections.

7. Cyclomatic complexity analysis of all code modules in application.
8. Keeping cyclomatic complexity <10 for critical software modules.
9. Automated test coverage analysis for all forms of testing.
10. Achieving defect potentials below 3.00 per function point.
11. Achieving >95% test coverage.
12. Achieving >97% DRE for all applications.
13. Achieving >99% DRE for critical applications.
14. Achieving <1% bad-fix injection (bad fixes are bugs in bug repairs).
15. Reuse of certified materials that approach zero-defect status.

The bottom line is that poor software quality is the main weakness of the software industry. But poor software quality can be eliminated by better education for project managers and technical staff, and by using quality methods of proven effectiveness. The good news is that high quality is faster and cheaper than poor quality.

Elimination of Bad Metrics and Adoption of Effective Software Metrics

The software industry has the worst metrics and worst measurement practices of any industry in human history. It is one of very few industries that cannot measure its own quality and its own productivity. This is professionally embarrassing.

Some of the troubling and inaccurate metrics used by the software industry are the following:

Cost per defect metrics penalize quality and makes the buggiest software look cheapest. There are no ISO or other standards for calculating cost per defect. Cost per defect does not measure the economic value of software quality. The urban legend that it costs 100 times as much to fix post-release defects as early defects is not true and is based on ignoring fixed costs. Due to fixed costs of writing and running test cases, cost per defect rises steadily because fewer and fewer defects are found. This is caused by a standard rule of manufacturing economics: "*if a process has a high percentage of fixed costs and there is a reduction in the units produced, the cost per unit will go up.*" This explains why cost per defects seems to go up over time even though actual defect repair costs are flat and do not change very much. There are of course very troubling defects that are expensive and time consuming, but these are comparatively rare.

Defect density metrics measure the number of bugs released to clients. There are no ISO or other standards for calculating defect density. One method counts only code defects released. A more complete method used by the author of this book includes bugs originating in requirements, architecture, design, and documents as well as code defects. The author's method also includes "bad fixes" or bugs in defect repairs themselves. About 7% of bug repairs contain new bugs. There is more than 500% variation between counting only released code bugs and counting bugs from all sources. For example requirements defects comprise about 20% of released software problem reports.

Lines of code (LOC) metrics penalize high-level languages and make low-level languages look better than they are. LOC metrics also make requirements and design invisible. There are no ISO or other standards for counting LOC metrics. About half of the papers and journal articles use physical LOC and half use logical LOC. The difference between counts of physical and logical LOC can top 500%. The overall variability of LOC metrics has reached an astounding 2,200% as measured by Joe Schofield, the former president of IFPUG! LOC metrics make requirements and design invisible and also ignore requirements and design defects, which outnumber code defects. Although there are benchmarks based on LOC, the intrinsic errors of LOC metrics make them unreliable. Due to lack of standards for counting LOC, benchmarks from different vendors for the same applications can contain widely different results. Appendix B provides a mathematical proof that LOC metrics do not measure economic productivity by showing 79 programming languages with function points and LOC in a side-by-side format.

SNAP point metrics are a new variation on function points introduced by IFPUG in 2012. The term SNAP is an awkward acronym for "software non-functional assessment process." The basic idea is that software requirements have two flavors: (1) functional requirements needed by users; (2) non-functional requirements due to laws, mandates, or physical factors such as storage limits or performance criteria. The SNAP committee view is that these non-functional requirements should be sized, estimated, and measured separately from function point metrics. Thus, SNAP and function point metrics are not additive, although they could have been. Having two separate metrics for economic studies is awkward at best and inconsistent with other industries. For that matter it seems inconsistent with standard economic analysis in every industry. Almost every industry has a single normalizing metric such as "cost per square foot" for home construction or "cost per gallon" for gasoline and diesel oil. As of 2017, none of the parametric estimation tools were fully integrated SNAP and it may be that they won't since the costs of adding SNAP are painfully expensive. As a rule of thumb, non-functional requirements are about equal to 15% of functional requirements, although the range is very wide.

Story point metrics are widely used for agile projects with "user stories." Story points have no ISO standard for counting or any other standard. They are highly ambiguous and vary by as much as 400% from company to company and project to project. There are few if any useful benchmarks using story points. Obviously story points can't be used for projects that don't utilize user stories so they are worthless for comparisons against other design methods.

Technical debt is a new metric and rapidly spreading. It is a brilliant metaphor developed by Ward Cunningham. The concept of "technical debt" is that topics deferred during development in the interest of schedule speed will cost more after release than they would have cost initially. However there are no ISO standards for technical debt and the concept is highly ambiguous. It can vary by over 500% from company to company and project to project. Worse, technical debt does not include all of the costs associated with poor quality and development short cuts. Technical debt omits canceled projects, consequential damages or harm to users, and the costs of litigation for poor quality.

Use case points are used by projects with designs based on "use cases" which often utilize IBM's Rational Unified Process (RUP). There are no ISO standards for use cases. Use cases are ambiguous and vary by over 200% from company to company and project to project. Obviously use cases are worthless for measuring projects that don't utilize use cases, so they have very little benchmark data. This is yet another attempt to imitate the virtues of function point metrics, only with somewhat less rigor and with imperfect counting rules as of 2015.

Velocity is an agile metric that is used for prediction of sprint and project outcomes. It uses historical data on completion of past work units combined with the assumption that future work units will be about the same. Of course it is necessary to know future work units for the method to operate. The concept of velocity is basically similar to the concept of using historical benchmarks for estimating future results. However as of 2017, velocity had no ISO standards and no certification.

There are no standard work units for velocity and these can be story points or other metrics such as function points or use case points, or even synthetic concepts such as "days per task." If agile projects used function points, then they could gain access to large volumes of historical data using activity-based costs, i.e. requirements effort, design effort, code effort, test effort, integration effort, documentation effort, etc. As long as agile continues to use quirky and unstandardized metrics without any certification exams, then agile productivity and quality will continue to be a mystery to clients who will no doubt be dismayed to find as many schedule delays and cost overruns as they had with waterfall.

As already stated in other chapters, there are 11 primary metrics and 10 supplementary metrics that allow software projects to be measured with about 1% precision.

The *only* software metrics that allow quality and productivity to be measured with 1% precision are these 11 primary software metrics and 10 supplemental metrics:

Primary Software Metrics for High Precision

1. Application size in function points including requirements creep.
2. Size of reusable materials (design, code, documents, etc.).
3. Activity-based costs using function points for normalization.
4. Work hours per month including paid and unpaid overtime.
5. Work hours per function point by activity.
6. Function points per month.
7. Defect potentials using function points (requirements, design, code, document, and bad fix defect categories).
8. DRE or the percentage of defects removed before release.
9. Delivered defects per function point.
10. Cost of quality (COQ).
11. Total cost of ownership (TCO).

Supplemental Software Metrics for High Precision

1. Software project taxonomy (nature, scope, class type).
2. Occupation groups (business analysts, programmers, testers, managers, QA, etc.).
3. Team experience levels (expert to novice).
4. CMMI level (1–5).
5. Development methodology used on application.
6. Programming language(s) used on application.
7. Complexity levels (problem, data, and code complexity).
8. User effort for internal applications.
9. Documents produced (type, pages, words, illustrations, etc.).
10. Meeting and communication costs.

What is important are the technical features of the metrics themselves and not the numbers of metric users. Even if 50,000 companies use "lines of code," it is still a bad metric that distorts reality and should be viewed as professional malpractice. Following are the characteristics of a sample of current software metrics:

	Function Points	Lines of Code	Story Points	Use-Case Points
Software Metric Attributes				
ISO standard?	Yes	No	No	No
OMG standard?	Yes	No	No	No
Professional associations?	Yes	No	No	No
Formal training?	Yes	No	No	No
Certification exam?	Yes	No	No	No
Automated counting?	Yes	Yes	No	No
Required by governments?	Yes	No	No	No
Good for productivity?	Yes	No	Yes	No
Good for quality?	Yes	No	No	No
Good for estimates?	Yes	No	Yes	No
Published conversion rules?	Yes	No	No	No
Accepted by benchmark groups?	Yes	Yes	No	No
Used for IT projects?	Yes	Yes	Yes	Yes
Used for web projects?	Yes	Yes	Yes	Yes
Used for cloud projects?	Yes	Yes	Yes	No
Used for embedded projects?	Yes	Yes	No	No
Used for systems software?	Yes	Yes	No	No
Used for telecom software?	Yes	Yes	No	No
Used for defense software?	Yes	Yes	No	No
Productivity Measures				
Activity-based costs?	Yes	No	No	No
Requirements productivity?	Yes	No	No	No
Design productivity?	Yes	No	No	No

(Continued)

	Function Points	Lines of Code	Story Points	Use-Case Points
Coding productivity?	Yes	Yes	No	No
Testing productivity?	Yes	Yes	No	No
Quality assurance productivity?	Yes	No	No	No
Technical writer productivity?	Yes	No	No	No
Project management productivity?	Yes	No	No	No
Net productivity of projects	Yes	Yes	Yes	Yes
Quality Measures				
Requirements defects?	Yes	No	No	No
Architecture defects?	Yes	No	No	No
Design defects?	Yes	No	No	No
Document defects?	Yes	No	No	No
Coding defects?	Yes	Yes	No	No
Bad fix defects?	Yes	Yes	No	No
Net quality of projects?	Yes	Yes	Yes	Yes

As can be seen, function point metrics are the only metrics that can be used for all software activities and for both quality and productivity analysis. This chapter uses IFPUG function points version 4.3, but other function point variations such as COSMIC, FISMA, and NESMA function points would produce similar but slightly different results.

Commissioning Annual Software Benchmark Studies

Software benchmarks are collections of data on software costs, schedules, staffing, quality, and technology usage that allow companies to compare results against similar projects in other companies. Usually the benchmarks are "sanitized" and do not reveal the names of the companies or projects themselves.

Major corporations should commission software benchmark studies about once a year in order to judge progress. Some companies such as IBM can produce their own internal benchmarks with high accuracy, but still commission external benchmarks to compare results against other companies.

However, most companies are incompetent in collecting historical data. Their data leaks and the average is only about 37% complete. This is why self-reported benchmark data often has higher productivity than benchmarks collected by professional benchmark consultants. Self-reported data "leaks" and is usually incomplete.

A more fundamental problem is that most enterprises simply do not record data for anything but a small subset of the activities actually performed. In carrying out interviews with project managers and project teams to validate and correct historical data, the author of this book has observed the following patterns of incomplete and missing data, using the 25 activities of a standard chart of accounts as the reference model (Table 1.10).

Benchmarks performed for projects starting today will also need to include the negative impacts of the corona virus. No doubt the virus is lowering productivity and will probably degrade quality, but it is too soon to know the full impact.

When the author of this book and his colleagues collect benchmark data, we ask the managers and personnel to try and reconstruct any missing cost elements. Reconstruction of data from memory is plainly inaccurate, but it is better than omitting the missing data entirely.

Unfortunately, the bulk of the software literature and many historical studies only report information to the level of complete projects, rather than to the level of specific activities. Such gross "bottom line" data cannot readily be validated and are almost useless for serious economic purposes.

As of 2020, there were about 40 companies and non-profit organizations that perform software benchmarks of various kinds. Some of the many forms of available software benchmarks include:

1. Compensation studies for software occupation groups.
2. Voluntary and involuntary attrition of software personnel.
3. Customer satisfaction for quality, reliability, etc.
4. Cyber-attack statistics for hacking, denial of service, data theft, etc.
5. Software productivity using function points per month and work hours per function point.
6. Software quality using defect potentials in function points and DRE.

Table 1.10   Gaps and Omissions Observed in Data for a Software Chart of Accounts

	Activities Performed	*Completeness of Historical Data*
1	Requirements	Missing or Incomplete
2	Prototyping	Missing or Incomplete
3	Architecture	Missing or Incomplete
4	Project planning	Missing or Incomplete
5	Initial analysis and design	Missing or Incomplete
6	Detail design	Incomplete
7	Design reviews	Missing or Incomplete
8	Coding	Complete
9	Reusable code acquisition	Missing or Incomplete
10	Purchased package acquisition	Missing or Incomplete
11	Code inspections	Missing or Incomplete
12	Independent verification and validation	Complete
13	Configuration management	Missing or Incomplete
14	Integration	Missing or Incomplete
15	User documentation	Missing or Incomplete
16	Unit testing	Incomplete
17	Function testing	Incomplete
18	Integration testing	Incomplete
19	System testing	Incomplete
20	Field testing	Missing or Incomplete
21	Acceptance testing	Missing or Incomplete
22	Independent testing	Complete
23	Quality assurance	Missing or Incomplete
24	Installation and training	Missing or Incomplete
25	Project management	Missing or Incomplete
Total project resources, costs		**Incomplete**

Usually software benchmarks are commissioned by individual business units rather than at the corporate level. Some companies spend over $5,000,000 per year on various kinds of benchmark studies, but may not realize this because the costs are scattered across various business and operating units.

The unexpected arrival of the corona virus in 2020 had caused a reduction in benchmarks for several years, since many software workers were at home and could probably not contribute benchmark data from their private home offices.

Table 1.11 shows some 40 software benchmark organizations circa 2020. The great majority of these are located in the United States, South America, or Europe. Asia is sparse on software benchmarks except for Japan, South Korea, and Malaysia. South America has large benchmark organizations in Brazil, and other more local benchmark groups in Mexico and Peru.

Benchmarks are hard to do with accuracy, but useful when done well. When done poorly, they add to the confusion about software productivity and quality that has blinded the software industry for more than 50 years.

Formal Best Practice Analysis of Software Tools, Methods, and Quality

The software literature has many articles and some books on software best practices. However, these usually lack quantitative data. To the author of this book, a "best practice" should improve quality or productivity by at least 10% compared to industry averages. A "worst practice" might degrade productivity and quality by 10%.

With over 28,000 projects to examine, the author of this book has published a number of quantitative tables and reports on software best (and worst) practices. Although we have evaluated about 335 methods and practices, the list is too big for convenience. A subset of 115 methods and practices shows best practices at the top and worst practices at the bottom. Namcook recommends using as many as possible from the top and avoiding the bottom (Table 1.12).

Because new practices come out at frequent intervals, companies need to have a formal method and practice evaluation group. At ITT, the Applied Technology Group evaluated existing and commercial tools, methods, and practices. The ITT Advanced Technology Group developed new tools and methods beyond the state of the art.

It is of minor historical interest that the Objective C programming language selected by Steve Jobs for all Apple software was actually

Table 1.11 Software Benchmark Providers 2020

1	4SUM Partners
2	Bureau of Labor Statistics, Department of Commerce
3	Capers Jones (Namcook Analytics LLC)
4	CAST Software
5	Congressional Cyber Security Caucus
6	Construx
7	COSMIC function points
8	Cyber Security and Information Systems
9	David Consulting Group
10	Economic Research Center (Japan)
11	Forrester Research
12	Galorath Incorporated
13	Gartner Group
14	German Computer Society
15	Hoovers Guides to Business
16	IDC
17	IFPUG
18	ISBSG Limited
19	ITMPI
20	Jerry Luftman (Stevens Institute)
21	Level 4 Ventures
22	Metri Group, Amsterdam
23	Namcook Analytics LLC
24	Price Systems
25	Process Fusion
26	QuantiMetrics
27	Quantitative Software Management (QSM)
28	Q/P Management Group
29	RBCS, Inc.
30	Reifer Consultants LLC

(Continued)

Table 1.11 (Continued)

31	Howard Rubin
32	SANS Institute
33	Software Benchmarking Organization (SBO)
34	Software Engineering Institute (SEI)
35	Software Improvement Group (SIG)
36	Software Productivity Research
37	Standish Group
38	Strassmann, Paul
39	System Verification Associates LLC
40	Test Maturity Model Integrated

developed by Dr. Tom Love and Dr. Brad Cox at the ITT Advanced Technology Group. When Alcatel acquired the ITT telecom research labs, the ownership of Objective C was transferred to Dr. Love at his new company.

Summary and Conclusions on Software Project Management

Software is viewed by a majority of corporate CEOs as the most troublesome engineering technology of the modern era. It is true that software has very high rates of canceled projects and also of cost and schedule overruns. It is also true that poor project management practices are implicated in these problems.

However, some companies have been able to improve software project management and thereby improve software results. These improvements need better estimates, better metrics and measures, and better quality control.

Since academic training in software project management is marginal, the best source of project management training is in-house education in large companies followed by professional education companies such as the Information Technology Metrics and Productivity Institute (ITMPI), and then by non-profit associations such as IFPUG, PMI, ASQ, etc.

The impact of the pandemic of 2020 on software corporations and projects is severe and no doubt will degrade productivity and quality.

Table 1.12 Software Technology Stack Scoring

	Methods and Practices in Technology Stack	*Value Scores*
1	Benchmarks (validated historical data from similar projects)	10.00
2	Defect potential <2.5	10.00
3	Defect removal efficiency (DRE) >99%	10.00
4	Estimates: activity-based cost estimates	10.00
5	Estimates: parametric estimation tools	10.00
6	Estimates: total cost of ownership (TCO) cost estimates	10.00
7	Formal and early quality predictions	10.00
8	Formal and early risk abatement	10.00
9	Inspection of all critical deliverables	10.00
10	Methods: patterns and >85% reuse of key deliverables	10.00
11	Metrics: defect potential measures	10.00
12	Metrics: defect removal efficiency (DRE) measures	10.00
13	Metrics: IFPUG function points	10.00
14	Metrics: SRM pattern matching sizing	10.00
15	Pre-requirements risk analysis	10.00
16	Static analysis of all source code	10.00
17	Automated project office (APO)	9.75
18	Metrics: bad-fix injections	9.70
19	Accurate cost tracking	9.50
20	Accurate defect tracking	9.50
21	Accurate status tracking	9.50
22	Estimates: cost of quality (COQ) estimates	9.25
23	Metrics: COSMIC function points	9.25
24	Metrics: FISMA function points	9.25
25	Metrics: NESMA function points	9.25
26	Metrics: cost of quality (COQ) measures	9.00
27	Metrics: defect detection efficiency (DDE) measures	9.00
28	Reusable test materials	9.00

(Continued)

Table 1.12 (Continued)

	Methods and Practices in Technology Stack	Value Scores
29	SEMAT usage on project	9.00
30	Test coverage >96%	9.00
31	Defect removal efficiency DRE >95%	8.75
32	Methods: disciplined agile delivery (DAD)	8.65
33	Mathematical test case design	8.60
34	CMMI 5	8.50
35	Methods: TSP/PSP	8.50
36	Test coverage tools used	8.50
37	Metrics: requirements growth before and after release	8.50
38	Metrics: deferred features	8.50
39	Methods: containers	8.40
40	Methods: DevOps	8.40
41	Methods: hybrid: (agile/TSP)	8.25
42	Automated requirements modeling	8.15
43	Methods: Git	8.10
44	Methods: Mashups	8.10
45	Methods: RUP	8.00
46	Methods: evolutionary development (EVO)	8.00
47	Metrics: automated function points	8.00
48	Reusable requirements	8.00
49	Reusable source code	8.00
50	Methods: hybrid (waterfall/agile)	7.80
51	Static analysis of text requirements	7.80
52	Methods: Kanban/Kaizen	7.70
53	Methods: iterative development	7.60
54	CMMI 4	7.50
55	Methods: service oriented models	7.50
56	Metrics: cyclomatic complexity tools	7.50
57	Requirements change tracking	7.50

Table 1.12 (Continued)

	Methods and Practices in Technology Stack	Value Scores
58	Reusable designs	7.50
59	Automated proofs of correctness	7.50
60	Methods: continuous development	7.40
61	Methods: quality function deployment (QFD)	7.35
62	CMMI 3	7.00
63	Methods: joint application design (JAD)	7.00
64	Methods: spiral development	7.00
65	Requirements change control board	7.00
66	Reusable architecture	7.00
67	Reusable user documents	7.00
68	Methods: extreme Programming	6.90
69	Metrics: FOG/Flesch readability scores	6.85
70	DRE >90%	6.50
71	Methods: agile <1000 function points	6.50
72	Methods: correctness proofs – automated	6.25
73	Automated testing	6.00
74	Certified quality assurance personnel	6.00
75	Certified test personnel	6.00
76	Defect potential 2.5–4.9	6.00
77	Maintenance: data mining	6.00
78	Metrics: earned value analysis (EVA)	6.00
79	Six-Sigma for software	5.50
80	ISO risk standards	5.00
81	Metrics: unadjusted function points	5.00
82	ISO quality standards	4.75
83	Maintenance: ITIL	4.75
84	Metrics: mark II function points	4.00
85	Requirements modeling – manual	3.00
86	Metrics: SNAP non-functional metrics	2.50

(Continued)

Table 1.12   (Continued)

	Methods and Practices in Technology Stack	*Value Scores*
87	CMMI 2	2.00
88	Estimates: phase-based cost estimates	2.00
89	Metrics: story point metrics	2.00
90	Metrics: technical debt measures	2.00
91	Metrics: use case metrics	1.00
92	CMMI 0 (not used)	0.00
93	CMMI 1	−1.00
94	Methods: correctness proofs – manual	−1.00
95	Test coverage <90%	−1.00
96	Benchmarks (unvalidated self-reported benchmarks)	−1.50
97	Testing by untrained developers	−2.00
98	Methods: waterfall development	−3.00
99	Methods: agile >5,000 function points	−4.00
100	Cyclomatic complexity >20	−6.00
101	Metrics: no productivity measures	−7.00
102	Methods: pair programming	−7.50
103	Methods: Cowboy development	−8.00
104	No static analysis of source code	−8.00
105	Test coverage not used	−8.00
106	Estimates: manual estimation >250 function points	−9.00
107	Inaccurate defect tracking	−9.00
108	Metrics: cost per defect metrics	−9.00
109	Inaccurate status tracking	−9.50
110	Defect potential >5.00	−10.00
111	DRE <85%	−10.00
112	Inaccurate cost tracking	−10.00
113	Metrics: lines of code for economic study	−10.00
114	Metrics: no function point measures	−10.00
115	Metrics: no quality measures	−10.00

Hopefully, the bright minds of the industry will develop effective methods for handling teams that work at home or remotely.

Suggested Readings on Software Project Management

Abran, A.; and Robillard, P.N.; "Function Point Analysis, An Empirical Study of its Measurement Processes"; *IEEE Transactions on Software Engineering*; Vol 22, No. 12; December 1996; pp. 895–909.

Abrain, Alain; *Software Estimating Models*; Wiley-IEEE Computer Society; 2015.

Abrain, Alain; *Software Metrics and Metrology*; Wiley-IEEE Computer Society; 2010.

Abrain, Alain; *Software Maintenance Management: Evolution and Continuous Improvement*; Wiley-IEEE Computer Society; 2008.

Baird, Linda M.; and Brennan, M. Carol; *Software Measurement and Estimation: A Practical Approach*; IEEE Computer Society Press/John Wiley & Sons, Los Alamitos, CA/Hoboken NJ; 2006; ISBN: 0-471-67622-5; 257 pages.

Boehm, Barry et al.; *Software Cost Estimating with Cocomo II*; Prentice Hall, Upper Saddle River, NJ; 2000; ISBN: 10-0137025769; 544 pages.

Boehm, Barry; *Software Engineering Economics*; Prentice Hall, Englewood Cliffs, NJ; 1981; 900 pages.

Brooks, Fred; *The Mythical Man-Month*; Addison Wesley, Reading, MA; 1974 rev.; 1995.

Bundshuh, Manfred; and Dekkers, Carol; *The IT Measurement Compendium; Estimating and Benchmarking Success with Functional Size Measurement*; Springer; 2008; ISBN: 10-3540681876; 644 pages.

Cohn, Mike; *Agile Estimating and Planning*; Prentice Hall PTR, Englewood Cliffs, NJ; 2005; ISBN: 0131479415.

Crosby, Phil; *Quality is Free*; New American Library, Mentor Books; New York, NY; 1979; 270 pages.

DeMarco, Tom; *Why Does Software Cost So Much?*; Dorset House, New York, NY; 1995; ISBN: 0-9932633-34-X; 237 pages.

Ebert, Christof; Dumke, Reiner; and Schmeitendorf, Andreas; *Best Practices in Software Measurement*; Springer; 2004; ISBN: 10-3540208674; 344 pages.

Fleming, Quentin W.; and Koppelman, Joel M.; *Earned Value Project Management*; 2nd ed.; Project Management Institute, New York, NY; 2000; ISBN: 10-1880410273; 212 pages.

Galorath, Daniel D.; and Evans, Michael W.; *Software Sizing, Estimation, and Risk Management: When Performance is Measured Performance Improves*; Auerbach, Philadelphia, AP; 2006; ISBN: 10-0849335930; 576 pages.

Gack, Gary; *Managing the Black Hole: The Executive's Guide to Project Risk*; Business Expert Publishing; 2010.

Garmus, David; and Herron, David; *Function Point Analysis*; Addison Wesley, Boston, MA; 2001; ISBN: 0-201069944-3; 363 pages.

Garmus, David; Russac Janet; and Edwards, Royce; *Certified Function Point Counters Examination Guide*; CRC Press; 2010.

Garmus, David; and Herron, David; *Measuring the Software Process: A Practical Guide to Functional Measurement*; Prentice Hall, Englewood Cliffs, NJ; 1995.

Gilb, Tom; and Graham, Dorothy; *Software Inspections*; Addison Wesley, Reading, MA; 1993; ISBN: 10-0201631814.

Glass, R.L.; *Software Runaways: Lessons Learned from Massive Software Project Failures*; Prentice Hall, Englewood Cliffs, NJ; 1998.

Harris, Michaael; Herron, David; and Iwanicki, Stacia; *The Business Value of IT: Managing Risks, Optimizing Performance, and Measuring Results*; CRC Press (Auerbach), Boca Raton, FL; 2008; ISBN: 13-978-1-4200-6474-2; 266 pages.

Hill, Peter; Jones Capers; and Reifer, Don; *The Impact of Software Size on Productivity*; International Software Standards Benchmark Group (ISBSG), Melbourne, Australia, September 2013.

Humphrey, Watts; *Managing the Software Process*; Addison Wesley, Reading, MA; 1989.

International Function Point Users Group (IFPUG); *IT Measurement – Practical Advice from the Experts*; Addison Wesley Longman, Boston, MA; 2002; ISBN: 0-201-74158-X; 759 pages.

Jacobsen, Ivar, Griss, Martin; and Jonsson, Patrick; *Software Reuse - Architecture, Process, and Organization for Business Success*; Addison Wesley Longman, Reading, MA; 1997; ISBN: 0-201-92476-5; 500 pages.

Jacobsen, Ivar et al; *The Essence of Software Engineering; Applying the SEMAT Kernel*; Addison Wesley Professional, Reading, MA; 2013.

Johnson, James et al; *The Chaos Report*; The Standish Group, West Yarmouth, MA; 2000.

Jones, Capers; *The Technical and Social History of Software Engineering*; Addison Wesley, Boston, MA; 2014.

Jones, Capers; and Bonsignour, Olivier; *The Economics of Software Quality*; Addison Wesley, Boston, MA; 2011.

Jones, Capers; *Software Engineering Best Practices*; McGraw Hill, New York; 2009; ISBN: 978-0-07-162161-8660.

Jones, Capers; *Applied Software Measurement*; 3rd ed.; McGraw Hill, New York; March 2008; ISBN: 978-0-07-150244-3; 668 pages.

Jones, Capers; *Estimating Software Costs*; McGraw Hill, New York; 2007; ISBN 13-978-0-07-148300-1.

Jones, Capers; *Program Quality and Programmer Productivity*; IBM Technical Report TR 02.764; IBM, San Jose, CA; January 1977.

Jones, Capers; "Sizing Up Software"; *Scientific American Magazine*; Vol. 279, No. 6; December 1998; pp 104–109.

Jones, Capers; *Software Assessments, Benchmarks, and Best Practices*; Addison Wesley Longman, Boston, MA; 2000; 659 pages.

Jones, Capers; *Conflict and Litigation Between Software Clients and Developers*; Version 6; Software Productivity Research, Burlington, MA; June 2006a; 54 pages.

Jones, Capers; "Software Project Management Practices: Failure Versus Success"; *Crosstalk*; Vol. 19, No. 6; June 2006b; pp 4–8.

Jones, Capers; *Patterns of Software System Failure and Success*; International Thomson Computer Press, Boston, MA; December 1995; ISBN: 1-850-32804-8; 250; 292 pages.

Jones, Capers; "Why Flawed Software Projects are not Cancelled in Time"; *Cutter IT Journal*; Vol. 10, No. 12; December 2003; pp. 12–17.

Kan, Stephen H.; *Metrics and Models in Software Quality Engineering*; 2nd ed.; Addison Wesley Longman, Boston, MA; 2003; ISBN: 0-201-72915-6; 528 pages.

Kaplan, Robert S.; and Norton, David B.; *The Balanced Scorecard*; Harvard University Press, Boston, MA; 2004; ISBN: 1591391342.

Love, Tom; *Object Lessons – Lessons Learned in Object-Oriented Development Projects*; SIG Books Inc., New York, NY; 1993; ISBN: 0-9627477-3-4; 266 pages.

Mark, Paulk et al; *The Capability Maturity Model; Guidelines for Improving the Software Process*; Addison Wesley, Reading, MA; 1995; ISBN: 0-201-54664-7; 439 pages.

McCabe, Thomas J.; "A Complexity Measure"; *IEEE Transactions on Software Engineering*; December 1976; pp. 308–320.

McConnell, Steve; *Software Estimation – Demystifying the Black Art*; Microsoft Press, Redmond, WA; 2006; ISBN: 10-0-7356-0535-1.

Parthasarathy, M.A.; *Practical Software Estimation – Function Point Methods for Insourced and Outsourced Projects*; Addison Wesley, Boston, MA; 2007; ISBN: 0-321-43910-4; 388 pages.

Pressman, Roger; *Software Engineering – A Practitioner's Approach*; McGraw Hill, New York, NY; 1982.

Putnam, Lawrence H.; *Measures for Excellence – Reliable Software On-Time Within Budget*; Yourdon Press, Prentice Hall, Englewood Cliffs, NJ; 1992; ISBN: 0-13-567694-0; 336 pages.

Putnam, Lawrence; and Myers, Ware; *Industrial Strength Software – Effective Management Using Measurement*; IEEE Press, Los Alamitos, CA; 1997; ISBN: 0-8186-7532-2; 320 pages.

Robertson, Suzanne; and Robertson, James; *Requirements-Led Project Management*; Addison Wesley, Boston, MA; 2005; ISBN: 0-321-18062-3.

Roetzheim, William H.; and Beasley, Reyna A.; *Best Practices in Software Cost and Schedule Estimation*; Prentice Hall PTR, Saddle River, NJ; 1998.

Royce, Walker; *Software Project Management – A Unified Framework*; Addison Wesley, Boston, MA; 1998.

Strassmann, Paul; *Governance of Information Management: The Concept of an Information Constitution*; 2nd ed.; (eBook); Information Economics Press, Stamford, CT; 2004.

Strassmann, Paul; *The Squandered Computer*; Information Economics Press, Stamford, CT; 1997.

Stutzke, Richard D.; *Estimating Software-Intensive Systems – Projects, Products, and Processes*; Addison Wesley, Boston, MA; 2005; ISBN: 0-301-70312-2; 917 pages.

Weinberg, Gerald; *Quality Software Management – Vol. 2: First-Order Measurement*; Dorset House Press, New York, NY; 1993; ISBN: 0-932633-24-2; 360 pages.

Wiegers, Karl A.; *Creating a Software Engineering Culture*; Dorset House Press, New York, NY; 1996; ISBN: 0-932633-33-1; 358 pages.

Wiegers, Karl E.; *Peer Reviews in Software – A Practical Guide*; Addison Wesley Longman, Boston, MA; 2002; ISBN: 0-201-73485-0; 232 pages.

Whitehead, Richard; *Leading a Development Team*; Addison Wesley, Boston, MA; 2001; ISBN: 10-0201675267; 368 pages.

Yourdon, Ed; *Outsource – Competing in the Global Productivity Race*; Prentice Hall PTR, Upper Saddle River, NJ; 2004; ISBN: 0-13-147571-1; 251 pages.

Yourdon, Ed; *Death March – The Complete Software Developer's Guide to Surviving "Mission Impossible" Projects*; Prentice Hall PTR, Upper Saddle River, NJ; 1997; ISBN: 0-13-748310-4.

Suggested Web Sites

http://www.IASAhome.org. This is the web site for the non-profit International Association of Software Architects (IASA). Software architecture is the backbone of all large applications. Good architecture can lead to applications whose useful life expectancy is 20 years or more. Questionable architecture can lead to applications whose useful life expectancy is less than 10 years, coupled with increasing complex maintenance tasks and high defect levels. The IASA is working hard to improve both the concepts of architecture and the training of software architects via a modern and extensive curriculum.

http://www.IIBA.org. This is the web site for the non-profit International Institute of Business Analysis. This institute deals with the important linkage between business knowledge and software that supports business operations. Among the topics of concern are the Business Analysis Body of Knowledge (BABOK), training of business analysts, and certification to achieve professional skills.

http://www.IFPUG.org. This is the web site for the non-profit International Function Point Users Group. IFPUG is the largest software metrics association in the world, and the oldest association of function point users. This web site contains information about IFPUG function points themselves, and also citations to the literature dealing with function points. IFPUG also offers training in function point analysis and administers. IFPUG also administers a certification program for analysts who wish to become function point counters.

http://www.ISBSG.org. This is the web site for the non-profit International Software Benchmark Standards Group. ISBSG, located in Australia, collects benchmark data on software projects throughout the world. The data is self-reported by companies using a standard questionnaire. About 4,000 projects comprise the ISBSG collection as of 2007, and the collection has been growing at a rate of about 500 projects per year. Most of the data is expressed in terms of IFPUG function point metrics, but some of the data is also expressed in terms of COSMIC function points, NESMA function points, Mark II function points, and several other function point variants. Fortunately the data in variant metrics is identified. It would be statistically invalid to include attempt to average IFPUG and COSMIC data, or to mix up any of the function point variations.

http://www.iso.org. This is the web site for the International Organization for Standardization (ISO). The ISO is a non-profit organization that sponsors and publishes a variety of international standards. As of 2007 the ISO published about a thousand standards a year, and the total published to date is approximately 17,000. Many of the published standards affect software. These include the ISO 9000-9004 quality standards and the ISO standards for functional size measurement.

http://www.namcook.com. This web site contains a variety of quantitative reports on software quality and risk factors. It also contains a patented high-speed sizing tool that can size applications of any size in 90 seconds or less. It also contains a catalog of software benchmark providers which currently lists 20 organizations that provide quantitative data about software schedules, costs, quality, and risks.

http://www.PMI.org. This is the web site for the Project Management Institute (PMI). PMI is the largest association of managers in the world. PMI performs research and collects data on topics of interest to managers in every discipline: software, engineering, construction, and so forth. This data is assembled into the well known Project Management Body of Knowledge or PMBOK.

http://www.ITMPI.org. This is the web site for the Information Technology Metrics and Productivity Institute. ITMPI is a wholly-owned subsidiary of Computer Aid Inc. The ITMPI web site is a useful portal into a broad range of measurement, management, and software engineering information. The ITMPI web site also provides useful links to many other web sites that contain topics of interest on software issues.

http://www.sei.cmu.edu. This is the web site for the Software Engineering Institute (SEI). The SEI is a federally-sponsored non-profit organization located on the campus of Carnegie Mellon University in Pittsburgh, PA. The SEI carries out a number of research programs dealing with software maturity and capability levels, with quality, risks, measurement and metrics, and other topics of interest to the software community.

http://www.stsc.hill.af.mil/CrossTalk. This is the web site of both the Air Force Software Technology Support Center (STSC) and also the CrossTalk journal, which is published by the STSC. The STSC gathers data and performs research into a wide variety of software engineering and software management issues. The CrossTalk journal is one of few technical journals that publish full-length technical articles of 4,000 words or more. Although the Air Force is the sponsor of STSC and CrossTalk, many topics are also relevant to the civilian community. Issues such as quality control, estimating, maintenance, measurement, and metrics have universal relevance.

Chapter 2

Wastage

Lost Time and Money Due to Poor Software Quality

Introduction

When the work patterns of software development and maintenance projects are analyzed, a surprising hypothesis emerges. Software quality is so poor that productivity is much lower than it should be. Poor quality shows up in three major software economic problems: (1) cancelled projects that are never released due to poor quality; (2) schedule delays due to poor quality extending test duration; and (3) excessive work on finding and fixing bugs, which often exceeds 60% of total software effort.

The amount of software effort spent on software projects that will be canceled due to excessive error content appears to absorb more than 20% of the U.S. software work force. In addition, about 60% of the U.S. software engineering work time centers on finding and fixing errors, which might have been avoided. Finally, software schedules for major applications are about 25% longer than they should be due to poor quality expanding testing intervals.

Out of a full software engineering working year, only about 48 days are spent on code development. About 53 days are spent on finding and fixing bugs in current applications. About 16 days are spent on canceled projects. About 15 days are spent on inspections and static analysis.

DOI: 10.1201/9781003193128-3

About 13 days are spent on bug repairs in legacy code, i.e. 97 days per year are essentially "wastage" spent on bugs that might have been prevented or removed inexpensively. No other major occupation appears to devote so much effort to canceled projects or to defect repairs as does software engineering.

> *Note that the corona virus of 2020 changed software engineering due to many factors such as working from home and the elimination of group activities such as inspections or staff meetings, unless they are done via Zoom or remotely. No doubt software productivity will decline and quality will become worse, but it is premature to know the actual losses that will accrue.*

Software is one of the most labor-intensive occupations of the 21st century (*The Technical and Social History of Software Engineering*, Jones, 2014). Software is also one of the most challenging business endeavors, since software projects are difficult to control and subject to a significant percentage of delays and outright cancellations. The primary reason for both software delays and cancellations is due to the large numbers of "bugs" or errors whose elimination can absorb more than 60% of the effort on really large software projects.

When the errors in software schedules and cost estimates are analyzed carefully, it can be seen that a major source of schedule slippage and cost overruns is the fact that the applications have so many bugs that they don't work or can't be released (*The Economics of Software Quality*, Jones and Bonsignour, 2011). A famous example of this phenomenon can be seen in the one-year delay in opening the Denver Airport due to errors in the software controlling the luggage handling system. Problems with excessive bugs or errors have also caused delays in many software application releases, even by such well-known companies and government agencies as Microsoft and the Department of Defense.

Canceled projects, schedule delays, and cost overruns all have a common origin: excessive defects that might be prevented, combined with labor-intensive defect removal methods such as testing and manual inspections.

Analyzing the Work Patterns of Software Engineers and Programmers

Software engineering is a very labor-intensive occupation. A key reason for the high labor content of software applications is because these applications are very complex and hence very error-prone.

A large number of severe errors or "bugs" in software applications have several unfortunate effects on the software industry:

1. A substantial number of software projects are cancelled due to high error rates.
2. Much of the development work of software engineering is defect removal.
3. Much of the maintenance work of software engineering is defect repair.

Using data gathered during Namcook's software assessments and benchmark studies, Table 2.1 shows the approximate number of software "projects" that are being undertaken in the United States during calendar year 2017. A software "project" is defined as the total effort assigned to developing or enhancing a specific software application.

Table 2.1 shows how a typical software engineer spends a calendar year. The background data for Table 2.1 comes from interviews and benchmarks carried out among the author's clients and also among software personnel at IBM and ITT since the author of this book worked at both companies.

Note that days spent finding and fixing bugs or working on canceled projects total to 97 annual work days while code development is only 48 annual work days. Worse, Agile is one of the newer and better methodologies. If the project had been done in Waterfall, even more days would have gone to finding and fixing bugs.

It is obvious that as of 2020, software engineering was out of kilter. Bug repairs constitute a far larger proportion of the work year than is satisfactory. It is also obvious that custom designs and manual coding are intrinsically error-prone and expensive.

What would be the results if instead of developing software as unique projects using manual labor, it were possible to construct software applications using libraries of about 85% standard and certified reusable components instead of 0% reuse?

Table 2.2 uses the same format as Table 2.1, but makes the assumption that the application is constructed from a library that allows 85% of the code to be in the form of certified reusable modules rather than hand coding and custom development (*Software Engineering Best Practices*, Jones, 2012).

Because the results in Table 2.2 are outside the envelope of current software engineering technology circa 2020, the date is changed to 2030 instead of 2020.

Table 2.1   2020 Distribution of Software Development Effort

(Assumes 1,000 function point projects; Agile development; 0% reuse; Java)		
(Assumes 132 hours per month; monthly costs of $10,000; CMMI 3; average skills)		
Activities	Work Days	Percent of Time
Regular weekends	104	28.49%
Testing and defect repairs	**53**	**14.52%**
New Code development	**48**	**13.15%**
Meetings and status tracking	24	6.58%
Producing paper documents	21	5.75%
Vacations and personal time	20	5.48%
Days spent on canceled projects	**16**	**4.38%**
Pre-test inspections/static analysis	**15**	**4.11%**
Bug repairs in legacy code	**13**	**3.56%**
Travel	12	3.29%
Training and classes	10	2.74%
Slack time between assignments	10	2.74%
Sick leave	10	2.74%
Public holidays	9	2.47%
Total	**365**	**100.00%**

Size in function points	1,000
Size in Java statements	53,000
Staff (development, test, mgt, etc.)	7
Schedule in calendar months	15.85
Work hours per function point	20.23
Function points per month	6.52
Costs per function point	**$1,532.42**
Total costs for project	**$1,532,423**
Defect potentials per function point	**3.50**
Defect potential	**3,500**

Table 2.1 (Continued)

Defect removal efficiency (DRE)	92.50%
Delivered defects per function point	0.26
Delivered defects	263
High-severity defects	39
Security flaws	6

Table 2.2 shows the kind of work pattern that software engineering needs to meet ever-growing business demands for new kinds of reliable software. The development schedule drops from 16.23 calendar months to 4.71 calendar months. High severity bugs drop from 39 to 2. These improvements are urgently needed to place the future of software engineering on a sound economic basis. It is obvious that software engineering needs to shift work away from defect repairs and failing projects and put more effort into effective development. Table 2.2 raises annual code development up to 119 work days per year in 2028 compared to only 48 work days per year in 2020.

Table 2.3 shows a side-by-side comparison between the 2020 and 2030 assumptions with 85% reuse for 2030.

As can be seen, there are major differences in the two scenarios due mainly to the assumption of 85% reuse circa 2030.

Tables 2.1, 2.2, and 2.3 show individual projects of 1,000 function points in size. It is also interesting to scale up the results to national levels. Table 2.4 shows the approximate U.S. software work force and the number of workers on projects that will be canceled and never delivered, mainly due to poor quality.

The data on the percent of projects cancelled within each size range is taken from the author's book on *Patterns of Software Systems Failure and Success* (Jones 1995) and updated using data from the more recent book, *The Economics of Software Quality* (Jones and Bonsigour, 2012) plus newer data from client studies done through mid-2017 as published in two new books from 2017: *Software Methodologies: A Quantified Comparison* (2016); *Software National and Industry Comparisons* (2017).

Very few small projects are canceled, but a majority of large systems are terminated without being completed. Although many reasons are associated with cancelled projects, the root cause for most is that they overran both budgets and schedules due to excessive error content. The

Table 2.2   2030 Distribution of Software Development Effort

(Assumes 1,000 function point projects; Agile development; 85% reuse; Java)		
(Assumes 132 hours per month; monthly costs of $10,000; CMMI 3; average skills)		
Activities	Work Days	Percent of Time
Regular weekends	104	28.49%
Testing and defect repairs	**8**	**2.18%**
New Code development	**119**	**32.60%**
Meetings and status tracking	24	6.58%
Producing paper documents	21	5.75%
Vacations and personal time	20	5.48%
Days spent on canceled projects	**2**	**0.66%**
Pre-test inspections/static analysis	**2**	**0.62%**
Bug repairs in legacy code	**13**	**3.56%**
Travel	12	3.29%
Training and classes	10	2.74%
Slack time between assignments	10	2.74%
Sick leave	10	2.74%
Public holidays	9	2.47%
Total	**365**	**100.00%**

Size in function points	1,000
Size in Java statements	53,000
Staff (development, test, mgt, etc.)	4
Schedule in calendar months	4.71
Work hours per function point	6.14
Function points per month	21.50
Costs per function point	**$465.11**
Total costs for project	**$465,105**
Defect potentials per function point	**0.53**
Defect potential	**525**

Table 2.2 (Continued)

Defect removal efficiency (DRE)	97.00%
Delivered defects per function point	0.02
Delivered defects	16
High-severity defects	2
Security flaws	0

delays and overruns are mainly due to poor quality, which stretches out testing far beyond expectations.

The next topic of interest is to quantify the staffing associated with six size plateaus, in order to determine the amount of software effort that appears to be wasted on projects that do not reach completion.

Table 2.4 shows the approximate numbers of U.S. software personnel assigned to the projects within each of the six main size plateaus. Obviously large systems, some of which have hundreds of software engineers, absorb the bulk of the available software personnel.

Table 2.4 shows that the software industry has major problems trying to develop applications >10,000 function points in size. In these larger size ranges, cancellations are a major economic problem, and the projects that are not canceled, all run late and exceed their budgets. Less than 5% of major systems have satisfactory conclusion.

Indeed for large systems that are outsourced, it looks like about 5% end up in court for breach of contract litigation. It is professionally embarrassing to have the same percentage of lawsuits as we have successful project outcomes!

Tables 2.1, 2.2, 2.3, and 2.4 present a troubling picture. Because cancelled projects are more frequent for large applications than for small,

Table 2.3 Comparison of the 2020 and 2030 Assumptions with 85% Reuse

	2020	2030	Difference
Activities	*Work Days*	*Work Days*	*Work Days*
Regular weekends	104	104	0
Testing and defect repairs	53	8	−45
New code development	48	119	71
Meetings and status tracking	24	24	0
Producing paper documents	21	21	0

(Continued)

Table 2.3 (Continued)

Activities	2020 Work Days	2030 Work Days	Difference Work Days
Vacations and personal time	20	20	0
Days spent on canceled projects	16	2	−14
Pre-test inspections/static analysis	15	2	−13
Bug repairs in legacy code	13	13	0
Travel	12	12	0
Training and classes	10	10	0
Slack time between assignments	10	10	0
Sick leave	10	10	0
Public holidays	9	9	0
Total	**365**	**365**	0
Annual wasted days	**97**	**25**	**−72**
Percent of certified reusable features	0.00%	85.00%	85.00%
Size in function points	1,000	1,000	0
Size in Java statements	53,000	53,000	0
Staff (development, test, mgt, etc.)	7.00	4.00	−3
Schedule in calendar months	15.85	4.71	−11.14
Work hours per function point	20.23	6.14	−14.09
Function points per month	6.52	21.5	14.98
Costs per function point	$1,532	**$465**	−1067.31
Total costs for project	$1,532,423	**$465,105**	−1067318
Defect potentials per function point	**3.5**	**0.53**	**−2.97**
Defect potential	**3,500**	525	**−2975**
Defect removal efficiency (DRE)	92.50%	**97.00%**	**4.50%**
Delivered defects per function point	0.26	**0.02**	−0.24
Delivered defects	263	**16**	−247
High-severity defects	39	**2**	−37
Security flaws	6	**0**	−6

Table 2.4   U.S. Software Personnel Circa 2020

Size in Function Points	Total Project Staff	Canceled Project Staff	Canceled Project Percent
1	75,000	375	0.50%
10	119,000	1,190	1.00%
100	250,000	10,000	4.00%
1,000	500,000	60,000	12.00%
10,000	1,580,000	474,000	30.00%
100,000	147,300	61,866	42.00%
1,000,000	50,000	32,500	65.00%
Total	**2,909,300**	**639,931**	**22.00%**

more than 22% of the available software personnel in the United States are working on projects that will not be completed!

Reuse of Certified Materials for Software Projects

As long as software applications are custom designed and coded by hand, software will remain a labor-intensive craft rather than a modern professional activity. Manual software development even with excellent methodologies cannot be much more than 15% better than average development due to the intrinsic limits in human performance and legal limits in the number of hours that can be worked without fatigue.

The best long-term strategy for achieving consistent excellence at high speed would be to eliminate manual design and coding in favor of construction from certified reusable components.

It is important to realize that software reuse encompasses many deliverables and not just source code. A full suite of reusable software components would include at least the following 10 items (*Software Engineering Best Practices*; Jones, 2010).

1. Reusable requirements.
2. Reusable architecture.
3. Reusable design.
4. Reusable code.
5. Reusable project plans and estimates.
6. Reusable test plans.
7. Reusable test scripts.

8. Reusable test cases.
9. Reusable user manuals.
10. Reusable training materials.

These materials need to be certified to near zero-defect levels of quality before reuse becomes safe and economically viable. Reusing buggy materials is harmful and expensive. This is why excellent quality control is the first stage in a successful reuse program.

The need for being close to zero defects and formal certification adds about 20% to the costs of constructing reusable artifacts and about 30% to the schedules for construction. However, using certified reusable materials subtracts over 80% from the costs of construction and can shorten schedules by more than 60%. The more times materials are reused, the greater their cumulative economic value.

Achieving Excellence in Software Quality Control

In addition to moving toward higher volumes of certified reusable components, it is also obvious from the huge costs associated with finding and fixing bugs that the software industry needs much better quality control than was common in 2020.

Excellent Quality Control

Excellent software projects have rigorous quality control methods that include formal estimation of quality before starting, full defect measurement and tracking during development, and a full suite of defect prevention, pre-test removal, and test stages. The combination of low defect potentials and high defect removal efficiency (DRE) is what software excellence is all about.

The most common companies that are excellent in quality control are usually the companies that build complex physical devices such as computers, aircraft, embedded engine components, medical devices, and telephone switching systems (*Software Engineering Best Practices*; Jones, 2010). Without excellence in quality, these physical devices will not operate successfully. Worse, failure can lead to litigation and even criminal charges. Therefore, all companies that use software to control complex physical machinery tend to be excellent in software quality.

Examples of organizations noted as excellent for software quality in alphabetical order include Advanced Bionics, Apple, AT&T, Boeing, Ford for engine controls, General Electric for jet engines, Hewlett Packard for embedded software, IBM for systems software, Motorola for electronics, NASA for space controls, the Navy for surface weapons, Raytheon, and Siemens for electronic components.

Companies and projects with excellent quality control tend to have low levels of code cyclomatic complexity and high test coverage, i.e. test cases cover >95% of paths and risk areas.

These companies also measure quality well and all know their DRE levels. (Any company that does not measure and know their DRE is probably below 85% in DRE.)

Excellence in software quality also uses pre-test inspections for critical materials (i.e. critical requirements, design, architecture, and code segments). Excellence in quality also implies 100% usage of pre-test static analysis for all new modules, for significant changes to modules and for major bug repairs. For that matter, static analysis is also valuable during the maintenance of aging legacy applications.

Excellent testing involves certified test personnel, formal test case design using mathematical methods such as design of experiments and a test sequence that includes at least: (1) unit test; (2) function test; (3) regression test; (4) performance test; (5) usability test; (6) system test; (7) beta or customer acceptance test. Sometimes additional tests such as supply-chain or security are also included.

Excellent quality control has DRE levels between about 97% for large systems in the 10,000 function point size range and about 99.6% for small projects <1,000 function points in size.

A DRE of 100% is theoretically possible but is extremely rare. The author of this book has only noted DRE of 100% in 10 projects out of a total of about 25,000 projects examined. As it happens, the projects with 100% DRE were all compilers and assemblers built by IBM and using >85% certified reusable materials. The teams were all experts in compilation technology and of course a full suite of pre-test defect removal and test stages were used as well.

Average Quality Control

In today's world, Agile is the new average and indeed a long step past waterfall development. Agile development has proven to be effective for smaller applications below 1,000 function points in size. Agile does not scale up well and is not a top method for quality. Indeed both Tables 2.1 and 2.2 utilize Agile since it was so common in 2015.

Agile is weak in quality measurements and does not normally use inspections, which has the highest DRE of any known form of defect removal. Inspections top 85% in DRE and also raise testing DRE levels.

Among the author's clients that use Agile, the average value for DRE ranges about 92%–94%. This is certainly better than the 85% to 90% industry average, but not up to the 99% actually needed to achieve optimal results.

Methods with stronger quality control than Agile include personal software process (PSP), team software process (TSP), and the rational unified process (RUP) which often top 97% in DRE) (*Applied Software Measurement*, Jones, 2008).

Some but not all agile projects use "pair programming" in which two programmers share an office and a work station and take turns coding while the other watches and "navigates." Pair programming is very expensive but only benefits quality by about 15% compared to single programmers. Pair programming is much less effective in finding bugs than formal inspections, which usually bring 3–5 personnel together to seek out bugs using formal methods. Critical inspection combined with static analysis has higher defect removal than pair programming at costs below 50% of pair programming.

Agile is a definite improvement for quality compared to waterfall development but is not as effective as the quality-strong methods of TSP and the RUP.

Average projects usually do not predict defects by origin and do not measure DRE until testing starts, i.e. requirements and design defects are under reported and sometimes invisible.

A recent advance since 1984 in software quality control now frequently used by average as well as advanced organizations is that of static analysis. Static analysis tools can find about 55%–65% of code defects, which is much higher than most forms of testing.

Many test stages such as unit test, function test, regression test, etc. are only about 35% efficient in finding code bugs, or find one bug out of three. This explains why 6–10 separate kinds of testing are needed.

The kinds of companies and projects that are "average" would include internal software built by hundreds of banks, insurance companies, retail and wholesale companies, and many government agencies at federal, state, and municipal levels.

Average quality control has DRE levels from about 85% for large systems up to 96% for small and simple projects.

Poor Quality Control

Poor quality control is characterized by weak defect prevention and almost a total omission of pre-test defect removal methods such as static analysis and formal inspections. Poor quality control is also characterized by inept and inaccurate quality measures which ignore front-end defects in requirements and design. There are also gaps in measuring code defects. For example, most companies with poor quality control have no idea how many test cases might be needed or how efficient various kinds of test stages are.

Companies with poor quality control also fail to perform any kind of up-front quality predictions so they jump into development without a clue as to how many bugs are likely to occur and what are the best methods for preventing or removing these bugs. Testing is usually by untrained, uncertified developers without using any formal test case design methods.

One of the main reasons for the long schedules and high costs associated with poor quality is the fact that so many bugs are found when testing starts that the test interval stretches out to two or three times longer than planned (*Estimating Software Costs*; Jones, 2007).

Some of the kinds of software that are noted for poor quality control include the Obamacare web site, municipal software for property tax assessments, and software for programmed stock trading, which has caused several massive stock crashes. Indeed government software projects tend to have more poor quality projects than corporate software by a considerable margin. For example, the author of this book has worked as an expert witness in lawsuits for poor quality for more state government software failures than any other industrial segment.

Poor quality control is often below 85% in DRE levels. In fact for canceled projects or those that end up in litigation for poor quality, the DRE levels may drop below 80%, which is low enough to be considered professional malpractice. In litigation where the author of this book has been an expert witness, DRE levels in the low 80% range have been the unfortunate norm.

Table 2.5   Distribution of DRE for 1,000 Projects

DRE	Projects	Percent
>99.00%	10	0.01
95%–99%	120	12.00
90%–94%	250	25.00
85%–89%	475	47.50
80%–85%	125	12.50
<80.00%	20	2.00
Totals	**1,000**	**100.00**

Table 2.5 shows the ranges in DRE noted from a sample of 1,000 software projects. The sample included systems and embedded software, web projects, cloud projects, information technology projects, and also defense and commercial packages.

As can be seen, high DRE does not occur often. This is unfortunate because projects that are above 95.00% in DRE have shorter schedules and lower costs than projects below 85.00% in DRE. The software industry does not measure either quality or productivity well enough to know this.

However, the most important economic fact about high quality is: ***Projects > 97% in DRE have shorter schedules and lower costs than projects < 90% in DRE***. This is because projects that are low in DRE have test schedules that are at least twice as long as projects with high DRE due to omission of pre-test inspections and static analysis!

Table 2.6 shows DRE for four application size plateaus and for six technology combinations.

As can be seen, DRE varies by size and also by technology stack. A combination of inspections, static analysis, and formal testing has the highest DRE values for all sizes.

The DRE metric was first developed by IBM circa 1970. It is normally calculated by measuring all defects found prior to release to customers,

Table 2.6 Software Defect Removal Efficiency (DRE)

	Note 1: Defect Removal Efficiency (DRE) is total removal before release				
	Note 2: Size is expressed in terms of IFPUG function points 4.3				
	Cases	100 DRE	1,000 DRE	10,000 DRE	100,000 DRE	Average
1	**Inspections, static analysis, formal testing**	99.60%	98.50%	97.00%	96.00%	97.78%
2	Inspections, formal testing	98.00%	97.00%	96.00%	94.50%	96.38%
3	Static analysis, formal testing	97.00%	96.00%	95.00%	93.50%	95.38%
4	Formal testing	93.00%	91.00%	90.00%	88.50%	90.63%
5	**Informal testing**	87.00%	85.00%	83.00%	80.00%	83.75%
	Average	94.92%	93.50%	92.20%	90.50%	92.78%

and then customer-reported defects for the first 90 days of usage (*The Economics of Software Quality*, Jones and Bonsignour, 2012).

As of 2020, DRE measures were used by dozens of high-technology companies, but were not widely used by government agencies or other industry segments such as banks, insurance, and manufacturing. However, DRE is one of the most useful of all quality measures. Namcook suggests that all companies and government agencies use "defect potentials" and "defect removal efficiency" on all projects. The phrase "defect potentials" also originated in IBM circa 1970 and is the sum total of bugs that originate in requirements, architecture, design, code, documents, and "bad fixes" or new bugs found in bug repairs themselves.

Formal testing implies certified test personnel and mathematical test case design such as use of "design of experiments." Informal testing implies untrained uncertified developers.

Note that the corona virus will eliminate group inspections in the same room, and will probably switch to Zoom inspections.

Table 2.7 shows the schedules in calendar months for the same combinations of application size plateaus and also for technology combinations.

As can be seen from Table 2.6, high quality does not add time to development. High quality shortens schedules because the main reason for schedule delays is too many bugs when testing starts, which stretches out test schedules by weeks or months (*Estimating Software Costs*, Jones, 2007).

Table 2.7 Software Schedules Related to Quality Control

	Note 1: Size is expressed in terms of IFPUG function points 4.3				
	Note 2: Schedule is expressed in terms of calendar months				
	Cases	100	1,000	10,000	100,000	Average
1	Inspections, static analysis, formal testing	5.50	12.88	30.20	70.79	29.84
2	Inspections, formal testing	5.75	13.80	33.11	79.43	33.03
3	Static analysis, formal testing	5.62	13.34	31.62	74.99	31.39
4	Formal testing	6.03	14.79	36.31	89.13	36.56
5	Informal testing	6.31	15.85	39.81	100.00	40.49
Average		**5.84**	**14.13**	**34.21**	**82.87**	**34.26**

Note: Namcook Analytics' Software Risk Master (SRM) tool can predict the results of any combination of defect prevention methods, pretest defect removal methods, and testing stages. SRM can also predict the results of 57 development methods, 79 programming languages, and the impact of all five levels of the CMMI.

Since one of the major forms of "wastage" involves canceled projects, Table 2.8 shows the impact of high quality on project cancellation rates. Since many cancelled projects are above 10,000 function points in size, only data for large systems is shown in Table 2.8.

As can be seen from Table 2.8, poor quality control and lack of pretest inspections and static analysis is a major cause of cancelled projects.

Table 2.9 shows the impact of quality control on software outsource litigation. The author of this book has been an expert witness in 15 breach of contract cases and has provided data to other testifying experts in about 50 other cases. In fact data from the author's book *The Economics of Software Quality* (Jones and Bonsignour, 2011) is used in many lawsuits, sometimes by both sides, because there is no other useful published source of quality data.

As can be seen, poor quality control on outsourced projects has an alarmingly high probability of ending up in court either because the projects are cancelled or because of major errors after deployment that prevent the owners from using the software as intended.

Table 2.10 shows the kinds of industries that are most likely to be found in each of the five levels of quality control. In general, the

Table 2.8 Impact of Software Quality on Cancellation

	Note 1: Size is expressed in terms of IFPUG function points 4.3					
	Note 2: Projects <10,000 function points are seldom canceled and not shown					
	Cases	*100*	*1,000*	*10,000*	*100,000*	*Average*
1	**Inspections, static analysis, formal testing**			**7.00%**	**14.00%**	**10.50%**
2	Inspections, formal testing			12.00%	24.00%	**18.00%**
3	Static analysis, formal testing			16.00%	32.00%	**24.00%**
4	Formal testing			43.00%	57.00%	**50.00%**
5	**Informal testing**			**72.00%**	**83.00%**	**77.50%**
Average				**30.00%**	**42.00%**	**36.00%**

Table 2.9   Impact of Software Quality on Litigation

	Cases	100	1,000	10,000	100,000	Average
	Note 1: Size is expressed in terms of IFPUG function points 4.3					
	Note 2: Data shows % of outsource projects in breach of contract litigation					
	Note 3: Most breach of contract litigation occurs >10,000 function points					
1	**Inspections, static analysis, formal testing**			2.00%	5.00%	3.50%
2	Inspections, formal testing			4.00%	12.00%	**8.00%**
3	Static analysis, formal testing			6.00%	17.00%	**11.50%**
4	Formal testing			12.00%	24.00%	**18.00%**
5	**Informal testing**			**24.00%**	**48.00%**	**36.00%**
Average				**9.60%**	**21.20%**	**15.40%**

industries with the best quality tend to be those that build complex physical devices such as medical equipment, aircraft, or telephone switching systems.

> *Note that the corona virus of 2020 has delayed court proceedings and is causing physical changes in court room structures such as plastic walls protecting the judge, witnesses, and attorneys. Jurors will no longer sit in a jury box side by side but probably will use Zoom from external locations elsewhere in the courthouse.*

The industries that bring up the bottom with frequently poor quality control include state, municipal, and federal civilian government groups (military software is fairly good in quality control), and also stock trading software. For that matter, tax software is not very good and there are errors in things like property tax and income tax calculations.

Table 2.10 shows trends but the data is not absolute. Some government groups are better than expected, but not very many. Namcook has data on over 70 industry sectors.

The final table in this chapter is taken from Chapter 7 of the author's book *The Economics of Software Quality* with Olivier Bonsignour; Jones 2011 as the co-author. Table 2.11 shows the approximate distribution of excellent, average, and poor software quality by application size.

Table 2.10 Industries Noted at Each Software Quality Level

	Note 1: Hi tech industries have the best quality control at all sizes	
	Note 2: Defense and avionics have good quality control	
	Note 3: All forms of civilian government have poor quality control	
	Note 4: Stock trading has poor quality control	
	Cases	*Industries*
1	Inspections, static analysis, formal testing	Medical devices
		Aircraft
		Telecomm
2	Inspections, formal testing	Airlines
		Pharmaceuticals
		Defense
3	Static analysis, formal testing	Open source
		Commercial software
		Automotive
4	Formal testing	Banks/insurance
		Health care
		Outsourcers
5	Informal testing	Retail
		Stock trading
		Government (all levels)

As can be seen, software quality declines as application size increased. This is due to the intrinsic complexity of large software applications, compounded by the lack of standard certified reusable components. It is also compounded by the omission of pre-test inspections and static analysis for many of the large applications above 10,000 function points in size.

Summary and Conclusions

Analysis of the work patterns of the software engineering world reveals a surprising fact. Much of the work of software engineering is basically "wasted" because it concerns either working on projects that will not be

Table 2.11   Distribution of Software Projects by Quality Levels

Function Points	(Sample = approximately 27,000 software projects to 2020)		
	Low Quality	*Average Quality*	*High Quality*
10	25.00%	50.00%	25.00%
100	30.00%	47.00%	23.00%
1,000	36.00%	44.00%	20.00%
10,000	**40.00%**	42.00%	**18.00%**
100,000	**43.00%**	45.00%	**12.00%**
Average	37.25%	**44.50%**	**18.25%**

completed or working on repairing defects that should not be present at all.

If the software community can be alerted to the fact that poor software engineering economics are due to poor quality, then we might be motivated to take defect prevention, defect removal, reusability, and risk analysis more seriously than they are taken today.

The impact of the corona virus on software engineering cannot yet be predicted in mid-2020. No doubt there will be an impact due to the elimination of staff meetings and face to face events such as inspections. Possibly Zoom or an equivalent can substitute but the author's experience with Zoom is that it is not yet an effective substitute for live meetings and especially for meetings where documents need to be shared and reviewed. The author of this book has never tried Zoom for software code inspection but he doubts if it will be easy.

Chapter 3

Root Causes of Poor Software Quality

Introduction

The software industry has a bad and justified reputation for poor quality and low reliability. A key reason for poor quality is that quality measurements are embarrassingly bad. Metrics such as cost per defect and lines of code distort reality and conceal software quality. Software measures omit important data, use hazardous metrics, and are not sufficient to show the effectiveness of various quality control methods such as static analysis, inspections, and testing.

Software quality depends upon two important variables. The first variable is that of "*defect potentials*" or the sum total of bugs likely to occur in requirements, architecture, design, code, documents, and "bad fixes" or new bugs in bug repairs. The second important measure is "*defect removal efficiency (DRE)*" or the percentage of bugs found and eliminated before release of software to clients.

The metrics of *defect potentials* and *defect removal efficiency (DRE)* were developed by IBM circa 1970 and are widely used by technology companies and also by insurance companies, banks, and other companies with large software organizations.

Poor software quality is an endemic problem of the software industry. Many large systems are canceled due to poor quality. Almost all large systems run late and are over budget due to poor quality. There are many lawsuits for poor quality. There are billions of dollars wasted by software customers due to customer damages caused by poor quality. There are also rapidly increasing numbers of cyber-attacks most due to poor software quality. Why do these endemic problems occur?

An important root cause is that most software quality companies are "one-trick-ponies" that only care about one subject. Some quality companies sell automated testing, some sell static analysis, some sell automated proofs, or whatever; no company sells a full suite of software quality tools and methods that encompass all sources of software defects and all forms of software defect removal.

Effective quality control needs a synergistic combination of defect prevention, pre-test defect removal, and formal testing with certified test personnel. Worse, most quality companies have zero empirical data as to the efficacy of their tools and methods. They make vast claims of better quality but provide no case studies or validated results.

Software quality data should be based on function point metrics because function points can show defects from all sources such as requirements, design, etc. Table 3.1 shows approximate U.S. averages for defect potentials for poor-quality and high-quality software projects.

If drugs and pharmaceutical products were released to the public with as little validation as software quality tools, the U.S. death rate would probably be twice what it actually is today.

Following is a list of 56 software topics that include defect origins, defect prevention methods, and defect removal stages that run from early requirements to post-delivery for a large system of a nominal 10,000 function points and 1,500 SNAP points in size in Java.

All of these 56 quality control factors are important for large systems in the 10,000 function point size range. The problem today is that no known software quality company sells more than one or two of these 56 quality methods or even knows about the others!

Few quality companies and even fewer of their clients know about the other factors! A narrow focus on testing and basic ignorance of the suite of effective software defect prevention and defect removal methods is an endemic and chronic problem of the software industry.

If a reader wanted to learn about all 56 quality factors, he or she would probably need a dozen courses from at least half a dozen software quality training companies because none of them cover the full spectrum of effective quality tools and methods or even know about them!

None of the major international standards such as ISO and IEEE standards on software quality are fully adequate because none of them ask for quantitative quality data and all ignore basic software quality factors such as defect potentials and DRE.

Table 3.1   Results of Poor-Quality and High Quality Software

		Poor Quality	High Quality
(Nominal 10,000 function points; 1,500 SNAP points)			
U.S. Software Defect Potentials per Function Point			
1	Requirements defects (functional and non-functional)	0.90	0.30
2	Architecture defects	0.20	0.05
3	Design defects	1.10	0.35
4	Code defects	1.55	0.60
5	Security flaw defects	0.35	0.10
6	Document defects	0.45	0.20
7	Bad fix defects (new bugs in bug repairs)	0.55	0.05
Total		**5.10**	**1.65**
Application Defect Removal Efficiency Results			
8	Defect removal efficiency (DRE)	91.00%	98.50%
9	Defects removed per function point	4.64	1.63
10	Defects removed – actual total	46,410	16,253
11	Defects delivered per function point	0.46	0.02
12	Defects delivered – actual total	4,590	247
13	High severity defects delivered per function point	0.46	0.02
14	High severity defects delivered – actual total	689	27
15	Security flaws delivered – actual total	55	1
Application Defect Prevention Stages			
16	Joint application design (JAD)	No	Yes
17	Prototype	Yes	Yes
18	Requirements models (primarily functional)	No	Yes
19	Quality function deployment (QFD)	No	Yes
20	Automated proofs	No	Yes
21	SEMAT (Software Engineering Methods and Theory)	No	Yes
22	Six-Sigma for software	No	Yes

(Continued)

Table 3.1 (Continued)

(Nominal 10,000 function points; 1,500 SNAP points)		Poor Quality	High Quality
23	Capability maturity model (CMMI) – defense only	No	No
Total		**1**	**7**
Application Pre-Test Defect Removal Stages			
24	Formal inspections of requirements	No	Yes
25	Formal inspection of architecture (large systems)	No	Yes
26	Formal inspections of design	No	Yes
27	Formal inspections of new/changed code	No	Yes
28	Formal quality assurance reviews	No	Yes
29	Pair programming (*not recommended*)	No	No
30	Independent verification & validation (defense only)	No	No
31	FOG readability index of requirements, design	No	Yes
32	Static analysis of application code and changed code	No	Yes
33	Ethical hackers on high-security software	No	Yes
34	Cyclomatic complexity analysis and reduction	No	Yes
35	SANS Institute defect category analysis and removal	No	Yes
Total		**1**	**10**
Application Test Defect Removal Stages			
36	Unit test – automated	Yes	Yes
37	New function test	Yes	Yes
38	Regression test – automated	Yes	Yes
39	Stress/performance test	Yes	Yes
40	Usability test	No	Yes
41	Component test	Yes	Yes
42	Independent test (defense only)	No	No
43	Security test	No	Yes
44	System test – automated	Yes	Yes
45	Multi-platform test	Yes	Yes
46	Global nationalization test	Yes	Yes

Table 3.1 (Continued)

(Nominal 10,000 function points; 1,500 SNAP points)		*Poor Quality*	*High Quality*
47	Beta/acceptance test	Yes	Yes
Total		**9**	**11**
Application Post-Release Quality Stages			
48	Static analysis of all code changes/bug repairs	No	Yes
49	Formal inspection of large changes	No	Yes
50	Cyber-attack defenses (firewalls, antivirus, etc.)	Yes	Yes
51	Penetration teams (high security applications)	No	Yes
52	Maintainability analysis of legacy applications	No	Yes
53	Test library analysis (defective test case removal)	No	Yes
54	Error-prone module (EPM) analysis and removal	No	Yes
55	Race-condition analysis and correction	No	Yes
56	Cyclomatic complexity analysis and correction	No	Yes
Total		**1**	**9**
Total Quality Control Factors		**19**	**53**

Software Quality Education Curricula

The curricula of the major software quality training companies are embarrassing because of the gaps, omissions, and topics that are not covered. Even worse not a single quality education company has actual quantified data on software defect origins, defect densities, defect prevention, or DRE levels.

You would have to go back almost 200 years in medical education to find such skimpy knowledge of the basic topics needed to train physicians as we have for training software quality and test personnel today.

You might take quality courses from companies such as Construx, from CAST, from IBM, from ITMPI, from SQE, from QAI, from the SANS Institute, from Parasoft, from Smart Bear, and probably from other local educators but these would probably be single-topic courses such as static analysis or automated testing. The courses, while useful by themselves, would not be part of a full software quality curriculum because none of the quality companies know enough about software quality to have effective overall curricula!

Worse, these courses even from major quality companies would lack quantitative data on defect potentials, DRE, bad-fix injections, error-prone modules, or any other of the critical topics that quality professionals should know about. The software industry is running blind due to the widespread lack of quantitative quality data.

Software quality data is available from some benchmark organizations such as Davids Consulting, Gartner Group, Namcook Analytics LLC, TIMetricas, Q/P Management Group/QSM, and several others. But the combined set of clients for all current quality benchmark organizations is less than 50,000 customers in an industry employing close to 20,000,000 people on a global basis.

Software quality data can be predicted by some parametric software estimation tools such as Software Risk Master (SRM), KnowledgePlan, SEER, SLIM, and COCOMO, but the combined market for all of these parametric tools is less than 25,000 customers in an industry employing almost 20,000,000 people on a global basis.

In other words, even companies that offer accurate quality data have comparatively few clients who are interested in that data, even though it could save companies and governments billions of dollars in reduced defect repairs and reduced cyber-attack recovery costs!

It is professionally embarrassing about how unsophisticated software quality education is compared to medical school curricula for training physicians.

You probably could not take courses on this set of 56 topics from any university because their curricula tend to deal only with a few of the more common methods and concentrate primarily on testing. I have yet to see a university with quantitative data on software defect volumes, severity levels, origins, or effective defect removal methods with quantitative results.

You might take some courses from non-profit associations such as the American Society for Quality (ASQ), the Society for Information Management (SIM), or the Project Management Institute (PMI). But no single organization in 2016 covers more than a small fraction of the total intellectual content of effective software quality control. None of the software non-profit organizations have quantitative data on defect volumes, severity levels, or DRE.

To illustrate the kind of quality education that is needed, Table 3.2 shows a sample curriculum for software quality assurance testing and Table 3.3 shows a sample curriculum for software test training.

In today's world, software quality assurance has an expanding role in cyber defenses and cyber-attack recovery. Software quality assurance

Table 3.2 Software Quality Assurance Curricula

	Software Quality Assurance Courses	Days	Value
1	Hazardous quality metrics: cost per defect	0.50	10.00
2	Hazardous quality metrics: lines of code	0.50	10.00
3	Hazardous quality metrics: technical debt	0.50	10.00
4	Hazardous quality metrics: story points	0.50	10.00
5	Effective quality metrics: function points	0.50	10.00
6	Effective quality metrics: defect removal %	0.50	10.00
7	Effective quality metrics: defect severity levels	0.50	10.00
8	Effective quality metrics: defect origin analysis	0.50	10.00
9	Emerging quality metrics: SNAP points	0.50	10.00
10	Overview of major software failures	1.00	10.00
11	Overview of major software cyber-attacks	1.00	10.00
12	Error prone module (EPM) analysis	1.00	10.00
13	Software defect detection efficiency (DDE)	1.00	10.00
14	Software defect removal efficiency (DRE)	1.00	10.00
15	Software defect tracking	1.00	10.00
16	Software defect prevention (JAD, QFD, etc.)	1.00	10.00
17	Software pre-test defect removal	1.00	10.00
18	Software test defect removal	1.00	10.00
19	Software requirements modeling	1.00	10.00
20	Functional and non-functional requirements	2.00	10.00
21	Software static analysis: text	1.00	10.00
22	Software static analysis: code	1.00	10.00
23	Software correctness proofs: manual	1.00	10.00
24	Software correctness proofs: automated	1.00	10.00
25	Software security and quality in 2016	2.00	10.00
26	Quality benchmarks: Namcook, Q/P, etc.	1.00	10.00
27	Software security inspections	3.00	10.00
28	Security flaw removal (hacking, test, etc.)	3.00	10.00

(Continued)

Table 3.2   (Continued)

	Software Quality Assurance Courses	Days	Value
29	Error prone module (EPM) analysis	2.00	9.95
30	Software test case design	2.00	9.75
31	Software test library management	1.00	9.75
32	Reducing bad-fix injections	1.00	9.75
33	Test case conflicts and errors	1.00	9.75
34	Software requirement inspections	1.00	9.75
35	Software design inspections	2.00	9.50
36	Software code inspections	2.00	9.50
37	Software test inspections	2.00	9.50
38	Defect removal using pair programming	1.00	9.50
39	Defect removal using container development	1.00	9.50
40	Defect removal using DevOps	2.00	9.50
41	Defect removal using TSP/PSP	2.00	9.00
42	Defect removal using Agile	2.00	9.00
43	Defect removal using RUP	2.00	9.00
44	Automated software testing	2.00	9.00
45	Quality assurance of software reuse	1.00	9.00
46	Quality assurance of COTS and ERP	1.00	9.00
47	Quality assurance of open source	1.00	9.00
48	Tools: quality assurance	1.00	9.00
49	Tools: defect prediction	1.00	9.00
50	Defect removal using Waterfall development	1.00	8.00
51	Cost of quality (COQ)	1.00	8.00
52	Overview of the CMMI	1.00	8.00
53	ISO and IEEE quality standards	1.00	7.00
54	Six Sigma: green belt	3.00	7.00
55	Six Sigma: black belt	3.00	7.00
Total		**70.50**	**9.49**

Table 3.3 Software Testing Courses

	Software Testing Courses	Days	Value
1	Test case design optimization	2.00	10.00
2	Test cases – design of experiments	2.00	10.00
3	Test cases – cause/effect graphing	2.00	10.00
4	Test cases and requirements	2.00	10.00
5	Risk-based test case design	2.00	10.00
6	Analysis of gaps and errors in test case designs	2.00	10.00
7	Cyclomatic complexity and test coverage	2.00	10.00
8	Test library control	2.00	10.00
9	Security testing overview	2.00	10.00
10	Advanced security testing	3.00	10.00
11	Test schedule estimating	1.00	10.00
12	Software defect potential estimating	1.00	10.00
13	Defect removal efficiency (DRE) measurement	1.00	10.00
14	Software build planning and control	1.00	10.00
15	Big data test design	2.00	10.00
16	Cloud test design	2.00	10.00
17	Removal of incorrect test cases	1.00	10.00
18	Test coverage analysis	1.00	9.50
19	Identifying error-prone modules (EPM)	2.00	9.50
20	Data base test design	1.00	9.50
21	Test case conflicts and errors	1.00	9.25
22	Static analysis and testing	1.00	9.00
23	Reducing bad-fix injections	1.00	9.00
24	Basic black box testing	1.00	9.00
25	Basic white box testing	1.00	9.00
26	Basic gray box testing	1.00	9.00
27	fundamentals or risk-based testing	1.00	9.00
28	Fundamentals of unit testing	1.00	9.00

(Continued)

Table 3.3   (Continued)

	Software Testing Courses	Days	Value
29	Fundamentals of regression testing	1.00	9.00
30	Fundamentals of component testing	1.00	9.00
31	Fundamentals of stress testing	1.00	9.00
32	Fundamentals of virus testing	2.00	9.00
33	Fundamentals of lab testing	1.00	9.00
34	Fundamentals of system testing	2.00	9.00
35	Fundamentals of external beta testing	1.00	9.00
36	Fundamentals of acceptance testing	1.00	9.00
37	Testing web applications	1.00	9.00
38	Tools: automated testing	2.00	9.00
39	Tools: test case design	1.00	9.00
40	Tools: test library control	1.00	9.00
41	Tools: defect tracking	1.00	9.00
42	Tools: complexity analysis	0.50	9.00
43	Tools: test coverage analysis	0.50	9.00
44	Fundamentals of reusable test materials	1.00	9.00
45	Testing Cloud, SOA, and SaaS	2.00	8.80
46	Testing COTS application packages	1.00	8.75
47	Testing ERP applications	1.00	8.75
48	Testing reusable functions	1.00	8.75
49	Supply chain testing	1.00	8.50
50	Function points for test measures	1.00	7.00
Total		**67.00**	**9.31**

personnel need much more knowledge on security topics than they did 30 years ago.

Today software testing has become a barrier to cyber-attacks so special attention is needed for testing software security flaws.

Between software quality assurance training and software test personnel training, there is a need to expand on both university curricula and the limited curricula from software quality companies, neither of which are fully adequate today.

If you wanted to acquire actual supporting tools for these 56 quality topics, you would probably need to go to at least 15 commercial quality companies, static analysis companies, and test tool companies and another half dozen open source quality groups.

Nobody sells all the tools that are needed to control software quality! Most quality tool vendors don't even know about effective quality tools other than the ones they sell. There are no software quality companies in 2017 that have the depth and breadth of medical companies such as McKesson or Johnson & Johnson.

The static analysis companies only sell static analysis; the testing companies only sell test tools; to get quality metrics and measurement tools you need additional vendors; to get ordinary defect tracking tools you need still other vendors; to get quality benchmark data you need another set of vendors; to get software quality predictions via commercial estimating tools you need yet another set of vendors.

The software industry has nothing like a Mayo Clinic where advanced medical treatments are available for a wide spectrum of medical conditions. In fact software quality control in 2016 is closer to the days 200 years ago when doctors were also barbers and sterile surgical procedures had not yet been discovered. Software has nothing even close to CAT scans and MRI exams for finding quality and security problems.

No known software company covers the full spectrum of software quality tools, technologies, topics, and effective quality methods, although a few large companies such as IBM, Microsoft, and Hewlett Packard may sell perhaps a 12 to 15 out of the set of 56.

No university has a truly effective software quality curriculum. In fact many universities still teach courses using "cost per defect" and "lines of code" metrics and hence have no accurate quality data available at all, since these metrics distort reality.

Of course no pharmaceutical company sells medicines for all diseases and no physicians can treat all medical conditions but physicians at least learn about almost all common medical conditions as a basic part of their education. There are also specialists available who can deal with uncommon medical conditions.

Medicine has the *Index Medicus* that provides an overall description of the use of thousands of prescription drugs, their side effects, and dosage. There is no exact equivalent to the Index Medicus for software bugs and their treatment, but the closest is probably Capers Jones' and Olivier Bonsignour's book on *The Economics of Software Quality*, published in 2012.

Medicine also has many wide-ranging books such as *Control of Communicable Diseases in Man* Published by the U.S. Surgeon General's office which show the scope of common infectious diseases such as polio and smallpox as well as their known treatments. Software has nothing like the breadth and depth of the medical literature.

A book recommended by the author of this book to all clients and colleagues is *The Social Transformation of American Medicine* by Paul Starr. This book won a Pulitzer Prize in 1982. It also won the Bancroft Prize. This book provides an excellent guide to how medicine was transformed from a poorly educated craft into one of the top learned professions in world history.

Surprisingly at one time about 150 years ago, medicine was even more chaotic than software is today. Medical schools did not require college degrees or even high-school graduation to enter. Medical students never entered hospitals during training because the hospitals used private medical staff. There was no monitoring of medical malpractice and quacks could become physicians. There were no medical licenses or board certifications.

There was no formal evaluation of prescription drugs before release and harmful substances such as opium could be freely prescribed. (A Sears-Roebuck catalog in the 1890s offered liquid opium as a balm for quieting noisy children. This product was available without prescription.)

Paul Starr's excellent book shows how the American Medical Association (AMA) transformed itself and also medical practice to improve medical education and introduce medical licenses and board certifications.

This book by Paul Starr provides a full guide for the set of steps needed by the software industry in order to become a true profession.

One of the interesting methods used by the AMA was reciprocal membership with all state medical societies. This had the effect of raising AMA membership from below 800 to more than 80,000 which finally gave physicians enough political clout to lobby for medical licenses. It would be interesting if the IEEE, SIM, ACM, and other software professional organizations also had reciprocal memberships instead of more or less competing.

Poor software quality is a sociological problem as well as a technology problem. Starr's book showed how medicine gradually improved both the sociology of medical practice and the underlying technology of medical offices and hospitals over about a 50-year period.

With Starr's book as a guide, software engineering might be able to accomplish the same results in less than 25 years instead of the 50 years required to professionalize medicine.

The three major problems facing the software industry are these:

1. Software has poor quality control due to lack of knowledge of effective software quality techniques.
2. Software has embarrassingly poor education on software quality due to lack of empirical data.
3. Software has embarrassingly bad and incomplete quality data due to use of ineffective and hazardous metrics such as "cost per defect," combined with the failure to use effective metrics such as function points and DRE.

The sad thing about poor software quality is that all three of these problems are treatable conditions that could be eliminated in less than 10 years if one or more major software companies became proactive in (1) effective quality metrics and measures, (2) fact-based education with quantitative data, and (3) expanded quality control that encompassed effective quality measures, effective defect prevention, effective pre-test defect removal, and effective formal testing.

The author's hope is that vaccinations and effective treatments for poor software quality will be developed soon such as vaccinations for smallpox and polio were developed, and antibiotics were developed for many bacterial infections. Dozens of companies worked toward a vaccine for COVID-19 which are now available and still expanding in 2021.

There are still untreatable medical conditions, but overall medicine has made huge advances in prevention and control of hundreds of formerly serious and common diseases. Software has not yet made any major advances in quality control although some modern methods such as static analysis hold promise.

References and Readings in Software Quality Control

Abrain, Alain; *Software Estimating Models*; Wiley-IEEE Computer Society; 2015.

Abrain, Alain; *Software Metrics and Metrology*; Wiley-IEEE Computer Society; 2010.

Abrain, Alain; *Software Maintenance Management: Evolution and Continuous Improvement*; Wiley-IEEE Computer Society; 2008.

Abrain, A.; and Robillard, P.N.; "Function Point Analysis: An Empirical Study of Its Measurement Processes"; *IEEE Transactions on Software Engineering*, Vol 22, No. 12; December 1996; pp. 895–909.

Albrecht, Allan; *AD/M Productivity Measurement and Estimate Validation*; IBM Corporation, Purchase, NY; May 1984.

Austin, Robert D.; *Measuring and Managing Performance in Organizations*; Dorset House Press, New York, NY; 1996; ISBN: 0-932633-36-6; 216 pages.

Beck, Kent; *Test-Driven Development*; Addison Wesley, Boston, MA; 2002; ISBN: 10-0321146530; 240 pages.

Black, Rex; *Managing the Testing Process: Practical Tools and Techniques for Managing Hardware and Software Testing*; Wiley; 2009; ISBN: 10-0470404159; 672 pages.

Boehm, Barry; *Software Engineering Economics*; Prentice Hall, Englewood Cliffs, NJ; 1981; 900 pages.

Brooks, Fred; *The Mythical Man-Month*, 1974 rev ed.; Addison-Wesley, Reading, MA; 1995.

Chelf, Ben; and Jetley, Raoul; *Diagnosing Medical Device Software Defects Using Static Analysis*; Coverity Technical Report, San Francisco, CA; 2008.

Chess, Brian; and West, Jacob; *Secure Programming with Static Analysis*; Addison Wesley, Boston, MA; 2007; ISBN: 13:978-0321424778; 624 pages.

Cohen, Lou; *Quality Function Deployment – How to Make QFD Work for You*; Prentice Hall, Upper Saddle River, NJ; 1995; ISBN: 10-0201633302; 368 pages.

Crosby, Philip B.; *Quality Is Free*; New American Library, Mentor Books, New York, NY; 1979; 270 pages.

Charette, Bob; *Software Engineering Risk Analysis and Management*; McGraw Hill, New York, NY; 1989.

Charette, Bob; *Application Strategies for Risk Management*; McGraw Hill, New York, NY; 1990.

Constantine, Larry L; *Beyond Chaos: The Expert Edge in Managing Software Development*; ACM Press; 2001.

DeMarco, Tom; *Peopleware: Productive Projects and Teams*; Dorset House, New York, NY; 1999; ISBN: 10-0932633439; 245 pages.

DeMarco, Tom; *Controlling Software Projects*; Yourdon Press, New York, NY; 1982; ISBN: 0-917072-32-4; 284 pages.

Everett, Gerald D.; and McLeod, Raymond; *Software Testing*; John Wiley & Sons, Hoboken, NJ; 2007; ISBN: 978-0-471-79371-7; 261 pages.

Ewusi-Mensah, Kweku; *Software Development Failures*; MIT Press, Cambridge, MA; 2003; ISBN: 0-26205072-2 276 pages.

Flowers, Stephen; *Software Failures: Management Failures; Amazing Stories and Cautionary Tales*; John Wiley & Sons; 1996.

Gack, Gary; *Managing the Black Hole: The Executives Guide to Software Project Risk*; Business Expert Publishing, Thomson, GA; 2010; ISBN: 10: 1-935602-01-9.

Gack, Gary; *Applying Six Sigma to Software Implementation Projects*; http://software.isixsigma.com/library/content/c040915b.asp.

Galorath, Dan; and Evans, Michael; *Software Sizing, Estimation, and Risk Management: When Performance is Measured Performance Improves*; Auerbach; Philadelphia, PA; 2006.

Garmus, David; and Herron, David; *Function Point Analysis – Measurement Practices for Successful Software Projects*; Addison Wesley Longman, Boston, MA; 2001; ISBN: 0-201-69944-3; 363 pages.

Gibbs, T. Wayt; "Trends in Computing: Software's Chronic Crisis"; *Scientific American Magazine*, Vol. 271, No. 3, International edition; September 1994; pp 72–81.

Gilb, Tom; and Graham, Dorothy; *Software Inspections*; Addison Wesley, Reading, MA; 1993; ISBN: 10: 0201631814.

Harris, Michael D.S., Herron, David; and Iwanacki, Stasia; *The Business Value of IT*; CRC Press, Auerbach Publications; 2009.

Hill, Peter R. *Practical Software Project Estimation*; McGraw Hill; 2010.

Hill, Peter; Jones Capers; and Reifer, Don; *The Impact of Software Size on Productivity*; International Software Standards Benchmark Group (ISBSG), Melbourne, Australia; September 2013.

Howard, Alan (Ed.); *Software Metrics and Project Management Tools*; Applied Computer Research (ACR), Phoenix, AZ; 1997; 30 pages.

Humphrey, Watts; *Managing the Software Process*; Addison Wesley, Reading, MA; 1989.

International Function Point Users Group (IFPUG); *IT Measurement – Practical Advice from the Experts*; Addison Wesley Longman, Boston, MA; 2002; ISBN: 0-201-74158-X; 759 pages.

Jacobsen, Ivar, Griss, Martin; and Jonsson, Patrick; *Software Reuse - Architecture, Process, and Organization for Business Success*; Addison Wesley Longman, Reading, MA; 1997; ISBN: 0-201-92476-5; 500 pages.

Jacobsen, Ivar et al; *The Essence of Software Engineering; Applying the SEMAT Kernel*; Addison Wesley Professional; 2013.

Jones, Capers; *Software Risk Master (SRM) tutorial*; Namcook Analytics LLC, Narragansett, RI; 2015a.

Jones, Capers; *Software Defect Origins and Removal Methods*; Namcook Analytics LLC, Narragansett, RI; 2015b.

Jones, Capers; *The Mess of Software Metrics*; Namcook Analytics LLC, Narragansett, RI; 2015c.

Jones, Capers; *The Technical and Social History of Software Engineering*; Addison Wesley; 2014.

Jones, Capers; and Bonsignour, Olivier; *The Economics of Software Quality*; Addison Wesley, Boston, MA; 2011; ISBN: 978-0-13-258220-9; 587 pages.

Jones, Capers; *Software Engineering Best Practices*; McGraw Hill, New York, NY; 2010; ISBN: 978-0-07-162161-8; 660 pages.

Jones, Capers; *Applied Software Measurement*, 3rd ed.; McGraw Hill; 2008; ISBN: 978=0-07-150244-3; 662 pages.

Jones, Capers; *Critical Problems in Software Measurement*; Information Systems Management Group; 1993a; ISBN: 1-56909-000-9; 195 pages.

Jones, Capers; *Software Productivity and Quality Today -- The Worldwide Perspective*; Information Systems Management Group; 1993b; ISBN: 156909-001-7; 200 pages.

Jones, Capers; *Assessment and Control of Software Risks*; Prentice Hall; 1994; ISBN: 0-13-741406-4; 711 pages.

Jones, Capers; *New Directions in Software Management*; Information Systems Management Group; n.d.; ISBN: 1-56909-009-2; 150 pages.

Jones, Capers; *Patterns of Software System Failure and Success*; International Thomson Computer Press, Boston, MA; December 1995; ISBN: 1-850-32804-8; 250; 292 pages.

Jones, Capers; "Sizing Up Software"; *Scientific American Magazine*, Vol. 279, No. 6; December 1998; pp. 104–111.

Jones, Capers; *Conflict and Litigation Between Software Clients and Developers*; Software Productivity Research Technical Report; Narragansett, RI; 2007a; 65 pages.

Jones, Capers; *Software Quality – Analysis and Guidelines for Success*; International Thomson Computer Press, Boston, MA; 1997a; ISBN: 1-85032-876-6; 492 pages.

Jones, Capers; *Estimating Software Costs*, 2nd ed.; McGraw Hill, New York, NY; 2007b; 700 pages.

Jones, Capers; *The Economics of Object-Oriented Software*; SPR Technical Report; Software Productivity Research, Burlington, MA; April 1997b; 22 pages.

Jones, Capers; *Software Project Management Practices: Failure Versus Success*; Crosstalk; October 2004.

Jones, Capers; *Software Estimating Methods for Large Projects*; Crosstalk; April 2005.

Kan, Stephen H.; *Metrics and Models in Software Quality Engineering*, 2nd ed.; Addison Wesley Longman, Boston, MA; 2003; ISBN: 0-201-72915-6; 528 pages.

Land, Susan K; Smith, Douglas B; and Walz, John Z; *Practical Support for Lean Six Sigma Software Process Definition: Using IEEE Software Engineering Standards*; Wiley-Blackwell; 2008; ISBN: 10: 0470170808; 312 pages.

McConnell, Steve; *Software Project Survival Guide*; Microsoft Press; 1997.

Mosley, Daniel J.; *The Handbook of MIS Application Software Testing*; Yourdon Press, Prentice Hall, Englewood Cliffs, NJ; 1993; ISBN: 0-13-907007-9; 354 pages.

Nandyal, Raghav; *Making Sense of Software Quality Assurance*; Tata McGraw Hill Publishing, New Delhi, India; 2007; ISBN: 0-07-063378-9; 350 pages.

Pressman, Roger; *Software Engineering – A Practitioner's Approach*, 6th ed.; McGraw Hill, New York, NY; 2005; ISBN: 0-07-285318-2.

Radice, Ronald A.; *High Qualitiy Low Cost Software Inspections*; Paradoxicon Publishing, Andover, MA; 2002; ISBN: 0-9645913-1-6; 479 pages.

Royce, Walker E.; *Software Project Management: A Unified Framework*; Addison Wesley Longman, Reading, MA; 1998; ISBN: 0-201-30958-0.

Starr, Paul; *The Social Transformation of American Medicine*; Basic Books; Perseus Group; 1982; ISBN: 0-465-07834-2. NOTE: This book won a Pulitzer Prize in 1982 and is highly recommended as a guide for improving both professional education and professional status. There is much of value for the software community.

Strassmann, Paul; *Information Payoff*; Information Economics Press, Stamford, CT; 1985.

Strassmann, Paul; *Governance of Information Management: The Concept of an Information Constitution*, 2nd ed.; (eBook); Information Economics Press, Stamford, CT; 2004.

Strassmann, Paul; *Information Productivity*; Information Economics Press, Stamford, CT; 1999.

Weinberg, Gerald M.; *The Psychology of Computer Programming*; Van Nostrand Reinhold, New York, NY; 1971; ISBN: 0-442-29264-3; 288 pages.

Weinberg, Gerald M.; *Becoming a Technical Leader*; Dorset House, New York, NY; 1986; ISBN: 0-932633-02-1; 284 pages.

Weinberg, Gerald. *Quality Software Management – Vol. 2: First-Order Measurement*; Dorset House Press, New York, NY; 1993; ISBN: 0-932633-24-2; 360 pages.

Wiegers, Karl A.; *Creating a Software Engineering Culture*; Dorset House Press, New York, NY; 1996; ISBN: 0-932633-33-1; 358 pages.

Wiegers, Karl E.; *Peer Reviews in Software – A Practical Guide*; Addison Wesley Longman, Boston, MA; 2002; ISBN: 0-201-73485-0; 232 pages.

Yourdon, Ed; *Outsource: Competing in the Global Productivity Race*; Prentice Hall PTR, Upper Saddle River, NJ; 2005; ISBN: 0-13-147571-1; 251 pages.

Yourdon, Ed; *Death March – The Complete Software Developer's Guide to Surviving "Mission Impossible" Projects*; Prentice Hall PTR, Upper Saddle River, NJ; 1997; ISBN: 0-13-748310-4; 218 pages.

Chapter 4

Defenses Against Breach of Contract Litigation

Introduction

From working as an expert witness in a number of lawsuits where large software projects were cancelled or did not operate correctly when deployed, six major problems occur repeatedly: (1) accurate estimates are not produced or are overruled; (2) accurate estimates are not supported by defensible benchmarks; (3) requirement changes are not handled effectively; (4) quality control is deficient; (5) progress tracking fails to alert higher management to the seriousness of the issues; (6) contracts themselves omit important topics such as change control and quality, or include hazardous terms.

Much of the software literature deals with "best practices." This book concentrates on "worst practices" or the factors that most often lead to failure and litigation.

For the purposes of this book, software "failures" are defined as software projects which met any of these attributes:

1. Termination of the project due to cost or schedule overruns.
2. Schedule or cost overruns in excess of 50% of initial estimates.
3. Applications which, upon deployment, fail to operate safely.
4. Law suits brought by clients for contractual non-compliance.

Although there are many factors associated with schedule delays and project cancellations, the failures that end up in court always seem to have six major deficiencies:

DOI: 10.1201/9781003193128-5

1. Accurate estimates were either not prepared or were rejected.
2. Accurate estimates were not supported by objective benchmarks.
3. Change control was not handled effectively.
4. Quality control was inadequate.
5. Progress tracking did not reveal the true status of the project.
6. The contracts omitted key topics such as quality and out of scope changes.

Readers are urged to discuss outsource agreements with their attorneys. This book is based on observations of actual cases, but the author of this book is not an attorney and the book is not legal advice. It is advice about how software projects might be improved to lower the odds of litigation occurring.

To begin the discussion of defenses against software litigation, let us consider the normal outcomes of 15 kinds of U.S. software projects. Table 4.1 shows the percentage of projects that are likely to be on time, late, or cancelled without being completed at all due to excessive cost or schedule overruns or poor quality.

As can be seen, schedule delays and cancelled projects are distressingly common among all forms of software in 2016. This explains why software is viewed by most CEOs as the least competent and least professional form of engineering of the current business world.

Note that the data in Table 4.1 is from benchmark and assessment studies carried out by the author of this book and colleagues between 1984 and 2016. Unfortunately, recent data since 2010 is not much better than older data before 1990. This is due to several reasons: (1) very poor measurement practices and distressingly bad metrics which prevent improvements from being widely known; (2) software continues to use custom designs and manual coding, both of which are intrinsically expensive and error prone. (Until the software industry adopts modern manufacturing concepts that utilize standard reusable components instead of custom-built artifacts, software can never be truly cost effective.)

Let us consider each of these six topics in turn.

Problem 1: Estimating Errors and Estimate Rejection

Although cost estimating is difficult, there are a number of commercial software parametric cost estimating tools that do a capable job: COCOMO III, CostXpert, ExcelerPlan, KnowledgePlan, True Price, SEER, SLIM, and the author's Software Risk Master ™ (SRM) are examples available in the United States.

In spite of the proven accuracy of parametric estimation tools and widespread availability, as of 2016 less than 20% of the author's clients

Table 4.1 Outcomes of U.S. Software Projects Circa 2016

	Application Types	On-Time	Late	Canceled
1	Scientific	68.00%	20.00%	12.00%
2	Smart phones	67.00%	19.00%	14.00%
3	Open source	63.00%	36.00%	7.00%
4	U.S. outsource	60.00%	30.00%	10.00%
5	Cloud	59.00%	29.00%	12.00%
6	Web applications	55.00%	30.00%	15.00%
7	Games and entertainment	54.00%	36.00%	10.00%
8	Offshore outsource	48.00%	37.00%	15.00%
9	Embedded software	47.00%	33.00%	20.00%
10	Systems and middleware	45.00%	45.00%	10.00%
11	Information technology (IT)	45.00%	40.00%	15.00%
12	Commercial	44.00%	41.00%	15.00%
13	Military and defense	40.00%	45.00%	15.00%
14	Legacy renovation	30.00%	55.00%	15.00%
15	Civilian government	27.00%	63.00%	10.00%
	Total applications	**50.13%**	**37.27%**	**13.00%**

used any formal estimating methods at all when we first carried out software process evaluation studies. It is alarming that 80% of U.S. software companies and projects in 2016 still lag in formal sizing and the use of parametric estimation tools.

However just because an accurate estimate can be produced using a commercial parametric estimating tool that does not mean that clients or executives will accept it. In fact from information presented during litigation, about half of the cases did not produce accurate estimates at all and did not use parametric estimating tools. Manual estimates tend toward optimism or predicting shorter schedules and lower costs than actually occur.

Problem 2: Missing Defensible Objective Benchmarks

Somewhat surprisingly, the other half of the cases in litigation had accurate parametric estimates, but these estimates were rejected and replaced by arbitrary forced "estimates" based on business needs rather than team abilities. These pseudo-estimates were not produced using parametric estimation tools but were arbitrary schedule demands by clients or top executives based on perceived business needs.

The main reason that the original accurate parametric estimates were rejected and replaced was the absence of supporting historical benchmark data. Without accurate history, even accurate estimates may not be convincing. A lack of solid historical data makes project managers, executives, and clients blind to the realities of software development.

Some foreign governments have improved contract accuracy by mandating function point metrics: the governments of Brazil, Japan, Malaysia, Mexico, and Italy require function point size and cost information for all government software contracts. Eventually, all governments will probably require function point metrics for contracts, but no doubt U.S. state governments and the U.S. Federal government will be among the last to do this since they lag in so many other software disciplines. The author of this book has been an expert witness in more lawsuits involving state governments than any other industry. Government software problems are often national news such as the delay of Obamacare.

Problem 3: Rapidly Changing Requirements

The average rate at which software requirements change is has been measured at 2% per month with a range between about 0.5% per calendar month and as high as 4% per calendar month. Thus for a project with a 12-month schedule, more than 10% of the features in the final delivery will not have been defined during the requirements phase. For a 36-month project, almost a third of the features and functions may have come in as afterthoughts.

The current state of the art for dealing with changing requirements includes the following:

- Estimating the number and rate of development changes before starting.
- Using function point metrics to quantify changes.
- A joint client/development change control board or designated domain experts.
- Model-based requirements methodologies.
- Calculating the FOG and Flesch readability indices of requirements.
- Full time involvement by user representatives for Agile projects.
- Use of joint application design (JAD) to minimize downstream changes.

- The use of quality function deployment (QFD) for quality requirements.
- Training in requirements engineering for business analysts and designers.
- Use of formal requirements inspections to minimize downstream changes.
- Use of formal prototypes to minimize downstream changes.
- Planned usage of iterative development to accommodate changes.
- Formal review of all change requests.
- Revised cost and schedule estimates for all changes >10 function points.
- Prioritization of change requests in terms of business impact.
- Formal assignment of change requests to specific releases.
- Use of automated change control tools with cross-reference capabilities.

Unfortunately in projects where litigation occurred, requirements changes were numerous but their effects were not properly integrated into cost, schedule, and quality estimates. As a result, unplanned slippages and overruns occurred.

Requirements changes will always occur for large systems. It is not possible to freeze the requirements of any real-world application, and it is naïve to think this can occur. Therefore, leading companies are ready and able to deal with changes, and do not let them become impediments to progress. For projects developed under contract, the contract itself must include unambiguous language for dealing with changes.

Problem 4: Poor Quality Control

It is dismaying to observe the fact that two of the most effective technologies in all of software are almost never used on projects that turn out to be disasters and end up in court. First, formal design and code inspections have a 50-year history of successful deployment on large and complex software systems. All "best in class" software producers utilize software inspections.

Second, the technology of static analysis has been available since 1984 and has proven itself to be effective in finding code bugs rapidly and early (although static analysis does not find requirements, architecture, and design problems).

Effective software quality control is the most important single factor that separates successful projects from delays and disasters. The reason for this is because finding and fixing bugs is the most expensive cost element for large systems, and takes more time than any other activity.

Both "defect potentials" and "defect removal efficiency" should be measured for every project. The "defect potentials" are the sum of all classes of defects, i.e. defects found in requirements, design, source code, user documents, and "bad fixes" or secondary defects. It would be desirable to include defects in test cases too, since there may be more defects in test libraries than in the applications being tested.

The phrase "defect removal efficiency" (DRE) refers to the percentage of defects found before delivery of the software to its actual clients or users. If the development team finds 900 defects and the users find 100 defects in a standard time period after release (normally 90 days), then it is obvious that the DRE is 90%.

The author of this book strongly recommends that DRE levels be included in all software outsource and development contracts, with 96% being a proposed minimum acceptable level of DRE. For medical devices and weapons systems, a higher rate of about 99% DRE should be written in to the contracts.

The U.S. average today is only about 92%. Agile projects average about 92%; waterfall are often below 85%. TSP and RUP are among the quality strong methods that usually top 96% in DRE.

A rate of 96% is a significant improvement over current norms. For some mission-critical applications, a higher level such as 99.8% might be required. It is technically challenging to achieve such high levels of DRE and it can't be done by testing alone.

Formal inspections and pre-test static analysis plus at least 8 forms of testing are needed to top 98% in DRE (1 unit test; 2 function test; 3 regression test; 4 component test; 5 performance test; 6 usability test; 7 system test; 8 acceptance or beta test.)

Table 4.2 shows combinations of quality control factors that can lead to high, average, or poor DRE.

For projects in the 10,000 function point size range, the successful ones accumulate development totals of around 4.0 defects per function point and remove about 98% of them before delivery to customers. In other words, the number of delivered defects is about 0.2 defects per function point or 800 total latent defects. Of these about, 10% or 80 would be fairly serious defects. The rest would be minor or cosmetic defects. Stabilization or the number of calendar months to achieve safe operation of the application would be about 2.5 months.

By contrast, the unsuccessful projects of 10,000 function points that end up in court accumulate development totals of around 6.0 defects per function point and remove only about 85% of them before delivery. The number of delivered defects is about 0.9 defects per function point

Table 4.2   Ranges of DRE for 1,000 Function Point Applications

Defect Removal Efficiency (DRE)		>99%	95%	<87%
1	Formal requirement inspections	Yes	No	No
2	Formal design inspections	Yes	No	No
3	Formal code inspections	Yes	No	No
4	Formal security inspections	Yes	No	No
5	Static analysis	Yes	Yes	No
6	Unit test	Yes	Yes	Yes
7	Function test	Yes	Yes	Yes
8	Regression test	Yes	Yes	Yes
9	Integration test	Yes	Yes	Yes
10	Usability test	Yes	Yes	No
11	Security test	Yes	Yes	No
12	System test	Yes	Yes	Yes
13	Acceptance test	Yes	Yes	Yes

or 9,000 total latent defects. Of these about 15% or 1,350 would be fairly serious defects. This large number of latent defects after delivery is very troubling for users. The large number of delivered defects is also a frequent cause of litigation. Stabilization or the number of calendar month to achieve safe operation of the application might stretch out to 18 months or more.

Unsuccessful projects typically omit design and code inspections and static analysis, and depend purely on testing. The omission of up-front inspections and static analysis cause four serious problems: (1) the large number of defects still present when testing begins slows down the project to a standstill; (2) the "bad fix" injection rate for projects without inspections is alarmingly high; (3) the overall DRE associated with only testing is not sufficient to achieve defect removal rates higher than about 85%; (4) applications that bypass both inspections and static analysis have a strong tendency to include error-prone modules.

Problem 5: Poor Software Milestone Tracking

Once a software project is underway, there are no fixed and reliable guidelines for judging its rate of progress. The civilian software industry has long utilized ad hoc milestones such as completion of design or completion of coding. However, these milestones are notoriously unreliable.

Tracking software projects requires dealing with two separate issues: (1) achieving specific and tangible milestones and (2) expending resources and funds within specific budgeted amounts.

Because software milestones and costs are affected by requirements changes and "scope creep," it is important to measure the increase in size of requirements changes, when they affect function point totals. However, there are also requirements changes that do not affect function point totals, which are termed "requirements churn." Both creep and churn occur at random intervals. Churn is harder to measure than creep and is often measured via "backfiring" or mathematical conversion between source code statements and function point metrics.

There are also "non-functional requirements" often due to outside influences. These can change abruptly and many are not under control of software groups. For example, a change in Federal or State laws may require changes to hundreds of applications including some that are under development.

As of today there are automated tools available that can assist project managers in recording the kinds of vital information needed for milestone reports. These tools can record schedules, resources, size changes, and also issues or problems.

Examples of tracking tools include Automated Project Office (APO), Microsoft project management suite, OmniTracker, Capterra, Jira, and in total perhaps 50 others with various capabilities. However in spite of the availability of these tools, less than 45% of the author's clients use any of them in our initial process evaluation studies.

For an industry now more than 65 years of age, it is somewhat surprising that there is no general or universal set of project milestones for indicating tangible progress. From the author's assessment and baseline studies, following are some representative milestones that have shown practical value.

Note that these milestones assume an explicit and formal review or inspection connected with the construction of every major software deliverable. Formal reviews and inspections have the highest DRE levels of any known kind of quality control activity, and are characteristics of "best in class" organizations.

The most important aspect of Table 4.3 is that every milestone is based on completing a review, inspection, or test. Just finishing up a document or writing code should not be considered a milestone unless the deliverables have been reviewed, inspected, or tested.

In the litigation where the author of this book worked as an expert witness, these criteria were not met. Milestones were very informal and

Table 4.3   Representative Tracking Milestones for Large Software Projects

1	Application sizing completed using both function points and code statements
2	Application risk predictions completed
3	Application size and risk predictions reviewed
4	Requirements document completed
5	Requirements document inspection completed
6	Initial cost estimate completed
7	Initial cost estimate review completed
8	Development plan completed
9	Development plan review completed
10	Cost tracking system initialized
11	Defect tracking system initialized
12	Prototype completed
13	Prototype review completed
14	Complexity analysis of base system (for enhancement projects)
15	Code restructuring of base system (for enhancement projects)
16	Functional specification completed
17	Functional specification review completed
18	Data specification completed
19	Data specification review completed
20	Logic specification completed
21	Logic specification review completed
22	Quality control plan completed
23	Quality control plan review completed
24	Change control plan completed
25	Change control plan review completed
26	Security plan completed
27	Security plan review completed
28	User information plan completed
29	User information plan review completed

(*Continued*)

Table 4.3 (Continued)

30	Code for specific modules completed
31	Code inspection for specific modules completed
32	Code for specific modules unit tested
33	Test plan completed
34	Test plan review completed
35	Test cases for specific test stage completed
36	Test case inspection for specific test stage completed
37	Test stage completed
38	Test stage review completed
39	Integration for specific build completed
40	Integration review for specific build completed
41	User information completed
42	User information review completed
43	Quality assurance sign off completed
44	Delivery to beta test clients completed
45	Delivery to clients completed

consisted primarily of calendar dates, without any validation of the materials themselves.

Also, the format and structure of the milestone reports were inadequate. At the top of every milestone report problems and issues or "red flag" items should be highlighted and discussed first. These "red flag" topics are those which are likely to cause schedule delays, cost overruns, or both.

During depositions and review of court documents, it was noted that software engineering personnel and many managers were aware of the problems that later triggered the delays, cost overruns, quality problems, and litigation. At the lowest levels, these problems were often included in weekly status reports or discussed at team meetings. But for the higher-level milestone and tracking reports that reached clients and executives, the hazardous issues were either omitted or glossed over.

A suggested format for monthly progress tracking reports delivered to clients and higher management would include these sections (Table 4.4).

Table 4.4   Suggested Format for Monthly Status Reports for Software Projects

1	Status of last month's "red flag" problems
2	New "red flag" problems noted this month
3	Change requests processed this month versus change requests predicted
4	Change requests predicted for next month
5	Size in function points for this month's change requests
6	Size in function points predicted for next month's change requests
7	Schedule impacts of this month's change requests
8	Cost impacts of this month's change requests
9	Quality impacts of this month's change requests
10	Defects found this month versus defects predicted
11	Defects predicted for next month
12	Costs expended this month versus costs predicted
13	Costs predicted for next month
14	Deliverables completed this month versus deliverables predicted
15	Deliverables predicted for next month

Although the suggested format somewhat resembles the items calculated using the earned value method, this format deals explicitly with the impact of change requests and also uses function point metrics for expressing costs and quality data.

An interesting question is the frequency with which milestone progress should be reported. The most common reporting frequency is monthly, although exception reports can be filed at any time that it is suspected that something has occurred that can cause perturbations. For example, serious illness of key project personnel or resignation of key personnel might very well affect project milestone completions, and this kind of situation cannot be anticipated. The same is true of natural phenomena such as hurricanes or earthquakes which can shut down businesses.

The simultaneous deployment of software sizing tools, estimating tools, planning tools, and methodology management tools can provide fairly unambiguous points in the development cycle that allow progress to be judged more or less effectively. For example, software sizing technology can now predict the sizes of both specifications and the volume of source code needed. Defect estimating tools can predict the numbers of bugs or errors that might be encountered and discovered. Although such milestones are not perfect, they are better than the former approaches.

Project management is responsible for establishing milestones, monitoring their completion, and reporting truthfully on whether the milestones were successfully completed or encountered problems. When serious problems are encountered, it is necessary to correct the problems before reporting that the milestone has been completed.

Failing or delayed projects usually lack serious milestone tracking. Activities are often reported as finished while work was still on-going. Milestones on failing projects are usually dates on a calendar rather than completion and review of actual deliverables.

Delivering documents or code segments that are incomplete, contain errors, and cannot support downstream development work is not the way milestones are used by industry leaders.

In more than a dozen legal cases involving projects that failed or were never able to operate successfully, project tracking was inadequate in every case. Problems were either ignored or brushed aside, rather than being addressed and solved.

Because milestone tracking occurs throughout software development, it is the last line of defense against project failures and delays. Milestones should be established formally and should be based on reviews, inspections, and tests of deliverables. Milestones should not be the dates that deliverables more or less were finished. Milestones should reflect the dates that finished deliverables were validated by means of inspections, testing, and quality assurance review.

Problem 6: Flawed Outsource Agreements that Omit Key Topics

In several of the cases where the author of this book has been an expert witness, the contracts themselves seemed flawed and omitted key topics that should have been included. Worse some contracts included topics that probably should have been omitted. Here are samples:

- In one case, the contract required that the software delivered by the vendor should have "zero defects." Since the application approached 10,000 function points in size, zero-defect software is beyond the current state of the art. The software as delivered did not have very many defects and in fact was much better than average, but it was not zero-defect software and hence the vendor was sued.

- A fixed-price contract had clauses for "out of scope" requirements changes. In this case, the client unilaterally added 82 major changes totaling about 3,000 new function points. But the contract did not define the phrase "out of scope" and the client asserted that the changes were merely elaborations to existing requirements and did not want to pay for them.
- In another fixed-price contract, the vendor added about 5,000 function points of new features very late in development. Here the client was willing to pay for the added features. However, features added after design and during coding are more expensive to build than features during normal development. In this case, the vendor was asking for additional payments to cover the approximate 15% increase in costs for the late features. Needless to say there should be a sliding scale of costs that goes up for features added 3, 6, 9, 12, or more months after the initial requirements are defined and approved by the client. The fee structure might be something like increase by 3%, 5%, 7% 12%, and 15% based on calendar month intervals.
- In several contracts where the plaintiff alleged poor quality on the part of the vendor, the contracts did not have any clauses that specified acceptable quality, such as DRE or maximum numbers of bugs found during acceptance test. In the absence of any contractual definitions of "poor quality," such charges are difficult to prove.

The bottom line is that clients, vendor, and their attorneys should be sure that all outsource contracts include clauses dealing with requirements changes, quality, delivered defects, and also penalties for schedule delays caused by vendor actions.

Note that the author of this book is not an attorney, and this is not legal advice. But it is obvious that every software outsource contract should include clauses for quality and for requirements changes, especially late requirements changes. Attorneys are needed for major outsource agreements.

Summary and Observations Based on Breach of Contract Litigation

Successful software projects can result from nothing more than avoiding the more serious mistakes that lead to disaster. A set of basic steps can lower the odds of a failing project followed by a lawsuit: (1) use parametric estimation tools and avoid manual estimates; (2) look at the actual benchmark results of similar projects; (3) make planning and estimating formal activities; (4) plan for and control creeping requirements; (5) use formal inspections as milestones for tracking project progress; (6) include pre-test static analysis and inspections in quality control; (7) collect accurate measurement data during your current project, to use with future projects; (8) make sure with your attorneys that contracts have suitable clauses for requirements growth and quality levels of delivered materials. Omitting these two topics can lead to very expensive litigation later.

Overcoming the risks shown here is largely a matter of opposites, or doing the reverse of what the risk indicates. Thus a well-formed software project will create accurate estimates derived from empirical data and supported by automated tools for handling the critical path issues. Such estimates will be based on the actual capabilities of the development team and will not be arbitrary creations derived without any rigor. The plans will specifically address the critical issues of change requests and quality control. In addition, monthly progress reports will also deal with these critical issues. Accurate progress reports are the last line of defense against failures.

Suggested Readings

Abrain, Alain; *Software Estimating Models*; Wiley-IEEE Computer Society; 2015.

Abrain, Alain; *Software Metrics and Metrology*; Wiley-IEEE Computer Society; 2010.

Abrain, Alain; *Software Maintenance Management: Evolution and Continuous Improvement*; Wiley-IEEE Computer Society; 2008.

Beck, Kent; *Test-Driven Development*; Addison Wesley, Boston, MA; 2002; ISBN: 10: 0321146530; 240 pages.

Black, Rex; *Managing the Testing Process: Practical Tools and Techniques for Managing Hardware and Software Testing*; Wiley; 2009; ISBN: 10 0470404159; 672 pages.

Boehm, Barry; *Software Engineering Economics*; Prentice Hall, Englewood Cliffs, NJ; 1981; 900 pages.

Brooks, Fred; *The Mythical Man-Month*, 1995 rev. ed.; Addison Wesley, Reading, MA; 1974.

Bundschuh, Manfred; and Dekkers, Carol; *The IT Metrics Compendium*; Springer; 2005.

Charette, Bob; *Software Engineering Risk Analysis and Management*; McGraw Hill, New York, NY; 1989.

Charette, Bob; *Application Strategies for Risk Management*; McGraw Hill, New York, NY; 1990.

DeMarco, Tom; *Controlling Software Projects*; Yourdon Press, New York, NY; 1982; ISBN: 0-917072-32-4; 284 pages.

Ebert, Christof; Dumke, Reinder; and Bundschuh, Manfred; *Best Practices in Software Measurement*; Springer; 2004.

Everett, Gerald D.; and McLeod, Raymond; *Software Testing – Testing Across the Entire Software Development Life Cycle*; IEEE Press; 2007.

Ewusi-Mensah, Kweku; *Software Development Failures*; MIT Press, Cambridge, MA; 2003; ISBN: 0-26205072-2; 276 pages.

Fernandini, Patricia L.; *A Requirements Pattern*; Addison Wesley, Boston, MA; 2002; ISBN: 0-201-73826-0.

Flowers, Stephen; *Software Failures: Management Failures; Amazing Stories and Cautionary Tales*; John Wiley & Sons; 1996.

Gack, Gary; *Managing the Black Hole: The Executives Guide to Software Project Risk*; Business Expert Publishing, Thomson, GA; 2010; ISBN: 10: 1-935602-01-9.

Galorath, Dan; and Evans, Michael; *Software Sizing, Estimation, and Risk Management: When Performance is Measured Performance Improves*; Auerbach; Philadelphia, PA; 2006.

Garmus, David; and Herron, David; *Function Point Analysis – Measurement Practices for Successful Software Projects*; Addison Wesley Longman, Boston, MA; 2001; ISBN: 0-201-69944-3; 363 pages.

Garmus, David; and Herron, David; *Measuring the Software Process: A Practical Guide to Functional Measurement*; Prentice Hall, Englewood Cliffs, NJ; 1995.

Garmus, David; Russac, Janet; and Edwards, Royce; *Certified Function Point Counters Examination Guide*; CRC Press; 2010.

Glass, R.L.; *Software Runaways: Lessons Learned from Massive Software Project Failures*; Prentice Hall, Englewood Cliffs, NJ; 1998a.

Gibbs, T. Wayt; "Trends in Computing: Software's Chronic Crisis"; *Scientific American Magazine*, 271, No. 3, International ed.; September 1994; pp. 72–81.

Gilb, Tom; and Graham, Dorothy; *Software Inspection*; Addison Wesley, Harlow UK; 1993; ISBN: 10: 0-201-63181-4.

Glass, R.L.; *Software Runaways: Lessons Learned from Massive Software Project Failures*; Prentice Hall, Englewood Cliffs, NJ; 1998b.

Harris, Michael D.S.; Herron, David; and Iwanicki, Stasia; *The Business Value of IT*; CRC Press, Auerbach, Boca Raton, FL; 2008; ISBN: 978-14200-6474-2.

Hill, Peter; Jones Capers; and Reifer, Don; *The Impact of Software Size on Productivity*; International Software Standards Benchmark Group (ISBSG), Melbourne, Australia, September 2013.

International Function Point Users Group (IFPUG); *IT Measurement – Practical Advice from the Experts*; Addison Wesley Longman, Boston, MA; 2002; ISBN: 0-201-74158-X; 759 pages.

Johnson, James; et al; *The Chaos Report*; The Standish Group, West Yarmouth, MA; 2000.

Jones, Capers; *The Technical and Social History of Software Engineering*; Addison Wesley, Boston, MA; 2015 (contains summaries of important software industry lawsuits such as anti-trust and patent violations).

Jones, Capers; "Studio 38 in Rhode Island – A Study of Software Risks"; 2012, published in various Rhode Island newspapers such as the Providence Journal, South County Independent, Narragansett Times, etc.

Jones, Capers; and Bonsignour, Olivier; *The Economics of Software Quality*; Addison Wesley, Boston, MA; 2011; ISBN: 10 0-13-258220-1; 587 pages.

Jones, Capers; *Software Engineering Best Practices*; McGraw Hill, New York, NY; 2010; ISBN: 978-0-07-162161-8; 660 pages.

Jones, Capers; *Applied Software Measurement*, 3rd ed.; McGraw Hill, New York, NY; 2008; ISBN: 978-0-07-150244-3; 662 pages.

Jones, Capers; *Assessment and Control of Software Risks*; Prentice Hall, Englewood Cliffs, NJ; 1994; ISBN: 0-13-741406-4; 711 pages.

Jones, Capers; *Patterns of Software System Failure and Success*; International Thomson Computer Press, Boston, MA; December 1995; ISBN: 1-850-32804-8; 250, 292 pages.

Jones, Capers; *Software Quality – Analysis and Guidelines for Success*; International Thomson Computer Press, Boston, MA; 1997; ISBN: 1-85032-876-6; 492 pages.

Jones, Capers; *Estimating Software Costs*; McGraw Hill, New York, NY; 2007a; ISBN: 13-978-0-07-148300-1.

Jones, Capers; *Software Assessments, Benchmarks, and Best Practices*; Addison Wesley Longman, Boston, MA; 2000; ISBN: 0-201-48542-7; 657 pages.

Jones, Capers; "Sizing Up Software"; *Scientific American Magazine*, Vol. 279, No. 6; December 1998; pp. 104–111.

Jones, Capers; *Conflict and Litigation Between Software Clients and Developers*; Software Productivity Research Technical Report, Narragansett, RI; 2007b; 65 pages.

Kan, Stephen H.; *Metrics and Models in Software Quality Engineering*, 2nd ed.; Addison Wesley Longman, Boston, MA; 2003; ISBN: 0-201-72915-6; 528 pages.

Pressman, Roger; *Software Engineering – A Practitioner's Approach*, 6th ed.; McGraw Hill, New York, NY; 2005; ISBN: 0-07-285318-2.

Radice, Ronald A.; *High Quality Low Cost Software Inspections*; Paradoxicon Publishing, Andover, MA; 2002; ISBN: 0-9645913-1-6; 479 pages.

Robertson, Suzanne; and Robertson, James; *Requirements-Led Project Management*; Addison Wesley, Boston, MA; 2005; ISBN: 0-321-18062-3.

Wiegers, Karl E.; *Peer Reviews in Software – A Practical Guide*; Addison Wesley Longman, Boston, MA; 2002; ISBN: 0-201-73485-0; 232 pages.

Yourdon, Ed; *Death March – The Complete Software Developer's Guide to Surviving "Mission Impossible" Projects*; Prentice Hall PTR, Upper Saddle River, NJ; 1997; ISBN: 0-13-748310-4; 218 pages.

Yourdon, Ed; *Outsource: Competing in the Global Productivity Race*; Prentice Hall PTR, Upper Saddle River, NJ; 2005; ISBN: 0-13-147571-1; 251 pages.

Web Sites

Information Technology Metrics and Productivity Institute (ITMPI), www.ITMPI.org

International Software Benchmarking Standards Group (ISBSG), www.ISBSG.org

International Function Point Users Group (IFPUG), www.IFPUG.org

Namcook Analytics LLC, www.Namcook.com

Namcook Analytics Blog, http://NamcookAnalytics.com

Reifer Consulting, www.Reifer.com

Software Engineering Institute (SEI), www.SEI.cmu.edu

Software Productivity Research (SPR), www.SPR.com

Suggested Web Sites

http://www.IASAhome.org. This is the web site for the non-profit International Association of Software Architects (IASA). Software architecture is the backbone of all large applications. Good architecture can lead to applications whose useful life expectancy is 20 years or more. Questionable architecture can lead to applications whose useful life expectancy is less than 10 years, coupled with increasing complex maintenance tasks and high defect levels. The IASA is working hard to improve both the concepts of architecture and the training of software architects via a modern and extensive curriculum.

http://www.IIBA.org. This is the web site for the non-profit International Institute of Business Analysis. This institute deals with the important linkage between business knowledge and software that supports business operations. Among the topics of concern are the Business Analysis Body of Knowledge (BABOK), training of business analysts, and certification to achieve professional skills.

http://www.IFPUG.org. This is the web site for the non-profit International Function Point Users Group. IFPUG is the largest software metrics association in the world, and the oldest association of function point users. This web site contains information about IFPUG function points themselves, and also citations to the literature dealing with function points. IFPUG also offers training in function point analysis and administers. IFPUG also administers a certification program for analysts who wish to become function point counters.

http://www.ISBSG.org. This is the web site for the non-profit International Software Benchmark Standards Group. ISBSG, located in Australia, collects benchmark data on software projects throughout the world. The data is self-reported by companies using a standard questionnaire. About 4,000 projects comprise the ISBSG collection as of 2007, and the collection has been growing at a rate of about 500 projects per year. Most of the data is expressed in terms of IFPUG function point metrics, but some of the data is also expressed in terms of COSMIC function points, NESMA function points, Mark II function points, and several other function point variants. Fortunately the data in variant metrics is identified. It would be statistically invalid to include attempt to average IFPUG and COSMIC data, or to mix up any of the function point variations.

http://www.iso.org. This is the web site for the International Organization for Standardization (ISO). The ISO is a non-profit organization that sponsors and publishes a variety of international standards. As of 2007 the ISO published about a thousand standards a year, and the total published to date is approximately 17,000. Many of the published standards affect software. These include the ISO 9000-9004 quality standards and the ISO standards for functional size measurement.

http://www.namcook.com. This web site contains a variety of quantitative reports on software quality and risk factors. It also contains a patented high-speed sizing tool that can size applications of any size in 90 seconds or less. It also contains a catalog of software benchmark providers which currently lists 20 organizations that provide quantitative data about software schedules, costs, quality, and risks.

http://www.PMI.org. This is the web site for the Project Management Institute (PMI). PMI is the largest association of managers in the world. PMI performs research and collects data on topics of interest to managers in every discipline: software, engineering, construction, and so forth. This data is assembled into the well known Project Management Body of Knowledge or PMBOK.

http://www.ITMPI.org. This is the web site for the Information Technology Metrics and Productivity Institute. ITMPI is a wholly-owned subsidiary of Computer Aid Inc. The ITMPI web site is a useful portal into a broad range of measurement, management, and software engineering information. The ITMPI web site also provides useful links to many other web sites that contain topics of interest on software issues.

http://www.sei.cmu.edu. This is the web site for the Software Engineering Institute (SEI). The SEI is a federally-sponsored non-profit organization located on the campus of Carnegie Mellon University in Pittsburgh, PA. The SEI carries out a number of research programs dealing with software maturity and capability levels, with quality, risks, measurement and metrics, and other topics of interest to the software community.

http://www.stsc.hill.af.mil/CrossTalk. This is the web site of both the Air Force Software Technology Support Center (STSC) and also the CrossTalk journal, which is published by the STSC. The STSC gathers data and performs research into a wide variety of software engineering and software management issues. The CrossTalk journal is one of few technical journals that publish full-length technical articles of 4,000 words or more. Although the Air Force is the sponsor of STSC and CrossTalk, many topics are also relevant to the civilian community. Issues such as quality control, estimating, maintenance, measurement, and metrics have universal relevance.

Chapter 5

The Mess of Software Metrics

Introduction

The software industry is one of the largest, wealthiest, and most important industries in the modern world. The software industry is also troubled by poor quality and very high cost structures due to the expense of software development, maintenance, and endemic problems with poor quality control.

Accurate measurements of software development and maintenance costs and accurate measurement of quality would be extremely valuable. But as of 2017, the software industry labors under a variety of nonstandard and highly inaccurate measures were compounded by very sloppy measurement practices. For that matter, there is little empirical data about the efficacy of software standards themselves.

The industry also lacks effective basic definitions for *"software productivity"* and *"software quality"* and uses a variety of ambiguous definitions that are difficult to predict before software is released and difficult to measure after the software is released. This chapter suggests definitions for both economic software productivity and software quality that are both predictable and measurable.

Note: The year 2017 marked the 30th anniversary of function point metrics. Function point metrics are the best available for measuring software economic productivity and software quality.

The software industry has become one of the largest and most successful industries in history. However, software applications are among the most expensive and error-prone manufactured objects in history.

Software needs a careful analysis of economic factors and much better quality control than is normally accomplished. In order to achieve these goals, software also needs accurate and reliable metrics and good measurement practices. Unfortunately, the software industry has ignored both.

The software industry has the worst metrics and measurement practices of any industry in human history. This is one of the reasons why the software industry has more failing projects than any other industry and a higher percentage large projects with cost and schedule overruns. It is also why a survey of CEOs in Fortune 500 companies reveals that software engineers are the least professional of any kind of engineers. Basically, the software industry has been running blind for over 60 years due to harmful metrics such as "cost per defect" and "lines of code" (LOC) both of which distort reality and conceal progress.

See Appendix A and Appendix B for the mathematical reasons why LOC and cost per defect do not measure either software development economic productivity or software quality economic value.

Fortunately, function point metrics do measure both economic productivity and software quality. Calendar year 2017 marked the 30th anniversary of the International Function Point Users Group (IFPUG), which has become the largest metrics association in the industry. Other forms of function point metrics such as COSMIC, FISMA, NESMA, and automated function points from CAST software are also popular. Collectively, function points are used for more software benchmarks than all other metrics combined. Table 5.1 shows comparative sizes in various metrics.

But more work is needed because today over half of software development companies and over 70% of government software organizations still use invalid metrics such as LOC and cost per defect.

Fortunately, a number of countries are starting to mandate function points for government contracts: Brazil, Malaysia, Italy, South Korea, and Japan. Others will probably do the same in future years.

This chapter deals with some of the most glaring problems of software metrics and suggests a metrics and measurement suite that can actually explore software economics and software quality with high precision. The suggested metrics can be predicted prior to development and then measured after release. The key metrics in this suite include (1) function points, (2) work hours per function point, (3) defect potentials using function points, (4) defect removal efficiency (DRE), and also three quality metrics (5) delivered defects per function point; (6) high-severity defects per function point; and (7) security flaws per function point.

Supplemental metrics include pre-release and post-release application growth using function points and dollar costs per function point for development, maintenance, cost of quality (COQ), and total cost of

Table 5.1   Variations in Software Size Metrics 2020

		Nominal Size	SNAP Size	% of IFPUG Size
(Based on 1,000 IFPUG 4.3 function points and Java language)				
(Sizes predicted by Software Risk Master (SRM))				
Metrics				
1	Automated code-based function points	1,070	142	107.00%
2	Automated UML-based function points	1,030	137	103.0%
3	Automated text-based function points	1,055	140	105.5%
4	Backfired function points	1,017	135	101.7%
5	Code size (logical statements)	53,000	7,049	NA
6	Code size (physical lines with comments, blanks)	145,750	19,385	NA
7	COSMIC function points	1,086	144	108.6%
8	Fast function points	970	129	97.0%
9	Feature points	1,000	133	100.0%
10	FISMA function points	1,020	136	102.0%
11	Full function points	1,170	156	117.0%
12	Function points light	967	129	96.7%
13	**IFPUG 4.3**	1,000	133	100.0%
14	IntegraNova function points	1,090	145	109.0%
15	Mark II function points	1,060	141	106.0%
16	NESMA function points	1,040	138	104.0%
17	Object-oriented function points (OOFP)	735	98	73.5%
18	RICE objects	4,439	590	443.9%
19	SCCQI function points	2,877	383	287.7%
20	Simple function points	975	130	97.5%
21	SNAP non-functional size metrics	133		13.3%
22	**SRM pattern matching function points**	1,000	133	100.0%
23	Story points	333	44	33.3%
24	Unadjusted function points	890	118	89.0%
25	Use-Case points	200	27	20.0%
26	Weighted micro function points	1,127	134	112.7%

ownership (TCO). Application size grows at about 1% per month during development and about 8% per year after release.

SNAP metrics for non-functional requirements are also discussed but there is very little data even today, although it is growing.

Following are descriptions of the more common software metric topics in alphabetical order:

Backfiring is a term that refers to mathematical conversion between LOC and function points. This method was first developed by A.J. Albrecht and colleagues during the original creation of function point metrics, since the IBM team had LOC data for the projects they used for function points. IBM used logical code statements for backfiring rather than physical LOC. There are no ISO standards for backfiring. Backfiring is highly ambiguous and varies by over 500% from language to language and company to company. A sample of "backfiring" is the ratio of about 106.7 statements in the procedure and data divisions of COBOL for one IFPUG function point. Consulting companies sell tables of backfire ratios for over 1000 languages, but the tables are not the same from vendor to vendor. Backfiring is not endorsed by any of the function point associations. Yet probably as many as 100,000 software projects have used backfiring because it is quick and inexpensive, even though very inaccurate with huge variances from language to language and programmer to programmer.

Benchmarks in a software context often refer to the effort and costs for developing an application. Benchmarks are expressed in a variety of metrics such as "work hours per function point," "function points per month," "lines of code per month," "work hours per KLOC," "story points per month," and many more. Benchmarks also vary in scope and range from project values, phase values, activity values, and task values. There are no ISO standards for benchmark contents. Worse, many benchmarks "leak" and omit over 50% of true software effort. The popular benchmark of "design, code, and unit test" termed DCUT contains only about 30% of total software effort. The most common omissions from benchmarks include unpaid overtime, management, and the work of part-time specialists such as technical writers and software quality assurance. Thus, benchmarks from various sources such as ISBSG, QSM, and others cannot be directly compared since they do not contain the same information. The best and most reliable benchmarks feature activity-based costs and include the full set of development tasks, i.e. requirements, architecture, business analysis, design, coding, testing, quality assurance, documentation, project management, etc.

Cost estimating for software projects is generally inaccurate and usually optimistic. About 85% of projects circa 2017 used inaccurate manual estimates. The other 15% used the more accurate parametric estimating tools of which the following were the most common estimating tools in 2015, shown in alphabetical order: COCOMO, COCOMO clones, CostXpert, ExcelerPlan, KnowledgePlan, SEER, SLIM, Software Risk Master (SRM), and TruePrice. A study by the author of this book that compared 50 manual estimates against 50 parametric estimates found that only 4 of the 50 manual estimates were within plus or minus 5% and the average was 34% optimistic for costs and 27% optimistic for schedules. For manual estimates, the larger the projects, the more optimistic the results. By contrast, 32 of the 50 parametric estimates were within plus or minus 5%, and the deviations for the others averaged about 12% higher for costs and 6% longer for schedules. Conservatism is the "fail safe" mode for estimates. The author's SRM tool has a patent-pending early sizing feature based on pattern matching that allows it to be used 30 to 180 days earlier than the other parametric estimation tools. It also predicts topics not included in the others such as litigation risks, costs of breach of contract litigation for the plaintiff and defendant, and document sizes and costs for 20 key document types such as requirements, design, user manuals, plans, and others. The patent-pending early sizing feature of SRM produces size in a total of 23 metrics including function points, story points, use-case points, logical code statements, physical LOC, and many others.

Cost per defect metrics penalize quality and makes the buggiest software look cheapest. There are no ISO or other standards for calculating cost per defect. Cost per defect does not measure the economic value of software quality. The urban legend that it costs 100 times as much to fix post-release defects as early defects is not true and is based on ignoring fixed costs. Due to fixed costs of writing and running test cases, cost per defect rises steadily because fewer and fewer defects are found. This is caused by a standard rule of manufacturing economics: "*If a manufacturing process has a high percentage of fixed costs and there is a reduction in the units produced, the cost per unit will go up.*" This explains why cost per defect seems to go up over time even though actual defect repair costs are flat and do not change very much. There are of course very troubling defects that are expensive and time consuming, but these are comparatively rare. Appendix A explains the problems of cost per defect metrics.

Defect removal efficiency (DRE) was developed by IBM circa 1970. The original IBM version of DRE measured internal defects found by developers and compared them to external defects found by clients in the first 90 days following release. If developers found 90 bugs and clients reported 10 bugs, the DRE is 90%. This measure has been in continuous use by hundreds of companies since about 1975. However, there are no ISO standards for DRE. The International Software Benchmark Standards Group (ISBSG) unilaterally changed the post-release interval to 30 days in spite of the fact that the literature on DRE since the 1970s was based on a 90-day time span, such as the author's 1991 version of *Applied Software Measurement* and his more recent book on *The Economics of Software Quality* with Olivier Bonsignour. Those with experience in defects and quality tracking can state with certainty that a 30-day time window is too short; major applications sometimes need more than 30 days of preliminary installation and training before they are actually used. Of course bugs will be found long after 90 days, but experience indicates that a 90-day interval is sufficient to judge the quality of software applications. A 30-day interval is not sufficient.

Earned value management (EVM) is a method of combining schedule, progress, and scope. It originated in the 1960s for government contracts and has since been applied to software with reasonable success. Although earned value is relatively successful, it really needs some extensions to be a good fit for software projects. The most urgent extension would be to link progress to quality and defect removal. Finding and fixing bugs is the most expensive software activity. It would be easy to include defect predictions and defect removal progress into the earned value concept. Another extension for software would be to include the specific documents that are needed for large software applications. If the earned-value approach included quality topics, it would be very useful for contracts and software outsource agreements. EVM is in use for defense software contracts, but the omission of quality is a serious problem since finding and fixing bugs is the most expensive single cost driver for software. The U.S. government requires earned value for many contracts. The governments of Brazil and South Korea require function points for software contracts. Most projects that end up in court for breach of contract do so because of poor quality. It is obvious that combining earned-value metrics, defect and quality metrics, and function point metrics would be a natural fit to all software contracts and would probably lead to fewer failures and better overall performance.

Defect density metrics measure the number of bugs released to clients. There are no ISO or other standards for calculating defect density. One method counts only code defects released. A more complete method used by the author includes bugs originating in requirements, architecture, design, and documents as well as code defects. The author's method also includes "bad fixes" or bugs in defect repairs themselves. There is more than a 500% variation between counting only released code bugs and counting bugs from all sources. For example requirements defects comprise about 20% of released software problem reports.

Function point metrics were invented by IBM circa 1975 and placed in the public domain circa 1978. Function point metrics do measure economic productivity using both *"work hours per function point"* and *"function points per month."* They also are useful for normalizing quality data such as "defects per function point." However, there are numerous function point variations and they all produce different results: Automatic, backfired, COSMIC, Fast, FISMA, IFPUG, Mark II, NESMA, Unadjusted, etc. There are ISO standards for COSMIC, FISMA, IFPUG, and NESMA. However in spite of ISO standards, all four produce different counts. Adherents of each function point variant claim "accuracy" as a virtue, but there is no cesium atom or independent way to ascertain accuracy so these claims are false. For example COSMIC function points produce higher counts than IFPUG function points for many applications but that does not indicate "accuracy" since there is no objective way to know accuracy.

Goal/Question metrics (GQM) were invented by Dr. Victor Basili of the University of Maryland. The concept is appealing. The idea is to specify some kind of tangible goal or target, and then think of questions that must be answered to achieve the goal. This is a good concept for all science and engineering and not just software. However, since every company and project tends to specify unique goals, the GQM method does not lend itself to either parametric estimation tools or to benchmark data collection. It would not be difficult to meld GQM with function point metrics and other effective software metrics such as DRE. For example, several useful goals might be *"How can we achieve defect potentials of less than 1.0 per function point?"* or *"How can we achieve productivity rates of 100 function points per month?"* Another good goal which should actually be a target for every company and every software project in the world would be *"How can we achieve more than 99% in defect removal efficiency (DRE)?"*

ISO/IEC standards are numerous and cover every industry, not just software. However, these standards are issued without any proof of efficacy. After release, some standards have proven to be useful, some are not so useful, and a few are being criticized so severely that some software consultants and managers are urging a recall such as the proposed ISO/IEC testing standard. ISO stands for the International Organization for Standards (in French) and IEC stands for International Electrical Commission. While ISO/IEC standards are the best known, there are other standard groups such as the Object Management Group (OMG) which recently published a standard on automatic function points. Here too there is no proof of efficacy prior to release. There are also national standards such as ANSI or the American National Standards Institute, and also military standards by the U.S. Department of Defense (DoD) and by similar organizations elsewhere. The entire topic of standards is in urgent need of due diligence and of empirical data that demonstrates the value of specific standards after issuance. In total there are probably several hundred standards groups in the world with a combined issuance of over 1000 standards, of which probably 50 apply to aspects of software. Of these only a few have solid empirical data that demonstrates value and efficacy.

Lines of code (LOC) metrics penalize high-level languages and make low-level languages look better than they are. LOC metrics also make requirements and design invisible. There are no ISO or other standards for counting LOC metrics. About half of the papers and journal articles use physical LOC and half use logical LOC. The difference between counts of physical and logical LOC can top 500%. The overall variability of LOC metrics has reached an astounding 2,200% as measured by Joe Schofield, the former president of IFPUG! LOC metrics make requirements and design invisible and also ignore requirements and design defects, which outnumber code defects. Although there are benchmarks based on LOC, the intrinsic errors of LOC metrics make them unreliable. Due to lack of standards for counting LOC, benchmarks from different vendors for the same applications can contain widely different results. Appendix B provides a mathematical proof that LOC metrics do not measure economic productivity by showing 79 programming languages with function points and LOC in a side-by-side format.

SNAP point metrics are a new variation on function points introduced by IFPUG in 2012. The term SNAP is an awkward acronym for "software non-functional assessment process." The basic idea is that software requirements have two flavors: (1) functional requirements needed by users; (2) non-functional requirements due to laws, mandates, or physical factors such as storage limits or performance criteria. The SNAP committee's view is that these non-functional requirements should be sized, estimated, and measured separately from function point metrics. Thus, SNAP and function point metrics are not additive, although they could have been. Having two separate metrics for economic studies is awkward at best and inconsistent with other industries. For that matter, it seems inconsistent with standard economic analysis in every industry. Almost every industry has a single normalizing metric such as "cost per square foot" for home construction or "cost per gallon" for gasoline and diesel oil. As of 2016, none of the parametric estimation tools had fully integrated SNAP, and it may be that they won't since the costs of adding SNAP are painfully expensive. As a rule of thumb, non-functional requirements are about equal to 15% of functional requirements, although the range is very wide.

Story point metrics are widely used for agile projects with "user stories." Story points have no ISO standard for counting or any other standard. They are highly ambiguous and vary by as much as 400% from company to company and project to project. There are few useful benchmarks using story points. Obviously, story points can't be used for projects that don't utilize user stories so they are worthless for comparisons against other design methods. The author's Software Risk Master (SRM) estimating tool converts story points to function points and agile sprints into a standard chart of accounts. These conversions allow agile to be compared side by side against DevOps, Iterative, Container development, waterfall, spiral, etc.

Taxonomy of software applications is needed to ensure "apples-to-apples" benchmark comparisons. Although there are several taxonomies for software, the one developed by the author of this book is useful for sizing, estimating, and benchmark data collection. It is a standard feature in the author's Software Risk Master (SRM) tool. The elements of the SRM taxonomy include: (1) country code, (2) region code, (3) city code, (4) industry code (we use the North American Industry Classification code or NAIC code), (5) project nature; (6) project scope, (7) project class, (8) project type, (9) project hardware platform, (10) problem complexity, (11) code complexity, and (12) data complexity. It happens that projects with identical taxonomies are usually very similar, which makes benchmark comparisons interesting and useful. We also include some additional topics of interest: (A) methodology chosen from a list of 50; (B) programming languages chosen from a list of 180; (C) project CMMI level; (D) team experience of several kinds; (E) project management experience; (F) client experience; and (G) reusable materials available.

Technical debt is a new metric and rapidly spreading. It is a brilliant metaphor developed by Ward Cunningham. The concept of "technical debt" is that topics deferred during development in the interest of schedule speed will cost more after release than they would have cost initially. However, there are no ISO standards for technical debt and the concept is highly ambiguous. It can vary by over 500% from company to company and project to project. Worse, technical debt does not include all of the costs associated with poor quality and development short cuts. Technical debt omits canceled projects, consequential damages or harm to users, and the costs of litigation for poor quality.

Use-case points are used by projects with designs based on "use cases" which often utilize IBM's Rational Unified Process (RUP). There are no ISO standards for use cases. Use cases are ambiguous and vary by over 200% from company to company and project to project. Obviously use cases are worthless for measuring projects that don't utilize use cases, so they have very little benchmark data. This is yet another attempt to imitate the virtues of function point metrics, only with somewhat less rigor and with imperfect counting rules as of 2015.

Velocity is an agile metric that is used for prediction of sprint and project outcomes. It uses historical data on completion of past work units combined with the assumption that future work units will be about the same. Of course it is necessary to know future work units for the method to operate. The concept of velocity is basically similar to the concept of using historical benchmarks for estimating future results. However as of 2015, velocity had no ISO standards and no certification. There are no standard work units, and these can be story points or other metrics such as function points or use-case points, or even synthetic concepts such as "days per task." If agile projects use function points, then they could gain access to large volumes of historical data using activity-based costs, i.e. requirements effort, design effort, code effort, test effort, integration effort, documentation effort, etc. Story points have too wide a range of variability from company to company and project to project; function points are much more consistent across various kinds of projects. Of course, COSMIC, IFPUG, and the other variants don't have exactly the same results.

Defining Software Productivity

For more than 200 years, the standard economic definition of productivity has been, "Goods or services produced per unit of labor or expense." This definition is used in all industries, but has been hard to use in the software industry. For software there is ambiguity in what constitutes our "*goods or services.*"

The oldest unit for software "goods" was a "*line of code*" or LOC. More recently, software goods have been defined as "*function points.*" Even more recent definitions of goods include "*story points*" and "*use-case points.*" The pros and cons of these units have been discussed and some will be illustrated in the appendices.

Another important topic taken from manufacturing economics has a big impact on software productivity that is not yet well understood even in 2017: fixed costs.

A basic law of manufacturing economics that is valid for all industries including software is the following:

> *When a development process has a high percentage of fixed costs, and there is a decline in the number of units produced, the cost per unit will go up.*

When a "*line of code*" is selected as the manufacturing unit and there is a switch from a low-level language such as assembly to a high-level language such as Java, there will be a reduction in the number of units developed.

But the non-code tasks of requirements and design act like fixed costs. Therefore, the cost per line of code will go up for high-level languages. This means that LOC is not a valid metric for measuring economic productivity as proven in Appendix B.

For software there are two definitions of productivity that match standard economic concepts:

1. *Producing a specific quantity of deliverable units for the lowest number of work hours.*
2. *Producing the largest number of deliverable units in a standard work period such as an hour, month, or year.*

In definition 1, deliverable goods are constant and *work hours are variable.*

In definition 2, *deliverable goods are variable* and work periods are constant.

The common metrics "*work hours per function point*" and "*work hours per KLOC*" are good examples of productivity definition 1.

The metrics *"function points per month"* and *"lines of code per month"* are examples of definition 2.

However for "lines of code," the fixed costs of requirements and design will cause apparent productivity to be reversed, with low-level languages seeming better than high-level languages, as shown by the 79 languages listed in Appendix B.

Definition 2 will also encounter the fact that the number of work hours per month varies widely from country to country. For example, India works 190 hours per month while the Netherlands work only 115 hours per month. This means that productivity definitions 1 and 2 will not be the same. A given number of work hours would take fewer calendar months in India than in the Netherlands due to the larger number of monthly work hours.

Table 5.2 shows the differences between *"work hours per function point"* and *"function points per month"* for 52 countries. The national work hour column is from the Organization of International Cooperation and Development (OECD). Table 5.1 assumes a constant value of 15 work hours per function point for an identical application in every country shown.

No one to date has produced a table similar to Table 5.1 for SNAP metrics, but it is obvious that work hours per SNAP point and SNAP points per month will follow the same global patterns as do the older function point metrics.

Of course differences in experience, methodologies, languages, and other variables also impact both forms of productivity. Table 5.1 shows that the two forms are not identical from country to country due to variations in local work patterns.

Defining Software Quality

As we all know, the topic of *"quality"* is somewhat ambiguous in every industry. Definitions for quality can encompass subjective aesthetic quality and also precise quantitative units such as numbers of defects and their severity levels.

Over the years software has tried a number of alternate definitions for quality that are not actually useful. For example, one definition for software quality has been *"conformance to requirements."*

Requirements themselves are filled with bugs or errors that comprise about 20% of the overall defects found in software applications. Defining quality as conformance to a major source of errors is circular reasoning and clearly invalid. We need to include requirements errors in our definition of quality.

Table 5.2 Comparison of Work Hours per FP and FP per Month

		OECD National Work Hours per Month	*Work Hours per Function Point*	*Function Points per Month*
1	India	190.00	15.00	13.47
2	Taiwan	188.00	15.00	13.20
3	Mexico	185.50	15.00	13.17
4	China	186.00	15.00	12.93
5	Peru	184.00	15.00	12.67
6	Colombia	176.00	15.00	12.13
7	Pakistan	176.00	15.00	12.13
8	Hong Kong	190.00	15.00	12.01
9	Thailand	168.00	15.00	11.73
10	Malaysia	192.00	15.00	11.73
11	Greece	169.50	15.00	11.70
12	South Africa	168.00	15.00	11.60
13	Israel	159.17	15.00	11.14
14	Viet Nam	160.00	15.00	11.07
15	Philippines	160.00	15.00	10.93
16	Singapore	176.00	15.00	10.92
17	Hungary	163.00	15.00	10.87
18	Poland	160.75	15.00	10.85
19	Turkey	156.42	15.00	10.69
20	Brazil	176.00	15.00	10.65
21	Panama	176.00	15.00	10.65
22	Chile	169.08	15.00	10.51
23	Estonia	157.42	15.00	10.49
24	Japan	145.42	15.00	10.49
25	Switzerland	168.00	15.00	10.45
26	Czech Republic	150.00	15.00	10.00
27	Russia	164.42	15.00	9.97

(Continued)

Table 5.2 (Continued)

		OECD National Work Hours per Month	Work Hours per Function Point	Function Points per Month
28	Argentina	168.00	15.00	9.91
29	Korea – South	138.00	15.00	9.60
30	**United States**	**149.17**	15.00	**9.47**
31	Saudi Arabia	160.00	15.00	9.44
32	Portugal	140.92	15.00	9.39
33	United Kingdom	137.83	15.00	9.32
34	Finland	139.33	15.00	9.29
35	Ukraine	156.00	15.00	9.20
36	Venezuela	152.00	15.00	9.10
37	Austria	134.08	15.00	8.94
38	Luxembourg	134.08	15.00	8.94
39	Italy	146.00	15.00	8.75
40	Belgium	131.17	15.00	8.74
41	New Zealand	144.92	15.00	8.68
42	Denmark	128.83	15.00	8.59
43	Canada	142.50	15.00	8.54
44	Australia	144.00	15.00	8.50
45	Ireland	127.42	15.00	8.49
46	Spain	140.50	15.00	8.42
47	France	123.25	15.00	8.22
48	Iceland	142.17	15.00	8.00
49	Sweden	135.08	15.00	7.97
50	Norway	118.33	15.00	7.89
51	Germany	116.42	15.00	7.76
52	Netherlands	115.08	15.00	7.67
Average		**155.38**	**15.00**	**10.13**

Another definition for quality has been *"fitness for use."* But this definition is ambiguous and cannot be predicted before the software is released, or even measured well after release.

It is obvious that a workable definition for software quality must be unambiguous and capable of being *predicted* before release and then *measured* after release and should also be *quantified* and not purely subjective.

Another definition for software quality has been a string of words ending in "…ility" such as reliability and maintainability. However laudable these attributes are, they are all ambiguous and difficult to measure. Further, they are hard to predict before applications are built.

The quality standard ISO/IEC 9126 includes a list of words such as portability, maintainability, reliability, and maintainability. It is astonishing that there is no discussion of defects or bugs. Worse, the ISO/IEC definitions are almost impossible to predict before development and are not easy to measure after release nor are they quantified. It is obvious that an effective quality measure needs to be predictable, measurable, and quantifiable.

Reliability is predictable in terms of mean time to failure (MTTF) and mean time between failures (MTBF). Indeed, these are standard predictions from the author's Software Risk Master (SRM) tool. However, reliability is inversely proportional to delivered defects. Therefore, the ISO quality standards should have included defect potentials, DRE, and delivered defect densities.

An effective definition for software quality that can be both predicted before applications are built and then measured after applications are delivered is: "***Software quality is the absence of defects which would either cause the application to stop working, or cause it to produce incorrect results.***"

Because delivered defects impact reliability, maintainability, usability, fitness for use, conformance to requirements, and also customer satisfaction any effective definition of software quality must recognize the central importance of achieving low volumes of delivered defects. Software quality is impossible without low levels of delivered defects no matter what definition is used.

This definition has the advantage of being applicable to all software deliverables including requirements, architecture, design, code, documents, and even test cases.

If software quality focuses on the prevention or elimination of defects, there are some effective corollary metrics that are quite useful.

The "***defect potential***" of a software application is defined as the sum total of bugs or defects that are likely to be found in requirements, architecture, design, source code, documents, and "bad fixes" or secondary bugs found in bug repairs themselves. The "defect potential" metric originated in IBM circa 1973 and is fairly widely used among technology companies.

The "*defect detection efficiency*" **(DDE)** is the percentage of bugs found prior to release of the software to customers.

The "*defect removal efficiency*" **(DRE)** is the percentage of bugs found and repaired prior to release of the software to customers.

DDE and DRE were developed in IBM circa 1973 but are widely used by technology companies in every country. As of 2017, the average DRE for the United States was about 92.50%. The best in class was about 99.75%. Worst case results were below 88.00% and projects this bad often end up in litigation.

DRE is normally measured by comparing internal bugs against customer reported bugs for the first 90 days of use. If developers found 90 bugs and users reported 10 bugs, the total is 100 bugs and DRE would be 90%.

Another corollary metric is that of "*defect severity.*" This is a very old metric dating back to IBM in the early 1960s. IBM uses four severity levels:

- Severity 1   Software is inoperable   <1%
- Severity 2   Major feature disabled or incorrect   <15%
- Severity 3   Minor error; software is usable   <40%
- Severity 4   Cosmetic error that does not affect results   <35%

To clarify these various terms, Table 5.3 shows defect potentials, and DRE for an application of 1,000 function points coded in the Java language using agile development. Table 5.3 uses even numbers to simplify the math. The author's Software Risk Master (SRM) tool predicts the same kinds of values for actual projects.

All of the values shown in Table 5.3 can be predicted before applications are developed and then measured after the applications are released. Thus, software quality can move from an ambiguous and subjective term to a rigorous and quantitative set of measures that can even be included in software contracts. Note that bugs from requirements and design cannot be quantified using lines of code or KLOC, which is why function points are the best choice for quality measurements. It is possible to retrofit LOC after the fact, but in real life, LOC is not used for requirements, architecture, and design bug predictions.

Note that Table 5.2 combines non-functional and functional requirements defects, which might be separate categories if SNAP metrics are

Table 5.3 Software Quality for 1000 Function Points, Java, and Agile Development

Defect Potentials	Number of Bugs	Defects per FP
Requirements defects	750	0.75
Architecture defects	150	0.15
Design defects	1,000	1.00
Code defects	1,350	1.35
Document defects	250	0.25
Sub total	**3,500**	**3.50**
Bad fixes	150	**0.15**
Total	**3,650**	**3.65**
Defect removal efficiency (DRE)	**97.00%**	**97.00%**
Defects removed	3,540	3.54
Defects delivered	**110**	**0.11**
High-severity delivered	**15**	**0.02**

used. However, in almost 100% of software requirements, documents studied by the author functional and non-functional requirements are both combined without any distinction in the requirements themselves.

Patterns of Successful Software Measurements and Metrics

Since the majority of global software projects are either not measured at all, only partially measured, or measured with metrics that violate standard economic assumptions, what does work? Following are discussions of the most successful combinations of software metrics available today in 2021.

Successful Software Measurement and Metric Patterns

1. Function points for normalizing productivity data.
2. Function points for normalizing quality data.
3. SNAP metrics for non-functional requirements (with caution).

4. Defect potentials based on all defect types normalized with function points.
5. Defect removal efficiency (DRE) based on all defect types.
6. Defect removal efficiency (DRE) including inspections and static analysis.
7. Defect removal efficiency (DRE) based on a 90-day post-release period.
8. Activity-based benchmarks for development.
9. Activity-based benchmarks for maintenance.
10. Cost of quality (COQ) for quality economics.
11. Total cost of ownership (TCO) for software economics.

Let us consider these 11 patterns of successful metrics.

Function Points for Normalizing Productivity Data

It is obvious that software projects are built by a variety of occupations and use a variety of activities including

1. Requirements
2. Design
3. Coding
4. Testing
5. Integration
6. Documentation
7. Management

The older LOC metric is worthless for estimating or measuring non-code work. Function points can measure every activity individually and also the combined aggregate totals of all activities.

Note that the new SNAP metric for non-functional requirements is not included. Integrating SNAP into productivity and quality predictions and measurements is still work in progress. Future versions of this chapter will discuss SNAP.

Function Points for Normalizing Software Quality

It is obvious that software bugs or defects originate in a variety of sources including but not limited to:

1. Requirements defects
2. Architecture defects
3. Design defects

4. Coding defects
5. Document defects
6. Bad fixes or defects in bug repairs

The older LOC metric is worthless for estimating or measuring non-code defects but function points can measure every defect source.

Defect Potentials Based on all Defect Types

The term "defect potential" originated in IBM circa 1965 and refers to the sum total of defects in software projects that originate in requirements, architecture, design, code, documents, and "bad fixes" or bugs in defect repairs. The older LOC metric only measures code defects, and they are only a small fraction of total defects. The current U.S. average distribution of defects based on about 26,000 projects is approximately as follows (Table 5.4):

There are of course wide variations based on team skills, methodologies, CMMI levels, programming languages, and other variable factors.

Defect Removal Efficiency (DRE) Based on All Defect Types

Since requirements, architecture, and design defects outnumber code defects, it is obvious that measures of DRE need to include all defect sources. It is also obvious to those who measure quality that getting rid of code defects is easier than getting rid of other sources. Following are representative values for DRE by defect source for an application of 1,000 function points in the C programming language:

Defect Sources	Defect Potential	DRE Percent	Delivered Defects
Requirements defects	1.00	85.00%	0.15
Architecture defects	0.25	75.00%	0.06
Design defects	1.25	90.00%	0.13
Code defects	1.50	97.00%	0.05
Document defects	0.50	95.00%	0.03
Bad fix defects	0.50	80.00%	0.10
Total	**5.00**	**89.80%**	**0.51**

As can be seen, DRE against code defects is higher than against other defect sources. But the main point is that only function point metrics

Table 5.4 Average Software Defect Potentials circa 2020 for the United States

• Requirements	0.70 defects per function point
• Architecture	0.10 defects per function point
• Design	0.95 defects per function point
• Code	1.15 defects per function point
• Security code flaws	0.25 defects per function point
• Documents	0.45 defects per function point
• Bad fixes	0.65 defects per function point
Total	**4.25 defects per function point**

can measure and include all defect sources. The older LOC metric is worthless for requirements, design, and architecture defects.

Defect Removal Efficiency Including Inspections and Static Analysis

Serious study of software quality obviously needs to include pre-test inspections and static analysis as well as coding.

The software industry has concentrated only on code defects and only on testing. This is short sighted and insufficient. The software industry needs to understand all defect sources and every form of defect removal including pre-test inspections and static analysis. The approximate DRE levels of various defect removal stages are shown in Table 5.5.

Since the costs of finding and fixing bugs in software have been the largest single expense element for over 60 years, software quality and defect removal need the kind of data shown in Table 5.5.

Defect Removal Efficiency Based on 90 Days after Release

It is obvious that measuring DRE based only on 30 days after release is insufficient to judge software quality:

Defects found before release	900	
Defects found in 30 days	5	99.45%
Defects found in 90 days	50	94.74%
Defects found in 360 days	75	92.31%

A 30-day interval after release will find very few defects since full usage may not even have begun due to installation and training. IBM selected a 90-day interval because that allowed normal usage patterns to unfold. Of course bugs continue to be found after 90 days and also the software may be updated. A 90-day window is a good compromise for measuring the DRE of the original version before updates begin to accumulate.

A 30-day window may be sufficient for small projects <250 function points. But anyone who has worked on large systems in the 10,000 to 100,000 function point size range knows that installation and training normally take about a month. Therefore, full production may not even have started in the first 30 days.

Activity-Based Benchmarks for Development

Today software development is one of the most labor-intensive and expensive industrial activities in human history. Building large software applications costs more than the cost of a 50-story office building or the cost of an 80,000-ton cruise ship.

Given the fact that large software applications can employ more than 500 personnel in a total of more than 50 occupations, one might think that the industry would utilize fairly detailed activity-based benchmarks to explore the complexity of modern software development.

But unfortunately, the majority of software benchmarks in 2017 were single values such as "work hours per function point," "function points per month," or "lines of code per month." This is not sufficient. Following are the kinds of activity-based benchmarks actually needed by the industry in order to understand the full economic picture of modern software development. Table 5.6 reflects a system of 10,000 function points and the Java programming language combined with an average team and iterative development.

Note that in real life, non-code work such as requirements, architecture, and design are not measured using LOC metrics. But it is easy to retrofit LOC since the mathematics are not complicated. Incidentally, the author's Software Risk Master (SRM) tool predicts all four values shown in Table 5.6 and also shows story points, use-case points, and in fact 23 different metrics.

The "cumulative results" show the most common benchmark form of single values. However, single values are clearly inadequate to show the complexity of a full set of development activities.

Note that agile projects with multiple sprints would use a different set of activities. But to compare agile projects against other kinds of

Table 5.5 Software Defect Potentials and Defect Removal Efficiency (DRE)

Note 1: The table how high-quality defect removal operations
Note 2: The table illustrates calculations from Software Risk Master ™ (SRM)

Application type	Embedded
Application size in function points	1,000
Application language	Java
Language level	6.00
Source lines per FP	53.33
Source lines of code	53,333
KLOC of code	53.33

Pre-Test Defect Removal Methods		Architect	Require	Design	Code	Document	Total
		Defects per Function Point	*Defects per Function Point*	*Defects per Function Point*	*Defects per Function Point*	*Defects per Function Point*	*Total*
	Defect potentials per FP	**0.35**	**0.97**	**1.19**	**1.47**	**0.18**	**4.16**
	Defect potentials	**355**	**966**	**1,189**	**1,469**	**184**	**4,163**
1	**Requirement inspection**	5.00%	87.00%	10.00%	5.00%	8.50%	25.61%
	Defects discovered	18	840	119	73	16	1,066
	Bad-fix injection	1	25	4	2	0	32
	Defects remaining	337	100	1,066	1,394	168	3,065

Pre-Test Defect Removal Activities

2	**Architecture inspection**	**85.00%**	10.00%	10.00%	2.50%	12.00%	14.93%
	Defects discovered	286	10	107	35	20	458
	Bad-fix injection	9	0	3	1	1	14
	Defects remaining	42	90	956	1,358	147	2,593
3	**Design inspection**	10.00%	14.00%	**87.00%**	7.00%	16.00%	37.30%
	Defects discovered	4	13	832	95	24	967
	Bad-fix injection	0	0	25	3	1	48
	Defects remaining	38	77	99	1,260	123	1,597
4	**Code inspection**	12.50%	15.00%	20.00%	85.00%	10.00%	70.10%
	Defects discovered	5	12	20	1,071	12	1,119
	Bad-fix injection	0	0	1	32	0	34
	Defects remaining	33	65	79	157	110	444
5	**Static analysis**	2.00%	2.00%	7.00%	**87.00%**	3.00%	33.17%
	Defects discovered	1	1	6	136	3	147
	Bad-fix injection	0	0	0	4	0	4
	Defects remaining	32	64	73	16	107	292
6	**IV & V**	10.00%	12.00%	**23.00%**	7.00%	18.00%	16.45%
	Defects discovered	3	8	17	1	19	48
	Bad-fix injection	0	0	1	0	1	1
	Defects remaining	29	56	56	15	87	243

(Continued)

Table 5.5 (Continued)

7 SQA review	10.00%	17.00%	17.00%	12.00%	12.50%	28.08%
Defects discovered	3	10	9	2	11	35
Bad-fix injection	0	0	0	0	0	2
Defects remaining	26	46	46	13	76	206
Pre-test DRE	**329**	**920**	**1,142**	**1,456**	**108**	**3,956**
Pre-test DRE %	**92.73%**	**95.23%**	**96.12%**	**99.10%**	**58.79%**	**95.02%**
Defects remaining	**26**	**46**	**46**	**13**	**76**	**207**

Test Defect Removal Stages

	Architect	Require	Design	Code	Document	Total
				Test Defect Removal Activities		
1 **Unit testing**	2.50%	4.00%	7.00%	35.00%	10.00%	8.69%
Defects discovered	1	2	3	5	8	18
Bad-fix injection	0	0	0	0	0	1
Defects remaining	25	44	43	8	68	188
2 **Function testing**	7.50%	5.00%	22.00%	37.50%	10.00%	12.50%
Defects discovered	2	2	9	3	7	23
Bad-fix injection	0	0	0	0	0	1
Defects remaining	23	42	33	5	61	164
3 **Regression testing**	2.00%	2.00%	5.00%	33.00%	7.50%	5.65%
Defects discovered	0	1	2	2	5	9
Bad-fix injection	0	0	0	0	0	0
Defects remaining	23	41	31	3	56	154

4	**Integration testing**	6.00%	20.00%	22.00%	**33.00%**	15.00%	16.90%
	Defects discovered	1	8	7	1	8	26
	Bad-fix injection	0	0	0	0	0	1
	Defects remaining	21	33	24	2	48	127
5	**Performance testing**	14.00%	2.00%	**20.00%**	18.00%	2.50%	7.92%
	Defects discovered	3	1	5	0	1	10
	Bad-fix injection	0	0	0	0	0	0
	Defects remaining	18	32	19	2	46	117
6	**Security testing**	12.00%	15.00%	**23.00%**	8.00%	2.50%	10.87%
	Defects discovered	2	5	4	0	1	13
	Bad-fix injection	0	0	0	0	0	0
	Defects remaining	16	27	15	2	45	104
7	**Usability testing**	12.00%	17.00%	15.00%	5.00%	**48.00%**	29.35%
	Defects discovered	2	5	2	0	22	30
	Bad-fix injection	0	0	0	0	1	1
	Defects remaining	14	22	12	2	23	72
8	**System testing**	16.00%	12.00%	18.00%	12.00%	**34.00%**	20.85%
	Defects discovered	2	3	2	0	8	15
	Bad-fix injection	0	0	0	0	0	0
	Defects remaining	12	20	10	1	15	57

(Continued)

Table 5.5 (Continued)

9		10.00%	5.00%	13.00%	10.00%	20.00%	11.55%
	Cloud testing						
	Defects discovered	1	1	1	0	3	7
	Bad-fix injection	0	0	0	0	0	0
	Defects remaining	10	19	9	1	12	51
10	**Independent testing**	12.00%	10.00%	11.00%	10.00%	23.00%	13.60%
	Defects discovered	1	2	1	0	3	7
	Bad-fix injection	0	0	0	0	0	0
	Defects remaining	9	17	8	1	9	44
11	**Field (Beta) testing**	14.00%	12.00%	14.00%	12.00%	34.00%	17.30%
	Defects discovered	1	2	1	0	3	8
	Bad-fix injection	0	0	0	0	0	0
	Defects remaining	8	15	7	1	6	36
12	**Acceptance testing**	13.00%	14.00%	15.00%	12.00%	24.00%	17.98%
	Defects discovered	1	2	1	0	2	6
	Bad-fix injection	0	0	0	0	0	0
	Defects remaining	7	13	6	1	3	30
	Test defects removed	**19**	**33**	**40**	**12**	**72**	**177**
	Testing efficiency %	**73.96%**	**72.26%**	**87.63%**	**93.44%**	**95.45%**	**85.69%**

Defects remaining	7	13	6	1	3	30
Total defects removed	348	953	1,183	1,468	181	4,133
Total bad-fix injection	10	29	35	44	5	124
Cumulative removal %	98.11%	98.68%	99.52%	99.94%	98.13%	99.27%
Remaining defects	7	13	6	1	3	30
High-severity defects	1	2	1	0	0	5
Security defects	0	0	0	0	0	1
Remaining defects per function point	0.0067	0.0128	0.0057	0.0009	0.0035	0.0302
Remaining defects per K function points	6.72	12.80	5.70	0.87	3.45	30.23
Remaining defects per KLOC	0.13	0.24	0.11	0.02	0.06	0.57

Table 5.6   Example of Activity-based Benchmark

Language	Java			
Function points	10,000			
Lines of code	533,333			
KLOC	533			
Development Activities	Work Hours per FP	FP per Month	Work Hours per KLOC	LOC per Month
1 Business analysis	0.02	7,500.00	0.33	400,000
2 Risk analysis/sizing	0.00	35,000.00	0.07	1,866,666
3 Risk solution planning	0.01	15,000.00	0.17	800,000
4 Requirements	0.38	350.00	7.08	18,667
5 Requirement. inspection	0.22	600.00	4.13	32,000
6 Prototyping	0.33	400.00	0.62	213,333
7 Architecture	0.05	2,500.00	0.99	133,333
8 Architecture. inspection	0.04	3,000.00	0.83	160,000
9 Project plans/estimates	0.03	5,000.00	0.50	266,667
10 Initial design	0.75	175.00	14.15	9,333
11 Detail design	0.75	175.00	14.15	9,333
12 Design inspections	0.53	250.00	9.91	13,333
13 Coding	4.00	33.00	75.05	1,760
14 Code inspections	3.30	40.00	61.91	2,133
15 Reuse acquisition	0.01	10,000.00	0.25	533,333
16 Static analysis	0.02	7,500.00	0.33	400,000
17 COTS package purchase	0.01	10,000.00	0.25	533,333
18 Open-source acquisition	0.01	10,000.00	0.25	533,333
19 Code security audit	0.04	3,500.00	0.71	186,667
20 Ind. verification & validation (IV&V).	0.07	2,000.00	1.24	106,667
21 Configuration control	0.04	3,500.00	0.71	186,667
22 Integration	0.04	3,500.00	0.71	186,667
23 User documentation	0.29	450.00	5.50	24,000

Table 5.6 (Continued)

Language	Java			
Function points	10,000			
Lines of code	533,333			
KLOC	533			
Development Activities	Work Hours per FP	FP per Month	Work Hours per KLOC	LOC per Month
24 Unit testing	0.88	150.00	16.51	8,000
25 Function testing	0.75	175.00	14.15	9,333
26 Regression testing	0.53	250.00	9.91	13,333
27 Integration testing	0.44	300.00	8.26	16,000
28 Performance testing	0.33	400.00	6.19	21,333
29 Security testing	0.26	500.00	4.95	26,667
30 Usability testing	0.22	600.00	4.13	32,000
31 System testing	0.88	150.00	16.51	8,000
32 Cloud testing	0.13	1,000.00	2.48	53,333
33 Field (Beta) testing	0.18	750.00	3.30	40,000
34 Acceptance testing	0.05	2,500.00	0.99	133,333
35 Independent testing	0.07	2,000.00	1.24	106,667
36 Quality assurance	0.18	750.00	3.30	40,000
37 Installation/training	0.04	3,500.00	0.71	186,667
38 Project measurement	0.01	10,000.00	0.25	533,333
39 Project office	0.18	750.00	3.30	40,000
40 Project management	4.40	30.00	82.55	1,600
Cumulative results	**20.44**	**6.46**	**377.97**	**349**

development methods, the agile results are converted into a standard chart of accounts shown by Table 5.4.

Note that there is no current data equivalent to Table 5.4 showing activity-based costs for SNAP metrics as of 2017. Indeed the IFPUG SNAP committee has not yet addressed the topic of activity-based costs.

Activity-Based Benchmarks for Maintenance

The word "maintenance" is highly ambiguous and can encompass no fewer than 25 different kinds of work. In ordinary benchmarks "maintenance" usually refers to post-release defect repairs. However, some companies and benchmarks also include enhancements. This is not a good idea since the funding for defect repairs and enhancements is from different sources and often the work is done by different teams (Table 5.7).

As with software development, function point metrics provide the most effective normalization metric for all forms of maintenance and enhancement work.

The author's Software Risk Master (SRM) tool predicts maintenance and enhancement for a three-year period. It can also measure annual maintenance and enhancements. The entire set of metrics is among the most complex. However, Table 5.8 illustrates a three-year pattern.

The mathematical algorithms for predicting maintenance and enhancements can work for 10 year periods, but there is little value in going past three years since business changes or changes in government laws and mandates degrade long-range predictions.

Cost of Quality (COQ) for Quality Economics

The cost of quality (COQ) metric is roughly the same age as the software industry, having originated in 1956 by Edward Feigenbaum. It was later expanded by Joseph Juran and then made very famous by Phil Crosby in his seminal book Quality is Free.

Quality was also dealt with fictionally in Robert M. Pirsig's famous book Zen and the Art of Motorcycle Maintenance. This book has become one of the best-selling books ever published and has been translated into many natural languages. It has sold over 5,000,000 copies. (By interesting coincidence Pirsig's regular work was as a software technical writer.)

Because COQ originated for manufacturing rather than for software, it needs to be modified slightly to be effective in a software context.

The original concepts of COQ include:

- Prevention costs
- Appraisal costs
- Internal failure costs
- External failure costs
- Total costs

Table 5.7 Major Kinds of Work Performed Under the Generic Term "Maintenance"

1	Major enhancements (new features of >20 function points).
2	Minor enhancements (new features of <5 function points).
3	Maintenance (repairing defects for good will).
4	Warranty repairs (repairing defects under formal contract).
5	Customer support (responding to client phone calls or problem reports).
6	Error-prone module removal (eliminating very troublesome code segments).
7	Mandatory changes (required or statutory changes).
8	Complexity or structural analysis (charting control flow plus complexity metrics).
9	Code restructuring (reducing cyclomatic and essential complexity).
10	Optimization (increasing performance or throughput).
11	Migration (moving software from one platform to another).
12	Conversion (changing the interface or file structure).
13	Reverse engineering (extracting latent design information from code).
14	Reengineering (transforming legacy application to modern forms).
15	Dead code removal (removing segments no longer utilized).
16	Dormant application elimination (archiving unused software).
17	Nationalization (modifying software for international use).
18	Mass updates such as Euro or Year 2000 Repairs.
19	Refactoring, or reprogramming applications to improve clarity.
20	Retirement (withdrawing an application from active service)
21	Field service (sending maintenance members to client locations).
22	Reporting bugs or defects to software vendors.
23	Installing updates received from software vendors.
24	Processing invalid defect reports.
25	Processing duplicate defect reports.

Table 5.8 Three-Year Maintenance, Enhancement, and Support Data

	Year 1	Year 2	Year 3	
	2013	2014	2015	3-Year Total
Enhancements (new features)				
Annual enhancement %	8.00%	200	216	233	649
Application growth in FP	2,500	2,700	2,916	3,149	3,149
Application growth in LOC	133,333	144,000	155,520	167,962	167,962
Cyclomatic complexity growth	10.67	10.70	10.74	10.78	10.78
Enhan. defects per FP	0.01	0.00	0.00	0.00	0.00
Enhan. defects delivered	21	1	1	1	23
Enhancement team staff	0	2.02	2.21	2.41	2.22
Enhancement (months)	0	24.29	26.51	28.94	79.75
Enhancement (hours)	0	3,206.48	3,499.84	3,820.47	10,526.78
Enhancement team costs	0	$273,279	$298,282	$325,608	$897,169
Function points per month		8.23	8.15	8.06	8.14
Work hours per function point		16.03	16.20	16.38	16.21
Enhancement $ per FP		$1,366.40	$1,380.93	$1,395.78	$1,381.79
Maintenance (defect repairs)				
Number of maintenance sites	1	1	1	1	1
Clients served per site	74	94	118	149	149
Number of initial client sites	3	4	5	6	6

		Year 1	Year 2	Year 3		3-Year Total
		2013	2014	2015		
Annual rate of increase	**15.00%**	22.51%	22.51%	22.51%		**20.63%**
Number of initial clients	**100**	128	163	207		**207**
Annual rate of increase	**20.00%**	27.51%	27.51%	27.51%		**25.63%**
Client sites added	0	1	1	1		3
Client sites lost	0	0	0	0		0
Net change	0	1	1	1		3
Year-end client sites	0	4	5	6		6
Clients added	0	28	36	46		110
Clients lost	0	−1	−1	−1		−3
Net change	0	28	35	45		107
Year-end clients	0	128	163	207		207
Customer defect/help requests						
Customer satisfaction	0	95.34%	99.42%	100.16%		**98.31%**
Customer help requests	0	67	62	60		189
Customer complaints	0	24	18	15		56
Enhancement bug reports	**0**	1	1	1		2
Original bug reports	**0**	8	5	3		16
High severity bug reports	**0**	1	1	0		2
Security flaws	**0**	1	0	0		0

(Continued)

Table 5.8 (Continued)

		Year 1	Year 2	Year 3	3-Year Total
		2013	2014	2015	
Bad fixes: bugs in repairs	0	0	0	0	0
Duplicate bug reports	0	8	7	6	22
Invalid bug reports	0	2	1	1	4
Abeyant defects	0	0	0	0	0
Total incidents	0	112	96	86	293
Complaints per FP	0	0.01	0.01	0.01	0.02
Bug reports per FP	0	0.00	0.00	0.00	0.01
High severity bugs per FP	0	0.00	0.00	0.00	0.00
Incidents per FP	0	0.04	0.04	0.03	0.12
Maintenance and support staff					
Customer support staff	0	0.31	0.33	0.38	0.34
Customer support (months)	0	3.72	4.01	4.56	12.29
Customer support (hours)	0	490.80	529.37	601.88	1,622.05
Customer support costs	0	$17,568	$18,949	$21,545	$58,062
Customer support $ per FP	0	$6.51	$6.50	$6.84	$6.62
Maintenance staff	0	1.83	1.80	1.77	1.80
Maintenance effort (months)	0	21.97	21.56	21.29	64.82
Maintenance effort (hours)	0	2,899.78	2,846.43	2,810.38	8,556.59
Maintenance (tech. debt)	0	$247,140	$242,593	$239,521	$729,255

| | | Year 1 | Year 2 | Year 3 | |
		2013	2014	2015	3-Year Total
Maintenance $ per FP	0	$91.53	$83.19	$76.06	$83.59
Management staff	0	0.22	0.22	0.22	0.22
Management effort (months)	0	2.69	2.66	2.67	8.02
Management effort (hours)	0	354.92	351.56	352.39	1,058.87
Management costs	0	$30,249	$29,963	$30,033	$90,245
Management $ per FP	0	$11.20	$10.28	$9.54	$10.34
Total maintenance staff	**0**	**2.36**	**2.35**	**2.38**	**2.36**
Total effort (months)	**0**	**28.37**	**28.24**	**28.52**	**85.13**
Total effort (hours)	**0**	**3,745.50**	**3,727.36**	**3,764.66**	**11,237.51**
Total maintenance $	**0**	**$294,957**	**$291,505**	**$291,099**	**$877,561**
Maintenance $ per FP	0	$117.98	$116.60	$116.44	$117.01
Maintenance hours per FP	0	1.39	1.28	1.20	1.29
Maintenance$ per defect	0	$32,865	$50,957	$82,650	$55,490.43
Maintenance $ per KLOC	0	$2,212	$2,186	$2,183	$6,582
Maintenance $ per incident	0	$2,637.01	$3,049.51	$3,375.50	$3,020.67
Incidents per support staff	0	360.99	286.03	226.96	873.98
Bug reports per staff member	0	11.57	8.52	6.42	26.51
Incidents per staff month	0	30.08	23.84	18.91	24.28
Bug reports per staff month	0	0.96	0.71	0.54	0.74

(Continued)

Table 5.8 (Continued)

		Year 1	Year 2	Year 3	3-Year Total
		2013	2014	2015	
(Maintenance + enhancement)					
Enhancement staff	0	2.02	2.21	2.41	2.22
Maintenance staff	0	2.36	2.35	2.38	2.36
Total staff	0	4.39	4.56	4.79	4.58
Enhancement effort (months)	0	24.29	26.51	28.94	79.75
Maintenance effort (months)	0	28.37	28.24	28.52	85.13
Total effort (months)	0	52.67	54.75	57.46	164.88
Total effort (hours)	0	6,951.97	7,227.19	7,585.12	21,764.29
Enhancement effort %	0	46.12%	48.43%	50.37%	48.37%
Maintenance effort %	0	53.88%	51.57%	49.63%	51.63%
Total effort %	0	100.00%	100.00%	100.00%	100.00%
Enhancement cost	0	$273,279	$298,282	$325,608	$897,169
Maintenance cost	0	$294,957	$291,505	$291,099	$877,561
Total cost	0	$568,237	$589,786	$616,707	$1,774,730
Enhancement cost %	0	48.09%	50.57%	52.80%	50.55%
Maintenance cost %	0	51.91%	49.43%	47.20%	49.45%
Total Cost	0	100.00%	100.00%	100.00%	100.00%
Maintenance + enhancement $ per FP		$210.46	$202.26	$195.82	$202.85
Maintenance + enhancement hours per FP		2.57	2.48	2.41	2.49

For software, a slightly modified set of topics for COQ include:

- Defect prevention costs (JAD, QFD, Kaizan, prototypes, etc.),
- Pre-test defect removal costs (inspections, static analysis, pair programming, etc.),
- Test defect removal costs (unit, function, regression, performance, system, etc.),
- Post-release defect repairs costs (direct costs of defect repairs),
- Warranty and damage costs due to poor quality (fines, litigation, indirect costs),

Using round numbers and even values to simplify the concepts, the COQ results for a 20,000 function point application with average quality and Java might be:

Defect prevention	$1,500,000
Pre-test defect removal	$3,000,000
Test defect removal	$11,000,000
Post-release repairs	$5,500,000
Damages and warranty costs	$3,000,000
Total Cost of Quality (COQ)	$24,000,000
COQ per function point	$1,200
COQ per KLOC	$24,000
COQ per SNAP point	Unknown as of 2020

If technical debt were included, but if not, the technical debt costs would probably be an additional $2,500,000. Among the issues with technical debt is that it focuses attention on a small subset of quality economic topics and of course does not deal with pre-release quality at all.

No doubt the corona virus of 2020 has had a negative impact on total cost of ownership due to working at home and not being able to meet with clients.

Total Cost of Ownership (TCO) for Software Economic Understanding

Because TCO cannot be measured or known until at least three years after release, it is seldom included in standard development benchmarks. The literature of TCO is sparse and there is very little reliable information. This is unfortunate because software TCO is much larger than the TCO of normal manufactured projects. This is due in part to poor quality control and in part to the continuous stream of enhancements which average about 8% per calendar year after the initial release and sometimes runs for periods of more than 30 calendar years.

Another issue with TCO is that since applications continue to grow, after several years, the size will have increased so much that the data needs to be renormalized with the current size. Table 5.9 illustrates a typical TCO estimate for an application that was 2,500 function points at delivery but grew to more than 3,000 function points after a three-year period:

Note that as of 2020 there is no current data on TCO cost per SNAP point, nor even on a method for integrating SNAP into TCO calculations

Table 5.9 Software Total Cost of Ownership (TCO) Estimates

	Staffing	*Effort*	*Costs*	*$ per FP at Release*	*% of TCO*
Development	7.48	260.95	$3,914,201	$1,565.68	46.17%
Enhancement	2.22	79.75	$897,169	$358.87	10.58%
Maintenance	2.36	85.13	$877,561	$351.02	10.35%
Support	0.34	12.29	$58,062	$23.22	0.68%
User costs	4.20	196.69	$2,722,773	$1,089.11	32.12%
Additional costs			$7,500	$3.00	0.09%
Total TCO	**16.60**	**634.81**	**$8,477,266**	**$3,390.91**	**100.00%**
Function points at release	2,500				
Function points after 3 years	3,149				
Lines of code after 3 years	167,936				
KLOC after 3 years	167.94				
TCO function points/staff month	**4.96**				
TCO work hours per function point	**26.61**				
TCO cost per function point	**$2,692**				
TCO cost per KLOC	**$50,479**				

due to the fact that SNAP has not yet been applied to maintenance, enhancements, and user costs.

Note that the TCO costs include normal development, enhancement, maintenance, and customer support but also user costs. For internal project users participate in requirements, reviews, inspections, and other tasks so their costs and contributions should be shown as part of TCO.

Note that customer support costs are low because this particular application had only 100 users at delivery. Eventually users grew to more than 200 but initial defects declined so number of customer support personnel was only one person part time. Had this been a high-volume commercial application with 500,000 users that grew to over 1,000,000 users customer support would have included dozens of support personnel and grown constantly.

Note that for internal IT and web projects, operational costs can also be included in total costs of ownership. However, operational costs are not relevant as TCO metrics for software that is run externally by external clients, such as software for automotive controls, avionics packages, medical devices such as cochlear implants, and commercial software sold or leased by companies such as Apple, Microsoft, IBM, and hundreds of others. It is also not a part of most open-source TCO studies.

Because applications grow at about 8% per year after release, the author of this book suggests renormalizing application size at the end of every calendar year or every fiscal year. Table 8 shows a total growth pattern for 10 years. It is obvious that renormalization needs to occur fairly often due to the fact that all software applications grow over time as shown in Table 5.10.

During development applications grow due to requirements creep at rates that range from below 1% per calendar month to more than 10% per calendar month. After release, applications grow at rates that range from below 5% per year to more than 15% per year. Note that for commercial software "mid-life kickers" tend to occur about every 4 years. These are rich collections of new features intended to enhance competiveness.

Needs for Future Metrics

There is little research in the future metrics needs for the software industry. Neither universities nor corporations have devoted funds or effort into evaluating the accuracy of current metrics or creating important future metrics.

Table 5.10   SRM Multi-Year Sizing Example

		Function Points	SNAP Points	Logical Code	
Nominal application size in IFPUG function points	10,000				
SNAP points	1,389				
Language	C				
Language level	2.50				
Logical code statements	1,280,000				
1	Size at end of requirements	10,000	1,389	1,280,000	
2	Size of requirement creep	2,000	278	256,000	
3	Size of planned delivery	12,000	1,667	1,536,000	
4	Size of deferred features	−4,800	(667)	(614,400)	
5	Size of actual delivery	7,200	1,000	921,600	
6	Year 1 usage	12,000	1,667	1,536,000	Kicker
7	Year 2 usage	13,000	1,806	1,664,000	
8	Year 3 usage	14,000	1,945	1,792,000	
9	Year 4 usage	17,000	2,361	2,176,000	Kicker
10	Year 5 usage	18,000	2,500	2,304,000	
11	Year 6 usage	19,000	2,639	2,432,000	
12	Year 7 usage	20,000	2,778	2,560,000	
13	Year 8 usage	23,000	3,195	2,944,000	Kicker
14	Year 9 usage	24,000	3,334	3,072,000	
15	Year 10 usage	25,000	3,473	3,200,000	

Kicker = Extra features added to defeat competitors.

Note: Simplified example with whole numbers for clarity.

Note: Deferred features usually due to schedule deadlines.

Some obvious needs for future metrics include:

1. Since companies own more data than software, there is an urgent need for a "*data point*" metric based on the logic of function point metrics. Currently, neither data quality nor the costs of data acquisition can be estimated or measured due to the lack of a size metric for data.
2. Since many applications such as embedded software operate in specific devices, there is a need for a "*hardware function point*" metric based on the logic of function points.
3. Since websites are now universal, there is a need for a "*website point*" metric based on the logic of function points. This would measure website contents.
4. Since risks are increasing for software projects, there is a need for a "*risk point*" metric based on the logic of function points.
5. Since cyber-attacks are increasing in number and severity, there is a need for a "*security point*" metric based on the logic of function points.
6. Since software value includes both tangible financial value and also intangible value, there is a need for a "*value point*" metric based on the logic of function points.
7. Since software now has millions of human users in every country, there is a need for a "*software usage point*" metric based on the logic of function points.

The goal would be to generate integrated estimates.

Every major university and every major corporation should devote some funds and effort to the related topics of metrics validation and metrics expansion. It is professionally embarrassing for one of the largest industries in human history to have the least accurate and most ambiguous metrics of any industry for measuring the critical topics of productivity and quality.

Table 5.11 shows a hypothetical table of what integrated data might look like from a suite of related metrics that include software function points, hardware function points, data points, risk points, security points, and value points.

Note that as of 2020, the SNAP metric had not yet fully integrated into total software economic analysis.

Summary and Conclusions

The current state of software metrics and measurement practices today is a professional embarrassment. The software industry continues to use

Table 5.11   Example of Multi-Metric Economic Analysis

Development Metrics	Number	Cost	Total
Function points	1,000	$1,000	$1,000,000
Data points	1,500	$500	$750,000
Hardware function points	750	$2,500	$1,875,000
Subtotal	**3,250**	**$1,115**	**$3,625,000**
Annual Maintenance Metrics			
Enhancements (micro function points)	150	$750	$112,500
Defects (micro function points)	750	$500	$375,000
Service points	5,000	$125	$625,000
Data maintenance	125	$250	$31,250
Hardware maintenance	200	$750	$150,000
Annual subtotal	**6,225**	**$179**	**$1,112,500**
Total cost of ownership (TCO)			
Development (development +5 years of usage)	3,250	$1,115	$3,625,000
Maintenance, enhancement, service	29,500	$189	$5,562,500
Data maintenance	625	$250	$156,250
Hardware maintenance	1,000	$750	$750,000
Application total TCO	**34,375**	**$294**	**$10,093,750**
Risk and Value Metrics			
Risk points	2,000	$1,250	$2,500,000
Security points	1,000	$2,000	$2,000,000
Subtotal	**3,000**	**$3,250**	**$4,500,000**
Value points	**45,000**	**$2,000**	**$90,000,000**
Net value	10,625	$7,521	$79,906,250
Return on investment (ROI)			**$8.92**

metrics proven mathematically to be invalid and which violate standard economic assumptions.

Most universities do not carry out research studies on metrics validity but merely teach common metrics whether they work or not.

Until the software industry has a workable set of productivity and quality metrics that are standardized and widely used, progress will

Table 5.12 Twenty-One Problems that Lack Effective Metrics and Data

1	How does agile quality and productivity compare to other methods?
2	Does agile work well for projects >10,000 function points?
3	How effective is pair programming compared to inspections and static analysis?
4	Do ISO/IEC quality standards have any tangible results in lowering defect levels?
5	How effective is the new SEMAT method of software engineering?
6	What are best productivity rates for 100, 1,000, 10,000, and 100,000 function points?
7	What are best quality results for 100, 1,000, 10,000, and 100,000 function points?
8	What are the best quality results for CMMI levels 1, 2, 3, 4, and 5 for large systems?
9	What industries have the best software quality results?
10	What countries have the best software quality results?
11	How expensive are requirements and design compared to programming?
12	Do paper documents cost more than source code for defense software?
13	What is the optimal team size and composition for different kinds of software?
14	How does data quality compare to software quality?
15	How many delivered high-severity defects might indicate professional malpractice?
16	How often should software size be renormalized because of continuous growth?
17	How expensive is software governance?
18	What are the measured impacts of software reuse on productivity and quality?
19	What are the measured impacts of unpaid overtime on productivity and schedules?
20	What are the measured impacts of adding people to late software projects?
21	How does SNAP work for COQ, TCO, and activity-based costs?

resemble a drunkard's walk. There are dozens of important topics that the software industry should know about but lacks effective data. Table 5.12 shows 21 samples where solid data would be valuable to the software industry:

These 21 issues are only the tip of the iceberg and dozens of other important topics are in urgent need of accurate predictions and accurate measurements. The software industry needs an effective suite of accurate and reliable metrics that can be used to predict and measure economic productivity and application quality. Until we have such a suite of effective metrics, software engineering should not be considered to be a true profession.

Appendix A: Problems with Cost per Defect Metrics

The cost-per-defect metric has been in continuous use since the 1960s for examining the economic value of software quality. Hundreds of journal articles and scores of books include stock phrases, such as *"it costs 100 times as much to fix a defect after release as during early development."*

Typical data for cost per defect varies from study to study but resembles the following pattern:

Defects found during requirements	=	$250
Defects found during design	=	$500
Defects found during coding and testing	=	$1,250
Defects found after release	=	$5,000

While such claims are often true mathematically, there are three hidden problems with cost per defect that are usually not discussed in the software literature:

1. Cost per defect penalizes quality and is always cheapest where the greatest numbers of bugs are found.
2. Because more bugs are found at the beginning of development than at the end, the increase in cost per defect is artificial. Actual time and motion studies of defect repairs show little variance from end to end.
3. Even if calculated correctly, cost per defect does not measure the true economic value of improved software quality. Over and above the costs of finding and fixing bugs, high quality leads to shorter development schedules and overall reductions in development costs. These savings are not included in cost per defect calculations, so the metric understates the true value of quality by several hundred percent.

The cost per defect metric has very serious shortcomings for economic studies of software quality. It penalizes high quality and ignores the major values of shorter schedules, lower development costs, lower maintenance costs, and lower warranty costs. In general, cost per defect causes more harm than value as a software metric. Let us consider the cost per defect problem areas using examples that illustrate the main points.

Why Cost per Defect Penalizes Quality

The well-known and widely cited "cost per defect" measure unfortunately violates the canons of standard economics. Although this metric is often used to make quality economic claims, its main failing is that it penalizes quality and achieves the best results for the buggiest applications.

Furthermore, when zero-defect applications are reached, there are still substantial appraisal and testing activities that need to be accounted for. Obviously, the "cost per defect" metric is useless for zero-defect applications.

As with KLOC metrics discussed in Appendix B, the main source of error is that of ignoring fixed costs. Three examples will illustrate how "cost per defect" behaves as quality improves.

In all three cases, A, B, and C, we can assume that test personnel work 40 hours per week and are compensated at a rate of $2,500 per week or $75.75 per hour using fully burdened costs. Assume that all three software features that are being tested are 100 function points in size and 5000 lines of code in size (5 KLOC).

Case A: Poor Quality

Assume that a tester spent 15 hours writing test cases, 10 hours running them, and 15 hours fixing 10 bugs. The total hours spent was 40 and the total cost was $2,500. Since 10 bugs were found, the cost per defect was $250. The cost per function point for the week of testing would be $25.00. The cost per KLOC for the week of testing would be $500.

Case B: Good Quality

In the second case, assume that a tester spent 15 hours writing test cases, 10 hours running them, and 5 hours fixing one bug, which was the only bug discovered.

However since no other assignments were waiting and the tester worked a full week 40 hours were charged to the project. The total cost for the week was still $2,500 so the cost per defect has jumped to $2,500.

If the 10 hours of slack time are backed out, leaving 30 hours for actual testing and bug repairs, the cost per defect would be $2,273.50 for the single bug. This is equal to $22.74 per function point or $454.70 per KLOC.

As quality improves, "cost per defect" rises sharply. The reason for this is that writing test cases and running them act like fixed costs. It is a well-known law of manufacturing economics that:

> *If a manufacturing cycle includes a high proportion of fixed costs and there is a reduction in the number of units produced, the cost per unit will go up.*

As an application moves through a full test cycle that includes unit test, function test, regression test, performance test, system test, and acceptance test, the time required to write test cases and the time required to run test cases stays almost constant, but the number of defects found steadily decreases.

Table 5.13 shows the approximate costs for the three cost elements of preparation, execution, and repair for the test cycles just cited using the same rate of $:75.75 per hour for all activities.

What is most interesting about Table 5.12 is that cost per defect rises steadily as defect volumes come down, even though Table 5.12 uses a constant value of 5 hours to repair defects for every single test stage! In other words, every defect identified throughout Table 5.1 had a constant cost of $378.25 when only repairs are considered.

In fact all three columns use constant values and the only true variable in the example is the number of defects found. In real life, of course, preparation, execution, and repairs would all be variables. But by making them constant, it is easier to illustrate the main point: ***cost per defect rises as numbers of defects decline***.

Since the main reason that cost per defect goes up as defects decline is due to the fixed costs associated with preparation and execution, it might be thought that those costs could be backed out and leave only defect repairs. Doing this would change the apparent results and minimize the errors, but it would introduce three new problems:

1. Removing quality cost elements that may total more than 50% of total quality costs would make it impossible to study quality economics with precision and accuracy.
2. Removing preparation and execution costs would make it impossible to calculate COQ because the calculations for COQ demand all quality cost elements.

Table 5.13 Cost per Defect for Six Forms of Testing

(Assumes $75.75 per Staff Hour for Costs)

	Writing Test Cases	Running Test Cases	Repairing Defects	Total Costs	Number of Defects	$ per Defect
Unit test	$1,250.00	$750.00	$18,937.50	$20,937.50	50	$418.75
Function test	$1,250.00	$750.00	$7,575.00	$9,575.00	20	$478.75
Regression test	$1,250.00	$750.00	$3,787.50	$5,787.50	10	$578.75
Performance test	$1,250.00	$750.00	$1,893.75	$3,893.75	5	$778.75
System test	$1,250.00	$750.00	$1,136.25	$3,136.25	3	$1,045.42
Acceptance test	$1,250.00	$750.00	$378.75	$2,378.75	1	$2,378.75

3. Removing preparation and execution costs would make it impossible to compare testing against formal inspections, because inspections do record preparation and execution as well as defect repairs.

Backing out or removing preparation and execution costs would be like going on a low-carb diet and not counting the carbs in pasta and bread, but only counting the carbs in meats and vegetables. The numbers might look good, but the results in real life would not be good.

Let us now consider cost per function point as an alternative metric for measuring the costs of defect removal. With the slack removed, the cost per function point would be $18.75. As can easily be seen, cost per defect goes up as quality improves, thus violating the assumptions of standard economic measures.

However, as can also be seen, testing cost per function point declines as quality improves. This matches the assumptions of standard economics. The 10 hours of slack time illustrate another issue: when quality improves defects can decline faster than personnel can be reassigned.

Case C: Zero Defects

In the third case, assume that a tester spent 15 hours writing test cases and 10 hours running them. No bugs or defects were discovered.

Because no defects were found, the "cost per defect" metric cannot be used at all. But 25 hours of actual effort were expended writing and running test cases. If the tester had no other assignments, he or she would still have worked a 40-hour week and the costs would have been $2,500.

If the 15 hours of slack time are backed out, leaving 25 hours for actual testing, the costs would have been $1,893.75. With slack time removed, the cost per function point would be $18.38. As can be seen again, testing cost per function point declines as quality improves. Here too, the decline in cost per function point matches the assumptions of standard economics.

Time and motion studies of defect repairs do not support the aphorism that "it costs 100 times as much to fix a bug after release as before." Bugs typically require between 15 minutes and 6 hours for repairing regardless of where they are found.

There are some bugs that are expensive and may takes several days to repair, or even longer. These are called "abeyant defects" by IBM. Abeyant defects are customer-reported defects which the repair center cannot recreate, due to some special combination of hardware and software at the client site. Abeyant defects comprise less than 5% of customer-reported defects.

Considering that cost per defect has been among the most widely used quality metrics for more than 50 years, the literature is surprisingly ambiguous about what activities go into "cost per defect." More than 75% of the articles and books that use cost per defect metrics do not state explicitly whether preparation and executions costs are included or excluded. In fact a majority of articles do not explain anything at all but merely show numbers without discussing what activities are included.

Another major gap is that the literature is silent on variations in cost per defect by severity level. A study done by the author of this book at IBM showed that these variations in defect repair intervals were associated with severity levels.

Table 5.14 shows the results of the study. Since these are customer-reported defects, "preparation and execution" would have been carried out by customers and the amounts were not reported to IBM. Peak effort for each severity level is highlighted in blue.

As can be seen, the overall average would be close to perhaps 5 hours, although the range is quite wide.

As a matter of minor interest, the most troublesome bug found by the author during the time he was a professional programmer was a bug found during unit test, which took about 18 hours to analyze and repair. The software application where the bug occurred was an IBM 1401 program being ported to the larger IBM 1410 computer. The bug involved one instruction, which was valid on both the 1401 and 1410. However, the two computers did not produce the same machine code. Thus, the bug could not be found by examination of the source code itself, since that was correct. The error could only be identified by examining the machine language generated for the two computers.

In Table 5.14, severity 1 defects mean that the software has stopped working. Severity 2 means that major features are disabled. Severity 3 refers to minor defects. Severity 4 defects are cosmetic in nature and do not affect operations. Invalid defects are hardware problems or customer errors inadvertently reported as software defects. A surprisingly large amount of time and effort goes into dealing with invalid defects although this topic is seldom discussed in the quality literature.

Yet another gap in the "cost per defect" literature is that of defect by origin. In Table 5.15 are shown the typical results by defect origin points for 20 common defect types.

Table 5.15 shows "find hours" separately from "repair hours." The "find" tasks involve analysis of bug symptoms and the hardware/software combinations in use when the bug occurred. The "repair" tasks as the name implies are those of fixing the bug once it has been identified, plus regression testing to ensure the repair is not a "bad fix."

Table 5.14 Defect Repair Hours by Severity Levels for Field Defects

	Severity 1	Severity 2	Severity 3	Severity 4	Invalid	Average
>40 hours	1.00%	3.00%	0.00%	0.00%	0.00%	0.80%
30–39 hours	3.00%	12.00%	1.00%	0.00%	1.00%	3.40%
20–29 hours	12.00%	20.00%	8.00%	0.00%	4.00%	8.80%
10–19 hours	22.00%	32.00%	10.00%	0.00%	12.00%	15.20%
1–9 hours	48.00%	22.00%	56.00%	40.00%	25.00%	38.20%
>1 hour	14.00%	11.00%	25.00%	60.00%	58.00%	33.60%
Total	**100.00%**	**100.00%**	**100.00%**	**100.00%**	**100.00%**	**100.00%**

Table 5.15 Defect Repairs by Defect Origins

	Defect Origins	Find Hours	Repair Hours	Total Hours
1	**Security defects**	**11.00**	**24.00**	**35.00**
2	Errors of omission	8.00	24.00	32.00
3	Hardware errors	3.50	28.00	31.50
4	Abeyant defects	5.00	23.00	28.00
5	Data errors	1.00	26.00	27.00
6	Architecture defects	6.00	18.00	24.00
7	Toxic requirements	2.00	20.00	22.00
8	Requirements defects	5.00	16.50	21.50
9	Supply chain defects	6.00	11.00	17.00
10	Design defects	4.50	12.00	16.50
11	Structural defects	2.00	13.00	15.00
12	Performance defects	3.50	10.00	13.50
13	Bad test cases	5.00	7.50	12.50
14	Bad fix defects	3.00	9.00	12.00
15	Poor test coverage	4.50	2.00	6.50
16	Invalid defects	3.00	3.00	6.00
17	**Code defects**	**1.00**	**4.00**	**5.00**
18	Document defects	1.00	3.00	4.00
19	User errors	0.40	2.00	2.40
20	Duplicate defects	0.25	1.00	1.25
Average		**3.78**	**12.85**	**16.63**

As can be seen, errors of omission, hardware errors, and data errors are the most expensive. Note also that errors caused by bad test cases and by "bad fixes" or secondary bugs in bug repairs themselves are more expensive than original code bugs. Note that even user errors and invalid defects require time for analysis and notifying clients of the situation.

The term "abeyant defects" originated in IBM circa 1965. It refers to defects that only occur for one client or one unique configuration of hardware and software. They are very hard to analyze and to fix.

Using Function Point Metrics for Defect Removal Economics

Because of the fixed or inelastic costs associated with defect removal operations, cost per defect always increases as the numbers of defects decline. Because more defects are found at the beginning of a testing cycle than after release, this explains why cost per defect always goes up later in the cycle.

An alternate way of showing the economics of defect removal is to switch from "cost per defect" and use "defect removal cost per function point." Table 5.14 uses the same basic information as Table 5.16, but expresses all costs in terms of cost per function point:

The advantage of *"defect removal cost per function point"* over *"cost per defect"* is that it actually matches the assumptions of standard economics. In other words, as quality improves and defect volumes decline, cost per function point tracks these benefits and also declines. High quality is shown to be cheaper than poor quality, while with cost per defect high quality is incorrectly shown as being more expensive.

However, quality has more benefits to software applications than just those associated with defect removal activities. The most significant benefit of high quality is that it leads to shorter development schedules

Table 5.16 Cost per Function Point for Six Forms of Testing

(Assumes $75.75 per Staff Hour for Costs) *(Assumes 100 Function Points in the Application)*					
	Writing Test Cases	*Running Test Cases*	*Repairing Defects*	*Total $ per F.P.*	*Number of Defects*
Unit test	$12.50	$7.50	$189.38	$209.38	50
Function test	$12.50	$7.50	$75.75	$95.75	20
Regression test	$12.50	$7.50	$37.88	$57.88	10
Performance test	$12.50	$7.50	$18.94	$38.94	5
System test	$12.50	$7.50	$11.36	$31.36	3
Acceptance test	$12.50	$7.50	$3.79	$23.79	1

and overall cheaper costs for both development and maintenance. The total savings from high quality are much greater than the improvements in defect removal expenses.

Let us consider the value of high quality for a large system in the 10,000 function point size range.

The Value of Quality for Large Applications of 10,000 Function Points

When software applications reach 10,000 function points in size, they are very significant systems that require close attention to quality control, change control, and corporate governance. In fact without careful quality and change control, the odds of failure or cancellation top 35% for this size range.

Note that as application size increases, defect potentials increase rapidly and DRE levels decline, even with sophisticated quality control steps in place. This is due to the exponential increase in the volume of paperwork for requirements and design, which often leads to partial inspections rather than 100% inspections. For large systems, test coverage declines and the number of test cases mounts rapidly but cannot usually keep pace with complexity (Table 5.17).

The glaring problem of cost per defect is shown in Table 5.16. Note that even though high quality reduced total costs by almost 50%, cost per defect is higher for the high-quality version than it is for the low-quality version. Note that cost per function point matches the true economic value of high quality, while "cost per defect" conceals the true economic value.

Cost savings from better quality increase as application sizes increase. The general rule is that the larger the software application, the more valuable quality becomes. The same principle is true for change control, because the volume of creeping requirements goes up with application size.

Appendix B: Side-by-Side Comparisons of 79 Languages using LOC and Function Points

This appendix provides side-by-side comparisons of 79 programming languages using both function point metrics and LOC metrics. Productivity is expressed using both hourly and monthly rates. The table assumes a constant value of 1,000 function points for all 79 languages. However, the number of LOC varies widely based on the specific language.

Table 5.17 Quality Value for 10,000 Function Point Applications

(Note: 10,000 Function Points = 1,250,000 C statements)			
	Average Quality	*Excellent Quality*	*Difference*
Defects per function point	6.00	3.50	−2.50
Defect potential	60,000	35,000	−25,000
Defect removal efficiency	84.00%	96.00%	12.00%
Defects removed	50,400	33,600	−16,800
Defects delivered	9,600	1,400	−8,200
Cost per defect	**$341**	**$417**	**$76**
Pre-release			
Cost per defect	**$833**	**$1,061**	**$227**
Post release			
Development schedule (calendar months)	40	28	−12
Development staffing	67	67	0.00
Development effort (staff months)	2,654	1,836	−818
Development costs	$26,540,478	$18,361,525	−$8,178,953
Function points per staff month	3.77	5.45	1.68
LOC per staff month	471	681	209.79
Maintenance staff	17	17	0
Maintenance effort (staff months)	800	117	−683.33
Maintenance costs (year 1)	$8,000,000	$1,166,667	-$6,833,333
Total effort (staff months)	3,454	1,953	−1501
Total cost	$34,540,478	$19,528,191	−$15,012,287
Total cost per staff member	$414,486	$234,338	−$180,147
Total cost per function point	**$3,454.05**	**$1,952.82**	**−$1,501.23**
Total cost per LOC	$27.63	$15.62	−$12.01
Average cost per defect	**$587**	**$739**	**$152**

Also held constant is the assumption for every language that the number of non-code work hours for requirements, architecture, design, documentation, and management is even 3,000 hours.

As can be seen, Appendix B provides a mathematical proof that LOC do not measure economic productivity. In Appendix B and in real life, economic productivity is defined as *"producing a specific quantity of goods for the lowest number of work hours."*

Function points match this definition of economic productivity, but LOC metrics reverse true economic productivity and make the languages with the largest number of work hours seem more productive than the languages with the lowest number of work hours. Of course results for a single language will not have the problems shown in Appendix B.

In the following table, "economic productivity" is shown in **green** and is the "lowest number of work hours to deliver 1000 function points." Economic productivity is **NOT** "increasing the number of lines of code per month."

Although not shown in the table, it also includes a fixed value of 3,000 hours of non-code work for requirements, design, documents, management, and the like. Thus "total work hours" in the table is the sum of code development + non-code effort. Since every language includes a constant value of 3,000 hours, this non-code effort is the "fixed cost" that drives up "cost per unit" when LOC declines. In real life, the non-code work is a variable, but it simplifies the math and makes the essential point easier to see: LOC penalizes high-level languages (Table 5.18).

It is obvious that in real life no one would produce 1,000 function points in machine language, JCL, or some of the other languages in the table. The table is merely illustrative of the fact that while function points may be constant and non-code hours are fixed costs, coding effort is variable and proportional to the amount of source code produced.

In Table 5.17, the exact number of KLOC can vary language to language, from team to team, and company to company. But that is irrelevant to the basic mathematics of the case. There are three aspects to the math:

Point 1: When a manufacturing process includes a high proportion of fixed costs and there is a reduction in the units produced, the cost per unit will go up. This is true for all industries and all manufactured products without exception.

Table 5.18 Side-by-Side Comparison of Function Points and Lines of Code Metrics

	Languages	Size in KLOC	Total Work Hours	Work Hours per FP	FP per Month	Work Months	Work Hours per KLOC	LOC per Month
1	Machine language	640.00	119,364	119.36	1.11	904.27	186.51	708
2	Basic Assembly	320.00	61,182	61.18	2.16	463.50	191.19	690
3	JCL	220.69	43,125	43.13	3.06	326.71	195.41	675
4	Macro Assembly	213.33	41,788	41.79	3.16	316.57	195.88	674
5	HTML	160.00	32,091	32.09	4.11	243.11	200.57	658
6	C	128.00	26,273	26.27	5.02	199.04	205.26	643
7	XML	128.00	26,273	26.27	5.02	199.04	205.26	643
8	Algol	106.67	22,394	22.39	5.89	169.65	209.94	629
9	Bliss	106.67	22,394	22.39	5.89	169.65	209.94	629
10	Chill	106.67	22,394	22.39	5.89	169.65	209.94	629
11	COBOL	106.67	22,394	22.39	5.89	169.65	209.94	629
12	Coral	106.67	22,394	22.39	5.89	169.65	209.94	629
13	Fortran	106.67	22,394	22.39	5.89	169.65	209.94	629
14	Jovial	106.67	22,394	22.39	5.89	169.65	209.94	629
15	GW Basic	98.46	20,902	20.90	6.32	158.35	212.29	622
16	Pascal	91.43	19,623	19.62	6.73	148.66	214.63	615
17	PL/S	91.43	19,623	19.62	6.73	148.66	214.63	615

	Languages	Size in KLOC	Total Work Hours	Work Hours per FP	FP per Month	Work Months	Work Hours per KLOC	LOC per Month
18	ABAP	80.00	17,545	17.55	7.52	132.92	219.32	602
19	Modula	80.00	17,545	17.55	7.52	132.92	219.32	602
20	PL/I	80.00	17,545	17.55	7.52	132.92	219.32	602
21	ESPL/I	71.11	15,929	15.93	8.29	120.68	224.01	589
22	Javascript	71.11	15,929	15.93	8.29	120.68	224.01	589
23	Basic (interpreted)	64.00	14,636	14.64	9.02	110.88	228.69	577
24	Forth	64.00	14,636	14.64	9.02	110.88	228.60	577
25	haXe	64.00	14,636	14.64	9.02	110.88	228.69	577
26	Lisp	64.00	14,636	14.64	9.02	110.88	228.69	577
27	Prolog	64.00	14,636	14.64	9.02	110.88	228.69	577
28	SH (shell scripts)	64.00	14,636	14.64	9.02	110.88	228.69	577
29	Quick Basic	60.95	14,082	14.08	9.37	106.68	231.04	571
30	Zimbu	58.18	13,579	13.58	9.72	102.87	233.38	566
31	C++	53.33	12,697	12.70	10.40	96.19	238.07	554
32	Go	53.33	12,697	12.70	10.40	96.19	238.07	554
33	Java	53.33	12,697	12.70	10.40	96.19	238.07	554
34	PHP	53.33	12,697	12.70	10.40	96.19	238.07	554

(Continued)

Table 5.18 (Continued)

	Languages	Size in KLOC	Total Work Hours	Work Hours per FP	FP per Month	Work Months	Work Hours per KLOC	LOC per Month
35	Python	53.33	12,697	12.70	10.40	96.19	238.07	554
36	C#	51.20	12,309	12.31	10.72	93.25	240.41	549
37	X10	51.20	12,309	12.31	10.72	93.25	240.41	549
38	Ada 95	49.23	11,951	11.95	11.05	90.54	242.76	544
39	Ceylon	49.23	11,951	11.95	11.05	90.54	242.76	544
40	Fantom	49.23	11,951	11.95	11.05	90.54	242.76	544
41	Dart	47.41	11,620	11.62	11.36	88.03	245.10	539
42	RPG III	47.41	11,620	11.62	11.36	88.03	245.10	539
43	CICS	45.71	11,312	11.31	11.67	85.69	247.44	533
44	DTABL	45.71	11,312	11.31	11.67	85.69	247.44	533
45	F#	45.71	11,312	11.31	11.67	85.69	247.44	533
46	Ruby	45.71	11,312	11.31	11.67	85.69	247.44	533
47	Simula	45.71	11,312	11.31	11.67	85.69	247.44	533
48	Erlang	42.67	10,758	10.76	12.27	81.50	252.13	524
49	DB2	40.00	10,273	10.27	12.85	77.82	256.82	514
50	LiveScript	40.00	10,273	10.27	12.85	77.82	256.82	514
51	Oracle	40.00	10,273	10.27	12.85	77.82	256.82	514
52	Elixir	37.65	9,845	9.84	13.41	74.58	261.51	505

	Languages	Size in KLOC	Total Work Hours	Work Hours per FP	FP per Month	Work Months	Work Hours per KLOC	LOC per Month
53	Haskell	37.65	9,845	9.84	13.41	74.58	261.51	505
54	Mixed Languages	37.65	9,845	9.84	13.41	74.58	261.51	505
55	Julia	35.56	9,465	9.46	13.95	71.70	266.19	496
56	M	35.56	9,465	9.46	13.95	71.70	266.19	496
57	OPA	35.56	9,465	9.46	13.95	71.70	266.19	496
58	Perl	35.56	9,465	9.46	13.95	71.70	266.19	496
59	APL	32.00	8,818	8.82	14.97	66.80	275.57	479
60	Delphi	29.09	8,289	8.29	15.92	62.80	284.94	463
61	Objective C	26.67	7,848	7.85	16.82	59.46	294.32	448
62	Visual Basic	26.67	7,848	7.85	16.82	59.46	294.32	448
63	ASP NET	24.62	7,476	7.48	17.66	56.63	303.69	435
64	Eiffel	22.86	7,156	7.16	18.45	54.21	313.07	422
65	Smalltalk	21.33	6,879	6.88	19.19	52.11	322.44	409
66	IBM ADF	20.00	6,636	6.64	19.89	50.28	331.82	398
67	MUMPS	18.82	6,422	6.42	20.55	48.65	341.19	387
68	Forte	17.78	6,232	6.23	21.18	47.21	350.57	377
69	APS	16.84	6,062	6.06	21.77	45.93	359.94	367
70	TELON	16.00	5,909	5.91	22.34	44.77	369.32	357

(Continued)

Table 5.18 (Continued)

	Languages	Size in KLOC	Total Work Hours	Work Hours per FP	FP per Month	Work Months	Work Hours per KLOC	LOC per Month
71	Mathematica9	12.80	5,327	5.33	24.78	40.36	416.19	317
72	TranscriptSQL	12.80	5,327	5.33	24.78	40.36	416.19	317
73	QBE	12.80	5,327	5.33	24.78	40.36	416.19	317
74	X	12.80	5,327	5.33	24.78	40.36	416.19	317
75	Mathematica10	9.14	4,662	4.66	28.31	35.32	509.94	259
76	BPM	7.11	4,293	4.29	30.75	32.52	603.69	219
77	Generators	7.11	4,293	4.29	30.75	32.52	603.69	219
78	Excel	6.40	4,164	4.16	31.70	31.54	650.57	203
79	IntegraNova	5.33	3,970	3.97	33.25	30.07	744.32	177
	Average	67.60	15,291	15.29	12.80	115.84	279.12	515

Point 2: When switching from a low-level programming language to a high-level programming language, the number of "units" produced will be reduced.

Point 3: The reduction in LOC metrics for high-level languages in the presence of the fixed costs for requirements and design will cause cost per LOC to go up and will also cause LOC per month to come down for high-level languages.

These three points are nothing more than the standard rules of manufacturing economics applied to software and programming languages.

Table 5.19 Percentages of Coding and Non-Coding Tasks

(Percent of Work Hours for Code and Non-Code)		
Languages		Non-Code Percent	Code Percent
1	Machine language	2.51%	97.49%
2	Basic Assembly	4.90%	95.10%
3	JCL	6.96%	93.04%
4	Macro Assembly	7.18%	92.82%
5	HTML	9.35%	90.65%
6	C	11.42%	88.58%
7	XML	11.42%	88.58%
8	Algol	13.40%	86.60%
9	Bliss	13.40%	86.60%
10	Chill	13.40%	86.60%
11	COBOL	13.40%	86.60%
12	Coral	13.40%	86.60%
13	Fortran	13.40%	86.60%
14	Jovial	13.40%	86.60%
15	GW Basic	14.35%	85.65%
16	Pascal	15.29%	84.71%
17	PL/S	15.29%	84.71%
18	ABAP	17.10%	82.90%
19	Modula	17.10%	82.90%
20	PL/I	17.10%	82.90%

(Continued)

Table 5.19   (Continued)

(Percent of Work Hours for Code and Non-Code)		
Languages	Non-Code Percent	Code Percent
21	ESPL/I	18.83%	81.17%
22	Javascript	18.83%	81.17%
23	Basic (interpreted)	20.50%	79.50%
24	Forth	20.50%	79.50%
25	haXe	20.50%	79.50%
26	Lisp	20.50%	79.50%
27	Prolog	20.50%	79.50%
28	SH (shell scripts)	20.50%	79.50%
29	Quick Basic	21.30%	78.70%
30	Zimbu	22.09%	77.91%
31	C++	23.63%	76.37%
32	Go	23.63%	76.37%
33	Java	23.63%	76.37%
34	PHP	23.63%	76.37%
35	Python	23.63%	76.37%
36	C#	24.37%	75.63%
37	X10	24.37%	75.63%
38	Ada 95	25.10%	74.90%
39	Ceylon	25.10%	74.90%
40	Fantom	25.10%	74.90%
41	Dart	25.82%	74.18%
42	RPG III	25.82%	74.18%
43	CICS	26.52%	73.48%
44	DTABL	26.52%	73.48%
45	F#	26.52%	73.48%
46	Ruby	26.52%	73.48%
47	Simula	26.52%	73.48%
48	Erlang	27.89%	72.11%
49	DB2	29.20%	70.80%
50	LiveScript	29.20%	70.80%

Table 5.19   (Continued)

(Percent of Work Hours for Code and Non-Code)			
Languages		*Non-Code Percent*	*Code Percent*
51	Oracle	29.20%	70.80%
52	Elixir	30.47%	69.53%
53	Haskell	30.47%	69.53%
54	Mixed Languages	30.47%	69.53%
55	Julia	31.70%	68.30%
56	M	31.70%	68.30%
57	OPA	31.70%	68.30%
58	Perl	31.70%	68.30%
59	APL	34.02%	65.98%
60	Delphi	36.19%	63.81%
61	Objective C	38.22%	61.78%
62	Visual Basic	38.22%	61.78%
63	ASP NET	40.13%	59.87%
64	Eiffel	41.92%	58.08%
65	Smalltalk	43.61%	56.39%
66	IBM ADF	45.21%	54.79%
67	MUMPS	46.71%	53.29%
68	Forte	48.14%	51.86%
69	APS	49.49%	50.51%
70	TELON	50.77%	49.23%
71	Mathematica9	56.31%	43.69%
72	TranscriptSQL	56.31%	43.69%
73	QBE	56.31%	43.69%
74	X	56.31%	43.69%
75	Mathematica10	64.35%	35.65%
76	BPM	69.88%	30.12%
77	Generators	69.88%	30.12%
78	Excel	72.05%	27.95%
79	IntegraNova	75.57%	24.43%
Average		**29.08%**	**70.92%**

The LOC metric originated in the 1950s when machine language and basic assembly were the only languages in use. In those early days, coding was over 95% of the total effort so the fixed costs of non-code work barely mattered. It was only after high-level programming languages began to reduce coding effort and requirements and design became progressively larger components that the LOC problems occurred. Table 5.19 shows the coding and non-coding percentages by language with the caveat that the non-code work is artificially held constant at 3,000 hours.

As can easily be seen for very low-level languages, the problems of LOC metrics are minor. But as language levels increase, a higher percentage of effort goes to non-code work while coding effort progressively gets smaller. Thus, LOC metrics are invalid and hazardous for high-level languages.

It might be thought that omitting non-code effort and only showing coding may preserve the usefulness of LOC metrics, but this is not the case. Productivity is still producing deliverable for the lowest number of work hours or the lowest amount of effort.

Producing a feature in 500 lines of Objective-C at a rate of 500 LOC per month has better economic productivity than producing the same feature in 1000 lines of Java at a rate of 600 LOC per month.

Objective-C took 1 month or 149 work hours for the feature. Java took 1.66 months or 247 hours. Even though coding speed favors Java by a rate of 600 LOC per month to 500 LOC per month for Objective-C, economic productivity clearly belongs to Objective-C because of the reduced work effort.

Function points were specifically invented by IBM to measure economic productivity. Function point metrics stay constant no matter what programming language is used. Therefore, function points are not troubled by the basic rule of manufacturing economics that when a process has fixed costs and the number of units goes down, cost per unit goes up. Function points are the same regardless of programming languages. Thus, in today's world of 2021, function point metrics measure software economic productivity, but LOC metrics do not.

References and Readings

Books and monographs by Capers Jones

1. Jones, Capers; *The Technical and Social History of Software Engineering.* Addison Wesley, 2014.
2. Jones, Capers; and Bonsignour, Olivier; *The Economics of Software Quality.* Addison Wesley, 2012.

3. Jones, Capers; *Software Engineering Best Practices*, 1st ed., McGraw Hill, 2010.
4. Jones, Capers; *Applied Software Measurement*, 3rd ed., McGraw Hill, 2008.
5. Jones, Capers; *Estimating Software Costs*, 2nd ed., McGraw Hill, 2007.
6. Jones, Capers; *Software Assessments, Benchmarks, and Best Practices*. Addison Wesley, 2000.
7. Jones, Capers; *Software Quality – Analysis and Guidelines for Success*. International Thomson Press, 1997.
8. Jones, Capers; *Patterns of Software Systems Failure and Success*. International Thomson Press, 1995.
9. Jones, Capers; *Assessment and Control of Software Risks*. Prentice Hall, 1993.
10. Jones, Capers; *Critical Problems in Software Measurement*. IS Mgt Group, 1993.

Monographs by Capers Jones 2012–2020 available from Namcook Analytics LLC

1. Comparing Software Development Methodologies
2. Corporate Software Risk Reduction
3. Defenses Against Breach of Contract Litigation
4. Dynamic Visualization of Software Development
5. Evaluation of Common Software Metrics
6. Function Points as a Universal Software Metric
7. Hazards of "Cost per Defect" Metrics
8. Hazards of "Lines of Code" Metrics
9. Hazards of "Technical Debt" Metrics
10. History of Software Estimation Tools
11. How Software Engineers Learn New Skills
12. Software Benchmark Technologies
13. Software Defect Origins and Removal Methods
14. Software Defect Removal Efficiency (DRE)
15. Software Project Management Tools

Books by Other Authors

Abrain, Alain; *Software Estimating Models*; Wiley-IEEE Computer Society; 2015.
Abrain, Alain; *Software Metrics and Metrology*; Wiley-IEEE Computer Society; 2010.
Abrain, Alain; *Software Maintenance Management: Evolution and Continuous Improvement*; Wiley-IEEE Computer Society, 2008.
Albrecht, Allan; *AD/M Productivity Measurement and Estimate Validation*; IBM Corporation, Purchase, NY; May 1984.
Barrow, Dean; Nilson, Susan; and Timberlake, Dawn; *Software Estimation Technology Report*; Air Force Software Technology Support Center, Hill Air Force Base, Utah; 1993.
Boehm, Barry; *Software Engineering Economics*; Prentice Hall, Englewood Cliffs, NJ; 1981; 900 pages.

Brooks, Fred; *The Mythical Man Month*; Addison-Wesley, Reading, MA; 1995; 295 pages.

Bundschuh, Manfred; and Dekkers, Carol; *The IT Measurement Compendium*; Springer-Verlag, Berlin; 2008; 643 pages.

Brown, Norm (Editor); *The Program Manager's Guide to Software Acquisition Best Practices*, Version 1.0; U.S. Department of Defense, Washington, DC; July 1995; 142 pages.

Chidamber, S.R.; and Kemerer, C.F.: "A Metrics Suite for Object Oriented Design"; *IEEE Transactions on Software Engineering*, Vol. 20; 1994; pp. 476–493.

Chidamber, S.R.; Darcy, D.P.; and Kemerer, C.F.; "Managerial Use of Object Oriented Software Metrics"; *Joseph M. Katz Graduate School of Business*, University of Pittsburgh, Pittsburgh, PA; Working Paper # 750; November 1996; 26 pages.

Cohn, Mike; *Agile Estimating and Planning*; Prentice Hall PTR, Englewood Cliffs, NJ; 2005; ISBN: 0131479415.

Conte, S.D.; Dunsmore, H.E.; and Shen, V.Y.; *Software Engineering Models and Metrics*; The Benjamin Cummings Publishing Company, Menlo Park, CA, 1986; ISBN: 0-8053-2162-4; 396 pages.

DeMarco, Tom; *Controlling Software Projects*; Yourdon Press, New York, NY; 1982; ISBN: 0-917072-32-4; 284 pages.

DeMarco, Tom; and Lister, Tim; *Peopleware*; Dorset House Press, New York, NY; 1987; ISBN: 0-932633-05-6; 188 pages.

DeMarco, Tom; *Why Does Software Cost So Much?*; Dorset House Press, New York, NY; 1995; ISBN: 0-932633-34-X; 237 pages.

DeMarco, Tom; *Deadline*; Dorset House Press, New York, NY; 1997.

Department of the Air Force; *Guidelines for Successful Acquisition and Management of Software Intensive Systems*; Vols. 1 and 2; Software Technology Support Center, Hill Air Force Base, UT; 1994.

Dreger, Brian; *Function Point Analysis*; Prentice Hall, Englewood Cliffs, NJ; 1989; ISBN: 0-13-332321-8; 185 pages.

Gack, Gary; *Managing the Black Hole – The Executives Guide to Project Risk*; The Business Expert Publisher, Thomson, GA; 2010; ISBSG: 10: 1-935602-01-2.

Galea, R.B.; *The Boeing Company: 3D Function Point Extensions*, Version 2.0, Release 1.0; Boeing Information Support Services, Seattle, WA; June 1995.

Galorath, Daniel D.; and Evans, Michael W.; *Software Sizing, Estimation, and Risk Management*; Auerbach Publications, New York, NY, 2006.

Garmus, David; and Herron, David; *Measuring the Software Process: A Practical Guide to Functional Measurement*; Prentice Hall, Englewood Cliffs, NJ; 1995.

Garmus, David; and Herron, David; *Function Point Analysis*; Addison Wesley Longman, Boston, MA; 1996.

Garmus, David; *Accurate Estimation; Software Development*; July 1996; pp 57–65.

Grady, Robert B.; *Practical Software Metrics for Project Management and Process Improvement*; Prentice Hall, Englewood Cliffs, NJ; 1992; ISBN: 0-13-720384-5; 270 pages.

Grady, Robert B.; and Caswell, Deborah L.; *Software Metrics: Establishing a Company-Wide Program*; Prentice Hall, Englewood Cliffs, NJ; 1987; ISBN: 0-13-821844-7; 288 pages.

Gulledge, Thomas R.; Hutzler, William P.; and Lovelace, Joan S. (Editors); *Cost Estimating and Analysis – Balancing Technology with Declining Budgets*; Springer-Verlag, New York, NY; 1992; ISBN: 0-387-97838-0; 297 pages.

Harris, Michael D.S.; Herron, David; and Iwanacki, Stasia; *The Business Value of IT*; CRC Press, Auerbach Publications; 2009.

Hill, Peter R.; *Practical Software Project Estimation*; McGraw Hill; 2010.

Howard, Alan (Editor); *Software Metrics and Project Management Tools*; Applied Computer Research (ACR), Phoenix, AZ; 1997; 30 pages.

Humphrey, Watts S.; *Managing the Software Process*; Addison Wesley Longman, Reading, MA; 1989.

Humphrey, Watts; *Personal Software Process*; Addison Wesley Longman, Reading, MA; 1997.

Kan, Stephen H.; *Metrics and Models in Software Quality Engineering*, 2nd ed.; Addison Wesley Longman, Boston, MA; 2003; ISBN: 0-201-72915-6; 528 pages.

Kemerer, Chris F.; "An Empirical Validation of Software Cost Estimation Models"; *Communications of the ACM*; 30; May 1987; pp. 416–429.

Kemerer, C.F.; "Reliability of Function Point Measurement – A Field Experiment"; *Communications of the ACM*, Vol. 36; 1993; pp 85–97.

Keys, Jessica; *Software Engineering Productivity Handbook*; McGraw Hill, New York, NY; 1993; ISBN: 0-07-911366-4; 651 pages.

Laird, Linda M.; and Brennan, Carol M.; *Software Measurement and Estimation: A Practical Approach*; John Wiley & Sons, Hoboken, NJ; 2006; ISBN: 0-471-67622-5; 255 pages.

Love, Tom; *Object Lessons*; SIGS Books, New York, NY; 1993; ISBN: 0-9627477 3-4; 266 pages.

Marciniak, John J. (Editor); *Encyclopedia of Software Engineering*; John Wiley & Sons, New York, NY; 1994; ISBN: 0-471-54002; in two volumes.

McCabe, Thomas J.; "A Complexity Measure"; *IEEE Transactions on Software Engineering*; December 1976; pp. 308–320.

McConnell; *Software Estimating: Demystifying the Black Art*; Microsoft Press, Redmund, WA; 2006.

Melton, Austin; *Software Measurement*; International Thomson Press, London, UK; 1995; ISBN: 1-85032-7178-7.

Mertes, Karen R.; *Calibration of the CHECKPOINT Model to the Space and Missile Systems Center (SMC) Software Database (SWDB)*; Thesis AFIT/GCA/ LAS/96S-11, Air Force Institute of Technology (AFIT), Wright Patterson AFB, Ohio; September 1996; 119 pages.

Mills, Harlan; *Software Productivity*; Dorset House Press, New York, NY; 1988; ISBN: 0-932633-10-2; 288 pages.

Muller, Monika; and Abram, Alain (Editors); *Metrics in Software Evolution*; R. Oldenbourg Vertag GmbH, Munich; 1995; ISBN: 3-486-23589-3.

Multiple authors; *Rethinking the Software Process*; (CD-ROM); Miller Freeman, Lawrence, KS; 1996. (This is a new CD ROM book collection jointly produced by the book publisher, Prentice Hall, and the journal publisher, Miller Freeman. This CD ROM disk contains the full text and illustrations of five Prentice Hall books: *Assessment and Control of Software Risks* by Capers Jones; *Controlling Software Projects* by Tom DeMarco; *Function Point Analysis* by Brian Dreger; *Measures for Excellence* by Larry Putnam and Ware Myers; and *Object-Oriented Software Metrics* by Mark Lorenz and Jeff Kidd.)

Park, Robert E. et al; *Software Cost and Schedule Estimating – A Process Improvement Initiative*; Technical Report CMU/SEI 94-SR-03; Software Engineering Institute, Pittsburgh, PA; May 1994.

Park, Robert E. et al; *Checklists and Criteria for Evaluating the Costs and Schedule Estimating Capabilities of Software Organizations*; Technical Report CMU/SEI 95-SR-005; Software Engineering Institute, Pittsburgh, PA; January 1995.

Paulk, Mark et al; *The Capability Maturity Model; Guidelines for Improving the Software Process*; Addison Wesley, Reading, MA; 1995; ISBN: 0-201-54664-7; 439 pages.

Perlis, Alan J.; Sayward, Frederick G.; and Shaw, Mary (Editors); *Software Metrics*; The MIT Press, Cambridge, MA; 1981; ISBN: 0-262-16083-8; 404 pages.

Perry, William E.; *Data Processing Budgets – How to Develop and Use Budgets Effectively*; Prentice Hall, Englewood Cliffs, NJ; 1985; ISBN: 0-13-196874-2; 224 pages.

Perry, William E.; *Handbook of Diagnosing and Solving Computer Problems*; TAB Books, Inc., Blue Ridge Summit, PA; 1989; ISBN: 0-8306-9233-9; 255 pages.

Pressman, Roger; *Software Engineering – A Practitioner's Approach*; McGraw Hill, New York, NY; 1982.

Putnam, Lawrence H.; *Measures for Excellence – Reliable Software On Time, Within Budget*; Yourdon Press, Prentice Hall, Englewood Cliffs, NJ; 1992; ISBN: 0-13-567694-0; 336 pages.

Putnam, Lawrence H.; and Myers, Ware; *Industrial Strength Software – Effective Management Using Measurement*; IEEE Press, Los Alamitos, CA; 1997; ISBN: 0-8186-7532-2; 320 pages.

Reifer, Donald (Editor); *Software Management*, 4th ed.; IEEE Press, Los Alamitos, CA; 1993; ISBN: 0 8186-3342-6; 664 pages.

Roetzheim, William H.; and Beasley, Reyna A.; *Best Practices in Software Cost and Schedule Estimation*; Prentice Hall PTR, Upper Saddle River, NJ; 1998.

Royce, W.E.; *Software Project Management: A Unified Framework*; Addison Wesley, Reading, MA; 1999.

Rubin, Howard; *Software Benchmark Studies For 1997*; Howard Rubin Associates, Pound Ridge, NY; 1997.

Shepperd, M.: "A Critique of Cyclomatic Complexity as a Software Metric"; *Software Engineering Journal*, Vol. 3; 1988; pp. 30–36.

Software Productivity Consortium; *The Software Measurement Guidebook*; International Thomson Computer Press; Boston, MA; 1995; ISBN: 1-850-32195-7; 308 pages.

St-Pierre, Denis; Maya, Marcela; Abran, Alain; and Desharnais, Jean-Marc; *Full Function Points: Function Point Extensions for Real-Time Software, Concepts and Definitions*; University of Quebec. Software Engineering Laboratory in Applied Metrics (SELAM); TR 1997-03; March 1997; 18 pages.

Strassmann, Paul; *The Squandered Computer*; The Information Economics Press, New Canaan, CT; 1997; ISBN: 0-9620413-1-9; 426 pages.

Stukes, Sherry; Deshoretz, Jason; Apgar, Henry; and Macias, Ilona; *Air Force Cost Analysis Agency Software Estimating Model Analysis*; TR-9545/008-2; Contract F04701-95-D-0003, Task 008; Management Consulting & Research, Inc., Thousand Oaks, CA; September 30, 1996.

Stutzke, Richard D.; *Estimating Software Intensive Systems*; Addison Wesley, Boston, MA; 2005.

Symons, Charles R.; *Software Sizing and Estimating – Mk II FPA (Function Point Analysis)*; John Wiley & Sons, Chichester; 1991; ISBN: 0 471-92985-9; 200 pages.

Thayer, Richard H. (Editor); *Software Engineering and Project Management*; IEEE Press, Los Alamitos, CA; 1988; ISBN: 0 8186-075107; 512 pages.

Umbaugh, Robert E. (Editor); *Handbook of IS Management*, 4th ed., Auerbach Publications, Boston, MA; 1995; ISBN: 0-7913-2159-2; 703 pages.

Whitmire, S.A.; "3-D Function Points: Scientific and Real-Time Extensions to Function Points"; Proceedings of the 1992 Pacific Northwest Software Quality Conference, June 1, 1992.

Yourdon, Ed; *Death March – The Complete Software Developer's Guide to Surviving "Mission Impossible" Projects*; Prentice Hall PTR, Upper Saddle River, NJ; 1997; ISBN: 0-13-748310-4; 218 pages.

Zells, Lois; *Managing Software Projects – Selecting and Using PC-Based Project Management Systems*; QED Information Sciences, Wellesley, MA; 1990; ISBN: 0-89435-275-X; 487 pages.

Zuse, Horst; *Software Complexity – Measures and Methods*; Walter de Gruyter, Berlin; 1990; ISBN: 3-11-012226-X; 603 pages.

Zuse, Horst; *A Framework of Software Measurement*; Walter de Gruyter, Berlin; 1997.

Software Benchmark Providers (listed in alphabetic order)

1. 4SUM Partners, www.4sumpartners.com
2. Bureau of Labor Statistics, Department of Commerce, www.bls.gov
3. Capers Jones (Namcook Analytics LLC), www.namcook.com
4. CAST Software, www.castsoftware.com

5. Congressional Cyber Security Caucus, https://cybercaucus-langevin.house.gov
6. Construx, www.construx.com
7. COSMIC Function Points, www.cosmicon.com
8. Cyber Security and Information Systems, https://s2cpat.thecsiac.com/s2cpat/
9. David Consulting Group, www.davidconsultinggroup.com
10. Forrester Research, www.forrester.com
11. Galorath Incorporated, www.galorath.com
12. Gartner Group, www.gartner.com
13. German Computer Society, http://metrics.cs.uni-magdeburg.de/
14. Hoovers Guides to Business, www.hoovers.com
15. IDC, www.IDC.com
16. ISBSG Limited, www.isbsg.org
17. ITMPI, www.itmpi.org
18. Jerry Luftman (Stevens Institute), http://howe.stevens.edu/index.php?id=14
19. Level 4 Ventures, www.level4ventures.com
20. Namcook Analytics LLC, www.namcook.com
21. Price Systems, www.pricesystems.com
22. Process Fusion, www.process-fusion.net
23. QuantiMetrics, www.quantimetrics.net
24. Quantitative Software Management (QSM), www.qsm.com
25. Q/P Management Group, www.qpmg.com
26. RBCS, Inc., www.rbcs-us.com
27. Reifer Consultants LLC, www.reifer.com
28. Howard Rubin, www.rubinworldwide.com
29. SANS Institute, www.sabs.org
30. Software Benchmarking Organization (SBO), www.sw-benchmark.org
31. Software Engineering Institute (SEI), www.sei.cmu.edu
32. Software Improvement Group (SIG), www.sig.eu
33. Software Productivity Research, www.SPR.com
34. Standish Group, www.standishgroup.com
35. Strassmann, Paul, www.strassmann.com
36. System Verification Associates LLC, http://sysverif.com
37. Test Maturity Model Integrated, www.experimentus.com

Chapter 6

Variations in Software Costs and Quality by Application Size

Introduction

Differences in function point size lead to very different kinds of development practices and to very different productivity rates at the low end compared to the high end. For example for some large systems, finding and fixing bugs and creating paper documents cost more than the code itself.

For successful results of large systems, early sizing and estimating using tools such as Software Risk Master (SRM) and careful progress and cost tracking using tools such as the Automated Project Office (APO) are required.

In many industries, building large products is not the same as building small products. Consider the differences in specialization and methods required to build a rowboat versus building an 80,000-ton cruise ship.

A rowboat can be constructed by a single individual using only hand tools. But a large modern cruise ship requires more than 350 workers including many specialists such a pipe fitters, electricians, steel workers, painters, and even interior decorators and a few fine artists.

Software follows a similar pattern: building large systems in the 10,000 to 100,000 function point range is more or less equivalent to

DOI: 10.1201/9781003193128-7

building other large structures such as ships, office buildings, or bridges. Many kinds of specialists are utilized and the development activities are quite extensive compared to smaller applications.

Table 6.1 illustrates the variations in development activities noted for the six size plateaus using the author's 25-activity checklist for development projects.

Below the plateau of 1,000 function points (which is roughly equivalent to 100,000 source code statements in a procedural language such as COBOL), less than half of the 25 activities are normally performed. But large systems in the 10,000 to 100,000 function point range perform more than 20 of these activities.

To illustrate these points, Table 6.2 shows quantitative variations in results for three size plateaus, 100, 1,000, and 10,000 function points.

As can be seen from Table 6.2 what happens for a small project of 100 function points can be very different from what happens for a large system of 10,000 function points. Note the presence of many kinds of software specialists at the large 10,000 function point size and their absence for the smaller sizes. As application size in function points goes up, a number of problems get worse (Table 6.3).

The software industry has done well for small projects but not for large systems. Function point metrics have been widely used for small applications but are seldom used above 10,000 function points due to the high cost and lengthy time interval required. There are several forms of high-speed function points such as pattern matching for new projects and automated counts for legacy applications, but manual counts by certified function point personnel remain the most common.

Summary and Conclusions

There are major differences in software development methods, software staffing, software quality, and software productivity between small applications of 100 function points and large systems of 10,000 function points or more. Small projects are generally successful and have fairly good quality and productivity. Large systems fail more often than they succeed and seldom have good quality and productivity.

Table 6.1 Development Activities for Six Project Size Plateaus

	Activities Performed	\multicolumn{6}{c}{*Function Points*}

	Activities Performed	*1*	*10*	*100*	*1,000*	*10,000*	*100,000*
1	Requirements	X	X	X	X	X	X
2	Prototyping				X	X	X
3	Architecture					X	X
4	Project plans				X	X	X
5	Initial design		X	X	X	X	X
6	Detail design			X	X	X	X
7	Design reviews					X	X
8	Coding	X	X	X	X	X	X
9	Reuse acquisition	X	X	X	X	X	X
10	Package purchase					X	X
11	Code inspections				X	X	X
12	Ind. verif. & valid.						
13	Change control				X	X	X
14	Formal integration				X	X	X
15	User documentation			X	X	X	X
16	Unit testing	X	X	X	X	X	X
17	Function testing			X	X	X	X
18	Integration testing				X	X	X
19	System testing				X	X	X
20	Beta testing					X	X
21	Acceptance testing				X	X	X
22	Independent testing						
23	Quality assurance						X
24	Installation/training				X	X	X
25	Project management			X	X	X	X
Activities		**4**	**5**	**9**	**18**	**22**	**23**

Table 6.2 Powers of Ten for 100, 1,000, and 10,000 Function Points

Size in Function Points		100	1,000	10,000
Examples		Medium Update	Smart Phone App	Local System
Team experience		Average	Average	Average
Methodology		Agile	Iterative	Hybrid
Sample size for this table		150	450	50
CMMI levels (0 = CMMI not used)		0	1	1
Monthly burdened costs		$10,000	$10,000	$10,000
Major Cost Drivers (rank order)	1	Coding	Bug repairs	Bug repairs
	2	Bug repairs	Coding	Paperwork
	3	Management	Paperwork	Coding
	4	Meetings	Management	Creep
	5	Paperwork	Meetings	Meetings
	6	0 integration	Integration	Integration
	7	0 creep	Creep	Management
Programming language		Java	Java	Java
Source statements per function point		53.00	53.00	53.00
Size in logical code statements (SRM default for LOC)		5,300	53,000	530,000
Size in logical KLOC (SRM default for KLOC)		5.30	53.00	530.00
Size in physical LOC (not recommended)		19,345	193,450	1,934,500
Size in physical KLOC (not recommended)		19.35	193.45	1,934.50
Client planned schedule in calendar months		5.25	12.50	28.00
Actual Schedule in calendar months		5.75	13.80	**33.11**
Plan/actual schedule difference		0.50	1.30	**5.11**

Table 6.2   (Continued)

Size in Function Points	100	1,000	10,000
Examples	Medium Update	Smart Phone App	Local System
Schedule slip percent	9.61%	10.43%	**18.26%**
Staff size (technical + management)	1.25	6.50	66.67
Effort in staff months	7.19	89.72	2,207.54
Work hours per month (U.S. value)	132	132	132
Unpaid overtime per month (software norms)	0	8	**16**
Effort in staff hours	949.48	11,843.70	291,395.39
IFPUG Function points per month	13.90	11.15	4.53
Work hours per function point	9.49	11.84	29.14
Logical Lines of code (LOC) per month (Includes executable statements and data definitions)	736.83	590.69	240.09
Physical lines of code (LOC) per month (Includes blank lines, comments, headers, etc.)	2,689.42	2,156.03	876.31
Requirements creep (total percent growth)	1.00%	6.00%	**15.00%**
Requirements creep (function points)	1	60	**1,500**
Probable deferred features to release 2	0.00	0.00	**2,500**
Client planned project cost	$65,625	$812,500	$18,667,600
Actual total project cost	$71,930	$897,250	$22,075,408
Plan/Actual cost difference	$6,305	$84,750	$3,407,808
Plan/Actual percent difference	8.77%	9.45%	15.44%

(Continued)

Table 6.2 (Continued)

Size in Function Points	100	1,000	10,000
Examples	Medium Update	Smart Phone App	Local System
Planned cost per function point	$656.25	$812.50	$1,866.76
Actual cost per function point	$719.30	$897.25	$2,207.54
Defect Potentials and Removal %			
Defect Potentials	**Defects**	**Defects**	**Defects**
Requirements defects	5	445	6,750
Architecture defects	0	1	27
Design defects	25	995	14,700
Code defects	175	2,150	30,500
Document defects	11	160	1,650
Bad fix defects	15	336	3,900
Total Defects	**231**	**4,087**	**57,527**
Defects per function point	2.31	4.09	5.75
Defect removal efficiency (DRE)	97.50%	96.00%	92.50%
Delivered Defects	6	163	4,313
High-severity defects	1	20	539
Security flaws	0	3	81
Delivered Defects per Function Point	0.06	0.16	0.43
Delivered defects per KLOC	1.09	3.08	8.14
Test Cases for Selected Tests	**Test Cases**	**Test Cases**	**Test Cases**
Unit test	101	1,026	10,461
Function test	112	1,137	11,592
Regression test	50	512	5,216
Component test	67	682	6,955
Performance test	33	341	3,477

Table 6.2   (Continued)

Size in Function Points	100	1,000	10,000
Examples	Medium Update	Smart Phone App	Local System
System test	106	1,080	11,012
Acceptance test	23	237	2,413
Total	**492**	**5,016**	**51,126**
Test cases per function point	4.92	5.02	5.11
Probable test coverage	95.00%	92.00%	87.00%
Probable peak cyclomatic complexity	12.00	15.00	>25.00
Document Sizing			
Document Sizes	**Pages**	**Pages**	**Pages**
Requirements	40	275	2,126
Architecture	17	76	376
Initial design	45	325	2,625
Detail design	70	574	5,118
Test plans	23	145	1,158
Development plans	6	55	550
Cost estimates	17	76	376
User manuals	38	267	2,111
HELP text	19	191	1,964
Courses	15	145	1,450
Status reports	20	119	1,249
Change requests	18	191	2,067
Bug reports	97	1,048	11,467
Total	**423**	**3,486**	**32,638**
Document set completeness	96.96%	91.21%	78.24%
Document pages per function point	4.23	3.49	3.26
Project Risks	**Risk %**	**Risk %**	**Risk %**
Cancellation	8.80%	14.23%	26.47%

(Continued)

Table 6.2   (Continued)

Size in Function Points	100	1,000	10,000
Examples	Medium Update	Smart Phone App	Local System
Negative ROI	11.15%	18.02%	33.53%
Cost overrun	9.68%	15.65%	34.00%
Schedule slip	10.74%	18.97%	38.00%
Unhappy customers	7.04%	11.38%	34.00%
Litigation	3.87%	6.26%	11.65%
Technical debt/high COQ	5.00%	16.00%	26.21%
Cyber-attacks	7.00%	9.75%	15.30%
Financial risk	9.00%	21.00%	41.00%
High warranty repairs/low maintainability	6.00%	14.75%	32.00%
Risk Average	**7.83%**	**14.60%**	**29.22%**
Project Staffing by Occupation Group	**100**	**1,000**	**10,000**
Programmers	1.91	6.23	43.53
Testers	1.85	5.66	38.58
Designers	0.51	2.13	18.00
Business analysts	0.00	2.13	9.00
Technical writers	0.44	1.05	7.00
Quality assurance	0.46	0.98	5.00
1st line managers	1.21	1.85	7.13
Data base administration	0.00	0.00	3.68
Project Office staff	0.00	0.00	3.19
Administrative support	0.00	0.00	3.68
Configuration control	0.00	0.00	2.08
Project librarians	0.00	0.00	1.72
2nd line managers	0.00	0.00	1.43
Estimating specialists	0.00	0.00	1.23
Architects	0.00	0.00	0.86
Security specialists	0.00	0.00	0.49

Table 6.2 (Continued)

Size in Function Points	100	1,000	10,000
Examples	Medium Update	Smart Phone App	Local System
Performance specialists	0.00	0.00	0.49
Function point counters	0.00	0.07	0.49
Human factors specialists	0.00	0.00	0.49
3rd line managers	0.00	0.00	0.36
Total staff	**6.37**	**20.11**	**148.42**

Table 6.3 Problems of Large Software Applications

1	Requirements completeness declines.
2	Requirements changes increase.
3	Document volumes grow rapidly.
4	Document completeness declines.
5	Defect potentials increase.
6	Defect removal efficiency (DRE) declines.
7	Numbers of test cases increase.
8	Test coverage declines.
9	Cyclomatic complexity goes up.
10	Risks of cancellation and delays go up alarmingly.
11	Function point counting costs go up.
12	Many large applications don't use function points.

References and Readings

Abran, A.; and Robillard, P.N.; "Function Point Analysis, an Empirical Study of Its Measurement Processes"; *IEEE Transactions on Software Engineering*, Vol. 22, No. 12; December 1996; pp. 895–909.

Bogan, Christopher E.; and English, Michael J.; *Benchmarking for Best Practices*; McGraw Hill, New York, NY; 1994; ISBN: 0-07-006375-3; 312 pages.

Gack, Gary; *Managing the Black Hole: The Executives Guide to Software Project Risk*; Business Expert Publishing, Thomson, GA; 2010; ISBN: 10: 1-935602-01-9.

Humphrey, Watts S.; *Managing the Software Process*; Addison Wesley Longman, Reading, MA; 1989.

IFPUG; *IFPUG Counting Practices Manual*, Release 6; International Function Point Users Group, Westerville, OH; April 2015; 105 pages.

Jones, Capers; *Quantifying Software: Global and Industry Perspectives*; CRC Press; 2017a.

Jones, Capers; and Bonsignour, Olivier; *The Economics of Software Quality*; Addison Wesley, Boston, MA; 2011; ISBN: 978-0-13-258220-9; 587 pages.

Jones, Capers; *A Ten-Year Retrospective of the ITT Programming Technology Center*; Software Productivity Research, Burlington, MA; 1988.

Jones, Capers; *A Guide to Selecting Software Measures and Metrics*; CRC Press; 2017b.

Jones, Capers; *Applied Software Measurement*, 3rd ed.; McGraw Hill; 2008.

Jones, Capers; *Assessment and Control of Software Risks*; Prentice Hall; 1994; ISBN: 0-13-741406-4; 711 pages.

Jones, Capers; *Becoming Best in Class*; Software Productivity Research, Burlington, MA; January 1998; 40 pages.

Jones, Capers; *Estimating Software Costs*, 2nd ed.; McGraw Hill; New York, NY; 2007.

Jones, Capers; *Patterns of Software System Failure and Success*; International Thomson Computer Press, Boston, MA; December 1995; ISBN: 1-850-32804-8; 250; 292 pages.

Jones, Capers; *Software Assessments, Benchmarks, and Best Practices*; Addison Wesley Longman, Boston, MA; 2000 (due in May of 2000); 600 pages.

Jones, Capers; *Software Engineering Best Practices*, 1st ed.; McGraw Hill; 2010.

Jones, Capers; *Software Methodologies, a Quantitative Guide*; CRC Press; 2017c.

Jones, Capers; *Software Quality – Analysis and Guidelines for Success*; International Thomson Computer Press, Boston, MA; 1997a; ISBN: 1-85032-876-6; 492 pages.

Jones, Capers; *The Economics of Object-Oriented Software*; Software Productivity Research, Burlington, MA; April 1997b; 22 pages.

Jones, Capers; *The Technical and Social History of Software Engineering*, Addison Wesley; 2014.

Kan, Stephen H.; *Metrics and Models in Software Quality Engineering*, 2nd ed.; Addison Wesley Longman, Boston, MA; 2003; ISBN: 0-201-72915-6; 528 pages.

McMahon, Paul; *15 Fundamentals for Higher Performance in Software Development*; PEM Systems; 2014.

Radice, Ronald A.; *High Quality Low Cost Software Inspections*; Paradoxicon Publishing, Andover, MA; 2002; ISBN: 0-9645913-1-6; 479 pages.

Wiegers, Karl A.; *Creating a Software Engineering Culture*; Dorset House Press, New York, NY; 1996; ISBN: 0-932633-33-1; 358 pages.

Yourdon, Ed; *Death March - The Complete Software Developer's Guide to Surviving "Mission Impossible" Projects*; Prentice Hall PTR, Upper Saddle River, NJ; 1997; ISBN: 0-13-748310-4; 218 pages.

Chapter 7

Advancing Software from a Craft to a Profession

Introduction

As of 2020 software is a major industry, but also a troubling industry. Software projects have many failures and even more cost and schedule overruns. Poor software quality remains an endemic problem, in part because software quality measures are generally incompetent.

Software education is deficient in teaching effective metrics and effective professional skills. In surveys of corporate CEOs and C-level executives by the author of this book, software engineering is regarded as the least professional and most troublesome form of engineering in major technology companies due to frequent failures and numerous cost and schedule overruns.

Unlike medical practice and other forms of engineering, the software industry has been running blind for over 60 years with little or no accurate quantitative data on productivity or quality and no empirical data that proves the value of software tools, methodologies, or programming languages. You can hardly be deemed a profession if you can't measure economic productivity or quality, or measure the effectiveness of the tools, languages, and methodologies in common use.

Software quality is weak due to poor quality measures. Since high quality leads to shorter schedules, lower costs, and reduced risks, quality improvement via measures of defect potentials and defect removal efficiency (DRE) is urgently needed.

DOI: 10.1201/9781003193128-8

Before dealing with the professional status or craft status of software engineering, the author of this book wants to recommend an important book that provides key insights into how a minor craft evolved into a true and major profession.

The book is *The Social Transformation of American Medicine*, Basic Books, 1982 by Paul Starr. It won a Pulitzer Prize for non-fiction in 1984 and also a Bancroft Prize in 1984.

In the 19th century, medicine was a craft with sparse and questionable academic training, no political power, and no licensing or board certifications. There were few medical schools and they had two-year curricula.

Medical schools did not require either college degrees or even high school graduation to attend. Essentially, the ability to pay the fees of these for-profit medical schools was the only criterion for admission. Many young physicians did not attend medical schools but worked as apprentices for older practicing physicians.

While in medical school student physicians never even entered hospitals because hospitals had their own closed groups of physicians and did not allow external physician at all. Even regular physicians could not visit their patients once they were admitted to hospitals. In England and some other countries women were barred from becoming physicians.

There were no state medical licenses and no board certifications. There were no regulations against medical malpractice, and not even any way to monitor or report bad medical decisions. Harmful drugs such as laudanum could be freely prescribed in spite of serious side effects such as opium addiction. In fact laudanum, liquid opium, was even available over the counter for calming down noisy children.

Paul Starr's book on medical transformation starts around 1760 and continues through 1980. At the start of the book, medical doctors were an offshoot of barbers and had little professional training other than apprenticeship with older doctors, mainly because of the lack of American medical schools.

The Wikipedia list of U.S. medical school start dates shows The University of Pennsylvania medical school starting in 1765, Columbia University in 1767, Harvard in 1782, Dartmouth in 1797, University of Maryland in 1807, Yale in 1810, and Brown University in 1811. It was not until after the Civil War that American medical schools began to increase in numbers and to top 100 academic medical institutions.

Paul Starr's book shows the gradual evolution of medical training and medical professionalism, including the interesting history of the American Medical Association (AMA).

In a nutshell, the AMA grew from a small inconsequential organization of a few hundred members to become a major professional association with over 235,000 members circa 2020. One of the methods used for this rapid growth was for the AMA to reach out to various state and local medical societies and offer reciprocal memberships.

This technique raised AMA membership from a few hundred physicians to over 80,000 in a few decades and began to give the AMA enough mass to lobby state governments for requiring medical licensing. The larger membership also gave the AMA enough power to influence medical school curricula and to even force the closure of some of the least competent medical schools.

It would also benefit software to have reciprocal memberships among the various software associations such as the Project Management Institute (PMI), the IEEE Software Engineering Society, the Society of Information Management (SIM), the Association of Computing Machinery (ACM), the International Function Point Users Group (IFPUG), and quite a few others. Reciprocal membership among the various function point groups (COSMIC, FISMA, IFPUG, NESMA, etc.) would be useful too.

It took almost 100 years for medicine to evolve from a craft into a leading profession. With Paul Starr's book as a guide, software engineering could probably evolve into a true profession in another 25 years or less, starting today.

What Are the Indicators of a Profession?

The Professional Standards Council says, in paraphrase, that a profession is *"A group of individuals who receive formal education in the knowledge of a field based on valid research, and who adhere to a code of ethical behavior."* Professionals should be able to *"apply their training and knowledge with high levels of competence and integrity."* All of us in software would do well to remember the line in the medical Hippocratic oath, *"first do no harm."* We should also remember Tom DeMarco's famous line, *"you can't manage what you can't measure."*

It is interesting that the Wikipedia list of professionals has over 100 job titles, but software engineering is not listed. Examples of some 15 of these professions include (Table 7.1).

All of these 15 have formal education based on large bodies of knowledge, and all require some kind of certification or licenses before professional work can be performed. Most require continuing education after starting work to keep current on the latest advances in the fields.

Software in 2020 has dozens of kinds of certification for specific tools and for general categories such as certified tester or certified quality assurance. However, there is little empirical data that shows certification

Table 7.1   Fifteen Professions Circa 2020

1	Accountants
2	Air line pilots
3	Anesthesiologists
4	Attorneys
5	Biologists
6	Chemists
7	Clergymen
8	Dentists
9	Engineers
10	Educators – college professors
11	Educators – school teachers
12	Nurses
13	Pharmacists
14	Physicians
15	Physicists

actually improves job performance, although education certainly should be helpful.

Why Software Engineering in Not Yet a Profession

Those of us who work in software can be proud of the many accomplishments created by software engineers including but not limited to medical diagnostic software, banking and financial software, operating systems and embedded software, military and defense software, and hundreds of other important applications.

However, software also has many canceled projects and a very large number of cost and schedule overruns. A survey by the author of CEOs and other C-level executives found that software was regarded by corporate CEOs and other executives as the least professional and least competent of any form of engineering. If our own CEOs don't regard us in software as professional, it is hard to claim that we are.

Lyman Hamilton, a former Chairman of ITT, noted in a public speech that it took about three years of on-the-job training before graduate software engineers could be trusted with serious projects, as opposed to about one year for other kinds of engineers such as mechanical, electrical, or telecommunications engineers.

For software to take the step from being a craft to becoming a true profession, we need to solve a number of critical endemic problems that have plagued software since the beginning (Table 7.2).

Let us evaluate these 15 professional needs in a bit more detail than just listing them in a table.

Topic 1: Reduce the Many Software Failures

Software projects are very risky. In fact large software projects seem to have the highest failure rates of any industry in human history. As software pioneer Dr. Gerald Weinberg observed years ago, "...*if buildings were built the way software is built, a woodpecker could destroy civilization...*"

From the author's examination of about 28,000 successful and unsuccessful software projects, failures are directly proportional to application size measured in IFPUG function points as shown in Table 7.3.

Below 1,000 function points, software projects are only slightly risky. Above 10,000 function points, they have perhaps the highest risk of any

Table 7.2   Fifteen Steps to Achieve Software Engineering Professional Status

1	Reduce the many software failures.
2	Reduce the many software cost and schedule overruns.
3	Improve poor software quality after deployment.
4	Improve poor software productivity and shorten schedules.
5	Improve poor software security and reduce cyber-attacks.
6	Stop using inaccurate and invalid metrics that distort reality.
7	Adopt accurate metrics and measurement practices.
8	Reduce inaccurate and optimistic estimates prior to starting.
9	Eliminate inaccurate status tracking during development.
10	Reduce high maintenance costs after deployment.
11	Reduce or eliminate frequent litigation from unhappy clients.
12	Improve undergraduate and graduate software education.
13	Improve post-graduate and on-the-job software education.
14	Introduce software licensing and board certification.
15	Move from custom manual software to standard reusable components.

Table 7.3   Software Failure % by Size

Size in IFPUG 4.3 FP	Failure Average
1	1.00%
10	1.86%
100	3.21%
1,000	10.14%
10,000	31.29%
100,000	47.57%
1,000,000	82.29%
Average	25.34%

manufactured product in human history. This does not speak well for the professionalism of software engineering.

Poor quality control is the main cause of software failure. Poor quality control, combined with unplanned requirements creep, can double planned schedules and these delays cause return on investment (ROI) to switch from positive to negative so projects are terminated without being completed.

Topic 2: Reduce Cost and Schedule Overruns

Of the software projects above 1,000 function points that are not canceled, about 70% run late and 60% exceed planned budgets. This is a key reason that CEOs and other C-level executives don't trust their software engineering teams.

Software cost and schedule estimates are usually excessively optimistic, due in part to the poor accuracy of informal manual estimates rather than to using accurate parametric estimates.

Poor quality control that stretches out test cycles and unplanned requirements creep in excess of 1% per calendar month are the two main causes of cost and schedule overruns.

Incidentally to calculate average U.S. software schedules, a simple rule of thumb is to raise application size in function points to the 0.4 power. The result will be the schedule in calendar months. For example 1,000 function points raised to the 0.4 power shows a schedule of 15.84 calendar months.

Projects with good technology stacks and expert teams could use a power exponent of 0.38. Projects with poor technology stacks and novice teams could use a power exponent of 0.42. Large defense projects which create about three times the volume of paper documents compared to civilian projects might use the 0.44 power, since paperwork is the #1 cost driver for defense software. Defense projects also have large volumes of non-functional requirements. One of the advantages of function point metrics is their ability to quantify software results better than the older lines of code metric.

It is theoretically possible for large companies to speed up development by dividing applications into independent components that can be built in different locations. It is also theoretically possible to transfer some aspects of development from location to location at the end of standard work shifts.

Hospitals operate 24 hours around the clock. One interesting feature that makes this possible is the accurate patient status data that allows the incoming team to see what actions were performed by the prior team.

Software has almost a total lack of accurate status information that would facilitate moving work from location to location. A few companies such as IBM and ITT have managed to do this, but both companies had to make major changes in project status monitoring.

Topic 3: Improve Software Quality after Deployment

A majority of large software systems have marginal to poor quality after deployment. A majority of companies and government agencies do not measure software quality or know the effectiveness of various kinds of defect removal activities such as inspections, static analysis, testing, etc.

A majority of universities have no empirical data on software quality control and hence are not able to teach state of the art methods to undergrads. Lack of quality measures and poor understanding of software quality control are two key reasons why software engineering is not yet a true profession but still a craft.

In order to improve software quality, two key factors need to improve: (1) defect potentials need to be reduced from today's average of about 4.25 per function point down below 2.50 per function point; (2) defect removal efficiency (DRE) needs to increase from today's average of about 92.5% to over 99.00%.

These quality results are based on observations of about 26,000 software projects combined with 15 lawsuits involving poor quality where the author of this book has been an expert witness.

Testing alone is not sufficient to achieve high quality because most forms of testing are only about 35% efficient or find one bug out of three. Static analysis is about 55% efficient and formal inspections are about 85% efficient. A synergistic combination of inspections, static analysis, and formal testing can top 99.50% defect removal efficiency (DRE). Even better, high DRE levels >99.00% also have shorter schedules and lower costs than low DRE < 85.00%.

Lowering defect potentials require advanced methods such as reuse of certified components that approach zero defects, requirements models, and automated proofs of correctness. These can lower defect potentials from over 4.25 bugs per function point down below 2.50 bugs per function point.

Topic 4: Improve Today's Low Software Development Productivity and Long Schedules

Custom software designs and manual coding are intrinsically slow, expensive, and error prone no matter what methodologies are used and what programming languages are used. Today in 2017 the U.S. average for software development productivity is only about 8.00 function points per staff month or 16.5 work hours per function point and software reuse is below 15% on average.

What the software industry needs to achieve are consistent productivity rates >25.00 function points per staff month or 5.28 work hours per function point. The only known way of achieving such high productivity rates is to shift from custom designs and manual coding to ever-larger percentages of certified reusable components.

Table 7.4 shows the impact of software reuse on a project of a nominal 1,000 function points in size coded in Java by average teams.

Methodologies such as agile are marginally better than older methodologies such as waterfall but are barely 15% better in terms of measured productivity and measured schedules. Modern languages such as Ruby and Python and Swift are better than older languages such as Fortran and COBOL but improve productivity and quality by less than 12%.

The only truly effective way of improving software productivity and quality at the same time is to eliminate custom designs and manual development and shift to construction from standard and certified reusable components.

Topic 5: Improve Poor Software Security and Reduce Cyber-Attacks

Software security and cyber-attacks are modern problems that are becoming more serious every day. The criminals who are attempting cyber-attacks are no longer individual hackers, but now members of sophisticated organized crime groups and even worse, operating under

Table 7.4   Impact of Software Reuse on Productivity and Quality

Reuse %	Wk hrs per FP	FP per Month	Defect Potential per FP	Defect Removal Percent	Delivered Defects per FP
95	2.07	63.63	1.25	99.75	0.003
85	2.70	48.94	1.68	98.25	0.029
75	3.51	37.65	2.10	96.78	0.068
65	4.56	28.96	2.53	95.33	0.118
55	5.93	22.28	2.95	93.90	0.180
45	7.70	17.14	3.38	92.49	0.253
35	10.01	13.18	3.80	91.10	0.338
25	13.02	10.14	4.23	89.74	0.434
15	16.92	7.80	4.65	88.39	0.540
5	22.00	6.00	5.08	87.06	0.656
0	33.00	4.00	5.50	85.76	0.783

the control of hostile military cyber-warfare units in countries such as North Korea and Iran.

Cyber security is a highly complex topic and every major company and government organization that builds or runs software needs both internal security teams and also access to top security consultants, plus links to government cyber-security specialists at the FBI, Homeland Security, and also State and Municipal government security groups.

Topic 6: Stop Using Inaccurate and Invalid Metrics That Distort Reality

The software industry has been running blind for over 60 years with bad metrics and bad measurement practices. The author of this book believes that the software industry has the worst metrics and measurement practices of any industry in human history.

It would be surprising if more than 5% of the readers of this book know their own company's actual productivity and quality levels at all using any metric. Less than 1.00% would know their productivity and quality results within 10% precision using function point metrics. Bad metrics and bad measurement practices are endemic problems for software and a professional embarrassment. Software can never be a true profession without knowing how to measure results with high accuracy.

This is too big a topic for a short article. Suffice it to say that the "lines of code" (LOC) metric penalizes high-level languages and makes requirements and design invisible. A metric that makes assembly language look better than Ruby or Swift is a professional embarrassment.

The "cost per defect" metric penalizes quality and is cheapest for the buggiest software. Applications with thousands of bugs have lower costs per defect than applications with only a few bugs.

Fixed costs are the reason for both problems. Every other industry except software knows that *if a development process has a high percentage of fixed costs and there is a decline in the number of units produced, the cost per unit will go up.*

If you use LOC as a unit and switch to a high level language, you reduce the number of units produced. But the work on requirements and design act like fixed costs and drive up cost per LOC.

If you use bugs as a unit and have effective quality control with static analysis and formal testing, the fixed costs of writing and running test cases drive up cost per defect. These are not just casual statements but have been proven mathematically.

Other hazardous but common software metrics include story points (undefined and highly erratic), use-case points (undefined and highly erratic), and technical debt, which no two companies seem to measure the same way in 2017. The author of this book regards poor metrics as a sign of professional malpractice, and software can't be a true profession until we adopt accurate metrics such as function points.

Topic 7: Adopt Accurate Metrics and Effective Measurement Practices

As of 2017 the best metrics for understanding software productivity are work hours per function point. This metric can be applied to individual activities as well as total projects, i.e. requirements, design, coding, and everything else can be measured to show the fine details of software development.

The best metrics for understanding software quality are defect potentials measured using function points combined with defect removal efficiency (DRE). DRE is the percentage of bugs found and eliminated prior to release of software to customers. The current U.S. average for DRE is only about 92.50% but best in class projects top 99.50%.

It is a matter of historical interest that all three of these effective metrics were developed within IBM during the years 1970–1975. IBM deserves thanks from the software industry for spending money on building a metrics family that allows high accuracy in both estimating projects before they start and measuring projects after they are delivered.

As to poor measurement practices, self-reported data tends to "leak" and omit over 50% of true software costs. Among the author's clients, the accuracy of self-reported development data is only about 37%.

The major omissions from self-reported data include unpaid overtime, project management costs, project office costs, and the work of part-time specialists such as quality assurance and technical writers.

Because self-reported data leaks, the best way of collecting accurate historical data is to use one of the commercial benchmark organizations of which there are about 35 in the United States and quite a few in Europe. These benchmark groups will assist clients in collecting data for 100% of work performed instead of just a small fraction of work such as "design, code, and unit test" (DCUT) which is only about 30% of total effort.

The major cost drivers for software include the costs of finding and fixing bugs and the costs producing paper documents. These costs should definitely be part of historical benchmark data, as well as coding costs and testing costs.

The International Function Point Users Group (IFPUG) introduced a new metric for non-functional requirements in 2012. This is the SNAP metric (Software Non-Functional Assessment Process). SNAP is too new to have much empirical data so it will not be discussed at this time. Non-functional requirements are things like government mandates such as Sarbanes-Oxley governance of financial applications. These add substantial costs but are not user requirements.

Topic 8: Improve Inaccurate and Optimistic Estimates before Starting Projects

As a disclosure to readers, the author of this book is the developer of 10 software parametric estimation tools. Six of these were proprietary and built for specific companies such as IBM, ITT, and AT&T. Four of these have been marketed commercially.

Below about 250 function points in size, manual estimates are done by experts and parametric estimates by Software Risk Master (SRM).

However as application size grows larger, manual estimates have a tendency to become progressively optimistic while parametric estimates tend to hold their accuracy up to 100,000 function points or larger.

If you build software applications below 250 function points, most forms of estimation are acceptable. But if you build large systems above 10,000 function points in size, you should stop using manual estimates and switch over to one or more of the commercial parametric estimation tools such as SRM. (Some leading companies also have formal software estimation teams.)

Topic 9: Eliminate Inaccurate Status Tracking

From working as an expert witness in a number of lawsuits where large software projects were cancelled or did not operate correctly when deployed, six major problems occur repeatedly: (1) accurate estimates are not produced or are overruled; (2) accurate estimates are not supported by defensible benchmarks; (3) requirements changes are not handled effectively; (4) quality control is deficient; (5) progress tracking fails to alert higher management to the seriousness of the issues; (6) contracts themselves omit important topics such as change control and quality, or include hazardous terms.

Depositions and discovery in these lawsuits found that software engineers and project managers were aware of the problems that later caused termination, but that monthly status reports did not alert higher management or clients to the existence of the problems. In fact in some cases, project management deliberately concealed the problems, perhaps in the hope that they could be solved before anyone found out about them.

The bottom line is that status tracking of large software applications needs significant improvement compared to 2017 averages. Automated project tracking tools and the use of project offices for large applications can improve this problem. But until project tracking reveals problems instead of concealing them, software cannot be deemed a true profession.

There are also effective automated project tracking tools available such as the Automated Project Office (APO) from Computer Aid Inc.

Topic 10: Reduce High Maintenance Costs after Deployment

As many readers know, for large software applications, more than 50% of total costs of ownership (TCO) occur after release rather than during development. While some of the costs are due to normal evolution and growth in functionality, the majority of the post-release costs are due to bug repairs for latent bugs in the application when it was delivered, plus the costs of "bad fixes."

A "bad fix" is a new bug accidentally included in bug repairs. The U.S. average for bad-fix injection in 2017 was that about 7% of bug repairs add new bugs. But with modules having high cyclomatic complexity of over 25, bad-fix injections can top 30%. Bad fixes are an endemic problem, but completely treatable by using static analysis tools on all bug repairs before integrating them. Unprofessional quality measures and unprofessional quality control are the causes of bad-fix injections.

Another huge post-release cost is that of dealing with "error-prone" modules (EPM). IBM discovered that bugs are not randomly distributed but clump in a small number of very buggy modules. Other companies such as AT&T and Raytheon also noted EPM, which occur in most large systems.

In general less than 3% of the modules in an application will contain over 50% of all bugs. Thus about half of post-release bug repair costs are for EPM, and they can and should have been eliminated prior to release.

A synergistic combination of defect prevention, pre-test defect removal such as static analysis and inspections, combined with formal testing and formal test case design such a using cause–effect graphs can completely eliminate EPM before software is released. Running cyclomatic complexity tools against all modules is important too. It is due in part to the very poor quality measurement practices of the software industry and poor quality control that most EPM are not discovered until too late. In fact quality measures are so bad that many companies have EPM but don't even know about them!

To achieve professional status, software should have less than 0.1% bad-fix injections and have zero error-prone modules (EPM) since both of these endemic problems have technical solutions available.

Topic 11: Reduce or Eliminate Litigation from Unhappy Clients

Among the author's clients who commissioned us to study outsourced projects, we found that about 70% of the projects were reasonably successful and both the vendor and the client were generally satisfied. But for 30% of the projects, there was considerable dissatisfaction by the clients for poor quality and schedule delays. For about 5% of the projects litigation was either about to happen or was in progress when we examined the projects. For quite a few projects, the author of this book was an expert witness in actual litigation.

Dissatisfaction and litigation occurs for other kinds of contracts such as home construction and home repairs, but software has more litigation than it should. Breach of contract litigation is the topic of this section, but software also has a lot of patent litigation and even some criminal litigation for things such as poor governance under Sarbanes-Oxley rules or causing death or injury as in the case of defective medical devices or automotive brake systems.

The root causes of breach of contract litigation seem to be four critical topics, all of which can be eliminated: (1) optimistic cost and schedule estimates before starting; (2) very poor status tracking during development; (3) inadequate quality control so that the application does not work well after deployment; (4) sloppy change control which tends to introduce "bad fixes" into software applications.

If software engineering were a true profession, all four of these common conditions that lead to litigation would be eliminated.

Topic 12: Improve Undergraduate and Graduate Software Education

About every two years, the author of this book does a study of software learning channels since there are quite a few of them. The study looks at effectiveness, convenience, costs, and other parameters. It is interesting that academic education does not rank very high among 17 learning channels as shown in Table 7.5.

As already noted, graduate software engineers seem to need more on-the-job training than other forms of engineering before doing major projects.

The fact that most graduate software engineers don't know the hazards of common metrics such as cost per defect and lines of code is a sign that academic training needs to be upgraded. Most graduates also don't know the measured defect removal efficiency (DRE) values for things like formal inspections, static analysis, and testing.

Compare these gaps in software education with what physicians know about the effectiveness of various medicines and therapy procedures. Software is running blind because poor metrics and poor measurement practices conceal progress and make it difficult to judge the effectiveness of tools, methods, languages, and other software performance factors.

Topic 13: Improve Post-Graduate and On-the-Job Software Education

A study by the author of this book some years ago on the impact of post-employment professional education on companies found an interesting result. Companies that provide 10 days of professional internal training per year show higher software productivity rates and better quality than companies of the same size and type that provide 0 days of training per year. In other words, devoting 10 days a year to professional education benefits software results, even though 10 work days are used for this purpose.

Some companies provide very impressive internal education programs for employees that the author thinks are often superior to

Table 7.5   Ranking of Software Learning Channels as of Spring 2020

Average Score	Form of Education	Cost Ranking	Efficiency Ranking	Effective-ness Ranking	Currency Ranking
3.00	Web browsing	1	1	9	1
3.25	Webinars/e-learning	3	2	6	2
3.50	Electronic books	4	3	3	4
5.25	In-house training	9	4	1	7
6.00	Self-study from CD/DVD	4	3	7	10
7.25	Vendor training	13	6	5	5
7.25	Commercial training	14	5	4	6
7.50	Wiki sites	2	9	16	3
8.25	Live conferences	12	8	8	5
9.00	Simulation web sites	8	7	13	8
10.25	Self-study from books	5	13	12	11
10.25	Journals	7	11	14	9
10.75	On-the-job training	11	10	10	12
11.75	Mentoring	10	12	11	14
12.00	Books	6	14	15	13
12.25	Undergraduate training	15	15	3	16
12.25	Graduate training	16	16	2	15

academic education. Examples of these companies with excellent internal post-employment professional training include IBM, AT&T, Microsoft, Amazon, Apple, and Google.

Topic 14: Introduce Software Licensing and Board Certification

Physicians, lawyers, and many kinds of engineers have licenses and also various kinds of board certifications. As of 2020 software has many kinds of certification, but generally no formal state licensing.

There are computer engineer and software engineer licenses that may be needed for consulting engineers who work for public agencies and need to sign or stamp official government documents. These allow successful applicants to use "P.E." for "professional engineer" when signing contracts or reports. However most kinds of software engineering personnel work under an industrial exemption clause and don't need licenses.

The basic issue is when and if software engineering licenses occur, what kinds of knowledge should be tested as part of the license process? Given the endemic problems that software has with poor quality control and bad metrics, it would be useful for software license exams to include topics such as knowledge of effective quality control and knowledge of effective quantification of software quality and productivity.

Topic 15: Move from Custom and Manual Development to Standard Reusable Components

Custom designs for software applications and manual coding by human programmers are intrinsically expensive, error-prone, and slow regardless of which programming languages are used and which development methodologies are used. Agile may be a bit faster than waterfall, but it is still slow compared to actual business needs.

The only effective solution for software engineering is to move away from manual custom development and toward construction of applications using standard certified and hardened reusable materials. The idea is to build software more like Ford builds automobiles on an assembly line rather than like the custom design and manual construction of a Formula 1 race car.

In fact when software reuse begins to top 75% on average, then the same thing can happen with software that has already happened with automotive construction: robotic software development tools can replace human analysts and human programmers for the portions of software constructed from standard reusable components. Human analysis and human programmers will still be needed for creating custom designs and custom code for novel features, but not for generic applications constructed from certified reusable components.

An ordinary passenger car and a Formula 1 race car have about the same number of mechanical parts, but the race car costs at least 10 times more to build due to the large volumes of skilled manual labor involved. The schedule would be more than 10 times longer as well. Custom designs and manual construction are intrinsically slow and expensive in every industry.

If you compare the costs and schedules of building an 50-story office building, a 50,000 ton cruise ship, and a 50,000 function point software system, the software is much more expensive and also much slower than the other two. When deployed the software is much less reliable than the other two and has many more defects that interfere with use than the other two. Worse, the software is much more likely to be attacked by external criminals seeking to steal data or interfere with software operation.

These problems are endemic but not impossible to cure. It is technically possible today in 2017 to build some software applications from standard reusable components. It is also possible to raise the immunity of software to external cyber-attack.

In the future, more and more standard components will expand the set of applications that can be assembled from certified standard parts free from security vulnerabilities rather than needing custom design and laborious manual coding that tend to introduce security flaws. Assembly from certified components can be more than 10 times faster and cheaper than the best manual methods such as agile, and also much more secure than today's norms where security vulnerabilities are rampant.

Topic 16: Develop Effective Methods for Working at Home Due To Corona Virus

The arrival of the corona virus in 2020 has disrupted hundreds of industries and put thousands of people out of work. The software and computing industries should take the lead in developing effective methods to stay productive and efficient in spite of the virus. Some obvious suggestions would be: improve the capabilities of Zoom meetings and other online tools so that it is easy to share documents while meetings are going on. This is necessary for design reviews and code inspections.

Summary and Conclusions on Software Professionalism

The author of this book has worked in software since about 1965 and has seen quite a few technical advances over the years. For example, he was at IBM during the period when function point metrics, formal inspections, and parametric estimation were first started, as well as the creation of the relational data base model.

He also saw the introduction of the Apple I computer and the introduction of Microsoft Windows, as well as the introduction the early IBM PC in 1981 followed by many others. He has seen the available programming languages expand from one (basic assembly) to over 1,000. He has seen the number of software methodologies grow from one (cowboy) to over 60 in 2020.

He has also seen the development of Software Engineering Methods and Theory (SEMAT) which attempts to put software engineering on a more reliable and repeatable basis by formalizing software development frameworks and concepts. SEMAT should be a useful approach to creating larger volumes of standard reusable components. Custom designs and manual coding will always be expensive and error prone.

In the past, the author of this book has worked as both the editor of a medical journal and of medical research papers for the Office of the Surgeon General and also as the editor and technical reviewer of a number of software journal articles and books for various publishers.

Medical papers devote about a third of the text to discussions of measures and metrics and include accurate quantified data. Software papers, on the other hand, devote hardly a paragraph to measures and metrics and seldom contain accurate quantified data.

As readers know, medical practice has been the top learned profession for over 100 years. By contrast, software is not even recognized as a true profession and is still classified as a craft circa 2020.

One reason for the low status of software is that software has failed to use effective metrics and measures. As a result, software has close to zero accurate data on software quality and productivity or the effectiveness of various methodologies and programming languages.

Software's current lack of a knowledge base of leading indicators for quality and costs is a professional embarrassment. Diagnosing software problems in 2017 was closer to medical diagnoses from 1817 before medicine adopted careful measures and accurate metrics.

From reading Paul Starr's book on the social transformation of American medical practice, it was interesting to see that medicine was as chaotic and inept 200 years ago as software is in 2017.

Medical practices circa 1820 were alarmingly similar to software practices circa 2020. Both were unlicensed, unregulated, unmeasured, and both mixed quackery and harmful practices with beneficial practices without patients or clients having any way of knowing which was which.

References and Readings on Software and Selected Texts on Medical Practice

Control of Communicable Diseases in Man; U.S. Public Health Service, published annually. This book provided the format for the author's first book on software risks, *Assessment and Control of Software Risks*. The format worked well for both medical diseases and software risks. The format included frequency of the conditions, severity of the conditions, methods of prevention, and methods of treatment. A few topics such as quarantine were not used for software risks, although with cyber-attacks increasing in frequency and severity quarantine should be considered for software that has been attacked by viruses or worms both of which are highly contagious.

Abran, A.; and Robillard, P.N.; "Function Point Analysis: An Empirical Study of Its Measurement Processes"; *IEEE Transactions on Software Engineering*, Vol 22, No. 12; December 1996; pp. 895–909.

Austin, Robert D.; *Measuring and Managing Performance in Organizations*; Dorset House Press, New York, NY; 1996; ISBN: 0-932633-36-6; 216 pages.

Black, Rex; *Managing the Testing Process: Practical Tools and Techniques for Managing Hardware and Software Testing*; Wiley; 2009; ISBN: 10: 0470404159; 672 pages.

Boehm, Barry; *Software Engineering Economics*; Prentice Hall, Englewood Cliffs, NJ; 1981; 900 pages.

Bogan, Christopher E.; and English, Michael J.; *Benchmarking for Best Practices*; McGraw Hill, New York, NY; 1994; ISBN: 0-07-006375-3; 312 pages.

Brooks, Fred; *The Mythical Man-Month*; Addison Wesley, Reading, MA, 1974 rev.; 1995.

Brown, Norm (Editor); *The Program Manager's Guide to Software Acquisition Best Practices*, Version 1.0; July 1995; U.S. Department of Defense, Washington, DC; 142 pages.

Campbell-Kelly, Martin; *A History of the Software Industry: from Airline Reservations to Sonic the Hedgehog*; The MIT Press, Cambridge, MA; 2003; ISBN: 0-262-03303-8; 372 pages.

Charette, Bob; *Application Strategies for Risk Management*; McGraw Hill, New York, NY; 1990.

Charette, Bob; *Software Engineering Risk Analysis and Management*; McGraw Hill, New York, NY; 1989.

Cohen, Lou; *Quality Function Deployment – How to Make QFD Work for You*; Prentice Hall, Upper Saddle River, NJ; 1995; ISBN: 10: 0201633302; 368 pages.

Constantine, Larry L.; *Beyond Chaos: The Expert Edge in Managing Software Development*; ACM Press, 2001.

Crosby, Philip B.; *Quality is Free*; New American Library, Mentor Books, New York, NY; 1979a; 270 pages.

Crosby, Philip B.; *Quality is Free*; New American Library, Mentor Books, New York, NY; 1979b; 270 pages.

Curtis, Bill; Hefley, William E.; and Miller, Sally; *People Capability Maturity Model*; Software Engineering Institute, Carnegie Mellon University, Pittsburgh, PA; 1995.

DeMarco, Tom; and Lister, Tim; *Waltzing with Bears: Managing Risks on Software Projects*; Dorset House Press, New York, NY; 2003.

DeMarco, Tom; *Peopleware: Productive Projects and Teams*; Dorset House Prees, New York, NY; 1999; ISBN: 10: 0932633439; 245 pages.

Department of the Air Force; *Guidelines for Successful Acquisition and Management of Software Intensive Systems*, Vols. 1–2; Software Technology Support Center, Hill Air Force Base, UT; 1994.

Dreger, Brian; *Function Point Analysis*; Prentice Hall, Englewood Cliffs, NJ; 1989; ISBN: 0-13-332321-8; 185 pages.

Gack, Gary; *Applying Six Sigma to Software Implementation Projects*; http://software.isixsigma.com/library/content/c040915b.asp.

Gack, Gary; *Managing the Black Hole: The Executives Guide to Software Project Risk*; Business Expert Publishing, Thomson, GA; 2010; ISBN: 10: 1-935602-01-9.

Gilb, Tom; and Graham, Dorothy; *Software Inspections*; Addison Wesley, Reading, MA; 1993; ISBN: 10: 0201631814.

Grady, Robert B.; and Caswell, Deborah L.; *Software Metrics: Establishing a Company-Wide Program*; Prentice Hall, Englewood Cliffs, NJ; 1987; ISBN: 0-13-821844-7; 288 pages.

Grady, Robert B.; *Practical Software Metrics for Project Management and Process Improvement*; Prentice Hall, Englewood Cliffs, NJ; 1992; ISBN: 0-13-720384-5; 270 pages.

Grady, Robert B.; *Successful Process Improvement*; Prentice Hall PTR, Upper Saddle River, NJ; 1997; ISBN: 0-13-626623-1; 314 pages.

Humphrey, Watts S.; *Managing the Software Process*; Addison Wesley Longman, Reading, MA; 1989.

IFPUG; *IFPUG Counting Practices Manual*, Release 6, International Function Point Users Group, Westerville, OH; April 2015; 105 pages.

Jacobsen, Ivar et al; *The Essence of Software Engineering; Applying the SEMAT Kernel*; Addison Wesley Professional, 2013.

Jacobsen, Ivar; Griss, Martin; and Jonsson, Patrick; *Software Reuse – Architecture, Process, and Organization for Business Success*; Addison Wesley Longman, Reading, MA; 1997; ISBN: 0-201-92476-5; 500 pages.

Jones, Capers; and Bonsignour, Olivier; *The Economics of Software Quality*; Addison Wesley, Boston, MA; 2011; ISBN: 978-0-13-258220-9; 587 pages.

Jones, Capers; *A Ten-Year Retrospective of the ITT Programming Technology Center*; Software Productivity Research, Burlington, MA; 1988.

Jones, Capers; *A Guide to Selecting Software Measures and Metrics*, CRC Press, 2017.

Jones, Capers; *Applied Software Measurement*, 3rd ed.; McGraw Hill, New York, NY; 2008.

Jones, Capers; *Assessment and Control of Software Risks*; Prentice Hall, 1994; ISBN: 0-13-741406-4; 711 pages.

Jones, Capers; *Becoming Best in Class*; Software Productivity Research, Burlington, MA; January 1998; 40 pages.

Jones, Capers; *Estimating Software Costs*, 2nd ed.; McGraw Hill, New York, NY; 2007.

Jones, Capers; *Patterns of Software System Failure and Success*; International Thomson Computer Press, Boston, MA; December 1995; ISBN: 1-850-32804-8; 250, 292 pages.

Jones, Capers; *Software Assessments, Benchmarks, and Best Practices*; Addison Wesley Longman, Boston, MA; 2000 (due in May of 2000); 600 pages.

Jones, Capers; *Software Engineering Best Practices*, 1st ed.; McGraw Hill, New York, NY; 2010.

Jones, Capers; *Software Quality – Analysis and Guidelines for Success*; International Thomson Computer Press, Boston, MA; 1997a; ISBN: 1-85032-876-6; 492 pages.

Jones, Capers; *The Economics of Object-Oriented Software*; Software Productivity Research, Burlington, MA; April 1997b; 22 pages.

Jones, Capers; *The Technical and Social History of Software Engineering*, Addison Wesley, 2014.

Kan, Stephen H.; *Metrics and Models in Software Quality Engineering*, 2nd ed.; Addison Wesley Longman, Boston, MA; 2003; ISBN: 0-201-72915-6; 528 pages.

Keys, Jessica; *Software Engineering Productivity Handbook*; McGraw Hill, New York, NY; 1993; ISBN: 0-07-911366-4; 651 pages.

Love, Tom; *Object Lessons*; SIGS Books, New York, NY; 1993; ISBN: 0-9627477 3-4; 266 pages.

McCabe, Thomas J.; "A Complexity Measure"; *IEEE Transactions on Software Engineering*; December 1976; pp. 308–320.

McConnell, Steve; *Software Project Survival Guide*; Microsoft Press; 1997.

McMahon, Paul; and Ambler, Scott; *15 Fundamentals for Higher Performance in Software Development*; PEM Systems; 2014.

Melton, Austin; *Software Measurement*; International Thomson Press, London, UK; 1995; ISBN: 1-85032-7178-7.

Multiple authors; *Rethinking the Software Process*; (CD-ROM); Miller Freeman, Lawrence, KS; 1996. (This is a new CD ROM book collection jointly produced by the book publisher, Prentice Hall, and the journal publisher, Miller Freeman. This CD ROM disk contains the full text and illustrations of five Prentice Hall books: *Assessment and Control of Software Risks* by Capers Jones; *Controlling Software Projects* by Tom DeMarco; *Function Point Analysis* by Brian Dreger; *Measures for Excellence* by Larry Putnam and Ware Myers; and *Object-Oriented Software Metrics* by Mark Lorenz and Jeff Kidd.)

Myers, Glenford; *The Art of Software Testing*; John Wiley & Sons, New York, NY; 1979; ISBN: 0-471-04328-1; 177 pages.

Paulk, Mark et al; *The Capability Maturity Model; Guidelines for Improving the Software Process*; Addison Wesley, Reading, MA; 1995; ISBN: 0-201-54664-7; 439 pages.

Perry, William E.; *Data Processing Budgets – How to Develop and Use Budgets Effectively*; Prentice Hall, Englewood Cliffs, NJ; 1985; ISBN: 0-13-196874-2; 224 pages.

Perry, William E.; *Handbook of Diagnosing and Solving Computer Problems*; TAB Books, Inc., Blue Ridge Summit, PA; 1989; ISBN: 0-8306-9233-9; 255 pages.

Pressman, Roger; *Software Engineering – A Practitioner's Approach*, 6th ed.; McGraw Hill, New York, NY; 2005; ISBN: 0-07-285318-2.

Putnam, Lawrence H.; and Myers, Ware; *Industrial Strength Software – Effective Management Using Measurement*; IEEE Press, Los Alamitos, CA; 1997; ISBN: 0-8186-7532-2; 320 pages.

Putnam, Lawrence H.; *Measures for Excellence – Reliable Software On Time, Within Budget*; Yourdon Press, Prentice Hall, Englewood Cliffs, NJ; 1992; ISBN: 0-13-567694-0; 336 pages.

Radice, Ronald A.; *High Qualitiy Low Cost Software Inspections*; Paradoxicon Publishing, Andover, MA; 2002; ISBN: 0-9645913-1-6; 479 pages.

Royce, Walker E.; *Software Project Management: A Unified Framework*; Addison Wesley Longman, Reading, MA; 1998; ISBN: 0-201-30958-0.

Rubin, Howard (Editor); *The Software Personnel Shortage*; Rubin Systems, Inc.; Pound Ridge, NY; 1998.

Rubin, Howard; *Software Benchmark Studies for 1997*; Howard Rubin Associates, Pound Ridge, NY; 1997.

Shepperd, M.: "A Critique of Cyclomatic Complexity as a Software Metric"; *Software Engineering Journal*, Vol. 3; 1988; pp. 30–36.

Starr, Paul; *The Social Transformation of American Medicine*; (Pulitzer Prize and Booker in 1984); Basic Books, 1982. This interesting book summarizes the steps used by the American Medical Association (AMA) to improve medical education and raise the professional status of physicians. The same sequence of steps would benefit software engineering.

Strassmann, Paul; *Governance of Information Management: The Concept of an Information Constitution*, 2nd ed.; (eBook); Information Economics Press, Stamford, CT; 2004.

Strassmann, Paul; *Information Payoff*; Information Economics Press, Stamford, Ct; 1985.

Strassmann, Paul; *Information Productivity*; Information Economics Press, Stamford, CT; 1999.

Strassmann, Paul; *The Squandered Computer*; The Information Economics Press, New Canaan, CT; 1997; ISBN: 0-9620413-1-9; 426 pages.

Stukes, Sherry; Deshoretz, Jason, Apgar, Henry; and Macias, Ilona; *Air Force Cost Analysis Agency Software Estimating Model Analysis*; TR-9545/008-2; Contract F04701-95-D-0003, Task 008; Management Consulting & Research, Inc.; Thousand Oaks, CA; September 30, 1996.

Symons, Charles R.; *Software Sizing and Estimating – Mk II FPA (Function Point Analysis)*; John Wiley & Sons, Chichester; 1991; ISBN: 0 471-92985-9; 200 pages.

Thayer, Richard H. (Editor); *Software Engineering and Project Management*; IEEE Press, Los Alamitos, CA; 1988; ISBN: 0 8186-075107; 512 pages.

Umbaugh, Robert E. (Editor); *Handbook of IS Management*, 4th ed.; Auerbach Publications, Boston, MA; 1995; ISBN: 0-7913-2159-2; 703 pages.

Weinberg, Gerald; *Quality Software Management – Vol. 2: First-Order Measurement*; Dorset House Press, New York, NY; 1993; ISBN: 0-932633-24-2; 360 pages.

Weinberg, Gerald M.; *The Psychology of Computer Programming*; Van Nostrand Reinhold, New York, NY; 1971; ISBN: 0-442-29264-3; 288 pages.

Weinberg, Gerald M.; *Becoming a Technical Leader*; Dorset House Press; New York, NY; 1986; ISBN: 0-932633-02-1; 284 pages.

Wiegers, Karl A.; *Creating a Software Engineering Culture*; Dorset House Press, New York, NY; 1996; ISBN: 0-932633-33-1; 358 pages.

BEST-CASE PATTERNS OF SOFTWARE DEVELOPMENT

This section shows patterns that lead to software success. The data comes from actual companies. The first chapter on Corporate Software Risk Reduction in a Fortune 500 company was based on a major telecom company whose chairman was troubled by repeated software failures.

The other chapters in this section deal with methods of achieving excellence, with measures that can prove excellence to C-level executives, and with continuing excellence through the maintenance cycle as well as for software development.

DOI: 10.1201/9781003193128-9

Chapter 8

Corporate Software Risk Reduction in a Fortune 500 Company

Introduction

Due to schedule delays, cost overruns, and several canceled software projects, the Chairman of a Fortune 500 company decided to bring in outside experts to identify major software risks and develop solutions for those risks.

Initially, the new risk abatement team reported directly to the Chairman, which is unusual but effective. The team visited more than 30 software locations in a dozen countries and met with many software managers and technical personnel.

As the risk abatement program moved into implementation, the head of the team became a corporate vice president and reported to the corporate chief technology officer (CTO). The Chairman remained an active participant and received frequent updates about progress of the risk abatement program throughout its progress.

The corporation was a conglomerate that had grown by acquisition. The major software groups did not know much about other groups elsewhere in the company. Many of the individual units were sophisticated in dealing with local projects. However, large and complex applications that required multisite coordination and cooperation were not usually successful.

The risk team identified a number of areas where improvements would be beneficial both for the individual units and for large multiunit applications. Among the proposed solutions were establishing corporate licenses for tools and methods; standardized quality measurements; and the introduction of pre-test quality control such as inspections and static analysis.

The risk abatement program operated for four years and achieved significant improvements in quality, productivity, and elimination of cost and schedule overruns.

This report describes the method and operation of the risk abatement program and summarizes the results. The final section of this report provides quantified data on the economic value of corporate software process improvement programs.

The chairman of a large manufacturing conglomerate was troubled by several major software failures of projects that were terminated without being completed. He was also troubled by the dissatisfaction expressed by customers in the quality of the software the corporation produced. He was further dissatisfied by the inability of internal software executives to explain why the problems occurred and what might be done to eliminate them.

At the time the corporation was about to embark on a very innovative new product line that would include sophisticated hardware components that were significantly ahead of competitive offerings and contained many unique and patented features. But in order to be effective in the market, the software that operated the products needed to be at state of the art levels in terms of quality, reliability, and security.

The chairman had serious doubts as to whether the software components would be able to meet the same quality and reliability criteria as the hardware components. Without top-quality software, the product lines could not be successful and might not operate well enough to even be marketed.

Given the track record of the company over the past five years, the chairman was also concerned that even if the software could be built well enough to operate effectively, it might be several years late and well over budget.

The chairman was both energetic and far sighted, and he recognized that software throughout the corporation needed to be converted from a liability into an asset. Following are discussions of the features of the corporate risk reduction program.

A National Talent Search

For a variety of reasons, the chairman felt that solving the corporation's software problems required expertise greater than what was available internally. To that end, he commissioned a national talent search for software executives who had been able to bring large and complex software products successfully to market.

An executive from IBM was selected to lead the corporate risk reduction program, but executives from other technical groups such as General Electric, the Air Force, and other technology enterprises were soon recruited.

Fact Finding and Software Assessments

At the time the risk reduction program started, the corporation had about 250,000 employees working in more than 30 countries. But no one knew how many software employees the corporation had.

In part this was due to the use of ambiguous job titles such as "member of the technical staff" in the more technical units. In part it was due to the fact that while financial reports from all units were consolidated, human resource data was largely local.

One of the first tasks of the risk-reduction team was to quickly visit all corporate locations that built software and carry out a census of software personnel, methodologies, tools, and other relevant information.

All of the findings were useful and some were surprising to the chairman and other officers. Here are a few typical data points.

At the time the project started, corporate software employment was about 10,000 total personnel.

Development	3,000
Maintenance	4,000
Support	2,000
Management	1,000
Total	**10,000**

These software workers were divided among some 50 locations in 20 countries. The top location had about 1,200 software personnel. Several locations had about 500 software personnel, and the remainder of the locations had smaller groups of 100 or more, with the very smallest location having only 10 software personnel.

Software Applications in Use

The corporate portfolio of software applications contained about 5,400 applications.

Internal Applications	
IT	1,500
Systems	900
Embedded	600
Support	400
Manufacturing	400
Sub Total	**3,800**
COTS Applications	1,300
Open source	100
User developed	200
Sub Total	**1,600**
Total	**5,400**

The overall size of the corporate portfolio at the time the risk study began was just over 7,000,000 function points using the method of the International Function Point Users Group (IFPUG) as the basis of the size calculation.

In the original study, size was determined by "backfiring" or mathematical conversion between source code counts and function points. Today in 2021, several methods exist for calculating function points in legacy applications. The Software Risk Master™ (SRM) tool developed by the author of this book is one. SRM can also size commercial packages such as Windows 7, Oracle, Linux, and essentially all others. Software Risk Master™ only takes about 1 minute and 30 seconds to size any application.

Other tools can analyze legacy code and extract business rules which can then be turned into a function point prediction. These data mining tools take about 5 to 10 minutes per application based on application size. However, these tools can't be used on commercial packages such as Oracle and SAP where the source code is not available. It is not clear if they support all of the 2,500 programming languages, but they do support at least 25 of the more common languages.

Another interesting fact that was discovered during the fact-finding assessments was that the total annual costs for the portfolio were about $1.5 billion per year. That by itself was not surprising, but several sub costs were alarming.

In the two years prior to the fact-finding assessment, the company had major and sometimes unbudgeted expenses for these topics.

Software bug repairs	$500,000,000
Cancelled projects	$68,000,000
Budget overruns	$67,000,000
Cyber attacks	$35,000,000
Cyber defenses	$30,000,000
Quality litigation	$15,000,000
Total	**$715,000,000**

More than 300,000 bugs were reported each year against the various applications in the corporate portfolio.

It was painfully obvious that quality control and security controls in software needed immediate improvements since almost 50 cents out of every dollar spent on software was going to defect repairs or security problems.

Some other findings were troubling but more easily fixed. A few samples of these other problems are as follows:

- There were no corporate licenses or purchase agreements with vendors of tools or methods. Each location or business unit negotiated their own contracts, so no one was gaining benefits from economies of scale.
- There was no corporate and very few unit measurement programs for either quality or productivity. No one at the corporate level had any idea of how the corporation compared to other similar corporations, or even how the operating units inside the corporation compared to each other.
- More than 75 different programming languages were in use throughout the corporation in random patterns.
- More than 25 different development methodologies were in use throughout the corporation in random patterns.
- More than 600 tools from more than 75 vendors were in use in random patterns. IBM was the largest single vendor because of the numbers of mainframes, but dozens of other companies also had contracts and provided products and services including SAP, Oracle, PeopleSoft, Computer Associates, Computer Sciences Corporation, MicroFocus, Mercury, and many others. Each unit had their own contracts rather than having a corporate contract that would provide economies of scale.
- The number of days of training provided to software personnel and software managers ranged from 0 to 3 days per year per person.

- Software personnel number had been increasing at 5% per year for the past five years, with no sign of any planned reductions in the future.

After the risk reduction team finished with the fact finding assessments, the next step was to prepare a presentation for the chairman, the board, and senior executives to discuss the logistics of risk reduction and process improvement.

The Initial Report to the Chairman

Since the chairman had a strong financial and accounting background, he understood and demanded accurate quantified data. One of the reasons he brought in outside executives to help in the risk reduction program was because there was a shortage of accurate quantified data about software in every aspect: personnel, quality, schedules, costs, occupation groups, and every other measurable topic either had no data at all or no reliable data.

The basic message to the chairman and the other corporate executives was essentially the following:

> *You have a current software headcount of about 10,000 people. The headcount has been growing at 5% per year and will continue to grow at that rate for at least five more years unless you intervene.*
>
> *In round numbers about 50 cents out of every dollar you spend on software goes to defect removal, canceled projects, or recovering from cyber-attacks. Your quality control methods lag the state of the art, as do your security methods.*
>
> *If the company continues on the current path in nine years you will have 15,000 software people and in 15 years you will have 20,000 software people. You will still be spending 50 cents out of every dollar on defect repairs and security problems.*
>
> *Your ability to successfully develop large applications >10,000 function points is currently inadequate. Small projects <1,000 function points are often successful. Too many large projects are terminated without completion and all of the rest of your large projects are at least 12 months late when delivered. Quality lags leading corporations and this is why you spend 50 cents out of every dollar finding and fixing bugs.*
>
> *If you fix quality now by using inspections, static analysis, models, better development methodologies, quality measurements, and better test methods and some additional tools you can free up about 40% of*

your current software work force for other tasks. These personnel can either reduce the corporate backlog to zero or they can assist on critical projects that might be short handed.

If you fix your quality and security problems you can stop increasing software personnel and reach a steady state at about 9,000 people, which is all the corporation really needs to support its overall population and growth plans.

If you fix your quality and security problems you will not have to worry that the software side of the company is less competent than the hardware side. They will both be at state of the art levels. This means that future hybrid products will not be held back by today's software problems.

It will cost about $15,000,000 the first year to improve quality, but you will get a positive return on this investment by the end of the second year. Quality can be improved by more than 25% per calendar year for at least five years in a row, and it is the only effective place to start because defect repairs are your major cost driver at the corporate level.

Although there was some discussion about logistical topics and the nature of the methods to be deployed, there was no disagreement to the essential message. The chairman approved and the risk-reduction activities commenced at once.

The overall set of internal software risk factors noted during the on-site assessments included the following 25 problems.

Corporate Software Risk Factors Found by the Initial Assessment

1. Project management: no annual training in state of the art methods.
2. Project management: no training in cost estimating.
3. Project management: no training in quality estimating.
4. Project management: no training in risk analysis.
5. Project management: no training in schedule planning.
6. Project management: lack of productivity measurements.
7. Project management: partial quality metrics.
8. Project management: total lack of productivity metrics.
9. Project management: incomplete milestone tracking.
10. Quality control: no use of formal design inspections.
11. Quality control: no use of formal code inspections.
12. Quality control: no use of static analysis tools.
13. Maintenance: no use of complexity analysis.

14. Maintenance: no use of code restructuring tools.
15. Maintenance: inconsistent use of defect tracking tools.
16. Maintenance: no use of inspections on enhancements.
17. No reuse program: requirements.
18. No reuse program: design.
19. No reuse program: source code.
20. No reuse program: test materials.
21. No reuse program: documentation.
22. No reuse program: project plans.
23. Office space: small open offices; high noise levels, many interruptions.
24. Insufficient meeting/breakout space for team meetings.
25. No large conference facility for lab meetings.

Unfortunately, these 25 problems are endemic in the software industry. The same set probably applies to about 85% of Fortune 500 companies even today in 2021.

Another part of the presentation was a proposal to build a major software engineering lab that could go beyond basic quality improvements and identify or develop software technologies at or beyond the current state of the art.

It is the role and structure of this software engineering lab that can serve as a possible model for other major corporations that are dissatisfied with the status quo of software and would like to reduce software risks on major applications.

The Corporate Risk Reduction Strategy: Fix Quality First

Because quality control and security control were visible weaknesses, they needed to be fixed first. That brings up an interesting question: how do you get a disparate corporate organization of 10,000 people scattered among some 50 locations to adopt better quality methods and also start quality measurements?

One of the first steps was to send out several pathfinders to the major software locations. These pathfinders gave presentations to senior management at the units which mirrored the corporate message:

> *You have X number of people and they are increasing at 5% per year. You are spending half of your budget on bug repairs and that will continue forever unless we can introduce better quality methods.*

We are not trying to force inspections, static analysis, and other new quality methods on your teams against their wills. We would like you to try the methods on an experimental basis and let the teams decide if the results are useful.

If your teams do like the methods we can then provide local training for everyone. We also have corporate licensing agreements that will give you a substantial discount compared to your local license agreements for a number of tools and some methods as well.

If your teams don't like the methods they don't have to use them, but you will be responsible for your total unit achieving the same quality levels as the units that do use them.

One of the best ways of introducing new methodologies, and especially methods such as inspections that require training, is to treat them as experiments with the understanding that if the teams don't like the results, they won't be forced to continue. As this happens, inspections are so effective that the teams almost always do want to continue.

If a few teams reject the idea at first, they soon notice that everyone is using the new methods and getting great results, so resistance does not last for long.

Measurement is a more difficult problem. Companies are very political and operating units often have rivalries with other operating units. A consolidated measurement program that tracked every unit using the same metrics is an alarming idea. The local managers are all afraid that they won't look as good as their rivals, so they will resist any attempt to measure performance. Their usual argument runs along these lines:

Measurement is very important and of course I support it. But our work is so different and so complex that I don't think it will work for us....

Since the risk-reduction team had no direct authority over unit managers, we had no way of insisting that measures take place at the individual units. However, the chairman had a personal interest in measurements and he made several calls to reluctant unit managers that convinced them to participate in the new corporate measurement program.

A final task for the pathfinders was to ask that each unit with a software group appoints a local software technology interface point that would communicate with the new software research group that was being formed. The reason for this is to have a firm contact point for mutual exchanges of technical and logistical information.

The corporate team would pass on new information about corporate licenses for tools and methodologies, and the unit reps would let the corporate group know about tools and methods that they might like to have evaluated for possible corporate licensing.

The overall targets for the corporate risk reduction program included the following 20 topics that spanned a four-year risk reduction time span:

Four-Year Software Risk Reduction Targets

1. Set aside 12 days a year for training in software management topics.
2. Set aside 10 days a year for training in software process improvement topics.
3. Establish local software "centers for excellence" in major software units.
4. Budget $10,000 per capita for improved tools and training over 4 years.
5. Achieve Level 3 status on the SEI CMM maturity scale.
6. No more than 5% difference between estimated schedules and real delivery dates.
7. No more than 5% difference between estimated costs and actual costs.
8. Raise defect removal efficiency above 97% as the corporate average.
9. Reduce defect potentials below 3.0 per function point as the corporate average.
10. Reduce development schedules or intervals by 50% from requirements until delivery.
11. Raise development productivity rates by more than 50%.
12. Reduce development costs by more than 40%.
13. Reduce maintenance costs by 50% for first two years of deployment.
14. Achieve more than 50% reusability by volume for design, code, and test artifacts.
15. Establish an in-house measurement department in every major software unit.
16. Publish monthly reports on software quality and defect removal.
17. Publish overall results in an annual "state of the art" report for group executives.
18. Change the office layouts to provide more small meeting rooms.
19. Attempt to improve the soundproofing of development office space.
20. Experiment with large-scale in-house webinars in place of lab meetings.

As can be seen, the corporate risk reduction strategy covered a wide range of software issues. However, since software engineering is not very sophisticated in 2021, it is necessary to deal with a wide variety of endemic problems.

Creating a Software Engineering Laboratory

A major aspect of the risk reduction program was the creation of a new software engineering laboratory reporting to the corporate vice president of technology. This lab was intended to provide support to all software units in North America, Europe, and the Pacific Rim.

This lab would eventually grow to a size of about 150 personnel. It was divided into a number of operating units with the following responsibilities:

Education

This was one of the first groups formed and one of the largest with a peak of about 50 personnel. This group was responsible for training corporate software groups in every country and every operating unit. Courses in inspections, design techniques, software reuse, quality measurements, cost estimating, and many others were included in their curricula. Eventually, about 30 courses were available for both technical personnel and management personnel.

The education teams travelled widely to many locations and provided courses on demand, and also courses that were necessary for quality improvement such as formal inspections and measurements.

External educators were also hired, and some of the following top experts in the world were used: Dr. Barry Boehm, Dr. Gerry Weinberg, Tom Gilb, Dr. Fred Brooks, and a number of others.

Applied Technology

The applied technology unit reached a peak of about 30 research personnel. It was responsible for examining and certifying methods and tools that would be helpful to the corporate software community. Once tools or methods were certified as being valuable, then corporate licenses would be drawn up with the assistance of the corporate purchasing and legal departments.

Examples of applied technology tools and methods included inspections, static analysis tools, automated test tools, cost estimating tools, requirements tools, requirements methods such as joint application design (JAD) and quality function deployment (QFD), design tools, design methods such as the unified modeling language (UML), and many others.

The applied technology group also supported corporate reusability programs by providing information to each operating unit about the availability of reusable artifacts that had been developed by every unit. Essentially, this group produced a catalog of corporate reusable software assets.

Advanced Technology

This unit reached a peak of about 20 research personnel. It was responsible for designing and building custom solutions that were in advance of the normal state of the art. This group built a very powerful object-oriented language, a proprietary design method, and several other innovative tools and methods.

Measurements

This unit reached a peak of about 12 personnel. One of the most visible gaps in the software groups throughout the corporation was the almost total lack of effective productivity and quality measurements. The most unique production of the measurement group was an annual report which was created at the same calendar time as the corporate annual report for shareholders, i.e. in the first quarter after the end of a fiscal year.

The annual software report summarized progress for every major operating unit, compared current year results to prior year results, and discussed plans for the next year. The annual report was distributed to the CEO, chairman, operating unit presidents, and all C level executives at the CIO, CTO level, and above. This report was a showcase for progress and demonstrated that investment in better software methods paid valuable dividends.

Because this annual report was a critical part of the corporate software risk reduction program, the following are some of the topics it contained:

- Demographic data of software employment in every operating unit.
- Benchmark results for annual productivity by operating unit and type of software.

- Benchmark results for annual quality by operating unit and type of software.
- Annual volumes of customer-reported defects sorted by several categories.
- Annual volumes of identified security flaws and security attacks.
- Annual expenses for defect repairs.
- Annual expenses for security problems.
- Comparisons of current year results to prior year results.
- Predictions of future year results compared to current year results.

Every company should produce such an annual report for executives. Although much of the data is proprietary and confidential, these annual reports are among the most effective tools for long-range risk reductions.

Communications

This unit reached a peak of about 20 people and fulfilled a variety of functions. They sponsored two large conferences per year. One conference was technical in nature and only open to corporate software personnel. This conference discussed proprietary technologies. The second conference was more public and selected customers, distinguished academics, and even some competitors were invited. This second conference was intended to be a showcase that illustrated the corporate commitment to state of the art software engineering practices.

In addition to conferences, the communications group published monthly newsletters, initiated a series of technical reports by software unit authors, and created a very sophisticated software journal that was modeled after Scientific American Magazine. This magazine had a two-fold purpose: (1) to provide a suitable venue for innovative information created by top researchers within the company and (2) to impress both clients and competitors with the software engineering expertise of the corporation. This two-fold purpose attracted new clients and also made it easy to attract top-gun software engineers away from competitors.

To encourage employees in various operating units to publish, a corporate policy was put in place that all royalties for technical books and articles published by corporate employees went to the employees. If the company tried to keep royalties under the Draconian terms of many employment agreements, no one would be motivated to write. Allowing authors to keep royalties is the policy adopted by most of the really innovative high technology companies.

In addition, the communications group could help with technical production issues such as graphics production which not all authors are comfortable doing.

Administration

Like every operating unit, the software engineering laboratory needed financial personnel, human resource personnel, secretarial support, and other standard logistical topics. This group fluctuated in size as demands increased.

Results of the Corporate Risk Reduction Program

Although there was some resistance to change at the beginning of the program, it soon began to be accepted because the quality improvements occurred within the first few months and continued to get better for four years.

Since quality improvements were the initial and primary target of the risk reduction program, Table 8.1 shows the approximate results for the program over a four-year period.

There were also improvements in development productivity, maintenance productivity, customer satisfaction, and team morale.

After four years of progress with the corporate risk reduction and process improvement program, there was a major corporate change. The corporation sold all of the high-technology business and their operating units and laboratories to another company. About 50% of total corporate personnel were part of this divestiture.

Table 8.1 Four-Year Improvement from Inspections and Testing Upgrades

Baseline	Defect Potential	Defect Removal	Delivered Defects	Percent Improvement
Month 0	5.25	83%	0.89	0.00%
Month 12	5.15	87%	0.67	75.01%
Month 24	4.65	92%	0.37	55.56%
Month 36	4.30	96%	0.17	46.24%
Month 48	3.60	98%	0.07	41.86%

Note: Table 8.1 expresses data using IFPUG function points.

The acquiring company decided to keep only the manufacturing facilities and close the research labs since they already had similar research labs of their own. As a result, the software engineering research lab and several other technical labs in both the U.S. and Europe were closed.

However, informal contacts with the operating units showed continued success from the risk reduction program.

The corporate risk reduction team established 50 goals that were targeted over a four-year period (Table 8.2).

These goals and their schedule timelines were shown and approved by the chairman and top officers as well as by unit executives.

Cost Justifying a Corporate Risk Reduction Program

A major corporate-wide risk reduction and process improvement program is of necessity, an expensive proposition. It requires funding approval at the highest level. It must also generate a positive return on investment by the end of the second year, and the ROI should continue to go up in future years. A well-planned corporate risk reduction program in an "average" Fortune 500 company should return at least $10.00 for every $1.00 spent over a four-year time window.

The most obvious value for a risk reduction program will be reduction in costs for software defect repairs, security attacks, and other negative cost elements.

However, a successful risk reduction program will have subtle and less obvious benefits. For example in this case study, the program would free up about 1,000 personnel from defect repair tasks and make them available for more productive work such as reducing the corporate backlog of applications.

Since a successful risk reduction program will lead to shorter schedules, this means quicker revenue streams for commercial products with software components as key features.

The total direct costs of the software risk reduction program for the software engineering lab was about $18,000,000 per year. This is a major expense and therefore needs to demonstrate a positive return on investment.

The operating unit costs across the 50 units with software were about $25,000.000 per year or roughly $2,500 per capita. These costs were for training and the deployment of selected tools and methods (Table 8.3).

As pointed out earlier, risk reduction and software process improvement are not inexpensive. In this case study, a total of $10,000 per capita was set aside for risk and process improvement expenses such as training, tool acquisition, consulting fees, etc.

Table 8.2 **Four-Year Sequence of Risk Reduction Tasks**

	Recommendations/Goals	Schedule Months
1	Evaluate security flaws in portfolio	1
2	Use security inspections for new apps	1
3	Evaluate agile before adoption	2
4	Use static analysis where possible	3
5	Include quality in outsource contracts	4
6	Use Code inspections >500 FP	4
7	Use Design inspections >1,000 FP	4
8	Use formal estimates >1,000 FP	6
9	Use formal milestones >1,000 FP	6
10	Deploy TSP/PSP on key projects	6
11	Deploy RUP on key IT projects	6
12	Establish corporate education curricula	6
13	Use formal defect tracking	7
14	Measure defect detection efficiency (DDE)	8
15	Measure defect removal efficiency (DRE)	8
16	Eliminate all error-prone modules	9
17	Use "data mining" on legacy apps	9
18	Use formal change control	9
19	Include quality in executive appraisals	12
20	Measure customer satisfaction	12
21	Measure delivered defects	12
22	Pilot studies of QFD	12
23	Pilot studies of SOA	12
24	Use JAD on IT >1,000 FP	12
25	Use six-sigma for embedded software	12
26	Use six-sigma for systems software	12
27	Achieve >95% defect removal	12
28	Improve defect repair time by 25%	12
29	Train 6 function point counters	12

Table 8.2 (Continued)

	Recommendations/Goals	Schedule Months
30	Provide 5 days of management training	12
31	Perform annual assessments	12
32	Perform annual benchmark studies	12
33	Reduce bad fixes to <2%	14
34	Adopt major ISO quality standards	14
35	Provide 10 days of staff training per year	18
36	Adopt function point metrics	18
37	Defect potentials <3.0 per FP	18
38	Provide 3 days of executive training	18
39	Quality improves >15% per year	24
40	Eliminate high-severity defects	24
41	Establish corporate skills inventory	24
42	Average > Level 3 on CMM	36
43	Improvement budget > $10,000 per cap.	36
44	Productivity gains >10% per year	36
45	Reduce Cost overruns <5%	36
46	Reduce Schedule slippage <5%	36
47	Requirements creep <0.5%	36
48	Cancelled projects = 0	48
49	Renovate critical applications	48
50	Achieve CMMI 5 in key units	48

The software personnel in the case study were stated to comprise 10,000 workers and managers, which implies that the total expenses for software process improvement activities amounted to $100,000,000 over a four-year period.

A cost of $100,000,000 over four years is a large number. That brings up the question of what kinds of savings will be generated? This question can be answered but it is a complex question because the savings will change every year.

Table 8.4 shows the current costs for various risk-related work activities and the projected savings from the risk reduction program.

Table 8.3   Annual Costs for the Risk Reduction Program

	Annual Costs
Software Research Lab costs	$18,000,000
Unit annual costs	$25,000,000
Total	**$43,000,000**

Table 8.4   Target Cost Reductions from the Corporate Risk Program

Major Software Risks	Annual Costs	Target Amount	Savings
Excessive bug repairs	$500,000,000	$75,000,000	$425,000,000
Cost overruns	$68,000,000	$10,000,000	$58,000,000
Schedule overruns	$67,000,000	$5,000,000	$62,000,000
Canceled projects	$50,000,000	$5,000,000	$45,000,000
Loss of customers	$25,000,000	$2,000,000	$23,000,000
Litigation: breach of contract	$15,000,000	$0	$15,000,000
Security attacks	$30,000,000	$3,000,000	$27,000,000
Total	**$755,000,000**	**$100,000,000**	**$655,000,000**

As can be seen from Tables 8.3 and 8.4, the corporate risk reduction program was expected to yield direct savings of about $655,000,000 per year for a cost of $43,000,000 per year. This is an ROI of about $15 for every $ 1 expended. However, there are additional and more subtle benefits that can also be calculated.

A software group with a total employment of 10,000 personnel will normally be able to develop about 420,000 function points per year and maintain about 1,250,000 function points per year. Although the situation is more complex in real life, let us assume that 50% of personnel are on the development side and 50% of the personnel are on the maintenance side. To further simplify, let us assume that half of the $100,000,000 for process improvements will go to the development side and half will go to the maintenance side.

Cost Recovery on the Development Side

Assume that the original baseline average productivity was 7 function points per staff month for development, which amounts to 84 function points per year per person. Assuming 5,000 development personnel and 84 function points per year, the annual rate of new work is 420,000 function points.

Since 5,000 personnel with fully burdened compensation rates of $120,000 per year have annual expenses of $600,000,000, it can be seen that the development cost per function point for the organization amounts to roughly $1,429 per function point for new function points added to the corporate inventory.

Without the process improvement program, the development group would have created 1,680,000 new function points over the four-year period shown in the case study. However, as a result of the improvement program, assume the average rate went from 7 to about 10 function points per month over the four-year improvement program.

Thus instead of creating 1,680,000 function points in four years, the same group of 5,000 development personnel would be able to create 600,000 function per year or 2,400,000 function points in the same four-year period.

Using only the principles of cost recovery, the 720,000 additional function points at a value of $1,429 per function point means additional corporate software assets worth $1,028,880,000 were created as a byproduct of an investment of $43,000,000 per year. These are not cost reductions but actual assets that might be added to the corporate books.

Because inspections and static analysis tools make significant improvements in software quality before testing begins, a major focus of improved performance will be in the test and quality control areas. It can be expected that fewer bugs will be found during testing, which can lead to fewer builds and fewer test runs, and hence fewer test personnel combined with much quicker test schedules.

Indeed improving quality exerts the greatest overall impact from process improvements. As a result of process improvements that include inspections and static analysis, probably 25% of test personnel will become available for other assignments.

Cost Recovery on the Maintenance Side

An even more significant aspect of cost recovery can be achieved on the maintenance side of the case study. Of the 5,000 personnel on the maintenance side, about 2,500 will be working on enhancements. Obviously, these personnel will be more productive too, so value will be associated with their higher output.

The other 2,500 maintenance personnel spend much of their time on software defect repairs. Now fixing bugs has been a necessary and expensive activity for software groups ever since the industry began.

Although bug repairs are needed to stay in business, every dollar spent on fixing bugs after a product is released is really a subtraction from the bottom line and should be viewed as a liability.

The greatly improved quality levels associated with the risk reduction and process improvement program will probably cut down the number of full-time staff working on bug repairs from 2,500 down to about 1,500 and hence free up 1,000 personnel for other assignments.

This means that the software risk reduction and process improvement program will unexpectedly free up about 10% of the total software employment, or a set of 1,000 experienced personnel, who are no longer going to be locked into heavy-duty bug repairs and customer support tasks.

This is the basis of the earlier statement that the corporation only needed 9,000 software people to support the operating units.

Assuming $120,000 a year for burdened compensation that was stated, this means a possible savings of $120,000,000 a year. The following are several options, which the corporate operating unit executives can consider as to how to best utilize the windfall of 1,000 spare personnel:

1. They can be reassigned to development and thereby raise software production by about 120,000 function points per year. At the assumed cost of $1,429 per function point, this would supply added value at a rate of $171,480,000 per year.
2. They could be assigned to maintenance projects not discussed in this report such as projects which have been put on hold due to lack of resources. Many companies have projects that are more or less frozen, and these include many enhancements to legacy applications. Thus, the windfall of extra maintenance staffing could be used to modernize many aging applications that might otherwise continue in some disrepair.
3. They can be "downsized" or transferred to other labs and locations within the company and removed from local payrolls. However, since most locations have a shortage of software personnel, this is unlikely to occur.

Empirical observations indicate that restructuring of aging applications and removal of error-prone modules can reduce overall maintenance costs by more than 50%. Expressed in terms of function point metrics, changes to existing applications can increase from about 15 function points per staff month to more than 30 function points per staff month. The number of customer-reported defects repaired per staff month can increase from about 8 to more than 12. The maintenance assignment scope, or amount of software maintained by one specialist, can increase from less than 1,000 to more than 3,000 function points.

In any case, the significant increase in software quality and resulting decrease in software defect repairs is one of the most valuable aspects of the process improvement program. Here too, returns in the vicinity of $15.00 can be projected for every $1.00 expended, although the exact ROI must be calculated for each company and each specific situation.

Asset Value of a Library of Reusable Artifacts

A typical Fortune 500 corporation owns a software portfolio or library that totals somewhere between 250,000 function points to more than 7,500,000 function points of software applications. The corporate portfolio for this case study totaled to about 7,000,000 function points.

Prior to the commencement of the formal risk reduction and process improvement program, about 15% of this volume was derived from reusable materials. However, much of the normal day to day reuse is in the form of "private" reuse by individual technical personnel. Private reuse may be valuable to individual programmers, but much of the value is invisible in the sense of having any tangible value on corporate books.

As a result of the emphasis on formal reuse as part of the planned risk reduction and process improvement program, the total volume of reusable artifacts owned by the enterprise may total to 500,000 function points after four years.

A library of certified reusable artifacts is a valuable corporate asset. However, the value of a library of reusable software assets may have tax consequences in the United States, so companies are advised to seek legal counsel about the implications of Internal Revenue Service Code Rule 482.

The essence of Rule 482 is that when one division or affiliate in a controlled group of related corporations such as a conglomerate or multinational company provides goods or services to another division, these goods or services may be treated by the IRS as though they were taxable income to the receiving division. This is potentially a "stake through the heart" of a formal corporate reuse program in multinational corporations.

For example, if Division A of Mega Company in San Jose supplies 1,000 function points of reusable artifacts to Division B in Boston, then the transfer may be treated as a taxable transaction by the IRS.

Of course, if the enterprise is not a U.S. corporation or if the transfers are made abroad, such as transferring reusable assets between London and Paris, then Rule 482 may not apply.

In any case, a formal library of reusable artifacts is a valuable corporate asset and that raises questions of how to determine the value. Since reusable artifacts are more difficult to develop than normal software, their costs are often about 30% to 50% higher than "normal" artifacts of the same nature.

Let us assume that the case study company has developed a library of 100,000 function points of reusable materials at an average cost of $2,000 per function point. Thus, the replacement value of these artifacts would amount to $200,000,000.

However, if each of these reusable artifacts is reused an average of 10 times, and each instance of reuse saves 70% of normal development costs, then the effective value of the library of reusable artifacts would amount to about $980,000,000. This value assumes a "normal" development cost of about $1,400 per function point where each reused function point saves 70% or $980.

As can be seen, calculating the real value of a library of reusable artifacts is a fairly complex situation. The replacement costs of the reusable assets themselves can be calculated fairly easily. However, the true business value of the library of reusable artifacts is more complex and requires analysis of normal development costs, the effectiveness of the reusable materials in reducing those costs, and the number of times each artifact is reused during its life expectancy.

These calculations assume reusable artifacts that are of zero-defect status. If any of the reusable artifacts contain serious flaws or bugs (say a latent year 2,000 bug embedded in a reusable module), then the value of the reusable artifact will be degraded by the recall and repair costs.

Adding Value through Shorter Development Schedules

One of the primary benefits of a software risk reduction and process improvement program is the ability to shorten typical software development schedules by 50% to 70% compared to the initial baseline. The main technology for achieving shorter schedules is of course having significant volumes of reusable artifacts available.

The direct beneficiaries of the shorter development schedules are the clients and users of the software applications that result. There may well be substantial financial benefits accruing from these shorter schedules, but the quantification of such values must be derived from the nature of the business activities that can commence earlier or from the business improvements that result from more rapid turnaround times.

For example, if a company can bring out a new product 50% faster than their main competitors as a result of their software process improvement activities, then no doubt significant business value and revenues will result. However, quantifying this value requires specific knowledge about the revenue stream of the product in question and does not lend itself to abstract generalization.

Adding Value through Higher Revenues

Thus far we have discussed value only in the form of cost recovery to recoup the $100,000,000 investment in risk reduction and process improvement by lowering in-house development costs and raising internal productivity rates.

However if some of the software is part of marketed products, or is itself commercially marketed, then the software process improvement program can also generate value by raising revenues.

The following three aspects of the process improvement program can benefit software-related revenue streams:

1. The shorter development schedules will get products to the market faster.
2. The higher quality levels will increase market shares.
3. The higher quality levels will reduce maintenance and warranty costs.

These three phenomena are both known to occur when software processes are improved, but their value is too specific to individual products and to focused markets to allow general rules of thumb to be developed.

Adding Value from Disaster Avoidance

Because many large software projects are cancelled or fail to perform when installed, an additional value of process improvement is that of avoiding the consequences of software disasters. Unfortunately, this kind of value is hard to quantify. When disasters do occur, their costs are highly visible. But if no disasters occur, then there is no way of being sure how many might have occurred under less stringent development practices.

For the U.S. as a whole, cancelled projects cost about 10% more than successfully completed projects of the same, but obviously provide zero value combined with massive losses. For large corporations that are building software applications >10,000 function points in size, one of the greatest value topics from process improvement is that of reduced risks of outright failure. For the company cited in this case study, cancelled projects would accrue costs of more than $1,600 per function point as opposed to only $1,400 per function point for successful projects.

Adding Value from Reduced Litigation Risk

The author of this book often works as an expert witness in software lawsuits where applications either did not get finished or worked so poorly when deployed as to be unusable. Litigation costs can be enormous, and litigation can absorb hundreds of staff and executive hours for several years. Here too the value of litigation avoidance is hard to quantify.

Adding Value from Improved Staff and Management Morale

No one likes to work on poorly planned and carelessly executed projects. Everyone likes to work on projects that are successful and yield good customer satisfaction. Therefore another form of value from process excellence is very high morale levels on the part of both managers and staff. This in turn yields very low voluntary attrition rates, and a very good "team spirit" among the software community. If voluntary employment declines from 3% per year to less than 1% per year, it is possible to quantify the savings in recruitment and training costs. However, collecting the data for this kind of value analysis is outside the scope of normal quality and productivity measurements.

Adding Value from Recruiting and Keeping Top-Ranked Personnel

One interesting phenomenon was first noted in the 1970s and remains true in 2011. Technical personnel who quit a company voluntarily are often the best qualified and have the highest appraisal scores. The following are two reasons for this: (1) top technical personnel are the most frustrated with poor performance and bad management; (2) top technical personnel are the ones most likely to be sought by other companies and professional recruiters. Therefore once a company gets a reputation in the industry as being a high-performance organization, they can attract the best people in the industry. Of course this means that companies with excellent technological prowess must also have good compensation and benefits plans.

Adding Value from Customer Loyalty

Customers quickly learn to avoid vendors with shoddy goods. Conversely, customers tend to buy multiple products from vendors with excellent manufacturing and customer support quality levels. Therefore, an investment in achieving software excellence will yield returns through customer loyalty. Here too the data for this kind of value analysis is outside the scope of normal quality and productivity measurements.

Overall Value from Effective Process Improvements

At the start of the four-year process improvement program, the corporation had 10,000 personnel and an annual budget of $1,200,000,000. After a few years 1,000 maintenance personnel became available for other work due to better quality. This is the basis for the earlier assertion that the company only needed 9,000 software personnel.

The tangible values of the improvement program were to increase annual function point production from 126,000 function points over a three-year period to 180,000 function points. The additional function points have a replacement value of more than $77,000,000.

The maintenance savings due to better quality freed up 100 maintenance personnel which indicate savings of $12,000,000 per year or about $28,000,000 for the three-year period (no savings occur for the first six months).

The asset value of a library of 100,000 reusable function points is about $200,000,000. Of course each reusable function point generates savings of about $980 each time it is utilized. Assuming an average of 10 reuses and reusable function points, the savings would be about $98,000,000.

Not all risk reduction and process improvement programs are as successful as the one discussed in this book. Indeed some are abandoned or have only minimal value. But a well-planned process improvement program can generate a wide array of both significant cost savings and also recurring revenues.

Summary and Conclusions

The phrase "software risk reduction" covers a very wide spectrum of methodologies, tools, quality control methods, project management functions, and enhanced volumes of reusable artifacts.

Although the literature on software risk reduction and process improvement is quite large and growing larger, much of the information is subjective and deals with qualitative factors. If the concept of risk reduction and software process improvement is going to become a permanent fixture of the software engineering world, then it must begin to augment subjective observations with quantitative information based on empirical baseline and benchmark studies.

This report covers some of the highlights of the economics of risk reduction software process improvement using a case study approach. But this report is intended simply to illustrate the basic structure of software process risk reduction economics. There is a continuing need for more extensive coverage in the software literature using both case studies and statistical analysis of software risk reduction and process improvement results.

Qualitative information is useful but not sufficient. Software risk reduction process improvements need to be firmly based on solid empirical findings.

Appendix A: Master List of 210 Corporate Software Risks

The following list of 210 software risks show how diverse software risks can be. Not only technical risks but also sociological and ethical risks are common.

One of the most widespread risk categories is that of "knowledge risks" or the fact that many software engineers and project managers are not properly trained for the work at hand (Table 8.A.1).

References and Readings

Gack, Gary; *Managing the Black Hole: The Executives Guide to Software Project Risk*; Business Expert Publishing, Thomson, GA; 2010; ISBN: 10: 1-935602-01-9.

Galorath, Dan; *Software Sizing, Estimating, and Risk Management: When Performance is Measured Performance Improves*; Auerbach Publishing, Philadelphia, PA; 2006; ISBN: 10: 0849335930; 576 pages.

Garmus, David; and Herron, David; *Function Point Analysis – Measurement Practices for Successful Software Projects*; Addison Wesley Longman, Boston, MA; 2001; ISBN: 0-201-69944-3; 363 pages.

Table 8.A.1   Master List of 210 Software Risk for 2020

		Severity
Health and Safety Risks		
1	Risk of application failure causing death	10.00
2	Risk of application failure causing serious illness or injuries	10.00
3	Risk of application violating FDA or other regulations	9.95
4	Risk of application failure damaging medical activates	9.90
5	Risk of application causing environmental damages	9.80
6	Risk of team fatigue due to excessive overtime	8.00
Security Risks		
7	Risk of loss or theft of proprietary source code	10.00
8	Risk of electromagnetic pulse shutting down software	10.00
9	Risk of application failure degrading national security	10.00
10	Risk of data theft from application	10.00
11	Risk of physical security breach at software locations	10.00
12	Risk of poor security flaw removal	9.90
13	Risk of security flaws in application	9.75
14	Risk of poor security flaw prevention	9.60
15	Risk of violating the 25 SANS coding problems	9.50
16	Risk of security flaws in uncertified reused code	9.50
17	Risk of deliberate "back door" traps placed by developers	9.00
18	Risk of theft of intellectual property	8.50
Quality Risks		
19	Risk of excessive defect levels: > 6.0 per function point	10.00
20	Risk of defect removal efficiency <85%	10.00
21	Risk of poor data quality with serious errors	9.90
22	Risk of inadequate defect removal methods, low efficiency	9.80
23	Risk of poor estimation of bugs, defect removal efficiency	9.50
24	Risk of premature application release with excessive bugs	9.50
25	Risk of not using pre-test inspections: requirements, design	9.50

(Continued)

Table 8.A.1 (Continued)

		Severity
26	Risk of poor test case and test script design methods	9.40
27	Risk of poor test library controls	9.40
28	Risk of testing with amateurs rather than professionals	9.40
29	Risk of high code complexity that raises "bad fixes" > 10%	9.25
30	Risk of error-prone modules in application	9.25
31	Risk of claiming to use inspections, but only partially	9.00
32	Risk of late and inadequate defect tracking	9.00
33	Risk of poor test coverage	8.75
34	Risk of poor quality in COTS packages	8.75
35	Risk of insufficient Quality Assurance (QA) reviews	8.75
36	Risk of poor quality in reused components	8.50
37	Risk of not using pre-test static analysis of source code	8.50
38	Risk of understaffing Quality Assurance	8.25
39	Risk of poor quality in outsourced projects	8.25
40	Risk of errors or bugs in test cases	8.00
41	Risk of low operational reliability	7.50
42	Risk of poor quality by open-source providers	7.50
43	Risk of duplicate test cases	7.00
Legal Risks		
44	Risks of patent litigation from competitors	10.00
45	Risk of Federal anti-trust litigation for dominant applications	10.00
46	Risk of inadequate warranties for quality and security	9.75
47	Risk of Sarbanes Oxley litigation	9.75
48	Risk of incurring contract penalties	9.50
49	Risk of poorly constructed contracts that leave out risks	9.50
50	Risk of poorly constructed contracts that leave out quality	9.50
51	Risk of former employees violating non-compete agreements	9.25
52	Risk of breach of contract litigation on outsourced projects	9.00
53	Risk of application failure causing violations of laws	9.00

Table 8.A.1 (Continued)

		Severity
54	Risk of "cease and desist" warnings of alleged patent flaws	8.25
Traditional Software Risks		
55	Risk of toxic requirements that should be avoided	10.00
56	Risk of inadequate progress tracking	9.80
57	Risk of development tasks interfering with maintenance	9.70
58	Risk of maintenance tasks interfering with development	9.50
59	Risk that designs are not kept updated after release	9.25
60	Risk of unstable user requirements growth >1% per month	9.25
61	Risk that requirements are not kept updated after release	9.25
62	Risk of clients forcing arbitrary schedules on team	9.10
63	Risk of omitting formal architecture for large systems	9.10
64	Risk of inadequate change control	9.00
65	Risk of executives forcing arbitrary schedules on team	8.80
66	Risk of not using a project office for large applications	8.75
67	Risk of missing requirements from legacy applications	8.50
68	Risk of missing user requirements due to user uncertainty	8.00
69	Risk of slow application response times	8.00
70	Risk of inadequate maintenance tools and workbenches	8.00
71	Risk of application performance problems	8.00
72	Risk of poor support by open-source providers	7.75
73	Risk of reusing code without test cases or related materials	7.00
74	Risk of excessive feature "bloat"	7.00
75	Risk of inadequate development tools	6.50
76	Risk of poor help screens and poor user manuals	6.00
77	Risk of slow customer support	6.00
78	Risk of inadequate functionality	6.00
Financial Risks		
79	Risk of application failure causing major financial loss	10.00
80	Risk of consequential damages > $1,000,000,000	10.00

(*Continued*)

Table 8.A.1 (Continued)

		Severity
81	Risk of project termination due to poor quality, overruns	10.00
82	Risk of features slipping from planned release	9.60
83	Risk of significant project cost overruns	9.50
84	Risk of project value dipping below project costs	9.50
85	Risk of "leakage" from software cost and historical data	9.00
86	Risk of bankruptcy by vendor	9.00
87	Risk of negative earned value for project	9.00
88	Risk of significant project schedule overruns	8.90
89	Risk of application failure causing moderate financial loss	8.75
90	Risk of cost overruns on outsourced projects	8.50
91	Risk of schedule delays on outsourced projects	8.50
92	Risk of unbudgeted costs from security attacks	8.35
93	Risk of unbudgeted costs from litigation	8.30
94	Risk of inadequate cost accounting	8.00
95	Risk of bankruptcy by client	8.00
96	Risk of application violating standard accounting practices	7.00
Business Risks		
97	Risk of missing critical market window	10.00
98	Risk of losing clients due to faulty software	9.95
99	Risk of application failure damaging business data	9.90
100	Risk of application failure damaging distribution	9.85
101	Risk of application failure damaging transportation	9.80
102	Risk of application failure affecting operation of equipment	9.80
103	Risk of application failure damaging retail activities	9.75
104	Risk of competitive applications with better features	9.75
105	Risk of application obsolescence before completion	9.70
106	Risk of application failure damaging law enforcement	9.70
107	Risk of application failure damaging government activities	9.60
108	Risk of application failure damaging communications	9.50

Table 8.A.1 (Continued)

		Severity
109	Risk of poor governance by executives	9.50
110	Risk of application failure damaging manufacturing	9.50
111	Risk of application failure damaging stock values	9.50
112	Risk of application failure shutting down vital equipment	9.25
113	Risk of rubber-stamp phase reviews without real oversight	9.20
114	Risk of poor or missing project historical data	8.50
115	Risk of executive and client dissatisfaction with project	8.50
116	Risk of poor support by COTS vendors	8.25
117	Risk of cost and schedule overruns for ERP deployment	8.25
Social Risks		
118	Risk of significant layoffs of project team	10.00
119	Risk of poor managers driving out top technical staff	10.00
120	Risk of termination for cause of key technical personnel	10.00
121	Risk of ignoring learning curve for new methodologies	10.00
121	Risk of voluntary attrition of key technical personnel	9.00
122	Risk of poorly planned organization structures	9.00
123	Risk of team sizes too small for application	9.00
124	Risk of too few personnel per manager (< 5)	9.00
125	Risk of too many personnel per manager (> 15)	9.00
126	Risk of poor organization structures	8.80
127	Risk of low team morale from excessive schedule pressure	8.00
128	Risk of poor communication among supply chain members	8.00
129	Risk of stakeholder disputes that change requirements	7.75
130	Risk of poor communications among team members	7.70
131	Risk of team size too large for application	7.00
132	Risk of low user satisfaction levels	7.00
133	Risk of inadequate user training for complex new software	7.00
134	Risk of poor communications with stakeholders	7.00
135	Risk of major management disagreements	6.50

(Continued)

Table 8.A.1 (Continued)

		Severity
136	Risk of strikes by unionized personnel	8.00
External Risks		
137	Risk of natural disaster affecting projects	8.00
138	Risk of loss of stakeholders or clients during development	7.00
139	Risk of accidental loss of key personnel during development	5.75
140	Risk of serious medical problems of key personnel	5.70
Ethical Risks		
141	Risk of fraudulent progress/status reports	10.00
142	Risk of project managers ignoring risks	9.50
143	Risk of project managers concealing risks from clients	9.50
144	Risk of non-compete violations by former employees	9.50
145	Risk of false claims by methodology enthusiasts	9.15
146	Risk of false claims of high CMMI levels	9.00
147	Risk of claiming to use a methodology, but not really doing so	8.50
148	Risk of false claims by outsource vendors	8.00
149	Risk of false claims by COTS vendors	8.00
Knowledge Risks		
150	Risk of users not fully understanding their own requirements	10.00
151	Risk of inadequate requirements analysis for large systems	10.00
152	Risk of adopting new methods as a cult rather than a technology	9.75
153	Risk of effective solutions not being known by managers	9.50
154	Risk of effective solutions not being known by team	9.75
155	Risk of inadequate sizing prior to funding project	9.70
156	Risk of inadequate schedule planning	9.60
157	Risk of late start in deploying risk solutions	9.50
158	Risk of manual estimates for large applications	9.50
159	Risk of excessive optimism in initial plans, estimates	9.50
160	Risk of estimates being rejected due to lack of benchmarks	9.45

Table 8.A.1 (Continued)

		Severity
161	Risk of using unsuitable development methodology	9.40
162	Risk of poor project oversight by clients	9.25
163	Risk of "good enough" fallacy applied to application	9.00
164	Risk of insufficient project management skills	9.00
165	Risk of poorly trained management personnel	9.00
166	Risk of inadequate user-error prevention	9.00
167	Risk of team skills not matching project needs	9.00
168	Risk of poorly trained maintenance personnel	8.60
169	Risk of inadequate defect prevention	8.50
170	Risk of poorly trained development personnel	8.50
171	Risk of poorly trained support personnel	8.40
172	Risk of poorly trained test personnel	8.25
173	Risk of application architectural flaws	8.25
174	Risk of inadequate user guides and HELP screens	8.00
175	Risk of poor usability and poor interfaces	8.00
176	Risk of poorly trained QA personnel	8.00
177	Risk of international misunderstandings for global projects	8.00
178	Risk of inadequate programming languages	7.75
179	Risk of insufficient technical skills	7.25
180	Risk of application violating international standards	5.50
Enterprise Risks		
181	Risks of obsolete or cumbersome enterprise architecture	10.00
182	Risks of difficult data migration from legacy applications	10.00
183	Risk of merger or takeover causing layoffs and cancellations	10.00
184	Risks from disconnected "stove pipe" applications	9.00
185	Risks of fragmented software ownership in enterprise	9.00
186	Risks of uncoordinated redundant applications and data	8.00
187	Risks of uncoordinated multinational development groups	

(Continued)

Table 8.A.1 (Continued)

		Severity
Merger, Acquisition, and Venture Capital Risks		
188	Risk of dilution of ownership due to multiple funding rounds	10.00
189	Risk of cutting R&D after mergers or venture investment	9.50
190	Risk of losing key personnel after mergers.	9.50
191	Risk of bankruptcy within three years of venture funding	9.50
192	Risk of inadequate due diligence prior to completion	9.00
193	Risk of eventual competition by dissatisfied personnel	9.00
194	Risk of poor integration of teams after mergers	9.00
195	Risk of venture-backed boards eliminating key technical staff	8.75
196	Risk of venture-backed boards damaging business prospects	8.50
197	Risk of bankruptcy within three years of mergers	7.50
Technology Risks		
198	Risk of hardware changes making application obsolete	9.00
199	Risk of hardware changes requiring extensive rework	8.50
200	Risk of related software changes requiring rework	8.00
201	Risk of supply chain changes requiring rework	7.00
202	Risk of standards changes requiring rework	7.00
203	Risk of unplanned directive to adopt multiple hardware platforms	7.00
204	Risk of withdrawal of hardware/software platforms	7.00
205	Risk of unplanned directive to adopt multiple software platforms	7.00
Embedded Software Risks		
206	Risk of software problems raising hardware liabilities	10.00
207	Risk of software problems causing unrepairable failures	10.00
208	Risk of software problems causing patent violations	10.00
209	Risk of software problems delaying hardware products	9.00
210	Risk of software raising hardware warranty costs	9.00
Averages		**8.85**

Gilb, Tom; and Graham, Dorothy; *Software Inspections*; Addison Wesley, Reading, MA; 1993; ISBN: 10: 0201631814.

Humphrey, Watts; *TSP – Leading a Development Team*; Addison Wesley, Boston, MA; 2006; ISBN: 0-321-34962-8; 307 pages.

Jones, Capers; *The Technical and Social History of Software Engineering*, Addison Wesley; 2014.

Jones, Capers; *Early Sizing and Early Risk Analysis*; Capers Jones & Associates LLC; Narragansett, RI; July 2011.

Jones, Capers; and Bonsignour, Olivier; *The Economics of Software Quality*; Addison Wesley Longman, Boston, MA; 2011; ISBN: 10: 0-13-258220-1; 585 pages.

Jones, Capers; *Software Engineering Best Practices*; McGraw Hill, New York, NY; 2010; ISBN: 978-0-07-162161-8; 660 pages.

Jones, Capers; *Applied Software Measurement*; McGraw Hill, New York, NY; 2008; ISBN: 978-0-07-150244-3; 662 pages.

Jones, Capers; *Estimating Software Costs*; McGraw Hill, New York, NY; 2007a; ISBN: 13: 978-0-07-148300-1.

Jones, Capers; *Software Assessments, Benchmarks, and Best Practices*; Addison Wesley Longman, Boston, MA; 2000; ISBN: 0-201-48542-7; 657 pages.

Jones, Capers; *Conflict and Litigation Between Software Clients and Developers*; Software Productivity Research, Inc.; Burlington, MA; September 2007b; 53 pages; (SPR technical report).

Kan, Stephen H.; *Metrics and Models in Software Quality Engineering*, 2nd ed.; Addison Wesley Longman, Boston, MA; 2003; ISBN: 0-201-72915-6; 528 pages.

Radice, Ronald A.; *High Quality Low Cost Software Inspections*; Paradoxicon Publishing, Andover, MA; 2002; ISBN: 0-9645913-1-6; 479 pages.

Royce, Walker; *Software Project Management – A Unified Framework*; Addison Wesley, Boston, MA; 1999; ISBN: 0-201-30958-0; 406 pages.

Wiegers, Karl E.; *Peer Reviews in Software – A Practical Guide*; Addison Wesley Longman, Boston, MA; 2002; ISBN: 0-201-73485-0; 232 pages.

Chapter 9

Achieving Software Excellence

As of the year 2021, software applications are the main operational component of every major business and government organization in the world. But software quality is still not good for a majority of these applications. Software schedules and costs are both frequently much larger than planned. Cyber-attacks are becoming more frequent and more serious.

This study discusses the proven methods and results for achieving software excellence. The book also provides quantification of what the term "excellence" means for both quality and productivity. Formal sizing and estimating using parametric estimation tools, excellent progress and quality tracking also using special tools, and a comprehensive software quality program can lead to shorter schedules, lower costs, and higher quality at the same time.

Introduction

Software is the main operating tool of business and government in 2019. But software quality remains marginal; software schedules and costs remained much larger than desirable or planned. Cancelled projects are about 35% in the 10,000 function point size range and about 5% of software outsource agreements end up in court in litigation. Cyber-attacks are increasing in numbers and severity. This short study identifies the major methods for bringing software under control and achieving excellent results.

The first topic of importance is to show the quantitative differences between excellent, average, and poor software projects in quantified form. Table 9.1 shows the essential differences between software excellence, average, and unacceptably poor results for a mid-sized project of 1,000 function points or about 53,000 Java statements.

The data comes from benchmarks performed by Namcook Analytics LLC. These were covered by non-disclosure agreements so specific companies are not shown. However, the "excellent" column came from telecom, high-technology, medical device companies; the average from insurance and manufacturing; and the poor column from state and local governments:

As stated the data in Table 9.1 comes from the author's clients, which consist of about 750 companies of whom 150 are Fortune 500 companies. About 40 government and military organizations are also clients, but the good and average columns in Table 9.1 are based on corporate results rather than government results. State and local governments provided data for the poor quality column.

Federal Government and defense software tend to have large overhead costs and extensive status reporting that are not found in the civilian sector. Some big defense projects have produced so much paperwork that there were over 1,400 English words for every Ada statement and the words cost more than the source code.

Note that the data in this report was produced using the Namcook Analytics Software Risk Master™ (SRM) tool. SRM can operate as an estimating tool prior to requirements or as a benchmark measurement tool after deployment.

At this point, it is useful to discuss and explain the main differences between the best, average, and poor results.

Software Sizing, Estimating, and Project Tracking Differences

High-quality projects with excellent results all use formal parametric estimating tools, perform formal sizing before starting, and have accurate status and cost tracking during development.

A comparative study by the author of this book on accuracy differences between manual estimates and parametric estimates showed that the manual estimates averaged about 34% optimistic for schedules and costs.

Table 9.1   Comparisons of Excellent, Average, and Poor Software Results

Topics	Excellent	Average	Poor
Monthly Costs			
(Salary + overhead)	$10,000	$10,000	$10,000
Size at Delivery			
Size in function points	1,000	1,000	1,000
Programming language	Java	Java	Java
Language Levels	6.25	6.00	5.75
Source statements per function point	51.20	53.33	55.65
Size in logical code statements	51,200	53,333	55,652
Size in KLOC	51.20	53.33	55.65
Certified reuse percent	20.00%	10.00%	5.00%
Quality			
Defect potentials	2,818	3,467	4,266
Defects per function point	2.82	3.47	4.27
Defects per KLOC	55.05	65.01	76.65
Defect removal efficiency (DRE)	**99.00%**	**90.00%**	**83.00%**
Delivered defects	**28**	**347**	**725**
High-severity defects	**4**	**59**	**145**
Security vulnerabilities	**2**	**31**	**88**
Delivered per function point	0.03	0.35	0.73
Delivered per KLOC	0.55	6.50	13.03
Key Quality Control Methods			
Formal estimates of defects	Yes	No	No
Formal inspections of deliverables	Yes	No	No
Static analysis of all code	Yes	Yes	No
Formal test case design	Yes	Yes	No
Testing by certified test personnel	Yes	No	No
Mathematical test case design	Yes	No	No

(Continued)

Table 9.1 (Continued)

Topics	Excellent	Average	Poor
Project Parameter Results			
Schedule in calendar months	12.02	13.80	18.20
Technical staff + management	6.25	6.67	7.69
Effort in staff months	75.14	92.03	139.98
Effort in staff hours	9,919	12,147	18,477
Costs in Dollars	**$751,415**	**$920,256**	**$1,399,770**
Cost per function point	$751.42	$920.26	$1,399.77
Cost per KLOC	$14,676	$17,255	$25,152
Productivity Rates			
Function points per staff month	13.31	10.87	7.14
Work hours per function point	9.92	12.15	18.48
Lines of code per staff month	681	580	398
Cost Drivers			
Bug repairs	**25.00%**	**40.00%**	**45.00%**
Paper documents	20.00%	17.00%	20.00%
Code development	35.00%	18.00%	13.00%
Meetings	8.00%	13.00%	10.00%
Management	12.00%	12.00%	12.00%
Total	**100.00%**	**100.00%**	**100.00%**
Methods, Tools, Practices			
Development Methods	TSP/PSP	Agile	Waterfall
Requirements Methods	JAD	Embedded	Interview
CMMI Levels	5	3	1
Work hours per month	132	132	132
Unpaid overtime	0	0	0
Team experience	Experienced	Average	Inexperienced
Formal risk analysis	Yes	Yes	No
Formal quality analysis	Yes	No	No
Formal change control	Yes	Yes	No

Table 9.1 (Continued)

Topics	Excellent	Average	Poor
Formal sizing of project	Yes	Yes	No
Formal reuse analysis	Yes	No	No
Parametric estimation tools	Yes	No	No
Inspections of key materials	Yes	No	No
Static analysis of all code	Yes	Yes	No
Formal test case design	Yes	No	No
Certified test personnel	Yes	No	No
Accurate status reporting	Yes	Yes	No
Accurate defect tracking	Yes	No	No
More than 15% certified reuse	Yes	Maybe	No
Low cyclomatic complexity	Yes	Maybe	No
Test coverage >95%	Yes	Maybe	No

Worse, manual estimating errors increased with application size. Below 250 function points, manual and parametric estimates were both within 5%. Above 10,000 function points, manual estimates were optimistic by almost 40%, while parametric estimates were often within 10%. Overall parametric estimates usually differed by less than 10% from actual results for schedules and costs, sometimes less than 5%, and were almost never optimistic.

The parametric estimation tools included COCOMO, Excelerator, KnowledgePlan, SEER, SLIM, Software Risk Master, and TruePrice. All of these parametric tools were more accurate than manual cost and schedule estimates for all size ranges and application types.

High-quality projects also track results with high accuracy for progress, schedules, defects, and cost accumulation. Some excellent projects use specialized tracking tools such as Computer Aid's Automated Project Office (APO) which was built to track software projects. Others use general tools such as Microsoft Project which supports many kinds of projects in addition to software.

Average projects with average results sometimes use parametric estimates but more often use manual estimates. However, some of the average projects did utilize estimating specialists, who are more accurate than untrained project managers.

Project tracking for average projects tends to be informal and use general-purpose tools such as Excel rather than specialized software tracking tools such as APO, Jira, Asana and others. Average tracking also "leaks" and tends to omit topics such as unpaid overtime and project management.

Poor quality projects almost always use manual estimates. Tracking of progress is so bad that problems are sometimes concealed rather than revealed. Poor quality cost tracking has major gaps and omits over 50% of total project costs. The most common omissions are unpaid overtime, project managers, and the work of part-time specialists such as business analysts, technical writers, and software quality assurance.

Quality tracking is embarrassingly bad and omits all bugs found before testing via static analysis or reviews, and usually omits bugs found during unit testing. Some poor-quality companies and government organizations don't track quality at all. Many others don't track until late testing or deployment.

Software Quality Differences for Best, Average, and Poor Projects

Software quality is the major point of differentiation between excellent results, average results, and poor results.

While software executives demand high productivity and short schedules, the vast majority do not understand how to achieve them. Bypassing quality control does not speed projects up: it slows them down.

The number one reason for enormous schedule slips noted in breach of contract litigation where the author of this book has been an expert witness is starting testing with so many bugs that test schedules are at least double their planned duration.

The major point of this book is: *High quality using a synergistic combination of defect prevention, pre-test inspections and static analysis combined with formal testing is fast and cheap.*

Poor quality is expensive, slow, and unfortunately far too common. Because most companies do not know how to achieve high quality, poor quality is the norm and at least twice as common as high quality.

High quality does not come from testing alone. It requires defect prevention such as Joint Application Design (JAD), quality function deployment (QFD) or embedded users; pre-test inspections and static analysis; and of course formal test case development combined with certified test personnel. New methods of test case development based on cause–effect graphs and design of experiments are quite a step forward.

The defect potential information in Table 9.1 includes defects from five origins: requirements defects, design defects, code defects, document defects, and "bad fixes" or new defects accidentally included in defect repairs. The approximate distribution among these five sources is as follows:

1. Requirements defects	15%
2. Design defects	30%
3. Code defects	40%
4. Document defects	8%
5. Bad fixes	7%
Total Defects	**100%**

Note that a "bad fix" is a bug in a bug repair. These can sometimes top 25% of bug repairs for modules with high cyclomatic complexity.

However, the distribution of defect origins varies widely based on the novelty of the application, the experience of the clients and the development team, the methodologies used, and programming languages. Certified reusable material also has an impact on software defect volumes and origins.

Table 9.2 shows approximate U.S. ranges for defect potentials based on a sample of 1,500 software projects that include systems software, web projects, embedded software, and information technology projects that range from 100 to 100,000 function points.

It is unfortunate that buggy software projects outnumber low-defect projects by a considerable margin.

Because the costs of finding and fixing bugs have been the #1 cost driver for the entire software industry for more than 50 years, the most important difference between excellent and mediocre results is in the areas of defect prevention, pre-test defect removal, and testing.

All three examples are assumed to use the same set of test stages, including:

1. Unit test
2. Function test
3. Regression test
4. Component test
5. Performance test
6. System test
7. Acceptance test

Table 9.2 Defect Potentials for 1,000 Projects

Defect Potentials	Projects	Percent
<1.00	5	0.50%
2 to 1	35	3.50%
3 to 2	120	12.00%
4 to 3	425	42.50%
5 to 4	350	35.00%
>5.00	65	6.50%
Total	**1,000**	**100.00%**

The overall defect removal efficiency (DRE) levels of these 7 test stages range from below 80% for the worst case up to about 95% for the best case.

Note that the seven test stages shown earlier are generic and used on a majority of software applications. Additional forms of testing may also be used and can be added to SRM for specific clients and specific projects:

1. Independent testing (mainly government and military software)
2. Usability testing (mainly software with complex user controls)
3. Performance testing (mainly real-time software)
4. Security testing
5. Limits testing
6. Supply-chain testing
7. Nationalization testing (for international projects)

Testing alone is not sufficient to top 95% in DRE. Pre-test inspections and static analysis are needed to approach or exceed the 99% range of the best case. Also requirements models and "quality-strong" development methods such as team software process (TSP) need to be part of the quality equation.

Excellent Quality Control

Excellent projects have rigorous quality control methods that include formal estimation of quality before starting, full defect measurement and tracking during development, and a full suite of defect prevention, pre-test removal, and test stages. The combination of low defect potentials and high DRE is what software excellence is all about.

The most common companies that are excellent in quality control are usually the companies that build complex physical devices such as computers, aircraft, embedded engine components, medical devices, and telephone switching systems. Without excellence in quality, these physical devices will not operate successfully. Worse, failure can lead to litigation and even criminal charges. Therefore, all companies that use software to control complex physical machinery tend to be excellent in software quality.

Examples of organizations noted as excellent software quality in alphabetical order include Advanced Bionics, Apple, AT&T, Boeing, Ford for engine controls, General Electric for jet engines, Hewlett Packard for embedded software, IBM for systems software, Motorola for electronics, NASA for space controls, the Navy for surface weapons, Raytheon, and Siemens.

Companies and projects with excellent quality control tend to have low levels of code cyclomatic complexity and high test coverage, i.e. test cases cover >95% of paths and risk areas.

These companies also measure quality well and all know their DRE levels. Any company that does not measure and know their DRE is probably below 85% in DRE.

Excellent quality control has DRE levels between about 97% for large systems in the 10,000 function point size range and about 99.6% for small projects <1,000 function points in size.

A DRE of 100% is theoretically possible but is extremely rare. The author has only noted DRE of 100% in 10 projects out of a total of about 25,000 projects examined. As it happens the projects with 100% DRE were all compilers and assemblers built by IBM and using >85% certified reusable materials. The teams were all experts in compilation technology and of course a full suite of pre-test defect removal and test stages were used as well.

Average Quality Control

In today's world, agile is the new average. Agile development has proven to be effective for smaller applications below 1,000 function points in size. Agile does not scale up well and is not a top method for quality. Agile is weak in quality measurements and does not normally use inspections, which have the highest DRE of any known form of defect removal. Disciplined agile development (DAD) can be used successfully on large systems where vanilla agile/scrum is not effective. Inspections top 85% in DRE and also raise testing DRE levels. Among the author's clients that use agile, the average value for DRE is about 92% to 94%. This is certainly better than the 85% to 90% industry average for waterfall projects, but not up to the 99% actually needed to achieve optimal results.

Some but not all agile projects use "pair programming" in which two programmers share an office and a work station and take turns coding while the other watches and "navigates." Pair programming is very expensive but only benefits quality by about 15% compared to single programmers. Pair programming is much less effective in finding bugs than formal inspections, which usually bring 3 to 5 personnel together to seek out bugs using formal methods.

Agile is a definite improvement for quality compared to waterfall development, but is not as effective as the quality-strong methods of TSP and the rational unified process (RUP) for larger applications >1,000 function points. An average agile project among the author's clients is about 275 function points. DAD is a good choice for larger information software applications.

Average projects usually do not know defects by origin and do not measure DRE until testing starts, i.e. requirements and design defects are under reported and sometimes invisible.

A recent advance in software quality control now frequently used by average as well as advanced organizations is that of static analysis. Static analysis tools can find about 55% of code defects, which is much higher than most forms of testing.

Many test stages such as unit test, function test, regression test, etc. are only about 35% efficient in finding code bugs, or find one bug out of three. This explains why 6 to 10 separate kinds of testing are needed.

The kinds of companies and projects that are "average" would include internal software built by hundreds of banks, insurance companies, retail and wholesale companies, and many government agencies at federal, state, and municipal levels.

Average quality control has DRE levels from about 85% for large systems up to 97% for small and simple projects.

Poor Quality Control

Poor quality control is characterized by weak defect prevention and almost a total omission of pre-test defect removal methods such as static analysis and formal inspections. Poor quality control is also characterized by inept and inaccurate quality measures which ignore front-end defects in requirements and design. There are also gaps in measuring code defects. For example, most companies with poor quality control have no idea how many test cases might be needed or how efficient various kinds of test stages are.

Companies or government groups with poor quality control also fail to perform any kind of up-front quality predictions so they jump into development without a clue as to how many bugs are likely to occur and what are the best methods for preventing or removing these bugs.

One of the main reasons for the long schedules and high costs associated with poor quality is the fact that so many bugs are found when testing starts that the test interval stretches out to two or three times longer than planned.

Some of the kinds of software that are noted for poor quality control include the Obamacare web site, municipal software for property tax assessments, and software for programmed stock trading, which has caused several massive stock crashes.

Poor quality control is often below 85% in DRE levels. In fact for canceled projects or those that end up in litigation for poor quality, the DRE levels may drop below 80%, which is low enough to be considered professional malpractice. In litigation where the author of this book has been an expert witness, DRE levels in the low 80% range have been the unfortunate norm.

Table 9.3 shows the ranges in DRE noted from a sample of 1,000 software projects. The sample included systems and embedded software, web projects, cloud projects, information technology projects, and also defense and commercial packages.

As can be seen, high DRE does not occur often. This is unfortunate because projects that are above 95.00% in DRE have shorter schedules and lower costs than projects below 85.00% in DRE. The software

Table 9.3   Distribution of DRE for 1,000 Projects

DRE	Projects	Percent
>99.00%	10	1.00%
95–99%	120	12.00%
90–94%	250	25.00%
85–89%	475	47.50%
80–85%	125	12.50%
<80.00%	20	2.00%
Total	**1,000**	**100.00%**

industry does not measure either quality or productivity well enough to know this.

However, the most important economic fact about high quality is: projects > 97% in DRE have shorter schedules and lower costs than projects < 90% in DRE. This is because projects that are low in DRE have test schedules that are at least twice as long as projects with high DRE due to omission of pre-test inspections and static analysis.

Reuse of Certified Materials for Software Projects

So long as software applications are custom designed and coded by hand, software will remain a labor-intensive craft rather than a modern professional activity. Manual software development even with excellent methodologies cannot be much more than 15% better than average development due to the intrinsic limits in human performance and legal limits in the number of hours that can be worked without fatigue.

The best long-term strategy for achieving consistent excellence at high speed would be to eliminate manual design and coding in favor of construction from certified reusable components.

It is important to realize that software reuse encompasses many deliverables and not just source code. A full suite of reusable software components would include at least the following 10 items:

Reusable Software Artifacts Circa 2019

1. Reusable requirements
2. Reusable architecture
3. Reusable design
4. Reusable code
5. Reusable project plans and estimates
6. Reusable test plans
7. Reusable test scripts
8. Reusable test cases
9. Reusable user manuals
10. Reusable training materials

These materials need to be certified to near zero-defect levels of quality before reuse becomes safe and economically viable. Reusing buggy materials is harmful and expensive. This is why excellent quality control is the first stage in a successful reuse program.

The need for being close to zero defects and formal certification adds about 20% to the costs of constructing reusable artifacts and about 30% to the schedules for construction. However, using certified reusable materials subtracts over 80% from the costs of construction and can shorten schedules by more than 60%. The more times materials are reused, the greater their cumulative economic value.

One caution to readers: reusable artifacts may be treated as taxable assets by the Internal Revenue Service. It is important to check this topic out with a tax attorney to be sure that formal corporate reuse programs will not encounter unpleasant tax consequences.

The three samples in Table 9.1 showed only moderate reuse typical for the start of 2016.

Excellent project	>25% certified reuse
Average project	+ −10% certified reuse
Poor projects	<5% certified reuse

In the future, it is technically possible to make large increases in the volumes of reusable materials. By around 2025, we should be able to construct software applications with perhaps 85% certified reusable materials. In fact some "mashup" projects already achieve 85% reuse, but the reused materials are not certified and some may contain significant bugs and security flaws.

Table 9.4 shows the productivity impact of increasing volumes of certified reusable materials. Table 9.4 uses whole numbers and generic values to simplify the calculations.

Software reuse from certified components instead of custom design and hand coding is the only known technique that can achieve order-of-magnitude improvements in software productivity. True excellence in software engineering must derive from replacing costly and error-prone manual work with construction from certified reusable components.

Because finding and fixing bugs is the major software cost driver, increasing volumes of high-quality certified materials can convert software from an error-prone manual craft into a very professional high-technology profession. Table 9.5 shows probable quality gains from increasing volumes of software reuse.

Since the current maximum for software reuse from certified components is only in the range of 15% or a bit higher, it can be seen that there is a large potential for future improvement.

Note that uncertified reuse in the form of mashups or extracting materials from legacy applications may top 50%. However, uncertified reusable materials often have latent bugs, security flaws, and even

Table 9.4 Productivity Gains from Software Reuse

(Assumes 1,000 function points and 53,300 LOC)					
Reuse Percent	*Months of Staff Effort*	*Function Points per Month*	*Work hours per Function Point*	*Lines of Code per Month*	*Project Costs*
0.00%	100	10.00	13.20	533	$1,000,000
10.00%	90	11.11	11.88	592	$900,000
20.00%	80	12.50	10.56	666	$800,000
30.00%	70	14.29	9.24	761	$700,000
40.00%	60	16.67	7.92	888	$600,000
50.00%	50	20.00	6.60	1,066	$500,000
60.00%	40	25.00	5.28	1,333	$400,000
70.00%	30	33.33	3.96	1,777	$300,000
80.00%	20	50.00	2.64	2,665	$200,000
90.00%	10	100.00	1.32	5,330	$100,000
100.00%	1	1,000.00	0.13	53,300	$10,000

Table 9.5 Quality Gains from Software Reuse

(Assumes 1,000 function points and 53,300 LOC)				
Reuse Percent	*Defects per Function Point*	*Defect Potential*	*Defect Removal Efficiency*	*Delivered Defects*
0.00%	5.00	1,000	90.00%	100
10.00%	4.50	900	91.00%	81
20.00%	4.00	800	92.00%	64
30.00%	3.50	700	93.00%	49
40.00%	3.00	600	94.00%	36
50.00%	2.50	500	95.00%	25
60.00%	2.00	400	96.00%	16
70.00%	1.50	300	97.00%	9
80.00%	1.00	200	98.00%	4
90.00%	0.50	100	99.00%	1
100.00%	–	1	99.99%	0

error-prone modules, so this is not a very safe practice. In several cases, the reused material was so buggy it had to be discarded and replaced by custom development.

Several emerging development methodologies such as "mashups" are pushing reuse values up above 90%. However, the numbers and kinds of applications built from these emerging methods are small. Reuse needs to become generally available with catalogs of standard reusable components organized by industries, i.e. banking, insurance, telecommunications, firmware, etc.

Software Methodologies

Unfortunately, selecting a methodology is more like joining a cult than making an informed technical decision. Most companies don't actually perform any kind of due diligence on methodologies and merely select the one that is most popular.

In today's world, agile is definitely the most popular. Fortunately, agile is also a pretty good methodology and much superior to the older waterfall method. However, there are some caveats about methodologies.

Agile has been successful primarily for smaller applications <1,000 function points in size. It has also been successful for internal applications where users can participate or be "embedded" with the development team to work our requirements issues.

Agile has not scaled up well to large systems >10,000 function points. Agile has also not been visibly successful for commercial or embedded applications where there are millions of users and none of them work for the company building the software so their requirements have to be collected using focus groups or special marketing studies.

A variant of agile that uses "pair programming" or two programmers working in the same cubical with one coding and the other "navigating" has become popular. However, it is very expensive since two people are being paid to do the work of one person. There are claims that quality is improved, but formal inspections combined with static analysis achieve much higher quality for much lower costs.

Another agile variation, extreme programming, in which test cases are created before the code itself is written has proven to be fairly successful for both quality and productivity, compared to traditional waterfall methods. However, both TSP and RUP are just as good and even better for large systems. Another successful variation on agile is DAD which expands the agile concept up above 5,000 function points.

There are more than 80 available methodologies circa 2016 and many are good; some are better than agile for large systems; some older methods such as waterfall and cowboy development are at the bottom of the effectiveness list and should be avoided on modern applications.

For major applications in the 10,000 function point size range and above, the TSP and the RUP have the best track records for successful projects and among the fewest failures. Table 9.6 ranks 50 current software development methodologies. The rankings show their effectiveness for small projects below 1,000 function points and for large systems above 10,000 function points. Table 9.1 is based on data from around 600 companies and 25,000 project results.

The green color highlights the methods with the most successful project outcomes. In general, the large-system methods are "quality strong" methodologies that support inspections and rigorous quality control. Some of these are a bit "heavy" for small projects although quality results are good. However, the overhead of some rigorous methods tends to slow down small projects.

Starting in 2014 and expanding fairly rapidly is the new "software engineering methods and theory" or SEMAT approach. This is not a "methodology" per se but new way of analyzing software engineering projects and applications themselves.

SEMAT has little or no empirical data as this book is written but the approach seems to have merit. The probable impact, although this is not yet proven, will be a reduction in software defect potentials and perhaps an increase in certified reusable components.

Unfortunately SEMAT seems to be aimed at custom designs and manual development of software, both of which are intrinsically expensive and error-prone. SEMAT would be better used for increasing the supply of certified reusable components. As SEMAT usage expands it will be interesting to measure actual results, which to date are purely theoretical.

Quantifying Software Excellence

Because the software industry has a poor track record for measurement, it is useful to show what "excellence" means in quantified terms.

Excellence in software quality combines defect potentials of no more than 2.50 bugs per function point combined with DRE of 99.00%. This means that delivered defects will not exceed 0.025 defects per function point.

By contrast, current average values circa 2021 are about 3.00 to 5.00 bugs per function point for defect potentials and only 90% to 94% DRE, leading to as many as 0.50 bugs per function point at delivery. There are

Table 9.6   Methodology Rankings for Small and Large Software Projects

	Small Projects	*Large Systems*
	<1,000 Function Points	*>10,000 Function Points*
1	Agile scrum	TSP/PSP
2	Crystal	Reuse-oriented
3	DSDM	Pattern-based
4	Feature driven (FDD)	IntegraNova
5	Hybrid	Product line engineering
6	IntegraNova	Model-driven
7	Lean	DevOps
8	Mashup	Service-oriented
9	Microsoft solutions	Specifications by example
10	Model-driven	Mashup
11	Object-oriented	Object-oriented
12	Pattern-based	Information engineering (IE)
13	Product line engineering	Feature driven (FDD)
14	PSP	Microsoft solutions
15	Reuse-oriented	Structured development
16	Service-oriented modeling	Spiral development
17	Specifications by example	T-VEC
18	Structured development	Kaizen
19	Test-driven development (TDD)	RUP
20	CASE	Crystal
21	Clean room	DSDM
22	Continuous development	Hybrid
23	DevOps	CASE
24	EVO	Global 24 hour
25	Information engineering (IE)	Continuous development
26	Legacy redevelopment	Legacy redevelopment
27	Legacy renovation	Legacy renovation
28	Merise	Merise

(*Continued*)

Table 9.6 (Continued)

Small Projects		Large Systems
<1,000 Function Points		*>10,000 Function Points*
29	Open-source	Iterative
30	Spiral development	Legacy data mining
31	T-VEC	Custom by client
32	Kaizen	CMMI 3
33	Pair programming	Agile scrum
34	Reengineering	Lean
35	Reverse engineering	EVO
36	XP	Open-source
37	Iterative	Reengineering
38	Legacy data mining	V-Model
39	Prototypes – evolutionary	Clean room
40	RAD	Reverse engineering
41	RUP	Prototypes – evolutionary
42	TSP/PSP	RAD
43	V-Model	Prince 2
44	Cowboy	Prototypes – disposable
45	Prince 2	Test-driven development (TDD)
46	Waterfall	Waterfall
47	Global 24 hour	Pair programming
48	CMMI 3	XP
49	Prototypes – disposable	Cowboy
50	Antipatterns	Antipatterns

projects that top 99.00% percent but the distribution is less than 5% of U.S. projects top 99% in DRE as of 2021.

Poor projects which are likely to fail and end up in court for poor quality or breach of contract often have defect potentials of >6.00 per function point combined with DRE levels <85%. Some poor projects deliver >0.75 bugs per function point and also excessive security flaws.

Excellence in software productivity and development schedules are not fixed values but varies with the size of the applications. Table 9.7 shows two "flavors" of productivity excellence: (1) the best that can be accomplished with 10% reuse and (2) the best that can be accomplished with 50% reuse.

As can be seen from Table 9.7, software reuse is the most important technology for improving software productivity and quality by really significant amounts. Methods, tools, CMMI levels, SEMAT, and other minor factors are certainly beneficial. However, as long as software applications are custom designed and hand coded, software will remain an expensive craft and not a true professional occupation.

The Metaphor of Technical Debt

Ward Cunningham's interesting metaphor of "technical debt" has become a popular topic in the software industry. The concept of technical debt is that in order to get software released in a hurry, short cuts and omissions occur that will need to repaired after release, for much greater cost, i.e. like interest builds up on a loan.

Although the metaphor has merit, it is not yet standardized and therefore can vary widely. In fact a common question at conferences is "what do you include in technical debt?"

Table 9.7   Excellent Productivity with Varying Quantities of Certified Reuse

	Schedule Months	Staffing	Effort Months	FP per Month
With <10% certified reuse				
100 function points	4.79	1.25	5.98	16.71
1,000 function points	13.80	6.25	86.27	11.59
10,000 function points	33.11	57.14	1,892.18	5.28
100,000 function points	70.79	540.54	38,267.34	2.61
With 50% certified reuse				
100 function points	3.98	1.00	3.98	25.12
1,000 function points	8.51	5.88	50.07	19.97
10,000 function points	20.89	51.28	1,071.43	9.33
100,000 function points	44.67	487.80	21,789.44	4.59

Technical debt is not a part of standard costs of quality. There are some other topics that are excluded also. The most important and also the least studied are "*consequential damages*" or actual financial harm to clients of buggy software. These show up in lawsuits against vendors and are known to attorneys and expert witnesses, but otherwise not widely published.

A major omission from technical debt circa 2016 is the cost of cyber-attacks and recovery from cyber-attacks. In cases where valuable data are stolen, cyber-attack costs can be more expensive than total development costs for the attacked application.

Another omission from both cost of quality (COQ) and technical are the costs of litigation and damage awards when software vendors or outsourcers are sued for poor quality. Table 9.8 puts all of these costs together to show the full set of costs that might occur for excellent quality, average quality, and poor quality. Note that Table 9.8 uses "defects per function point" for the quality results.

As of early 2019 almost 85% of the true costs of poor quality software were invisible and not covered by either technical debt or standard "cost of quality" (COQ). No one has yet done a solid study of the damages of poor quality to clients and users but these costs are much greater than internal costs.

This is a topic that should be addressed by both the CMMI and the SEMAT approach, although neither has studied consequential damages.

Table 9.8 Technical Debt and Software Quality for 1,000 Function Points

	High Quality	*Average Quality*	*Poor Quality*
Defect potential	2	4	6
Removal efficiency	99.00%	92.00%	80.00%
Delivered defects	0.02	0.32	1.2
Post-release defect repair $	$5,000	$60,000	$185,000
Technical debt problems	1	25	75
Technical debt costs	$1,000	$62,500	$375,000
Excluded from Technical Debt			
Consequential damages	$0.00	$281,250	$2,437,500
Cyber-attack costs	$0.00	$250,000	$5,000,000
Litigation costs	$0.00	$2,500,000	$3,500,000
Total Costs of Quality (COQ)	**$6,000**	**$3,153,750**	**$11,497,500**

No data has yet been published on the high costs of litigation for poor quality and project failures, or even the frequency of such litigation.

The author of this book has been an expert witness in 15 cases for project failure or poor quality, and therefore has better data than most on litigation frequencies and costs. Also the author's SRM tool has a standard feature that predicts probable litigation costs for both the plaintiff and defendant in breach of contract litigation.

Table 9.8 illustrates two important but poorly understood facts about software quality economics.

1. *High quality software is faster and cheaper to build than poor quality software; maintenance costs are many times cheaper; and technical debt is many times cheaper.*
2. *Poor quality software is slower and more expensive to build than high-quality software; maintenance costs are many times more expensive; and technical debt is many times more expensive.*

Companies that skimp on quality because they need to deliver software in a hurry don't realize that they are slowing down software schedules; not speeding them up.

High quality also causes little or no consequential damages to clients, and the odds of being sued are below 1%, as opposed to about 15% for poor quality software built by outsource vendors. Incidentally state governments seem to have more litigation for failing projects and poor quality than any other industry sector.

High-quality projects are also less likely to experience cyber-attacks because many of these attacks are due to latent security flaws in deployed software. These flaws might have been eliminated prior to deployment if security inspections and security testing plus static analysis had been used.

For software projects, high quality is more than free; it is one of the best investments companies can make. High quality has a large and positive return on investment (ROI). Poor quality software projects have huge risks of failure, delayed schedules, major cost overruns, and more than double the cost per function point compared to high quality.

Stages in Achieving Software Excellence

Readers are probably curious about the sequence of steps needed to move from "average" to "excellent" in software quality. They are also curious about the costs and schedules needed to achieve excellence. Following are short discussions of the sequence and costs needed for a company with about 1,000 software personnel to move from average to excellent results.

Stage 1: Quantify Your Current Software Results

In order to plan improvements rationally, all companies should know their current status using effective quantified data points. This means that every company should measure and know the following topics:

1. Defect potentials
2. Defect severity levels
3. Defects per function point
4. Defect detection efficiency (DDE)
5. Defect removal efficiency (DRE)
6. Cyclomatic complexity of all applications
7. Error-prone modules (EPM) in deployed software
8. Test coverage of all applications
9. Test cases and test scripts per function point
10. Duplicate or incorrect test cases in test libraries
11. Bad-fix injection rates (bugs in defect repairs)
12. The existence or absence of error-prone modules in operational software
13. Customer satisfaction with existing software
14. Defect repair turnaround
15. Technical debt for deployed software
16. Cost of quality (COQ)
17. Security flaws found before release and then after deployment
18. Current set of defect prevention, pre-test, and test quality methods in use
19. The set of software development methodologies in use for all projects
20. Amount of reusable materials utilized for software projects

For a company with 1,000 software personnel and a portfolio of perhaps 3,000 software applications, this first stage can take from two to three calendar months. The effort would probably be in the range of 15 to 25 internal staff months, plus the use of external quality consultants during the fact-finding stage.

The most likely results will be the discovery that defect potentials top 3.5 per function point and DRE is below 92%. Other likely findings will include <80% test coverage and cyclomatic complexity that might be >50 for key modules. Probably a dozen or more error-prone modules will be discovered. Quantitative goals for every software company should be to have defect potentials <2.5 per function point combined with DRE levels >97% for every software project, and above 99% for mission-critical software projects. Software reuse will probably be <15% and mainly be code modules that are picked up informally from other applications.

The analogy for this stage would be like going to a medical clinic for a thorough annual medical check-up. The check-up does not cure any medical problems by itself, but it identifies the problems that physicians will need to cure, if any exist.

Once the current quality results have been measured and quantified, it is then possible to plan rational improvement strategies that will reduce defect potentials and raise DRE to approximate 99% levels.

Stage 2: Begin to Adopt State of the Art Quality Tools and Methods

Software excellence requires more than just adopting a new method such as agile and assuming everything will get better. Software excellence is the result of a web of related methods and tools that are synergistic.

The second stage, which occurs as the first stage is ending, and perhaps overlaps the last month, is to acquire and start to use proven methods for defect prevention, pre-test defect removal, and formal testing.

This stage can vary by the nature and size of the software produced. Real-time and embedded applications will use different tools and methods compared to web and information technology applications. Large systems will use different methods than small applications. However, a nucleus of common techniques is used for all software. These include the following:

Formal Sizing, Estimating, and Tracking

1. Use parametric estimation tools on projects >250 function points.
2. Carry out formal risk analysis before starting.
3. Use formal tracking of progress, quality, and costs.

Defect Prevention

1. Joint application design (JAD).
2. Quality function deployment (QFD).
3. Requirements models.
4. Formal reuse programs.
5. Formal defect measurements.
6. Data mining of legacy applications for lost requirements.

7. Training and certification of quality personnel.
8. Acquisition of defect measurements tools and methods.
9. Formal methodology analysis and selection for key projects.
10. Formal quality and defect estimation before projects start.

Pre-test Defect Removal

1. Static analysis of all legacy applications.
2. Static analysis of all new applications.
3. Static analysis of all changes to applications.
4. Inspections of key deliverables for key projects (requirements, design, code, etc.).
5. Automated proofs of correctness for critical features.

Test Defect Removal

1. Formal test case design, often using design of experiments or cause–effect graphs.
2. Acquisition of test coverage tools.
3. Acquisition of cyclomatic complexity tools.
4. Review of test libraries for duplicate or defective test cases.
5. Formal training of test personnel.
6. Certification of test personnel.
7. Planning optimal test sequences for every key project.
8. Measuring test coverage for all projects.
9. Measuring cylomatic complexity for all code
10. Formal test and quality measures of all projects

This second stage normally lasts about a year and includes formal training of managers, development personnel, quality assurance personnel, test personnel, and other software occupation groups.

Because there is a natural tendency to resist changes, the best way of moving forward is to treat the new tools and methods as experiments. In other words, instead of directing that certain methods such as inspections be used, treat them as experiments and make it clear that if the inspections don't seem useful after trying them out, the teams will not be forced to continue with them. This is how IBM introduced inspections in the 1970s, and the results were so useful that inspections became a standard method without any management directives.

This second stage will take about a year for a company with 1,000 software personnel and more or less time for larger or smaller organizations. Probably all technical personnel will receive at least a week of training and so will project managers.

Probably the costs during this phase due to training and learning curves can top $1,000 per staff member. Some costs will be training; others will be acquisitions of tools. It is difficult to establish a precise cost for tools due to the availability of a large number of open-source tools that have no costs.

Improvements in quality will start to occur immediately during stage 2. However due to learning curves, productivity will drop down slightly for the first 4 months due to having formal training for key personnel. But by the end of a year, productivity may be 15% higher than when the year started. Defect potentials will probably drop by 20% and DRE should go up by >7% from the starting point, and top 95% for every project.

Stage 3: Continuous Improvements Forever

Because stages 1 and 2 introduce major improvements, some interesting sociological phenomena tend to occur. One thing that may occur is that the technical and management leaders of stages 1 and 2 are very likely to get job offers from competitive companies or from other divisions in large corporations.

It sometimes happens that if the stage 1 and 2 leaders are promoted or change jobs, their replacements may not recognize the value of the new tools and methods. For example many companies that use inspections and static analysis find that defects are much reduced compared to previous years.

When quality improves significantly unwise managers may say, *"why keep using inspections and static analysis when they are not finding many bugs?"* Of course if the inspections and static analysis stop, the bug counts will soon start to climb back up to previous levels and DRE will drop down to previous levels.

In order to keep moving ahead and staying at the top, formal training and formal measurements are both needed. Annual training is needed and also formal training of new personnel and new managers. Companies that provide 5 or more days of training for software personnel have higher annual productivity than companies with zero days of training.

When the ITT Corporation began a successful 4-year improvement program, one of the things that was part of their success was an annual report for corporate executives. This report was produced on the same schedule as the annual corporate financial report to shareholders, i.e. in the first quarter of the next fiscal year.

The ITT annual reports showed accomplishments for the prior year; comparisons to earlier years; and projected accomplishments for the following year. Some of the contents of the annual reports included:

1. Software personnel by division.
2. Software personnel by occupation groups.
3. Year-by-year COQ.
4. Total costs of software ownership (TCO).
5. Changes in software personnel by year for three years.
6. Average and ranges of defect potentials.
7. Average and ranges of DRE.
8. Three-year running averages of defect potentials and DRE.
9. Customer satisfaction year by year.
10. Plans for the next fiscal year for staffing, costs, quality, etc.

ITT was a large corporation with over 10,000 software personnel located in a number of countries and more than 25 software development labs. As a result, the overall corporate software report was a fairly large document of about 50 pages in size.

For a smaller company with a staffing of about 1,000 personnel, the annual report would probably be in the 20-page size range.

Once software is up to speed and combines high quality and high productivity, that opens up interesting business questions about the best use of the savings. For example, ITT software personnel had been growing at more than 5% per year for many years. Once quality and productivity improved, it was clear that personnel growth was no longer needed. In fact the quality and productivity were so good after a few years that perhaps 9,000 instead of 10,000 could build and maintain all needed software.

Some of the topics that need to be considered when quality and productivity improve are related to what is the best use of resources no longer devoted to fixing bugs. Some of the possible uses include:

- Reduce corporate backlogs to zero by tackling more projects per year.
- Move into new kinds of applications using newly available personnel no longer locked into bug repairs.
- Allow natural attrition to lower overall staffing down to match future needs.

For commercial software companies expanding into new kinds of software and tackling more projects per year are the best use of available personnel that will be freed up when quality improves.

For government software or for companies that are not expanding their businesses, then probably allowing natural attrition to reduce staffing might be considered. For large organizations, transfers to other business units might occur.

One thing that would be a sociological disaster would be to have layoffs due to the use of improved technologies that reduced staffing needs. In this case resistance to changes and improvements would become a stone wall and progress would stop cold.

Since most companies have large backlogs of applications that are awaiting development, and since most leading companies have needs to expand software into new areas, the best overall result would be to use the available personnel for expansion

Stage three will run for many years. The overall costs per function point should be about 30% lower than before the improvement program started. Overall schedules should be about 25% shorter than before the improvement program started.

Defect potentials will be about 35% lower than when the improvement program started and corporate DRE should top 97% for all projects and 99% for mission critical projects.

Going Beyond Stage 3 into Formal Reuse Programs

As mentioned previously in this report, custom designs and manual coding are intrinsically expensive and error-prone no matter what methodologies are used and what programming languages are used.

For companies that need peak performance, moving into a full and formal software reuse program can achieve results even better than Stage 3.

Summary and Conclusions

Because software is the driving force of both industry and government operations, it needs to be improved in terms of both quality and productivity. The most powerful technology for making really large improvements in both quality and productivity will be from eliminating costly custom designs and labor-intensive hand coding, and moving toward manufacturing software applications from libraries of well-formed standard reusable components that approach zero-defect quality levels.

Today's best combinations of methods, tools, and programming languages are certainly superior to waterfall or cowboy development using unstructured methods and low-level languages. But even the best current methods still involve error-prone custom designs and labor-intensive manual coding.

References and Readings

Abran, A.; and Robillard, P.N.; "Function Point Analysis: An Empirical Study of Its Measurement Processes"; *IEEE Transactions on Software Engineering*, Vol. 22, No. 12; December 1996; pp. 895–909.

Austin, Robert D.; *Measuring and Managing Performance in Organizations*; Dorset House Press, New York, NY; 1996; ISBN: 0-932633-36-6; 216 pages.

Black, Rex; *Managing the Testing Process: Practical Tools and Techniques for Managing Hardware and Software Testing*; Wiley; 2009; ISBN: 10 0470404159; 672 pages.

Bogan, Christopher E.; and English, Michael J.; *Benchmarking for Best Practices*; McGraw Hill, New York, NY; 1994; ISBN: 0-07-006375-3; 312 pages.

Brown, Norm (Editor); *The Program Manager's Guide to Software Acquisition Best Practices*; Version 1.0; U.S. Department of Defense, Washington, DC; July 1995; 142 pages.

Cohen, Lou; *Quality Function Deployment – How to Make QFD Work for You*; Prentice Hall, Upper Saddle River, NJ; 1995; ISBN: 10: 0201633302; 368 pages.

Crosby, Philip B.; *Quality is Free*; New American Library, Mentor Books, New York, NY; 1979; 270 pages.

Curtis, Bill; Hefley, William E.; and Miller, Sally; *People Capability Maturity Model*; Software Engineering Institute, Carnegie Mellon University, Pittsburgh, PA; 1995.

Department of the Air Force; *Guidelines for Successful Acquisition and Management of Software Intensive Systems*, Vols. 1–2; Software Technology Support Center, Hill Air Force Base, UT; 1994.

Dreger, Brian; *Function Point Analysis*; Prentice Hall, Englewood Cliffs, NJ; 1989; ISBN: 0-13-332321-8; 185 pages.

Gack, Gary; *Managing the Black Hole: The Executives Guide to Software Project Risk*; Business Expert Publishing, Thomson, GA; 2010; ISBN: 10: 1-935602-01-9.

Gack, Gary; *Applying Six Sigma to Software Implementation Projects*; http://software.isixsigma.com/library/content/c040915b.asp.

Gilb, Tom; and Graham, Dorothy; *Software Inspections*; Addison Wesley, Reading, MA; 1993; ISBN: 10: 0201631814.

Grady, Robert B.; *Practical Software Metrics for Project Management and Process Improvement*; Prentice Hall, Englewood Cliffs, NJ; 1992; ISBN: 0-13-720384-5; 270 pages.

Grady, Robert B. & Caswell, Deborah L.; *Software Metrics: Establishing a Company-Wide Program*; Prentice Hall, Englewood Cliffs, NJ; 1987; ISBN: 0-13-821844-7; 288 pages.

Grady, Robert B.; *Successful Process Improvement*; Prentice Hall PTR, Upper Saddle River, NJ; 1997; ISBN: 0-13-626623-1; 314 pages.

Humphrey, Watts S.; *Managing the Software Process*; Addison Wesley Longman, Reading, MA; 1989.

IFPUG; *IFPUG Counting Practices Manual*, Release 4, International Function Point Users Group, Westerville, OH; April 1995; 83 pages.

Jacobsen, Ivar; Griss, Martin; and Jonsson, Patrick; *Software Reuse – Architecture, Process, and Organization for Business Success*; Addison Wesley Longman, Reading, MA; 1997; ISBN: 0-201-92476-5; 500 pages.

Jacobsen, Ivar et al; *The Essence of Software Engineering; Applying the SEMAT Kernel*; Addison Wesley Professional; 2013.

Jones, Capers; *The Technical and Social History of Software Engineering*, Addison Wesley; 2014.

Jones, Capers; and Bonsignour, Olivier; *The Economics of Software Quality*, Addison Wesley Longman, Reading, MA; 2011a.

Jones, Capers; *Estimating Software Costs*, 2nd ed.; McGraw Hill; New York, NY; 2007.

Jones, Capers; *Software Engineering Best Practices*; McGraw Hill, New York, NY; 2010a.

Jones, Capers; and Bonsignour, Olivier; *The Economics of Software Quality*; Addison Wesley, Boston, MA; 2011b; ISBN: 978-0-13-258220-9; 587 pages.

Jones, Capers; *A Ten-Year Retrospective of the ITT Programming Technology Center*; Software Productivity Research, Burlington, MA; 1988.

Jones, Capers; *Applied Software Measurement*; McGraw Hill, 3rd ed.; 2008.

Jones, Capers; *Software Engineering Best Practices*; McGraw Hill, 1st ed.; 2010b.

Jones, Capers; *Assessment and Control of Software Risks*; Prentice Hall; 1994; ISBN: 0-13-741406-4; 711 pages.

Jones, Capers; *Patterns of Software System Failure and Success*; International Thomson Computer Press, Boston, MA; December 1995; ISBN: 1-850-32804-8; 250, 292 pages.

Jones, Capers; *Software Assessments, Benchmarks, and Best Practices*; Addison Wesley Longman, Boston, MA; 2000 (due in May of 2000); 600 pages.

Jones, Capers; *Software Quality – Analysis and Guidelines for Success*; International Thomson Computer Press, Boston, MA; 1997a; ISBN: 1-85032-876-6; 492 pages.

Jones, Capers; *The Economics of Object-Oriented Software*; Software Productivity Research, Burlington, MA; April 1997b; 22 pages.

Jones, Capers; *Becoming Best in Class*; Software Productivity Research, Burlington, MA; January 1998; 40 pages.

Kan, Stephen H.; *Metrics and Models in Software Quality Engineering*, 2nd ed.; Addison Wesley Longman, Boston, MA; 2003; ISBN: 0-201-72915-6; 528 pages.

Keys, Jessica; *Software Engineering Productivity Handbook*; McGraw Hill, New York, NY; 1993; ISBN: 0-07-911366-4; 651 pages.

Love, Tom; *Object Lessons*; SIGS Books, New York, NY; 1993; ISBN: 0-9627477 3-4; 266 pages.

McCabe, Thomas J.; "A Complexity Measure"; *IEEE Transactions on Software Engineering*; December 1976; pp. 308–320.

McMahon, Paul; *15 Fundamentals for Higher Performance in Software Development*; PEM Systems; 2014.

Melton, Austin; *Software Measurement*; International Thomson Press, London, UK; 1995; ISBN: 1-85032-7178-7.

Multiple authors; *Rethinking the Software Process*; (CD-ROM); Miller Freeman, Lawrence, KS; 1996. (This is a new CD ROM book collection jointly produced by the book publisher, Prentice Hall, and the journal publisher, Miller Freeman. This CD ROM disk contains the full text and illustrations of five Prentice Hall books: *Assessment and Control of Software Risks* by Capers Jones; *Controlling Software Projects* by Tom DeMarco; *Function Point Analysis* by Brian Dreger; *Measures for Excellence* by Larry Putnam and Ware Myers; and *Object-Oriented Software Metrics* by Mark Lorenz and Jeff Kidd.)

Paulk, Mark et al; *The Capability Maturity Model; Guidelines for Improving the Software Process*; Addison Wesley, Reading, MA; 1995; ISBN: 0-201-54664-7; 439 pages.

Perry, William E.; *Data Processing Budgets – How to Develop and Use Budgets Effectively*; Prentice Hall, Englewood Cliffs, NJ; 1985; ISBN: 0-13-196874-2; 224 pages.

Perry, William E.; *Handbook of Diagnosing and Solving Computer Problems*; TAB Books, Inc.; Blue Ridge Summit, PA; 1989; ISBN: 0-8306-9233-9; 255 pages.

Putnam, Lawrence H.; *Measures for Excellence – Reliable Software On Time, Within Budget*; Yourdon Press, Prentice Hall, Englewood Cliffs, NJ; 1992; ISBN: 0-13-567694-0; 336 pages.

Putnam, Lawrence H.; and Myers, Ware; *Industrial Strength Software – Effective Management Using Measurement*; IEEE Press, Los Alamitos, CA; 1997; ISBN: 0-8186-7532-2; 320 pages.

Radice, Ronald A.; *High Qualitiy Low Cost Software Inspections*; Paradoxicon Publishing, Andover, MA; 2002; ISBN: 0-9645913-1-6; 479 pages.

Royce, Walker E.; *Software Project Management: A Unified Framework*; Addison Wesley Longman, Reading, MA; 1998; ISBN: 0-201-30958-0.

Rubin, Howard; *Software Benchmark Studies For 1997*; Howard Rubin Associates, Pound Ridge, NY; 1997.

Rubin, Howard (Editor); *The Software Personnel Shortage*; Rubin Systems, Inc.; Pound Ridge, NY; 1998.

Shepperd, M.: "A Critique of Cyclomatic Complexity as a Software Metric"; *Software Engineering Journal*, Vol. 3; 1988; pp. 30–36.

Strassmann, Paul; *The Squandered Computer*; The Information Economics Press, New Canaan, CT; 1997; ISBN: 0-9620413-1-9; 426 pages.

Stukes, Sherry; Deshoretz, Jason; Apgar, Henry; and Macias, Ilona; *Air Force Cost Analysis Agency Software Estimating Model Analysis*; TR-9545/008-2; Contract F04701-95-D-0003, Task 008; Management Consulting & Research, Inc.; Thousand Oaks, CA; September 30, 1996.

Symons, Charles R.; *Software Sizing and Estimating – Mk II FPA (Function Point Analysis)*; John Wiley & Sons, Chichester; 1991; ISBN: 0 471-92985-9; 200 pages.

Thayer, Richard H. (Editor); *Software Engineering and Project Management*; IEEE Press, Los Alamitos, CA; 1988; ISBN: 0 8186-075107; 512 pages.

Umbaugh, Robert E. (Editor); *Handbook of IS Management*, 4th ed.; Auerbach Publications, Boston, MA; 1995; ISBN: 0-7913-2159-2; 703 pages.

Weinberg, Gerald; *Quality Software Management – Vol. 2: First-Order Measurement*; Dorset House Press, New York, NY; 1993; ISBN: 0-932633-24-2; 360 pages.

Wiegers, Karl A.; *Creating a Software Engineering Culture*; Dorset House Press, New York, NY; 1996; ISBN: 0-932633-33-1; 358 pages.

Yourdon, Ed; *Death March – The Complete Software Developer's Guide to Surviving "Mission Impossible" Projects*; Prentice Hall PTR, Upper Saddle River, NJ; 1997; ISBN: 0-13-748310-4; 218 pages.

Zells, Lois; *Managing Software Projects – Selecting and Using PC-Based Project Management Systems*; QED Information Sciences, Wellesley, MA; 1990; ISBN: 0-89435-275-X; 487 pages.

Zvegintzov, Nicholas; *Software Management Technology Reference Guide*; Dorset House Press, New York, NY; 1994; ISBN: 1-884521-01-0; 240 pages.

Chapter 10

Early Sizing and Estimating of Software Projects

Introduction

Most methods of software sizing and estimating are based on software requirements and design documents, or on the source code itself. For both new applications and enhancements, this means that substantial funds will have been expended before sizing and estimating take place. Early sizing and estimating pay handsome dividends due to better results for on-schedule and within-budget projects, as shown in Table 10.1 in this chapter.

Namcook Analytics has developed a new method of early software sizing and estimating based on pattern matching that can be used prior to requirements. This new method permits very early estimates and very early risk analysis before substantial investments are made.

Software sizing and estimating have been weak areas of software engineering since the industry began. Even today a majority of the world's software projects use educated guesses for sizing and inaccurate and optimistic manual estimates instead of accurate automated parametric estimates. Large companies are more sophisticated than small companies and tend to have more sophisticated sizing and estimating methods and tools. It is useful to look at sizing and estimating methods since the software industry began:

DOI: 10.1201/9781003193128-12

1950 to 1959

Sizing was based on lines of code (LOC) (usually physical). Estimating was a combination of guesswork and sparse historical data. In this era, assembly was the only language at the beginning of the decade so LOC still worked.

1960 to 1969

Sizing was based on LOC. Estimating was still based on guesswork but some companies such as IBM collected useful historical data that were helpful in estimation. Projects grew larger so estimating requirements and design became important. Languages such as COBOL, Algol, and others were developed and LOC metrics started to encounter problems such as difficulty in counting LOC for projects with multiple languages.

1970 to 1979

By the end of this decade, over 80 programming languages were in existence and LOC metrics were proven to be inaccurate and unreliable by IBM. LOC metrics can't measure requirements and design, which by 1979 were more expensive than code itself. Also, LOC metrics penalize high-level languages such as APL and PL/I.

IBM was the first company to perform a formal study of the errors and problems with LOC metrics, which occurred about 1972 with the author of this book as the primary IBM researcher. This study and the proof of LOC failure led IBM to fund the development of function point metrics.

Due to major problems and proven errors with LOC metrics, IBM created the function point metric for sizing and estimating software projects.

In 1973 the author of this book developed IBM's first parametric estimation tool, which was coded in APL by Dr. Charles Turk. Also during this decade, other estimating pioneers such as Dr. Barry Boehm, Dr. Howard Rubin, Frank Freiman, and Dr. Larry Putnam developed early parametric estimation tools.

Function points were put into the public domain by IBM in 1979 and expanded all over the world. By the end of this decade, many leading organizations such as IBM, ITT, TRW, RCA, and the Air Force used proprietary parametric estimation tools and also used function point metrics. The technique of "backfiring" or mathematical conversion from source code to function points was developed by IBM in this decade and began to be used for sizing legacy applications.

1980 to 1989

During this decade, function points became a major global metric for sizing and estimating. The author's SPQR/20 estimation tool released in 1984 was the world's first parametric estimation tool based on function points. It was also the first that included sizing for all deliverables (requirements, design, code, test cases, etc.). The inventor of function point metrics, A.J. Albrecht, had retired from IBM and came to work for the author.

Only function point metrics support sizing of requirements, design, user documents, and test cases; this cannot be done using LOC metrics. Other parametric estimating tools such as CheckPoint, COCOMO, Estimacs, KnowledgePlan, SEER, SLIM, etc. also entered the commercial market.

Most major companies used either commercial or proprietary parametric estimation by the end of this decade. The author of this book designed proprietary estimation tools under contract for several telecommunication companies and also taught software sizing and estimation at AT&T, Bell Northern, GTE, ITT, Motorola, Nippon Telephone, Nokia, Pacific Bell, Siemens, Sprint, and others.

The International Function Point User's Group (IFPUG) was created in Canada and began to provide certification examinations to ensure accurate function point counts. IFPUG later moved its headquarters to the United States.

1990 to 1999

Due to the initial success and value of IFPUG function points, this decade saw the creation of a number of function point metric "clones" that differed somewhat in their counting rules. Some of these functional metric clones include in alphabetical order: COSMIC function points, engineering function points, fast function points, feature points, FISMA function points, NESMA function points, story points, unadjusted function points, and use-case points. Most of these use counting rules similar to IFPUG but have various additional rules or changed rules. This causes more confusion than value. It also introduced a need for conversion rules between the various functional metrics, such as the conversion rules built into Software Risk Master (SRM).

The International Software Benchmark Standards Group (ISBSG) was created in 1997 and began to provide software benchmark data using only function points. Lines-of-code data is hazardous and unreliable for benchmarks.

Other benchmark providers also began to offer benchmarks such as the author's former company, Software Productivity Research (SPR).

Two former vice presidents at SPR also formed software benchmark companies after SPR was sold in 1998.

Although function point metrics were widely used and were accurate when counted by certified personnel, they were also slow and expensive. An average certified function point counter can count about 500 function points per day, which limited the use of function points to small projects.

By the end of this decade, most U.S. telecom companies employed or contracted with between 5 and 12 certified function point counters.

2000 to 2010

Function point metrics had become the global basis of software benchmarks and were widely used in parametric estimation tools. However, the slow counting speeds and high costs of manual function point analysis led to research in easier and faster methods of function point analysis.

Many companies developed function point tools that provided mathematical support for the calculations. These speeded up function point counting from about 500 function points per day to more than 1,000 function points per day.

Several companies (CAST Software and Relativity Technologies) developed automated function point counting tools. These tools examined source code from legacy applications and created function points based on this code analysis. These tools only work for applications where code exists, but instead of 500 function points per day they can top 50,000 function points per day.

In 2012 IFPUG issued the new SNAP metric (software non-functional assessment process). This metric has been added to the Namcook sizing method.

The author and Namcook Analytics developed a proprietary sizing method based on pattern matching that is part of the SRM estimating tool. This method uses a formal taxonomy and then extracts size data from the Namcook knowledge base for projects that have the same taxonomy pattern.

The Namcook sizing method is included in the SRM estimating tool. SRM sizing is unique in being able to size and estimate projects before requirements, or 30–180 days earlier than any other known method.

The SRM method is the fastest available method of sizing and averages about 1.8 minutes to size any application. Of course measured speed varies with the sizes of the applications themselves, but SRM can size at speeds of well over 300,000 function points per day.

SRM sizing is also unique in being able to predict size in a total of 23 metrics at the same time: all forms of function points, logical and physical LOC, story points, use-case points, and even RICE objects for ERP packages.

SRM also collects new benchmark data every month, because estimating tools need continuous updates to their knowledge bases to stay current with technical changes such as cloud computing, SaaS, estimating social network software, and other technology innovations. In fact the commercial estimating companies all collect benchmark data for the same reason.

The State of the Art of Sizing and Estimating from 2010 to 2020

In 2020, the corona virus pandemic arrived in the United States. Many companies have shifted to work at home. Group activities such as reviews and inspections were done remotely via Zoom instead of using face to face meetings in conference rooms. No doubt productivity declined and quality lowered as well. It is too soon to know the exact magnitude to the disruption.

As of 2020, the state of the art varied with the size and sophistication of the company. Large technology companies such as medical devices, computers, avionics, telecommunications etc. typically use multiple sizing and estimating methods and look for convergence. Most employ or use function point counters. Most technology companies use high-end commercial estimation tools such as SRM or have built their own proprietary estimation tools. Some smaller companies and universities use the open-source COCOMO estimating tool, which is available without cost.

Mid-sized companies and companies in the banking, insurance, and other areas are not quite as sophisticated as the large technology companies. It is interesting that the Bank of Montreal was the first major company to use function points and was a founder of IFPUG.

However, a recent survey of over 100 companies found that function point metrics were now dominant for estimating and benchmarks in the U.S., Europe, Japan, and Brazil and these countries have many more function point users than other metrics such as story points or the older LOC metrics. About 70% of mid-sized companies still use manual estimates but about 30% use one or more parametric estimating tools such as SRM.

Many agile projects use manual estimates combined with the "story point metric." Unfortunately, story points have no ISO or OMG standards and vary by hundreds of percent from company to company. They are almost useless for benchmarks due to the low quantity of available data and the poor accuracy of story points for either estimates or measurements.

In 2012, a new metric for non-functional requirements called "SNAP" was created by IFPUG and is now starting to be used. However as of 2016, this metric is so new that not a great deal of data exists, nor do all companies use it. This metric needs additional definitions and continued analysis.

Small companies with less than 100 employees only build small applications where risks are low. About 90% of these companies use manual estimates. Most are too small to afford function point consultants and too small to afford commercial estimating tools so they tend to use backfiring and convert code size into function points. They still need function points because all reliable benchmarks are based on function point metrics. Some small companies use COCOMO because it is free, even though it was originally calibrated for defense software. Table 10.1 shows the economic advantages of using automated sizing and estimating tools such as SRM.

As can be seen, early sizing and estimating using a tool such as SRM can lead to much better on-time and within-budget performance than older manual estimating methods or delayed estimates after requirements are completed.

Table 10.1 Results of Early Sizing and Estimating (Assumes 1000 Function Points and Java Code)

	On-Time Delivery	In Budget Delivery	Defect Removal Efficiency	$ per Function Point
Automated sizing and estimating before Requirements	95.00%	95.00%	97.50%	$950
Automated sizing and estimating after Requirements	80.00%	87.00%	92.50%	$1,100
Manual sizing and estimating after requirements	55.00%	60.00%	88.00%	$1,350
No formal sizing or estimating	44.00%	38.00%	85.00%	$1,800

Hazards of Older Metrics

Even some users of function point metrics are not fully aware of the problems with older metrics. Following paragraphs are short summaries of metric hazards in alphabetical order:

Automated function points several companies such as CAST Software and Relativity Technologies have marketed automated function point tools that derive function point totals from an analysis of source code. These tools have no published accuracy data. They also can only be used on legacy software and cannot be used for early sizing and estimating of new software applications before code exists.

Cost per defect penalizes quality and is cheapest for the buggiest software. This phenomenon was discovered circa 1972 by the author of this book and colleagues at IBM. Cost per defect cannot be used at all for zero-defect software. The cost per defect for software with 1,000 released defects will be much cheaper than the same software with only 10 defects. Cost per defect is useless for zero-defect software, which should be the goal of all projects. Defect removal costs per function point provide a much better basis for studying software quality economics than cost per defect.

Design, code, and unit test (DCUT) metrics are embarrassingly bad. The sum total of effort for design, code, and unit test is less than 37% of total software effort. Using DCUT is like measuring only the costs of the foundations and framing of a house, and ignoring the walls, roof, electrical systems, plumbing, etc. Only the software industry would use such a poor metric as DCUT. All projects should measure <u>every</u> activity: business analysis, requirements, architecture, design, documentation, quality assurance, management, etc.

Lines of code (LOC) metrics cannot measure non-coding work such as requirements, architecture, design, and documentation which are more expensive than the code itself. Coding on large systems may only comprise 30% of total costs. LOC cannot measure bugs in requirements and design, which often are more numerous than coding bugs. Even worse, LOC metrics penalize high-level languages and make low-level languages such as assembly and C look better than high-level languages such as Visual Basic and Ruby. Also, many languages use buttons or controls and allow "programming" without even using LOC. LOC has no ISO standard counting rules (physical and logical code are counted about equally), and also no certification exams. There are automatic counting tools for LOC but these vary in what they count. Finally, an average application in 2015 uses at least two languages and sometimes up to a dozen different programming languages. Code counting for multiple programming languages is very complex and slow. Typical combinations are Java, HTML, MySQL, and possibly others as well.

Technical debt by Ward Cunningham is a brilliant metaphor but not yet an effective metric. Technical debt has no ISO standards and no certification exams. Among the author's clients, technical debt varies by more than 200% between companies and projects. Worse, technical debt only covers about 17% of the total costs of poor quality. Missing with technical are canceled projects that are never delivered; consequential damages to users; litigation costs for poor quality; and court awards to plaintiffs for damages caused by poor quality.

Story point metrics are widely used with agile projects. However, story points have no ISO standards or OMG standards and no certification exams. Among the author's clients story points vary by more than 400% between companies and projects. There are few if any benchmarks based on story points.

Use-case metrics are widely used with RUP projects. However use-case points have no ISO standards and no certification exams. Among the author's clients, use-case points vary by more than 100% between companies and projects. There are few if any benchmarks based on use-case points.

Overall function point metrics provide the most stable and effective metrics for analyzing software quality economics, software productivity, and software value. The major forms of function points have ISO standards and certification exams unlike the older and hazardous metrics discussed above.

As illustrated elsewhere in this chapter, the detailed metrics used with function points include but are not limited to the following points (Table 10.2).

All 30 of these sizing features were included in the SRM sizing methodology as of 2019.

Metrics Used with Function Point Analysis

The counting rules for function points are available from the various function point associations and are too complicated to discuss here. If a company wants to learn function point counting, the best methods are to either hire certified function point counters or send internal personnel to learn function point analysis and take a certification exam offered by the function point associations.

Table 10.2 Software Risk Master (SRM) Function Point and SNAP Usage Circa 2020

1	Predicting size in function points, SNAP, LOC, and a total of 23 metrics.
2	Early sizing and risk analysis via pattern matching before full requirements.
3	Sizing of internal, COTS, and open-source applications.
4	Sizing and estimating both new projects and legacy repairs and renovations.
5	Sizing and estimating 15 types of software (web, IT, embedded, defense, etc.).
6	Source code sizing for 84 programming languages and combinations of languages.
7	Sizing requirements creep during development (>1% per calendar month).
8	Sizing post-release requirements growth for up to 10 years (>8% per year).
9	Sizing defect potentials per function point/SNAP point (requirements, design, code, etc.).
10	Defect prevention efficiency (DPE) for JAD, QFD, modeling, reuse, etc.
11	Defect removal efficiency (DRE) for pre-test and test defect removal methods.
12	Document sizing for 30 document types (requirements, design, architecture, etc.).
13	Sizing test cases per function point and per SNAP point for all forms of testing.
14	Estimating delivered defects per function point and per SNAP point.
15	Activity-based costs for development.
16	Activity-based costs for user effort on internal projects.
17	Activity-based costs for maintenance.
18	Activity-based costs for customer support.
19	Activity-based costs for enhancements.
20	Occupation-group effort for 25 common software skills (coders, testers, analysts, etc.).
21	Total cost of ownership (TCO) including cyber-attack costs.
22	Cost of quality (COQ) for software applications including cyber-attacks and litigation.
23	Estimating the newer technical debt metric which is ambiguous in 2016.
24	Risk probabilities for 30 common software risk factors (delays, overruns, cancellation).

(Continued)

Table 10.2 (Continued)

25	Estimating productivity and quality results for 60 software development methodologies.
26	Estimating ERP deployment, customization, and training costs.
27	Software litigation costs for failing outsource projects (both plaintiff and defendant).
28	Estimating venture funding rounds, investment, equity dilution for software startups.
29	Estimating cyber-attack deterrence and recovery costs (new in 2016).
30	Portfolio sizing for corporate portfolios (>5000 applications,10,000,000 function points, and 1,500,000 SNAP points) including internal, COTS, and open-source.

The current IFPUG counting rule manual is available from the IFPUG organization and is about 125 pages in size: too big to summarize here. Counting rules are also available from other function point communities such as COSMIC, FISMA, NESMA, etc.

Once the function point total for an application is known, then function points can be used with a variety of useful supplemental metrics to examine productivity, quality, costs, etc.

The following are some of the leading metrics used with function points in alphabetical order:

Assignment Scope

This is the amount of work typically assigned to a software team member. It can be expressed using function points or natural metrics such as pages of documents and LOC. For example, a technical writer might be assigned a user manual of 200 pages. Since software user manuals average about 0.15 pages per function point that would be an assignment scope of 30 function points.

Typical assignment scopes using function points for a project of 1,000 function points would be:

Requirements	=	460 function points
Design	=	345 function points
Coding	=	130 function points
Testing	=	150 function points

This kind of data is available for 40 activities from Namcook Analytics LLC. This data is a standard feature of SRM but limited to 7 activities.

Cost per Function Point

As of 2020, cost per function point is one of the most widely used economic metrics in the world. Several national governments such as Brazil and South Korea demand cost per function point in all bids and software contracts. India uses cost per function point to attract business to Indian outsource companies. The cost per function point metric can be used for full projects and also for individual activities such as requirements, design, coding, etc.

There are several cautions about this metric however. For long-range projects that may take more than 5 years inflation needs to be factored in. For international projects that may include multiple countries local costs and currency conversions need to be factored in. In the U.S. as of 2015 development costs per function point range from less than $500 for small internal projects to more than $3,000 for large defense projects.

Cost per function point varies from project to project. Assuming a cost structure of $10,000 per month and 1,000 function points typical costs per function point would be:

Requirements	=	$41.79
Design	=	$66.87
Coding	=	$393.89
Testing	=	$236.34

Here too these are standard results from SRM. This kind of data is available for 40 activities from Namcook Analytics LLC. SRM shows 7 activities.

Defect Potentials

Defect potentials are the sum total of bugs that are likely to be found in requirements, architecture, design, code user documents, and bad fixes or secondary bugs in bug repairs. U.S. totals for defect potentials range from <2.00 defects per function point to >6.00 defects per function point. This metric is also used for specific defect categories. Requirements defects per function point range from <0.25 per function point to >1.15 per function point. The full set of defect potentials include defects in requirements, architecture, design, code, documents, and "bad fixes" or secondary bugs in defect repairs themselves. There are also defects in test cases, but these are very seldom studied so there is not enough available data to include test-case defects in defect potentials as of 2016.

Defect potentials are ONLY possible with function point metrics because LOC metrics cannot be used for requirements and design defects. Typical values for defect potentials in function points circa 2019 are shown in Table 10.3.

As can be seen, defect potentials include bugs in many sources and not just code. As can be seen, requirements, architecture, and design defects outnumber code defects. Defect potential estimation is a standard feature for SRM.

Defect Removal Efficiency (DRE)

This metric does not use function points themselves, but rather shows the percentage of defect potentials removed before release. Typical values would be 80% of requirements defects are removed before release but 98% of code defects. SRM predicts both defect potentials and individual removal efficiency levels for requirements defects, architecture defects, code defects, document defects, and bad-fix injections.

Typical values for DRE are as follows:

Requirements defects	=	75%
Design defects	=	85%
Architecture defects	=	90%
Code defects	=	97%

Table 10.3   Average Software Defect Potentials circa 2020 for the United States

•Requirements	0.70 defects per function point
•Architecture	0.10 defects per function point
•Design	0.95 defects per function point
•Code	1.15 defects per function point
•Security code flaws	0.25 defects per function point
•Documents	0.45 defects per function point
•Bad fixes	0.65 defects per function point
Total	**4.25 defects per function point**

Defect removal efficiency is a standard feature of SRM. DRE in SRM includes (1) pre-test inspections, (2) static analysis, (3) desk checking, and (4) pair programming.

Test DRE is shown for six kinds of testing: (1) unit, (2) regression, (3) component, (4) performance, (5) system, and (6) acceptance.

Function Points per Month

This is a common productivity metric but one that needs to be adjusted for countries, industries, and companies. Work-hours-per-function-point is more stable from country to country. The typical number of work hours in the U.S. is 132 hours per month; in India it is about 190 hours per month; in Germany it is about 116 hours per month. Thus, the same number of work hours would have different values for function points per month. Assume a small project took exactly 500 work hours. For India, this project would take 2.63 months; for the U.S. 3.78 months; for Germany 4.31 months. The metric of work hours per function point is stable across all countries, but function points per month (and the older LOC per month) vary widely from country to country.

Production Rate

This metric is the amount of work a software team member can perform in a given time period such as an hour, day, week, or month. This metric can be expressed using function points or natural metrics such as LOC or pages. For example a technical writer might be able to write 50 pages per month. A programmer may be able to code 1,000 LOC per month. A tester may be able to run 500 test cases per month, and so on. The same activities can also be measured using work hours per function point, or a combination of function points and natural metrics.

Requirements Creep

Because applications add new requirements and new features during development, size must be adjusted from time to time. Requirements grow and change at measured rates of between 1% per calendar month and about 4% per calendar month. Thus, an application sized at 1,000 function points at the end of requirements may grow to 1,100 function points by delivery. Software keeps growing after release, and the same application may grow to 1,500 function points after three or four years of use. SRM predicts growth and can also measure it. (This is not a feature of most parametric estimation tools.)

Work Hours per Function Point

This is a very common metric for software productivity. It has the advantages of being the same in every country and also of being useful with every software development activity. SRM uses this as a standard metric for all estimates as shown subsequently:

1. Requirements	=	0.60 work hours per function point
2. Design	=	0.90 work hours per function point
3. Coding	=	5.00 work hours per function point
4. Testing	=	3.50 work hours per function point
5. Quality	=	0.50 work hours per function point
6. Documents	=	0.40 work hours per function point
7. Management	=	2.00 work hours per function point
Total	**=**	**12.90 work hours per function point**

Note: these values are just examples and not intended for use in actual estimates. There are wide ranges for every activity. Also, the example only shows 7 activities, but similar data is available from Namcook Analytics LLC for 40 activities.

The same metric or work hours per function point can also be used to measure user costs for internal user effort, training costs for customers and team members, and even marketing and sales effort for commercial software packages. It can also be used for customer support, bug repairs, and even project management.

Function points are a powerful and useful metric but need additional metrics in order to actually estimate and measure real projects.

Application Sizing Using Pattern Matching

The unique Namcook pattern-matching approach is based on the same methodology as the well-known Trulia and Zillow data bases for real-estate costs.

With the real-estate data bases, home buyers can find the costs, taxes, and other information for all listed homes in all U.S. cities. They can specify "patterns" for searching such as size, lot size, number of rooms, etc.

The main topics used for software pattern matching in the Namcook SRM tool are given in Table 10.4.

Table 10.4   Patterns for Application Sizing and Risk Analysis

1	Local average team salary and burden rates.
2	Paid and unpaid overtime planned for projects.
3	Planned start date for the project.
4	Desired delivery date for the project.
5	Country or countries where the software will be built.
6	Industry for which the software is intended.
7	Locations where the software will be built (states, cities).
8	Experience levels for clients, team, management.
9	Development methodologies that will be used (Agile, RUP,TSP, etc.)*.
10	CMMI level of the development group*.
11	Programming language(s) that will be used (C#, C++, Java, SQL, etc.)*.
12	Amount of reusable materials available (design, code, tests etc.)*.
13	Nature of the project (new, enhancement, etc.)*.
14	Scope of the project (subprogram, program, departmental system, etc.)*.
15	Class of the project (internal use, open-source, commercial, etc.)*.
16	Type of the project (embedded, web application, client–server, etc.)*.
17	Problem complexity ranging from very low to very high*.
18	Code complexity ranging from very low to very high*.
19	Data complexity ranging from very low to very high*.
20	Number of anticipated users (for maintenance estimates).

* Factors used for pattern analysis for sizing

All of these topics are usually known well before requirements. All of the questions are multiple choice questions except for the start date and compensation and burden rates. Default cost values are provided for situations where such cost information is not known or is proprietary. This might occur if multiple contractors are bidding on a project and they all have different cost structures.

The answers to the multiple-choice questions form a "pattern" that is then compared against a Namcook knowledge base of more than 25,000 software projects. As with the real-estate data bases, software projects that have identical patterns usually have about the same size and similar results in terms of schedules, staffing, risks, and effort.

Sizing via pattern matching can be used prior to requirements and therefore perhaps 6 months earlier than most other sizing methods. The method is also very quick and usually takes less than 5 minutes per project. With experience, the time required can drop down to less than 2 minutes per project.

The pattern-matching approach is very useful for large applications >10,000 function points where manual sizing might take weeks or even months. With pattern matching, the actual size of the application does not affect the speed of the result and even massive applications in excess of 100,000 function points can be sized in a few minutes or less.

The method of sizing by pattern matching is metric neutral and does not depend upon any specific metric. However, due to the fact that a majority of the author's clients use function point metrics as defined by the International Function Point Users Group (IFPUG), the primary metric supported is that of IFPUG function points counting rules 4.2. There are of course more projects measured using IFPUG function points than those available using other metrics.

Many additional metrics can also be based on sizing via SRM pattern matching including but not limited to metrics given in Table 10.5.

The pattern-matching approach depends upon the availability of thousands of existing projects to be effective. However now that function point metrics have been in use for more than 48 years, there are thousands of projects available.

One additional feature of pattern matching is that it can provide size data on requirements creep and on deferred functions. Thus the pattern-matching method predicts size at the end of the requirements phase, creeping requirements, size at delivery, and also the probable number of function points that might have to be deferred to achieve a desired delivery date.

In fact the pattern-matching approach does not stop at delivery but can continue to predict application growth year by year for up to 10 years after deployment.

The ability to size open-source and commercial applications or even classified weapons systems is a unique feature of sizing via pattern matching. Table 10.6 shows 100 software applications sized via pattern matching with an average speed of about 1.8 minutes per application.

The ability to size open-source and commercial applications or even classified weapons systems is a unique feature of sizing via pattern matching and also unique to SRM.

No other sizing method can be used without access to at least published requirements. The unique patter-matching size technique of SRM is the only one that can size software without detailed inner knowledge. This is because SRM uses external patterns.

Note that SRM sizing is a proprietary trade secret and not available to the public. However, a visit to the Namcook web site www.Namcook.com

Table 10.5   Metrics Supported by Namcook Pattern Matching

1	IFPUG function points
2	Automated code-based
3	Automated UML-based
4	Backfired function points
5	Non-functional SNAP points based on SNAP rules
6	COSMIC function points
7	FISMA function points
8	NESMA function points
9	Simple function points
10	Mark II function points
11	Unadjusted function points
12	Function points "light"
13	Engineering function points
14	Feature points
15	Use-case points
16	Story points
17	Lines of code (logical statements)
18	Lines of code (physical lines)
19	RICE objects
20	Micro function points
21	Logical code statements
22	Physical lines of code
23	Additional metrics as published

includes a trial version that is run-limited but can produce several project sizes before the limits are reached.

Early Risk Analysis

One of the main purposes of early sizing is to be able to identify software risks early enough to plan and deploy effective solutions. This is why Namcook calls its sizing and estimating tool "Software Risk Master" (SRM).

Table 10.6   Sizes of 100 Software Applications

	Applications (Note: SRM sizing takes about 1.8 minutes per application for sizing (patent-pending)	Size in Function Points	SNAP Non-function Points	Size in Logical Code
		IFPUG 4.3	*IFPUG*	*Statements*
1	IBM Future System FS/1 (circa 1985 not completed)	515,323	108,218	68,022,636
2	Star Wars missile defense	352,330	42,280	32,212,992
3	World-wide military command and control (WWMCCS)	307,328	56,856	28,098,560
4	U.S. Air Traffic control	306,324	59,121	65,349,222
5	Israeli air defense system	300,655	63,137	24,052,367
6	North Korean border defenses	273,961	50,957	25,047,859
7	Iran's air defense system	260,100	46,558	23,780,557
8	SAP	253,500	32,070	18,480,000
9	Aegis destroyer C&C	253,088	49,352	20,247,020
10	Oracle	229,434	29,826	18,354,720
11	Windows 10 (all features)	198,050	21,786	12,675,200
12	Obamacare web (all features)	107,350	5,720	12,345,250
13	Microsoft Office Professional 2010	93,498	10,285	5,983,891
14	Airline reservation system	38,392	5,759	6,142,689
15	North Korean Long-Range Missile controls	37,235	4,468	5,101,195
16	NSA code decryption	35,897	3,590	3,829,056
17	FBI Carnivore	31,111	2,800	3,318,515
18	FBI fingerprint analysis	25,075	3,260	2,674,637
19	NASA space shuttle	23,153	3,010	2,116,878
20	VA Patient monitoring	23,109	3,004	4,929,910
21	Data Warehouse	21,895	2,846	1,077,896

Table 10.6 (Continued)

	Applications (Note: SRM sizing takes about 1.8 minutes per application for sizing (patent-pending)	Size in Function Points	SNAP Non-function Points	Size in Logical Code
		IFPUG 4.3	*IFPUG*	*Statements*
22	NASA Hubble controls	21,632	2,163	1,977,754
23	Skype	21,202	3,392	1,130,759
24	Shipboard gun controls	21,199	4,240	1,938,227
25	American Express billing	20,141	3,223	1,432,238
26	M1 Abrams battle tank operations	19,569	3,131	1,789,133
27	Apple I Phone v6 operations	19,366	2,518	516,432
28	IRS income tax analysis	19,013	2,472	1,352,068
29	Cruise ship navigation	18,896	2,456	1,343,713
30	MRI medical imaging	18,785	2,442	1,335,837
31	Google search engine	18,640	2,423	1,192,958
32	Amazon web site	18,080	2,350	482,126
33	State wide child support	17,850	2,321	952,000
34	Linux	17,505	2,276	700,205
35	FEDEX shipping controls	17,378	2,259	926,802
36	Tomahawk cruise missile	17,311	2,250	1,582,694
37	Denver Airport luggage (original)	17,002	2,166	1,554,497
38	Inventory management	16,661	2,111	1,332,869
39	EBAY transaction controls	16,390	2,110	1,498,554
40	Patriot missile controls	16,239	2,001	1,484,683
41	IBM IMS data base	15,392	1,939	1,407,279
42	Toyota robotic manufacturing	14,912	1,822	3,181,283
43	Android operating system	14,019	1,749	690,152
44	Quicken 2015	13,811	1,599	679,939

(Continued)

Table 10.6 (Continued)

	Applications (Note: SRM sizing takes about 1.8 minutes per application for sizing (patent-pending)	Size in Function Points	SNAP Non-function Points	Size in Logical Code
		IFPUG 4.3	IFPUG	Statements
45	State transportation ticketing	12,300	1,461	656,000
46	State Motor vehicle registrations	11,240	1,421	599,467
47	Insurance claims handling	11,033	1,354	252,191
48	SAS statistical package	10,927	1,349	999,065
49	Oracle CRM Features	10,491	836	745,995
50	DNA Analysis	10,380	808	511,017
51	EZPass vehicle controls	4,751	594	253,400
52	Cat scan medical device	4,575	585	244,000
53	Chinese submarine sonar	4,500	522	197,500
54	Microsoft Excel 2007	4,429	516	404,914
55	Citizens bank on-line	4,017	655	367,224
56	MapQuest	3,969	493	254,006
57	Bank ATM controls	3,917	571	208,927
58	NVIDIA graphics card	3,793	464	151,709
59	Lasik surgery (wave guide)	3,625	456	178,484
60	Sun D-Trace utility	3,505	430	373,832
61	Microsoft Outlook	3,450	416	157,714
62	Microsoft Word 2007	3,309	388	176,501
63	Adobe Illustrator	2,507	280	178,250
64	SpySweeper antispyware	2,227	274	109,647
65	Norton anti-virus software	2,151	369	152,942
66	Microsoft Project 2007	2,108	255	192,757
67	Microsoft Visual Basic	2,068	247	110,300

Table 10.6 (Continued)

Applications (Note: SRM sizing takes about 1.8 minutes per application for sizing (patent-pending)	Size in Function Points IFPUG 4.3	SNAP Non-function Points IFPUG	Size in Logical Code Statements
68	All-in-one printer	1,963	231	125,631
69	AutoCAD	1,900	230	121,631
70	Garmin hand-helc GPS	1,858	218	118,900
71	Intel Math function library	1,768	211	141,405
72	PBX switching system	1,658	207	132,670
73	Motorola cell phone contact list	1,579	196	144,403
74	Seismic analysis	1,564	194	83,393
75	Sidewinder missile controls	1,518	188	60,730
76	Apple I Pod	1,507	183	80,347
77	Property tax assessments	1,492	179	136,438
78	Mozilla Firefox (original)	1,450	174	132,564
79	Google Gmail	1,379	170	98,037
80	Digital camera controls	1,344	167	286,709
81	IRA account management	1,340	167	71,463
82	Consumer credit report	1,332	165	53,288
83	Sun Java compiler	1,310	163	119,772
84	All in one printer driver	1,306	163	52,232
85	Laser printer driver	1,285	162	82,243
86	JAVA compiler	1,281	162	91,096
87	Smart bomb targeting	1,267	150	67,595
88	Wikipedia	1,257	148	67,040
89	Casio atomic watch with compass, tides	1,250	129	66,667

(Continued)

Table 10.6 (Continued)

Applications (Note: SRM sizing takes about 1.8 minutes per application for sizing (patent-pending)		Size in Function Points	SNAP Non-function Points	Size in Logical Code
		IFPUG 4.3	IFPUG	Statements
90	Cochlear implant (embedded)	1,250	135	66,667
91	APAR analysis and routing	1,248	113	159,695
92	Computer BIOS	1,215	111	86,400
93	Automobile fuel injection	1,202	109	85,505
94	Anti-lock brake controls	1,185	107	63,186
95	Ccleaner utility	1,154	103	73,864
96	Hearing aid (multi program)	1,142	102	30,448
97	LogiTech cordless mouse	1,134	96	90,736
98	Instant messaging	1,093	89	77,705
99	Twitter (original circa 2009)	1,002	77	53,455
100	Denial of service virus	866	–	79,197
Averages		**42,682**	**6,801**	**4,250,002**

If risks are not identified until after the requirements are complete, it is usually too late to make changes in development methods.

25 major risks where application size has been proven to be a major factor in application costs, schedules, and quality include but are not limited to those shown in the Table 10.7.

All 25 of these software risks are proportional to application size, so early sizing is a useful precursor for risk avoidance and risk mitigation. In estimating mode, SRM predicts the odds of these risks occurring and in measurement mode can measure their impact on completed projects.

There are also many risks that are not directly related to project size: bankruptcies, theft of intellectual property, cyber-attacks

Table 10.7   Software Risks Related to Application Size

1	Project cancellations
2	Project cost overruns
3	Project schedule delays
4	Creeping requirements (>1% per month)
5	Deferred features due to deadlines (>20% of planned features)
6	High defect potentials
7	Low defect removal efficiency (DRE)
8	Latent security flaws in application when released
9	Error-prone modules (EPM) in applications
10	High odds of litigation for outsource contract projects
11	Low customer satisfaction levels
12	Low team morale due to overtime and over work
13	Inadequate defect tracking which fails to highlight real problems
14	Inadequate cost tracking which omits major expense elements
15	Long learning curves by maintenance and support teams
16	Frequent user errors when learning complex new systems
17	Post-release cyber-attacks (denial of service, hacking, data theft, etc.)
18	High cost of learning to use the application (COL)
19	High cost of quality (COQ)
20	High technical debt
21	High maintenance costs
22	High warranty costs
23	Excessive quantities of rework
24	Difficult enhancement projects
25	High total cost of ownership (TCO)

on applications, loss of key personnel, and many more. In total the Namcook Analytics LLC master list of current software risks includes a total of 210 software risk factors. Of course starting in 2020 there is the new risk of teams catching the corona virus, which is currently unpredictable.

Lifetime Sizing with Software Risk Master™

Although this chapter concentrates on quality and the initial release of a software application, the SRM sizing algorithms actually create 15 size predictions. The initial prediction is for the nominal size at the end of requirements. SRM also predicts requirements creep and deferred functions for the initial release.

After the first release, SRM predicts application growth for a 3-year period but internally growth is predicted for 10 years. However after 3 years, business changes become so critical that Namcook limits the results to a 3-year window.

To illustrate the full set of SRM size predictions, Table 10.8 shows a sample application with a nominal starting size of 10,000 function points. All of the values are in round numbers to make the patterns of growth clear.

As can be seen from Table 10.8, software applications do not have a single fixed size, but continue to grow and change for as long as they are being used by customers or clients. Therefore, productivity and quality data needs to be renormalized from time to time. Namcook suggests renormalization at the beginning of every fiscal or calendar year.

Economic Modeling with Software Risk Master

Because SRM can predict the results of any methodology used for any size and kind of software project, it is in fact a general economic model that can show the total cost of ownership (TCO) and the cost of quality (COQ) for a variety of software development methods and practices.

For example, SRM can show immediate results in less than one minute for any or all of the more than 60 developments; for any combination of 84 programming languages; and for work patterns in any of more than 50 countries.

Following are the 20 most common methodologies used by SRM customers as of 2016 in alphabetical order:

1. Agile development
2. Capability Maturity Model Integrated (CMMI)™ – all 5 levels
3. Extreme programming (XP)
4. Feature-driven development (FDD)
5. Formal inspections (combined with other methods)
6. Hybrid development (features from several methods)
7. Information Engineering (IE)
8. Iterative development

Table 10.8   SRM Multi-Year Sizing Example

Patent Application 61434091. February 2012.

		Function Points	SNAP Points	Logical Code	
	Nominal application size in IFPUG function points	10,000			
	SNAP points	1,389			
	Language	C			
	Language level	2.50			
	Logical code statements	1,280,000			
1	Size at end of requirements	10,000	1,389	1,280,000	
2	Size of requirement creep	2,000	278	256,000	
3	Size of planned delivery	12,000	1,667	1,536,000	
4	Size of deferred features	−4,800	(667)	(614,400)	
5	Size of actual delivery	7,200	1,000	921,600	
6	Year 1 usage	12,000	1,667	1,536,000	Kicker
7	Year 2 usage	13,000	1,806	1,664,000	
8	Year 3 usage	14,000	1,945	1,792,000	
9	Year 4 usage	17,000	2,361	2,176,000	Kicker
10	Year 5 usage	18,000	2,500	2,304,000	
11	Year 6 usage	19,000	2,639	2,432,000	
12	Year 7 usage	20,000	2,778	2,560,000	
13	Year 8 usage	23,000	3,195	2,944,000	Kicker
14	Year 9 usage	24,000	3,334	3,072,000	
15	Year 10 usage	25,000	3,473	3,200,000	

Kicker = Extra features added to defeat competitors.

Note: Simplified example with whole numbers for clarity.

Note: Deferred features usually due to schedule deadlines.

    9. Lean software development (alone or in combination)
10. Mashup software development
11. Model-driven development
12. Open-source development models
13. Personal software process (PSP)
14. Rational unified process (RUP)
15. Reusable components and artifacts (various levels of reuse)
16. SCRUM (alone or with other methods)
17. Spiral development
18. Team software process (TSP)
19. Test driven development (TDD)
20. Waterfall development

It takes less than one minute to switch SRM from one methodology to another, so it is possible to examine and evaluate 10–20 alternatives methods in less than half an hour. This is not a feature of most other parametric estimation tools.

Software Risk Master can also model any level of development team experience, management experience, tester experience, and even client experience.

Software Risk Master can also show the results of any of 84 different programming language or combination of programming languages for more than 79 languages such as ABAP, Ada, APL, Basic, C, C#, C++, CHILL, COBOL, Eiffel, Forth, Fortran, HTML, Java, Javascript, Julia, Objective C, PERL, PHP, PL/I, Python, Ruby, Smalltalk, SQL, Visual Basic, and many other languages. In theory, SRM could support all 2,500 programming languages, but there is very little empirical data available for many of these.

To add clarity to the outputs, SRM can show identical data for every case, such as showing a sample application of 1,000 function points and then changing methods, programming languages, CMMI levels, and team experience levels. Using the same data and data formats allows side-by-side comparisons of different methods and practices.

This allows clients to judge the long-range economic advantages of various approaches for both development and TCO.

The Future of Sizing and Estimating Software with Function Points

Every year since 1975 more and more companies have adopted function point metrics; fewer and fewer companies are using LOC, story points, cost per defect, and other ambiguous and hazardous metrics.

The governments of Brazil and Korea already use function points for government software contracts (Korea sent a delegation to Namcook Analytics to discuss this policy.) Other countries such as Italy and Malaysia are also planning to use function points for contracts (the author of this book is an advisor to the Malaysian software testing organization and knows that Malaysia is considering function points for contracts).

Outside of the United States, the 25 countries with the most certified function point counters and the widest usage of function points among technology companies include:

Countries Expanding Use of Function Points 2019		
1	Argentina	
2	Australia	
3	Belgium	
4	**Brazil**	**Required for government contracts**
5	Canada	
6	China	
7	Finland	
8	France	
9	Germany	
10	India	
11	**Italy**	**Required for government contracts**
12	**Japan**	**Required for government contracts**
13	**Malaysia**	**Required for government contracts**
14	Mexico	
15	Norway	
16	Peru	
17	Poland	
18	Singapore	
19	**South Korea**	**Required for government contracts**
20	Spain	
21	Switzerland	
22	Taiwan	

(Continued)

(Continued)

Countries Expanding Use of Function Points 2019		
23	The Netherlands	
24	United Kingdom	
25	United States	

It is interesting that several countries with large numbers of technology companies have not utilized function point metrics to the same degree as the 25 countries shown earlier. Some of the countries that do not seem to have internal function point user groups as of 2019 (although this is uncertain) include in alphabetical order: China, Russia, Saudi Arabia, and the Ukraine.

Because software is important in all countries and function points are the best metric for estimating and measuring software quality, costs, and productivity, it can be expected by about 2025 that every industrial country in the world will use function point metrics and have internal function point user groups.

Even today in 2020, Namcook receives requests for function point data from over 45 countries per year including several such as China, Colombia, Cuba, Jordan, Pakistan, Russia, Saudi Arabia, and Viet Nam which are just starting to examine the usefulness of function point metrics.

For economic analysis and quality analysis of software, function points are the best available metric and already have more benchmark data than all other metrics combined.

Summary and Conclusions

Large software projects are among the most risky business ventures in history. The failure rate of large systems is higher than other kinds of manufactured products. Cost overruns and schedule delays for large software projects are endemic and occur on more than 75% of large applications. Indeed about 35% of large systems >10,000 function points are cancelled and not delivered: one of the most expensive forms of business failure in history.

Early sizing via pattern matching and function point metrics combined with early risk analysis can improve the success rates of large software applications due to alerting mangers and software teams to potential hazards while there is still time enough to take corrective actions prior to expending significant funds.

References and Readings

Jones, Capers; *A Guide to Selecting Software Measures and Metrics*; CRC Press; 2017a.

Jones, Capers; *Software Methodologies, a Quantitative Guide*; CRC Press; 2017b.

Jones, Capers; *Quantifying Software: Global and Industry Perspectives*; CRC Press; 2017c.

Jones, Capers; *The Technical and Social History of Software Engineering*; Addison Wesley; 2014.

Jones, Capers; and Bonsignour, Olivier; *The Economics of Software Quality*; Addison Wesley Longman, Boston, MA; 2011; ISBN: 10: 0-13-258220-1; 585 pages.

Jones, Capers; *Software Engineering Best Practices*; McGraw Hill, New York, NY; 2010; ISBN: 978-0-07-162161-8; 660 pages.

Jones, Capers; *Applied Software Measurement*; McGraw Hill, New York, NY; 2008; ISBN: 978-0-07-150244-3; 662 pages.

Jones, Capers; *Estimating Software Costs*; McGraw Hill, New York, NY; 2007a; ISBN: 13: 978-0-07-148300-1.

Jones, Capers; *Software Assessments, Benchmarks, and Best Practices*; Addison Wesley Longman, Boston, MA; 2000; ISBN: 0-201-48542-7; 657 pages.

Jones, Capers; *Conflict and Litigation Between Software Clients and Developers*; Software Productivity Research, Inc.; Burlington, MA; September 2007b; 53 pages; (SPR technical report).

Additional Literature

Abran, Alain; *Software Estimating Models*; Wiley-IEEE Computer Society; 2015.

Abran, Alain; *Software Metrics and Metrology*; Wiley-IEEE Computer Society; 2010.

Abran, Alain; *Software Maintenance Management: Evolution and Continuous Improvement*; Wiley-IEEE Computer Society; 2008.

Abran, Alain; and Dumke, Reiner R.; *Innovations in Software Measurement*; Shaker-Verlag, Aachen, DE; 2005; ISBN: 3-8322-4405-0; 456 pages.

Abran, Alain; Bundschuh, Manfred; Dumke, Reiner; Ebert, Christof; and Zuse, Horst; *Software Measurement News*; Vol. 13, No. 2; October 2008 (periodical).

Bundschuh, Manfred; and Dekkers, Carol; *The IT Measurement Compendium*; Springer-Verlag, Berlin, DE; 2008; ISBN: 978-3-540-68187-8; 642 pages.

Chidamber, S.R. & Kemerer, C.F.; "A Metrics Suite for Object-Oriented Design"; *IEEE Trans. On Software Engineering*; Vol. SE20, No. 6; June 1994; pp. 476–493.

Dumke, Reiner; Braungarten, Rene; Büren, Günter; Abran, Alain; and Cuadrado-Gallego, Juan J.; (editors); *Software Process and Product Measurement*; Springer-Verlag, Berlin; 2008; ISBN: 10: 3-540-89402-0; 361 pages.

Ebert, Christof; and Dumke, Reiner; *Software Measurement: Establish, Extract, Evaluate, Execute*; Springer-Verlag, Berlin, DE; 2007; ISBN: 978-3-540-71648-8; 561 pages.

Gack, Gary; *Managing the Black Hole: The Executives Guide to Software Project Risk*; Business Expert Publishing, Thomson, GA; 2010; ISBN: 10: 1-935602-01-9.

Gack, Gary; *Applying Six Sigma to Software Implementation Projects*; http://software.isixsigma.com/library/content/c040915b.asp.

Galorath, Dan; and Evans, Michael; *Software Sizing, Estimation, and Risk Management*; Auerbach Publications, Boca Raton, FL; 2006.

Garmus, David; and Herron, David; *Measuring the Software Process: A Practical Guide to Functional Measurement*; Prentice Hall, Englewood Cliffs, NJ; 1995.

Garmus, David; and Herron, David; *Function Point Analysis – Measurement Practices for Successful Software Projects*; Addison Wesley Longman, Boston, MA; 2001; ISBN: 0-201-69944-3; 363 pages.

Gilb, Tom; and Graham, Dorothy; *Software Inspections*; Addison Wesley, Reading, MA; 1993; ISBN: 10: 0201631814.

Harris, Michael D.S., Herron, David; and Iwanicki, Stasia; *The Business Value of IT*; CRC Press, Auerbach; Boca Raton, FL; 2008; ISBN: 978-14200-6474-2.

International Function Point Users Group (IFPUG); *IT Measurement – Practical Advice from the Experts*; Addison Wesley Longman, Boston, MA; 2002; ISBN: 0-201-74158-X; 759 pages.

Kemerer, C.F.; "Reliability of Function Point Measurement – A Field Experiment"; *Communications of the ACM*; Vol. 36; 1993; pp. 85–97.

Parthasarathy, M.A.; *Practical Software Estimation – Function Point Metrics for Insourced and Outsourced Projects*; Infosys Press, Addison Wesley, Upper Saddle River, NJ; 2007; ISBN: 0-321-43910-4.

Putnam, Lawrence H.; *Measures for Excellence – Reliable Software On Time, Within Budget*; Yourdon Press, Prentice Hall, Englewood Cliffs, NJ; 1992; ISBN: 0-13-567694-0; 336 pages.

Putnam, Lawrence H.; and Myers, Ware; *Industrial Strength Software – Effective Management Using Measurement*; IEEE Press, Los Alamitos, CA; 1997; ISBN: 0-8186-7532-2; 320 pages.

Royce, Walker; *Software Project Management – Unified Framework*; Addison Wesley, Boston, MA; 1999.

Stein, Timothy R.; *The Computer System Risk Management Book and Validation Life Cycle*; Paton Press, Chico, CA; 2006; ISBN: 10: 1-9328-09-5; 576 pages.

Chapter 11

Optimizing Software Defect Removal Efficiency (DRE)

Introduction

Note: The corona virus pandemic of 2020 introduced changes into software development practices. Team meetings and inspections started using Zoom or with participants wearing masks for safety.

Software quality depends upon two important variables. The first variable is that of "defect potentials" or the sum total of bugs likely to occur in requirements, architecture, design, code, documents, and "bad fixes" or new bugs in bug repairs. Defect potentials are measured using function points, since "lines of code" (LOC) cannot deal with requirements and design defects.

The second variable is "defect removal efficiency" (DRE) or the percentage of bugs found and eliminated before release of software to clients. Defect potentials and DRE metrics were developed by IBM circa 1973 and are widely used by technology companies. Function point metrics were also invented by IBM during the same time period.

The metrics of "*defect potentials*" and "*defect removal efficiency (DRE)*" are useful quality metrics developed by IBM circa 1973 and widely used by technology companies as well as by banks, insurance companies, and other organizations with large software staffs. These metrics were selected for Software Risk Master (SRM) because they are the most accurate for predicting overall software quality results.

DOI: 10.1201/9781003193128-13

Defect potentials are the sum total of bugs found in requirements, architecture, design, code, and other sources of error. The approximate U.S. average for software defect potentials is shown in Table 11.1 using IFPUG function points version 4.3. Function point metrics were also invented by IBM in the same time period circa 1973.

Function points were invented by A.J. Albrecht and colleagues at IBM White Plains. Defect potential and DRE metrics were developed by Michael Fagan, Ron Radice, Capers Jones, and other IBM personnel at IBM Kingston and IBM San Jose to validate the effectiveness of inspections. Function point metrics, defect potential metrics, and DRE metrics were placed in the public domain by IBM.

Function points have become global metrics and responsibility for counting rules passed to the International Function Point Users Group (IFPUG).

Defect potentials and DRE metrics are widely used by technology companies but do not have a formal user group as of 2017. However, these metrics are frequently used in software benchmarks produced by organizations such as the International Software Benchmark Group (ISBSG) and Namcook Analytics LLC. These metrics are also standard outputs from the SRM estimation tool, which was used to produce Table 11.3 in this chapter.

Note that the phrase "bad fix" refers to new bugs accidentally introduced in bug repairs for older bugs. The current U.S. average for bad-fix injections is about 7%, i.e. 7% of all bug repairs contain new bugs. For modules that are high in cyclomatic complexity and for "error prone modules," bad-fix injections can top 75%.

Table 11.1   Average Software Defect Potentials circa 2017 for the United States

• Requirements	0.70 defects per function point
• Architecture	0.10 defects per function point
• Design	0.95 defects per function point
• Code	1.15 defects per function point
• Security code flaws	0.25 defects per function point
• User Documents	0.45 defects per function point
• Bad fixes	0.65 defects per function point
Total	**4.25 defects per function point**

Defect potentials are of necessity measured using function point metrics. The older "lines of code" metric cannot show requirements, architecture, and design defects not any other defect outside the code itself. As of 2015 function points were the most widely used software metric. There are more benchmarks using function point metrics than all other metrics put together.

The overall U.S. range in defect potentials runs from about 1.50 per function point to more than 6.00 per function point. Factors that influence defect potentials include team skills, development methodologies, CMMI levels, programming languages, and defect prevention techniques such as joint application design (JAD) and quality function deployment (QFD).

Defect removal efficiency is also a powerful and useful metric. Every important project should top 99% in DRE, but few do. The current U.S. range in DRE is from below 80% for projects that use no pre-test defect removal and only a few test stages. The highest measured DRE to date is about 99.95%, and this level required pre-test inspections, static analysis, and at least 8 test stages. The current U.S. average in DRE is just over 92% which is only marginal. All projects should top 97% and the best should top 99%.

DRE is measured by keeping track of all bugs found internally during development, and comparing these to customer-reported bugs during the first 90 days of usage. If internal bugs found during development total 95 and customers report 5 bugs, DRE is 95%.

Table 11.2 shows U.S. software average DRE ranges by application size measured in IFPUG function points.

Table 11.2   U.S. Software Average DRE Ranges by Application Size

Function Points	Best	Average	Worst
1	99.95%	97.00%	94.00%
10	99.00%	96.50%	92.50%
100	98.50%	95.00%	90.00%
1,000	96.50%	94.50%	87.00%
10,000	94.00%	89.50%	83.50%
100,000	91.00%	86.00%	78.00%
Average	**95.80%**	**92.20%**	**86.20%**

As can be seen, DRE comes down as application size goes up. For that matter, defect potentials go up with application size. Large systems above 10,000 function points are very risky due to high defect potentials and low DRE values.

Table 11.3 shows the approximate DRE values for common pre-test and test methods although there are variations for each method and also for the patterns of methods used. Note that Table 11.3 omits architecture bugs due to the small size of the example of only 1,000 function points.

Table 11.3 assumes top-level experts, the quality-strong "team software process" (TSP) methodology, the Java programming language, and CMMI level 5. Therefore, defect potentials are well below current U.S. averages.

To illustrate the principles of optimal defect prevention, pre-test removal, and test defect removal. Table 11.3 shows a sequence of pre-test and test stages that will top 99% in DRE. Table 11.3 illustrates 1,000 function points and about 53,000 Java statements. Table 11.3 is taken from the quality output predictions of SRM.

DRE measures can be applied to any combination of pre-test and testing stages. The U.S. norm is to use static analysis before testing and six kinds of testing: unit test, function test, regression test, performance test, system test, and acceptance test. This combination usually results in about 95% DRE.

Critical software for medical devices, avionics packages, weapons systems, telecommunications switching systems, operating systems and other software that controls complex physical devices use full pre-test inspections and static analysis plus at least eight kinds of testing. These applications need to top 99% in DRE in order to operate safely.

In order to top 99% in DRE Table 11.2 shows several forms of defect prevention and includes inspections as an important pre-test removal method. Formal inspections have the highest DRE of any known method, and over 50 years of empirical data.

Due to the 2020 corona virus, inspections still need to be done remotely via Zoom in 2021, which reduces efficiency.

Due to inspections, static analysis, and formal testing by certified test personnel, the DRE for code defects can top 99.75%. It is harder to top 99% for requirements and design bugs since both resist testing and can only be found via inspections, or by text static analysis.

Summary and Conclusions

The combination of defect potential and DRE measures provide software engineering and quality personnel with powerful tools for predicting

Table 11.3   DRE > 99%

	Defects
Requirements defect potential	134
Design defect potential	561
Code defect potential	887
Document defect potential	135
Total Defect Potential	1,717
Per function point	1.72
Per KLOC	32.20

	Efficiency	Remainder	Bad Fixes	Costs
Defect Prevention				
Joint Application Design (JAD)	27%	1,262	5	$28,052
Quality Function Deployment	30%	888	4	$39,633
Prototype	20%	713	2	$17,045
Models	68%	229	5	$42,684
Subtotal	**86%**	**234**	**15**	**$127,415**
Pre-Test Removal				
Desk check	27%	171	2	$13,225
Static analysis	55%	78	1	$7,823
Inspections	93%	5	0	$73,791
Subtotal	**98%**	**6**	**3**	**$94,839**
Test Removal				
Unit	32%	4	0	$22,390
Function	35%	2	0	$39,835
Regression	14%	2	0	$51,578
Component	32%	1	0	$57,704
Performance	14%	1	0	$33,366
System	36%	1	0	$63,747

(Continued)

Table 11.3   (Continued)

		Defects		
Acceptance	17%	1	0	$15,225
Subtotal	**87%**	**1**	**0**	**$283,845**
				Costs
Pre-Release Costs		1,734	3	$506,099
Post-Release Repairs (Technical Debt)		1	0	$658
Maintenance Overhead				$46,545
Cost of Quality (COQ)				$553,302
Defects delivered	1			
High severity	0			
Security flaws	0			
High severity %	11.58%			
Delivered per FP	0.001			
High severity per FP	0.000			
Security flaws per FP	0.000			
Delivered Per KLOC	0.014			
High severity per KLOC	0.002			
Security flaws per KLOC	0.001			
Cumulative Removal Efficiency	**99.96%**			

and measuring all forms of defect prevention and all forms of defect removal.

Function point metrics are the best choice for normalizing defect potentials since they can include the defects found in requirements, architecture, design, and other non-code defect origins. The older LOC metric can only measure code defects which are usually less than 50% of total defects.

Introduction

From data collected by the author of this book during software assessment and benchmark studies, there are major differences in the patterns of software tool usage between "leading" and "lagging" enterprises. Leading enterprises are defined as those in the top quartile of the companies evaluated in terms of software productivity, schedule adherence, and quality results. Lagging enterprises are those in lower quartile.

The most significant differences noted between laggards and leaders are in the areas of project management tools, quality assurance tools, and testing tools. Leaders tend to exceed laggards by a ratio of about 15 to 1 in the volumes of tools associated with project management and quality control. The function point metric is proving to be a useful analytical tool for evaluating the capacities of software tool suites.

Function point metrics provide a very useful tool for comparing and evaluating software tools in all categories. In this chapter, software tools are categorized as follows:

Project Management Tools

These are tools aimed at the software management community. These tools are often concerned with predicting the costs, schedules, and quality levels prior to development of software projects and also collecting historical data from completed projects.

Software Engineering Tools

The set of software engineering tools are those used by programmers or software engineering personnel. There are many tools in this family, and they cover a variety of activities commencing with requirements analysis and proceeding through design, coding, change control, static analysis, and personal testing such as unit test.

Software Maintenance Engineering Tools

The tools in this family are aimed at stretching out the lives of aging legacy software applications. These tools are concerned with topics such as reverse engineering, code restructuring, defect tracking, reengineering, and other activities that center on existing applications. More modern "maintenance workbenches" provide support for full renovation of legacy applications.

Software Quality Assurance Tools

The tools in the software quality assurance (SQA) set are aimed at defect prediction, prevention, defect tracking, and the other "traditional" activities of SQA teams within major corporations.

Software Testing and Static Analysis Tools

The family of testing tools has been expanding rapidly, and the vendors in this family have been on a wave of mergers and acquisitions. The test tool market place is expanding fairly rapidly, and new tools are being marketed at an increasing pace. New kinds of tools such as automated test tools and static analysis tools have joined the traditional family of test tools.

Software Documentation Tools

Every software project requires some kind of documentation support, in terms of user's guides, reference manuals, HELP text, and other printed matter. The more sophisticated software projects have a substantial volume of graphics and illustrations too, and may also use hypertext links to ease transitions from topic to topic.

Various kinds of software engineering and project management tools are used by all software professionals between 2 and 7 hours per day, every day. Because so much of the work of modern software engineering involves using tools, the usage patterns and effectiveness of tools needs greater study than the software engineering literature has provided thus far.

Commercial Tools

There are hundreds or even thousands of commercial tools available for software development, software project management, maintenance, testing, quality control and other key activities associated with software projects. There are also hundreds of proprietary, internal tools which companies build for their own use but not for sale to others.

Every single working day, software engineers, project managers, testers, and other software professionals make use of tools between 2 hours and 7 hours per day, every day. In fact without using various kinds of tools software engineering would not even exist as an occupation.

However, the software literature has provided very little in the way of quantitative analysis about either usage patterns or the overall impact of tools on software productivity and quality. This chapter is an attempt to bring the issue of tool usage to the attention of software engineering and project management researchers.

Many commercial software tool vendors make advertising claims about the power of their tools in terms of increasing software development productivity, quality, or shortening schedules. Many of these claims are not supported by empirical data and most appear to be exaggerated in greater or lesser degree. Indeed, the exaggerations by tool vendors did much to discredit the value of Computer Aided Software Engineering (CASE) which tended to promise more than it performed.

Considering the importance of software to business and industry, it is surprising that the topic of software tool usage has been under-reported in the software literature. Indeed, since about 1990 much of the software engineering literature has been devoted to the subject of "software process improvement" and tools have been regarded as a minor background issue. Tools alone do not distinguish between leaders and laggards, but tool usage is a significant supplemental factor.

The author's current company, Namcook Analytics LLC, performs both qualitative assessments and quantitative benchmark studies for clients. A part of the analysis is collecting data on the numbers and kinds of tools utilized for software development, project management, and other related activities.

In addition, we also record data on software productivity, quality, schedules, and other quantitative aspects of software performance as well as qualitative data on the methods and processes utilized. As of 2016, the total number of software projects in our knowledge base is rapidly pushing past 26,000 and the total number of client organizations from which we have collected data is approaching 600 companies and some government agencies.

Table 11.4 shows the variety of tools used by one of the author's clients on a large financial application of about 5,000 function points in size. Table 11.4 shows the many different kinds of tools used circa 2016.

As can be seen, tool usage circa 2018 is complex and involves dozens of tool vendors.

In analyzing this data, we perform multiple regression studies on the factors that influence the outcomes of software projects. Although the software development process is indeed a key issue, tools also exert a major impact. This chapter discusses some of the differences in the patterns of tool usage noted between "lagging" organizations and "leading"

Table 11.4 Tools used for Finance Software Project

	Tasks	Tools Utilized
1	Architecture	QEMU
2	Automated test	HP QuickTest Professional
3	Benchmarks	ISBSG, Namcook, Q/P Mgt Group, Davids
4	Coding	Eclipse, Slickedit
5	Configuration	Perforce
6	Cost estimate	Software Risk Master (SRM), SEER, SLIM
7	Cost tracking	Automated project office (APO), MS Project
8	Cyclomatic	BattleMap
9	Debugging	GHS probe
10	Defect tracking	Bugzilla
11	Design	Projects Unlimited
12	Earned value	DelTek Cobra
13	ERP	Microsoft Dynamics
14	Function points 1	Software Risk Master (SRM)
15	Function points 2	Function point workbench
16	Function points 3	CAST automated function points
17	Graphics design	Visio
18	Inspections	SlickEdit
19	Integration	Apache Camel
20	ISO tools	ISOXpress
21	Maintenance	Mpulse
22	Manual test	DevTest
23	Milestone track	KIDASA Software Milestone Professional
24	Progress track	Jira, Automated project office (APO)
25	Project mgt.	Automated project office (APO)
26	Quality estimate	Software Risk Master (SRM)
27	Requirements	Rational Doors
28	Risk analysis	Software Risk Master (SRM)
29	Source code size 1	Software Risk Master (SRM)

Table 11.4   (Continued)

	Tasks	*Tools Utilized*
30	Source code size 2	Unified code counter (UCC)
31	SQA	NASA Goddard ARM tool
32	Static analysis	Kiuwan
33	Support	Zendesk
34	Test coverage	Software Verify suite
35	Test library	DevTest
36	Value analysis	Excel and Value Stream Tracking

organizations. In terms of tool usage, the most significant differences between laggards and leaders are in the domains of project management tools and quality control tools.

Performance of Lagging, Average, and Leading Projects

Before discussing the impact of tools, it is useful to provide some background data on the results which we associate with lagging, average, and leading software projects. In our measurement studies, we use the function point metric for data normalization, and this chapter assumes version 4.3 of the function point counting rules published by the International Function Point Users Group (IFPUG). Function points have substantially replaced the older "lines of code" (LOC) metric for all quantitative benchmark studies, since the LOC metric is not useful for large-scale studies involving multiple programming languages. We have not yet incorporated the newer SNAP metric for non-functional requirements into these studies due to the lack of data and the ambiguity of the SNAP metric. Neither do we use story points or use-case points since neither has any ISO standards, and the results vary by over 400% from company to company.

Note that similar kinds of studies could be done using COSMIC function points, Finnish function points (FISMA), Netherlands function points (NESMA), or some of the other functional size variations. The size results would probably differ by about 15% from the current study. Other metrics such as story points and use-case points do not seem particularly well suited for tool analysis.

In our quantitative benchmark studies, as might be expected, the majority of projects are "average" in terms of productivity, quality, and schedule results. What this chapter concentrates on are the extreme ends of the data we collect: the outlying projects that are either much better than average or much worse than average. There are more insights to be gained by analysis of the far ends of the spectrum than by examining the projects that cluster around the center.

Let us consider what it means for a software project to be considered "average" or "leading" or "lagging" in quantitative terms. Although many attributes can be included, in this short chapter only six key factors are discussed.

1. The length of software development schedules.
2. Productivity rates expressed in function points per staff month.
3. Defect potentials expressed in function points.
4. Defect removal efficiency levels.
5. Delivered defect levels.
6. Rank on the capability maturity model (CMMI) of the Software Engineering Institute (SEI).

In general, the set of leading companies are better in all of these factors than either the average or lagging groups. That is, their schedules are shorter, their quality levels are better, and they place higher on the SEI CMMI.

Average Software Projects

Because schedules vary with project size, the development schedules of average software projects can be approximated by raising the function point total of the project to the 0.4 power. This calculation yields the approximate number of calendar months for development between start of requirements and delivery to clients. Thus, for a project of 1,000 function points, raising that size to the 0.4 power yields a development schedule from start of requirements until deployment that would be roughly 15.8 calendar months.

The defect potential or number of possible bugs that might be found for average projects totals to about 4.50 bugs per function point. This is the sum of bugs or defects found in five deliverable artifacts: requirements, design, source code, user documents, and "bad fixes" or secondary defects introduced while fixing other defects. The cumulative DRE before delivery to clients is about 85% to perhaps 92%, so the number of bugs still latent at the time of delivery is about 0.75 bugs per function point.

Software development productivity rates vary with the size and nature of the application but are typically in the range of 6 to 10 function points per staff month for projects in the average zone.

Although the CMMI published by the SEI is based on qualitative rather than quantitative results, the data shown here for average projects is representative of projects that are at Level 1 of the CMM, but not far from Level 2.

Leading Software Projects

Software projects in the upper quartile of our data base have shorter schedules, higher quality levels, and higher productivity rates simultaneously. This is not surprising, because the costs, effort, and time to find software defects is usually the largest cost driver and the most significant barrier to rapid development schedules.

To approximate the development schedule for projects in the upper quartile, raise the function point total of the application to the 0.35 power to generate the number of calendar months from requirements to deployment. For a sample project of 1,000 function points in size, this calculation yields a result of about 11.2 calendar months from start of requirements until deployment.

The defect potential or number of possible bugs that might be found for leading projects is well below average, and runs to less than about 3.0 bugs per function point. The cumulative DRE before delivery to clients is about 95% to 99%, so the number of bugs still latent at the time of delivery is about 0.15 bugs per function point or even lower.

The reduced levels of defect potentials stem from better methods of defect prevention, while the elevated rates of DRE are always due to the utilization of formal design reviews and code inspections. Testing alone is insufficient to achieve defect removal rates higher than about 90% so all of the top-ranked quality organizations utilize inspections also.

Here too the productivity rates vary with the size and nature of the application but are typically in the range of 10 to 20 function points per staff month for projects in the upper quartile. The maximum rate can exceed 30 function points per staff month.

In terms of the CMMI published by the SEI, the data for the upper quartile shown is representative of projects that are at well into Level 3 of the CMMI, or higher.

Lagging Software Projects

Software projects in the lower quartile of our data base are troublesome, and there is also a known bias in our data. Many projects that would be in the lower quartile if the project went all the way to completion are cancelled, and hence not studied in any depth. Therefore the projects discussed here are those which were completed, but which were well below average in results.

The effect of this situation is to make the lagging projects, as bad as they are, look somewhat better than would be the case if all of the cancelled projects were included in the same set. Unfortunately in our consulting work, we are seldom asked to analyze projects that have been terminated due to excessive cost and schedule overruns. We are often aware of these projects, but our clients do not ask to have the projects included in the assessment and benchmark studies that they commission us to perform.

To approximate the development schedule for projects in the lower quartile, raise the function point total of the application to the 0.45 power to generate the number of calendar months from requirements to deployment. For a sample project of 1,000 function points in size, this calculation yields a result of about 22.4 calendar months.

The defect potential or number of possible bugs that are found for lagging projects is well above average, and runs to more than about 7.0 bugs per function point. The cumulative DRE before delivery to clients is only about 75%, so the number of bugs still latent at the time of delivery is an alarming 1.75 bugs per function point. Needless to say, lagging projects have severe quality problems, unhappy users, and horrendous maintenance expenses.

As will be discussed later, the lagging projects usually have no quality assurance tools or SQA teams, and may also be careless and perfunctory in testing as well.

For laggards too, the productivity rates vary with the size and nature of the application, but are typically in the range of 1.0 to 5.0 function points per staff month, although some projects in the lower quartile achieve only a fraction of a function point per staff month. The minimum rate we've measured is 0.13 function points per staff month. The best results from the laggard group seldom approach 10 function points per staff month.

In terms of the CMMI published by the SEI, the data for the lower quartile is representative of projects that are at well back at the rear of Level 1 of the CMM.

A Taxonomy of Software Tool Classes

This chapter is concerned with fairly specialized tools which support software projects in specific ways. There are of course scores of general-purpose tools used by millions of knowledge workers such as word processors, spreadsheets, data bases, and the like. These general-purpose tools are important, but are not covered in the following chapter in depth because they are not really aimed at the unique needs of software projects.

Because tool usage is under-reported in the software literature, there is no general taxonomy for discussing the full range of tools which can be applied to software projects or are deployed within software organizations. In this chapter, the author of this book has developed the following taxonomy for discussing software-related tools.

Project Management Tools

These are tools aimed at the software management community. These tools are often concerned with predicting the costs, schedules, and quality levels prior to development of software projects. The set of management tools also includes tools for measurement and tracking, budgeting, and other managerial activities that are performed while software projects are underway. In other words, some project management tools perform estimates and point to the future; others measure results and point to the past. Both kinds are needed.

Note that there are a number of tools available for personnel functions such as appraisals. However, these are generic tools and not aimed specifically at project management or control of software projects themselves and hence are not dealt with in this chapter. There are also payroll and benefits accumulation tools, but these deal with personnel topics and not with software engineering so they are not included either.

Software Engineering Tools

The set of software engineering tools are those used by programmers or software engineering personnel. There are many tools in this family, and they cover a variety of activities commencing with requirements analysis and proceeding through design, coding, change control, static analysis, and personal testing such as unit test.

Examples of the tools in the software engineering family include design tools, compilers, assemblers, and the gamut of features now available under the term "programming support environment."

Numerically, there are more vendors and more kinds of tools within the software engineering family than any of the other families of tools discussed in this chapter. The software engineering tools family has several hundred vendors and several thousand projects in the United States alone, and similar numbers in Western Europe. Significant numbers of tools and tool vendors also occur in the Pacific Rim and South America.

Software Maintenance Engineering Tools

The tools in this family are aimed at stretching out the lives of aging legacy software applications. These tools are concerned with topics such as reverse engineering, code restructuring, defect tracking, reengineering, and other activities that center on existing applications. More modern "maintenance workbenches" provide support for full renovation of legacy applications.

Although the family of maintenance tools is increasing, it has been an interesting phenomenon that maintenance tools have never been as plentiful nor as well marketed as software development tools.

The impact of two massive maintenance problems, the year 2000 and the Euro-currency conversion, triggered a burst of new maintenance tools circa 1995–1999. For perhaps the first time in software's history, the topic of maintenance began to achieve a level of importance equal to new development.

Software Quality Assurance Tools

The tools in the SQA set are aimed at defect prediction, prevention, defect tracking, and the other "traditional" activities of SQA teams within major corporations.

It is an unfortunate aspect of the software industry that the family of quality-related tools was small during the formative years of the software occupation, during the 1960s and 1970s. In recent years, the numbers of quality-related tools have been increasing fairly rapidly, although SQA tools are still found primarily only in large and sophisticated corporations. Incidentally, as a class, software quality groups are often understaffed and underfunded.

Software Testing and Static Analysis Tools

The family of testing tools has been expanding rapidly, and the vendors in this family have been on a wave of mergers and acquisitions. The test tool market place is expanding fairly rapidly, and new tools are being marketed at an increasing pace. New kinds of tools such as automated test tools and static analysis tools have joined the traditional family of test tools.

The test tool community is logically related to the SQA community, but the two groups are not identical in their job functions nor in the tools which are often utilized, although there are of course duplications of tools between the two job categories.

In recent years, a new class of tools called "static analysis tool" have joined traditional testing tools, although usually marketed by companies outside of traditional testing. Static analysis tools have a high efficiency in finding bugs and are cost-effective when run prior to testing. In fact, some of the structural defects found by static analysis tools are very difficult to find using normal testing tools and methods.

A wave of mergers and acquisitions has been sweeping through the test and quality tool domain. As a result, test and quality assurance tools are now starting to be marketed by larger corporations than was formerly the case, which may increase sales volumes. For many years, test and quality assurance tools were developed and marketed by companies that tended to be small and undercapitalized.

Software Documentation Tools

Every software project requires some kind of documentation support, in terms of user's guides, reference manuals, HELP text, and other printed matter. The more sophisticated software projects have a substantial volume of graphics and illustrations too, and may also use hypertext links to ease transitions from topic to topic.

For modern applications offered in the form of "software as a service" (SaaS) or web-enabled office suites such as those by Google, all of the documentation is now online and available primarily from web sites.

The topic of documentation tools is undergoing profound changes under the impact of the World Wide Web and the Internet. Also the topic of work-flow management and newer technologies such as HTML, web authoring tools, and hypertext links are beginning to expand, the world of documentation from "words on paper" to a rich multi-media experience where online information may finally achieve the long-delayed prominence which has been talked about for almost 50 years.

References and Readings

Beck, Kent; *Test-Driven Development*; Addison Wesley, Boston, MA; 2002; ISBN: 10: 0321146530; 240 pages.

Black, Rex; *Managing the Testing Process: Practical Tools and Techniques for Managing Hardware and Software Testing*; Wiley, Hoboken, NJ; 2009; ISBN: 10: 0470404159; 672 pages.

Cohen, Lou; *Quality Function Deployment – How to Make QFD Work for You*; Prentice Hall, Upper Saddle River, NJ; 1995; ISBN: 10: 0201633302; 368 pages.

Everett, Gerald D.; and McLeod, Raymond; *Software Testing*; John Wiley & Sons, Hoboken, NJ; 2007; ISBN: 978-0-471-79371-7; 261 pages.

Gack, Gary; *Managing the Black Hole: The Executives Guide to Software Project Risk*; Business Expert Publishing, Thomson, GA; 2010; ISBN: 10: 1-935602-01-9.

Gilb, Tom; and Graham, Dorothy; *Software Inspections*; Addison Wesley, Reading, MA; 1993; ISBN: 10: 0201631814.

Jones, Capers; and Bonsignour, Olivier; *The Economics of Software Quality*; Addison Wesley, Boston, MA; 2011; ISBN: 978-0-13-258220-9; 587 pages.

Jones, Capers; *Software Engineering Best Practices*; McGraw Hill, New York, NY; 2010; ISBN: 978-0-07-162161-8;660 pages.

Jones, Capers; *Applied Software Measurement*, 3rd ed.; McGraw Hill, New York, NY; 2008; ISBN: 978-0-07-150244-3; 662 pages.

Jones, Capers; *Estimating Software Costs*, 2nd ed.; McGraw Hill, New York, NY; 2007; 700 pages.

Kan, Stephen H.; *Metrics and Models in Software Quality Engineering*, 2nd ed.; Addison Wesley Longman, Boston, MA; 2003; ISBN: 0-201-72915-6; 528 pages.

Nandyal, Raghav; *Making Sense of Software Quality Assurance*; Tata McGraw Hill Publishing, New Delhi, India; 2007; ISBN: 0-07-063378-9; 350 pages.

Radice, Ronald A.; *High Qualitiy Low Cost Software Inspections*; Paradoxicon Publishing, Andover, MA; 2002; ISBN: 0-9645913-1-6; 479 pages.

Wiegers, Karl E.; *Peer Reviews in Software – A Practical Guide*; Addison Wesley Longman, Boston, MA; 2002; ISBN: 0-201-73485-0; 232 pages.

Chapter 12

Tool Usage on Best-Case, Average, and Worst-Case Projects

This section of the chapter discusses the ranges and variations of tools noted on lagging, average, and leading projects. Three primary kinds of information are reported in this section.

1. Variances in the numbers of tools used in lagging and leading projects.
2. Variances in the function point totals of the lagging and leading tool suites.
3. Variances in the daily hours of usage by software engineers and managers.

The count of the numbers of tools is simply based on assessment and benchmark results and our interviews with project personnel. Although projects vary, of course, deriving the counts of tools is reasonably easy to perform.

The sizes of the tools expressed in function points are more difficult to arrive at, and have a larger margin of error. For some kinds of tools such as cost estimating tools, actual sizes are known in both function point and lines of code forms because the author's company builds such tools.

DOI: 10.1201/9781003193128-14

For many tools, however, the size data is only approximate and is derived either from "backfiring" which is conversion from lines of code to function points, or from analogy with tools of known sizes. The size ranges for tools in this chapter are interesting, but not particularly accurate. The purpose of including the function point size data is to examine the utilization of tool features in lagging and leading projects.

In general, the lagging projects depend to a surprising degree on manual methods and have rather sparse tool usage in every category except software engineering, where there are comparatively small differences between the laggards and the leaders.

Project Management Tools on Lagging and Leading Projects

The differences in project management tool usage are both significant and striking. The lagging projects typically utilize only 3 general kinds of project management tools, while the leading projects utilize 18. Indeed, the project management tool family is one of the key differentiating factors between lagging and leading projects.

In general, the managers on the lagging projects typically use manual methods for estimating project outcomes, although quite a few may use schedule planning tools such as Microsoft Project. However, project managers on lagging projects tend to be less experienced in the use of planning tools and to utilize fewer of the available features. The sparseness of project management tools does much to explain why so many lagging software projects tend to run late, to exceed their budgets, or to behave in more or less unpredictable fashions. Table 12.1 shows project management tool ranges.

It is interesting that project managers on successful project tend to utilize tools about 4 hours per work day. On average projects the usage is about 2.5 hours per work day. On lagging projects, barely an hour per day is devoted to tool usage.

By contrast, the very significant use of project management tools on the leading projects results in one overwhelming advantage: "No surprises." The number of on-time projects in the leading set is far greater than in the lagging set, and all measurement attributes (quality, schedules, productivity, etc.) are also significantly better.

Table 12.1 Numbers and Size Ranges of Software Project Management Tools

(Tool sizes are expressed in terms of IFPUG function points, version 4.3)			
Project Management Tools	*Lagging*	*Average*	*Leading*
1	Project planning	1,000	1,250	3,000
2	Project cost estimating			3,000
3	Statistical analysis			3,000
4	Methodology management		750	3,000
5	Reusable feature analysis			2,000
6	Quality estimation			2,000
7	Assessment support		500	2,000
8	Project office support		500	2,000
9	Project measurement			1,750
10	Portfolio analysis			1,500
11	Risk analysis			1,500
12	Resource tracking	300	750	1,500
13	Governance tools			1,500
14	Value analysis		350	1,250
15	Cost variance reporting	500	500	1,000
16	Personnel support	500	500	750
17	Milestone tracking		250	750
18	Budget support		250	750
19	Function point analysis		250	750
20	Backfiring: LOC to FP			300
21	Earned value analysis		250	300
22	Benchmark data collection			300
Subtotal		**1,800**	**4,600**	**30,000**
Tools		**4**	**12**	**22**

Differences in the software project management domain are among the most striking in terms of the huge differential of tool usage between the laggards and leaders. Variances in the number of tools deployed is about 7 to 1 between the leaders and the laggards, while variances in the tool capacities expressed in function points has a ratio of approximately 17 to 1 between the leaders and the laggards. These differences are far greater than almost any other category of tool.

Software Engineering Tools on Lagging and Leading Projects

The set of software engineering tools deployed has the smallest variance of any tool category between the leaders and the laggard classes. In general, unless a critical mass of software engineering tools are deployed, software can't be developed at all so the basic needs of the software community have built up a fairly stable pattern of software engineering tool usage.

Table 12.2 shows the numbers and size ranges of software engineering tools deployed, but as can easily be seen, the variations are surprisingly small between the lagging, average, and leading categories.

Software engineering is the most intense occupation in terms of tool usage. There is comparatively little difference between lagging, average, and leading projects in terms of daily hours of tool usage: somewhere between 5 and 9 hours per working day, every day.

There are some differences in software engineering tool usage, of course, but the differences are very minor compared to the much more striking differences in the project management and quality assurance categories.

The overall features and sizes of software engineering tools have been increasing as tool vendors add more capabilities. About 10 years ago, when the author first started applying function point metrics to software tools, no software engineering tools were larger than 1,000 function points in size, and the total volume of function points even among the leading set was only about 10,000 function points. A case can be made that the power or features of software engineering tools have tripled over the last 10 years.

As can be seen in Table 12.2, although there are some minor differences in the tool capacities between the leaders and the laggards, the differences in the number of software engineering tools deployed are almost non-existent.

A very common pattern noted among assessment and benchmark studies is for the software development teams and tool suites to be fairly

Table 12.2 Numbers and Size Ranges of Software Engineering Tools

(Tool sizes are expressed in terms of IFPUG function points, version 4.3)			
Software Engineering Tools	*Lagging*	*Average*	*Leading*
1	Compilers	3,500	3,500	3,500
2	Program generators		3,500	3,500
3	Design tools	1,000	1,500	3,000
4	Code editors	2,500	2,500	2,500
5	GUI design tools	1,500	1,500	2,500
6	Assemblers	2,000	2,000	2,000
7	Configuration control	750	1,000	2,000
8	Source code control	750	1,000	1,500
9	Static analysis		1,000	1,500
10	Automated testing		1,000	1,500
11	Data modeling	750	1,000	1,500
12	Debugging tools	500	750	1,250
13	Data base design	750	750	1,250
14	Capture/playback	500	500	750
15	Library browsers	500	500	750
16	Reusable code analysis			750
Subtotal		**15,000**	**22,000**	**29,750**
Tools		**12**	**14**	**16**

strong, but the project management and quality tool suites to be fairly weak. This pattern is often responsible for major software disasters, such as the long delay in opening up the Denver Airport because the luggage-handling software was too buggy to be put into full production.

Software Maintenance Engineering Tools on Lagging and Leading Projects

When the focus changes from development to maintenance (defined here as the combination of fixing bugs and making minor functional enhancements), the tool differentials between the leaders and the laggards are much more significant than for development software engineering.

For many years, software maintenance has been severely understated in the software literature and severely underequipped in the tool markets. Starting about 10 years ago, the numbers of software personnel working on aging legacy applications began to approach and in some cases exceed the numbers of personnel working on brand new applications. This phenomenon brought about a useful but belated expansion in software maintenance tool suites. Table 12.3 shows the variations in software maintenance engineering tools.

Personnel on leading software maintenance projects tend to use tools more than 4 hours per day. Laggards use tools less than 2 hours per day, while personnel on average projects use tools about 3 hours per day.

As the overall personnel balance began to shift from new development to maintenance, software tool vendors began to wake up to the fact that a potential market was not being tapped to the fullest degree possible.

The differences between the leaders and the laggards in the maintenance domain are fairly striking and include about a 4 to 1 differential in numbers of tools deployed, and a 13 to 1 differential in the function point volumes of tools between the leaders and the laggards.

The emergence of two massive business problems had a severe impact on maintenance tools and on maintenance personnel as well. The year 2000 software problem and the ill-timed Euro-currency conversion work both triggered major increases in software maintenance tools that can deal with these specialized issues.

Other issues that affect maintenance work include the use of COTS packages, the use of open-source applications, and the emergence of Software as a Service. Also the Information Technology Infrastructure Library (ITIL) has also impacted both maintenance and customer support tools.

Between about 2000 and 2016, industry maintenance "leaders" tend to have almost twice the maintenance tool capacities as those available prior the elevation of maintenance to a major occupation.

Software Quality Assurance Tools on Lagging and Leading Projects

When the software quality assurance tool suites are examined, one of the most striking differences of all springs into focus. Essentially, the projects and companies in the "laggard" set have either no software

Table 12.3   Numbers and Size Ranges of Maintenance Engineering Tools

(Tool sizes are expressed in terms of IFPUG function points, version 4.3)				
Maintenance Engineering Tools		*Lagging*	*Average*	*Leading*
1	Maintenance work benches		1,500	3,500
2	Reverse engineering		1,000	3,000
3	Reengineering		1,250	3,000
4	ITIL support tools		1,000	3,000
5	Configuration control	500	1,000	2,000
6	Code restructuring			1,500
7	Customer support		750	1,250
8	Debugging tools	750	750	1,250
9	Defect tracking	500	750	1,000
10	Complexity analysis			1,000
11	Error-prone module analysis		500	1,000
12	Incident management	250	500	1,000
13	Reusable code analysis		500	750
Subtotal		**1,750**	**9,500**	**23,250**
Tools		**4**	**11**	**13**

quality assurance function at all or no more than one kind of tool in use, as shown in Table 12.4.

Quality assurance provides the greatest contrast between tool usage and lack of tool usage. Quality assurance personnel on leading projects use tools almost 5 hours per day and only about 2 hours per day on average projects. For lagging projects, tools might not even be used. If they are, usage is seldom more than 1 hour per day.

By contrast, the leaders in terms of delivery, schedule control, and quality all have well-formed independent software quality assurance groups that are supported by powerful and growing tool suites.

Unfortunately, even leading companies are sometimes understaffed and underequipped with software quality assurance tools. In part, this is due to the fact that so few companies have software measurement and metrics programs in place that the significant business value of achieving high levels of software quality is often unknown to the management and executive community.

Table 12.4   Numbers and Size Ranges of Software Quality Assurance Tools

(Tool sizes are expressed in terms of IFPUG function points, version 4.3)			
Quality Assurance Tools	*Lagging*	*Average*	*Leading*
1	Quality estimation tools			2,000
2	Quality measurement tools		750	1,500
3	Six-sigma analysis			1,250
4	Data quality analysis			1,250
5	QFD support			1,000
6	TQM support			1,000
7	Inspection support			1,000
8	Reliability estimation			1,000
9	Defect tracking	250	750	1,000
10	Complexity analysis		500	1,000
Subtotal		**250**	**1,500**	**12,000**
Tools		**1**	**3**	**10**

Several tools in the quality category are identified only by their initials and need to have their purpose explained. The set of tools identified as "QFD support" are those which support the special graphics and data analytic methods of the "quality function deployment" methodology.

The set of tools identified as "TQM support" are those which support the reporting and data collection criteria of the "total quality management" methodology.

The other tools associated with the leaders are the tools of the trade of the software quality community: tools for tracking defects, tools to support design and code inspections, quality estimation tools, reliability modeling tools, and complexity analysis tools.

Complexity analysis tools are fairly common, but their usage is much more frequent among the set of leading projects than among either average or lagging projects. Complexity analysis is a good starting point prior to beginning complex maintenance work such as error-prone module removal.

Another good precursor tool class prior to starting major maintenance tasks would be to run static analysis tools on the entire legacy application. However, a caveat is that static analysis tools only support about 25 languages out of the approximate 2,500 programming languages in existence. Static analysis is available for common languages such as C, C++, C#, Java, COBOL, FORTRAN, and some others. Static analysis is not available for the less common languages used for legacy applications such as JOVIAL, CMS2, CHILL, or CORAL.

Unfortunately, since the laggards tend to have no quality assurance tools at all, the use of ratios is not valid in this situation. In one sense, it can be said that the leading projects have infinitely more software quality tools than the laggards, but this is simply because the lagging set often have zero quality tools deployed.

Software Testing Tools on Lagging and Leading Projects

Although there are significant differences between the leading and lagging projects in terms of testing tools, even the laggards test their software and hence have some testing tools available.

Note that there is some overlap in the tools used for testing and the tools used for quality assurance. For example, both test teams and software quality assurance teams may both utilize complexity analysis tools.

Incidentally, testing by itself has never been fully sufficient to achieve defect removal efficiency levels in the high 90% range. All of the "best in class" software quality organizations use a synergistic combination of requirements inspections, static analysis, design and code inspections, and multiple testing stages. This combined approach can lead to defect removal efficiency levels that may top 99% in best-case situations and always top the current U.S. average of 85% or so (Table 12.5).

Modern testing is highly dependent on tool usage. On leading projects, test tools are used almost 7 hours per business day; about 5 hours on average projects; and perhaps 4 hours per day even on lagging projects. Testing circa 2010 is intensely automated.

The differences in numbers of test tools deployed range by about 3.5 to 1 between the leading and lagging projects. However, the tool capacities vary even more widely, and the range of tool volumes is roughly 16 to 1 between the leaders and the laggards.

This is one of the more interesting differentials because all software projects are tested and yet there are still major variations in numbers of test tools used and test tool capacities. The leaders tend to employ full-time and well-equipped testing specialists while the laggards tend to assign testing to development personnel, who are often poorly trained and poorly equipped for this important activity.

Table 12.5 Numbers and Size Ranges of Software Testing Tools

(Tool sizes are expressed in terms of IFPUG function points, version 4.3)			
Testing Tools	*Lagging*	*Average*	*Leading*
1	Test case generation			1,500
2	Automated test tools			1,500
3	Complexity analysis		500	1,500
4	Static analysis tools		500	1,500
5	Data quality analysis			1,250
6	Defect tracking	500	750	1,000
7	Test library control	250	750	1,000
8	Performance monitors		750	1,000
9	Capture/playback		500	750
10	Test path coverage			350
11	Test case execution			350
Subtotal		750	3,750	11,700
Tools		3	6	11

For a more extensive discussion of the differences between leaders and laggards in terms of both quality assurance and testing refer to the author's book *Software Quality – Analysis and Guidelines for Success* (Jones 1996) and the more recent *Software Engineering Best Practices* (Jones 2010).

These books also discuss variations in the numbers and kinds of testing activities performed, and also variations in the use of defect tracking tools, use of formal design and code inspections, quality estimation, quality measurements, and many other differentiating factors.

Unfortunately, none of the major vendors of test tools and only a few of the vendors of quality assurance tools have any empirical data on software quality or provide information on defect removal efficiency levels. The subject of how many bugs can actually be found by various kinds of review, inspection, and test is the most important single topic in the test and quality domain, but the only published data on defect removal tends to come from software measurement and benchmark companies rather than from test tool and quality tool companies.

Software Documentation Tools on Lagging and Leading Projects

Almost all software projects require documentation, but very few are documented extremely well. The set of documentation tools is undergoing profound transformation as online publishing and the World Wide Web begin to supplant conventional paper documents.

Note that some of these tools included here in the documentation section are also used for requirements, specifications, plans, and other documents throughout the software development cycle. For example, almost every knowledge worker today makes use of "word processing" tools, so these tools are not restricted only to the software documentation domain.

As online publishing grows, this category is interesting in that the "average" and "leading" categories are fairly close together in terms of document tool usage. However, the laggards are still quite far behind in terms of both numbers of tools and overall capacities deployed (Table 12.6).

There had not been a great deal of difference in tool usage among writers and illustrators as of 2018. All three projects, lagging, average, and leading, tend to use tools between 4 and 6 hours per business day.

As web publishing becomes more common, it is likely that conventional paper documents will gradually be supplanted by online documents. The advent of the "paperless office" has been predicted for years but stumbled due to the high costs of storage.

Now that optical storage is exploding in capacities and declining in costs, optical online storage is now substantially cheaper than paper storage, so the balance is beginning to shift toward online documentation and the associated tool suites.

In the documentation domain, the variance between the leaders and the laggards is 1.5 to 1 in the number of tools deployed, and almost 2 to 1 in the volumes of tools deployed. The differences in the documentation category are interesting, but not so wide as the differentials for project management and quality assurance tools.

Overall Tool Differences between Laggards and Leaders

To summarize this analysis of software tool differentials between lagging and leading organizations, Table 12.7 shows the overall numbers of tools noted in our assessment and benchmark studies. Table 12.7 shows the largest ratios between leaders and laggards at the top.

Table 12.6 Numbers and Size Ranges of Software Documentation Tools

(Tool sizes are expressed in terms of IFPUG function points, version 4.3)				
Documentation Support Tools		Lagging	Average	Leading
1	Word processing	3,000	3,000	3,000
2	Web publishing	2,000	2,500	3,000
3	Desktop publishing	2,500	2,500	2,500
4	Graphics support	500	500	2,500
5	Multimedia support	–	750	2,000
6	Grammar checking	–	–	500
7	Dictionary/thesaurus	500	500	500
8	Hypertext support	–	250	500
9	Web publishing	200	400	500
10	Scanning	–	–	300
11	Spell checking	200	200	200
Subtotal		**8,900**	**10,600**	**15,500**
Tools		**7**	**9**	**11**

As can be seen, there is roughly a 2.5 to 1 differential in the numbers of tools deployed on leading projects as opposed to the numbers of tools on lagging projects. The major differences are in the project management and quality assurance tools, where the leaders are very well equipped indeed and the laggards are almost exclusively manual and lack most of the effective tools for both project management and quality control purposes.

When tool capacities are considered, the range of difference between the lagging and leading sets of tools is even more striking, and the range between leaders and laggards jumps up to about a 4.3 to 1 ratio.

The use of function point totals to evaluate tool capacities is an experimental method with a high margin of error, but the results are interesting. Although not discussed in this chapter, the author's long-range studies over a 10-year period has found a substantial increase in the numbers of function points in all tool categories.

Table 12.7   Ratios Between Tools Used by Lagging Project Compared to Leading Projects

Total Tools Utilized	Lagging	Average	Leading	Ratios
Quality assurance tools	1	3	10	1–10.0
Project management tools	4	12	22	1–5.5
Testing tools	3	6	11	1–3.6
Maintenance tools	4	11	13	1–2.6
Testing tools	3	6	11	1–3.6
Documentation support tools	7	9	11	1–1.4
Total	31	55	83	1–2.5

It is not completely clear if the increase in functionality is because of useful new features, or merely reflects the "bloat" which has become so common in the software world. For selected categories of tools such as compilers and programming environments, many of the new features appear to be beneficial and quite useful.

The added features in many project management tools such as cost estimating tools, methodology management tools, and project planning tools are also often giving valuable new capabilities which were long needed.

For other kinds of tools, however, such as word processing, at least some of the new features are of more questionable utility and appear to have been added for marketing rather than usability purposes.

Table 12.8 shows the overall differences in tool capacities using function point metrics as the basis of the comparison. Table 12.7 shows the largest differences in function point tool usage at the top.

It is painfully obvious that lagging projects use inaccurate manual estimates and are very poor in software quality control. No wonder laggards are troubled by cancelled projects, cost overruns, lengthy schedule delays, and very bad quality after deployment.

Summary and Conclusions

Although software tools have been rapidly increasing in terms of numbers and features, the emphasis on software process improvement in the software engineering literature has slowed down research on software tool usage.

Table 12.8   Ratio of Tool Features Used by Lagging Project Compared to Leading Projects

(Tool sizes are expressed in terms of IFPUG function points, version 4.3)				
Total Tool Function Points	Lagging	Average	Leading	Ratios
Quality assurance tools	250	1,500	12,000	1–48.0
Project management tools	1,800	4,600	30,000	1–16.6
Testing tools	750	3,750	11,700	1–15.6
Maintenance engineering tools	1,750	9,500	23,250	1–13.2
Software engineering tools	15,000	22,000	29,750	1–1.9
Documentation support tools	8,900	10,600	15,500	1–1.7
Total	**28,200**	**51,950**	**122,200**	**1–4.3**

Both software processes and software tools have significant roles to play in software engineering, and a better balance is needed in research studies that can demonstrate the value of both tools and process activities.

The use of function point metrics for exploring software tool capacities is somewhat experimental, but the results to date have been interesting and this method may well prove to be useful.

Long-range analysis by the author of this book over a 10-year period using function point analysis has indicated that software tool capacities have increased substantially, by a range of about 3 to 1. It is not yet obvious that the expansion in tool volumes has added useful features to the software engineering world, or whether the expansion simply reflects the "bloat" that has been noted in many different kinds of software applications.

However, modern quality control tools such as static analysis and modern project management tools such as parametric cost estimates do add significant value in terms of improved software results.

References and Readings

Garmus, David; and Herron, David; *Function Point Analysis – Measurement Practices for Successful Software Projects*; Addison Wesley Longman, Boston, MA; 2001; ISBN: 0-201-69944-3; 363 pages.

Howard, Alan (editor); *Software Productivity Tool Catalogs*; (in seven volumes); Applied Computer Research (ACR), Phoenix, AZ; 1997; 300 pages.

International Function Point Users Group (IFPUG); *IT Measurement – Practical Advice from the Experts*; Addison Wesley Longman, Boston, MA; 2002; ISBN: 0-201-74158-X; 759 pages.

Jones, Capers; *Function Point Metrics and Software Usage Patterns*; Capers Jones & Associates, Narragansett, RI; December 2009.

Jones, Capers; *The Technical and Social History of Software Engineering*; Addison Wesley Longman, Boston, MA; 2014.

Jones, Capers; and Bonsignour, Olivier; *The Economics of Software Quality*; Addison Wesley Longman, Boston, MA; 2011; ISBN: 10: 0-13-258220-1; 585 pages.

Jones, Capers; *Software Engineering Best Practices*; McGraw Hill, New York, NY; 2010; ISBN: 978-0-07-162161-8; 660 pages.

Jones, Capers; *Applied Software Measurement*, 3rd ed.; McGraw Hill, New York, NY; March 2008; ISBN: 978-0-07-150244-3; 668 pages.

Jones, Capers; *Estimating Software Costs*; McGraw Hill, New York, NY; 2007; ISBN: 13-978-0-07-148300-1.

Jones, Capers; *Software Assessments, Benchmarks, and Best Practices*; Addison Wesley Longman, Boston, MA; 2000; ISBN: 0-201-48542-7; 657 pages.

Jones, Capers; *Assessment and Control of Software Risks*; Prentice Hall; 1994; ISBN: 0-13-741406-4; 711 pages.

Jones, Capers; *Patterns of Software System Failure and Success*; International Thomson Computer Press, Boston, MA; December 1995; ISBN: 1-850-32804-8; 250, 292 pages.

Jones, Capers; *Software Quality – Analysis and Guidelines for Success*; International Thomson Computer Press, Boston, MA; 1997; ISBN: 1-85032-876-6; 492 pages.

Jones, Capers; "Sizing Up Software"; *Scientific American Magazine*, Vol. 279, No. 6; December 1998; pp. 104–111.

Kan, Stephen H.; *Metrics and Models in Software Quality Engineering*, 2nd ed.; Addison Wesley Longman, Boston, MA; 2003; ISBN: 0-201-72915-6; 528 pages.

Pressman, Roger; *Software Engineering – A Practitioner's Approach*, 6th ed.; McGraw Hill, New York, NY; 2005; ISBN: 0-07-285318-2.

Chapter 13

Geriatric Care for Aging Software

Introduction

Software has been a mainstay of business and government operations for more than 60 years. As a result, all large enterprises utilize aging software in significant amounts. Some Fortune 500 companies exceed 10,000,000 function points or 500,000,000 in the total volume of their corporate software portfolios. Much of this software is now more than 15 years old, and some important aging applications such as air traffic control are more than 35 years old.

Maintenance of aging software tends to become more difficult and expensive year by year since annual updates gradually destroy the original structure of the applications and increase its entropy and cylomatic complexity. On average the cyclomatic complexity of aging software applications increases by as much as 1% per calendar year due to numerous minor and a few major changes.

Aging software also becomes larger each year as changes increase function point totals and also total volumes of source code. Aging software often has large inclusions of "dead code" that used to perform useful function but which have been bypassed by newer changes. Dead code tends to make maintenance more complex and harder to perform.

Another attribute of aging software is that of a steady increase in "bad fix" injections. Bad fixes are new bugs accidentally included in repairs of reported bugs. The U.S. average for bad-fix injections is about 1.50% for new applications, but increases steadily over time as system

DOI: 10.1201/9781003193128-15

structure decays and becomes more complex. After 20 years of continuous usage, software bad fix injections can top 7.00%. In a few extreme cases, bad fixes on aging legacy applications have topped 20.00% per year.

Aging software may also contain troublesome regions with very high error densities called "error-prone modules." Error prone modules are so complex and troublesome that they need to be surgically removed and replaced by modern error-free code segments.

There are also sociological issues with maintenance of aging software. Many software engineers prefer to work on new development because it is more glamorous. Also, some companies unwisely pay maintenance engineers lower salaries than development engineers. Because maintenance is less popular than new development, it has become a major field of software outsourcing. Over 50% of aging, U.S. software applications are now maintained by outsource vendors rather than by an organization's own software staff. In general, maintenance outsourcing has been successful for both clients and outsource vendors, some of whom specialize in "managed maintenance."

Some leading companies such as IBM pay development and maintenance personnel equally and allow transfers back and forth.

Many popular methodologies such as agile are ineffective for handling updates to aging legacy applications. Technologies that can be useful for providing geriatric care to aging legacy software include frequent and widespread use of static analysis tools, manual inspections of critical code segments, and identification and surgical removal of error-prone modules. Maintenance-friendly methodologies such as team software process (TSP) are also useful.

In today's world, more than 50% of the global software population is engaged in modifying existing applications rather than writing new applications. This fact by itself should not be a surprise, because whenever an industry has more than 50 years of product experience, the personnel who repair existing products tend to outnumber the personnel who build new products. For example, there have long been more automobile mechanics in the United States who repair automobiles than there are personnel employed in building new automobiles.

The imbalance between software development and maintenance is opening up new business opportunities for software outsourcing groups. It is also generating a significant burst of research into tools and methods for improving software maintenance performance.

Maintenance and renovation of legacy software plays a major role in "brownfield" development, which involves carefully building new applications in an environment where they will need to interface with scores of older applications.

Brownfield development is analogous to putting up an office building in an urban environment where the site is surrounded by other office buildings whose occupants cannot be disrupted, nor the surrounding structures damaged during new construction.

What Is Software Maintenance?

The word "maintenance" is surprisingly ambiguous in a software context. In normal usage, it can span some 23 forms of modification to existing applications. The two most common meanings of the word maintenance include: (1) defect repairs; (2) enhancements or adding new features to existing software applications.

Although software enhancements and software maintenance in the sense of defect repairs are usually funded in different ways and have quite different sets of activity patterns associated with them, many companies lump these disparate software activities together for budgets and cost estimates.

The author of this book does not recommend the practice of aggregating defect repairs and enhancements, but this practice is very common. Consider some of the basic differences between enhancements or adding new features to applications and maintenance or defect repairs as shown in Table 13.1.

Because the general topic of "maintenance" is so complicated and includes so many different kinds of work, some companies merely lump all forms of maintenance together and use gross metrics such as the

Table 13.1   Key Differences between Maintenance and Enhancements

Enhancements New features)	Maintenance (Defect repairs)	
Funding source	Clients	Absorbed
Requirements	Formal	None
Specifications	Formal	None
Inspections	Formal	None
User documentation	Formal	None
New function testing	Formal	None
Regression testing	Formal	Minimal

overall percentage of annual software budgets devoted to all forms of maintenance summed together.

This method is crude but can convey useful information. Organizations which are proactive in using geriatric tools and services can spend less than 30% of their annual software budgets on various forms of maintenance, while organizations that have not used any of the geriatric tools and services can top 60% of their annual budgets on various forms of maintenance.

The kinds of maintenance tools used by lagging, average, and leading organizations are shown in Table 13.2. Table 13.2 is part of a larger study that examined many different kinds of software engineering and project management tools (1).

It is interesting that the leading companies in terms of maintenance sophistication not only use more tools than the laggards, but they use more of their features as well. The function point values in Table 13.2 refer to the capabilities of the tools that are used in day to day maintenance operations. The leaders not only use more tools, but they do more with them.

Before proceeding, let us consider 23 discrete topics that are often coupled together under the generic term "maintenance" in day to day

Table 13.2   Numbers and Size Ranges of Maintenance Engineering Tools

(Size data expressed in terms of function point metrics)			
Maintenance Engineering	*Lagging*	*Average*	*Leading*
Reverse engineering		1,000	3,000
Reengineering		1,250	3,000
Code static analysis			1,500
Configuration control	500	1,000	2,000
Test support		500	1,500
Customer support		750	1,250
Debugging tools	750	750	1,250
Defect tracking	500	750	1,000
Complexity analysis			1,000
Mass update search engines		500	1,000
Function Point Subtotal	**1,750**	**6,500**	**16,500**
Number of Tools	**3**	**8**	**10**

discussions, but which are actually quite different in many important respects (2) (Table 13.3).

Although the 23 maintenance topics are different in many respects, they all have one common feature that makes a group discussion possible: They all involve modifying an existing application rather than starting from scratch with a new application.

Table 13.3   Major Kinds of Work Performed under the Generic Term "Maintenance"

1	Major Enhancements (new features of >50 function points)
2	Minor Enhancements (new features of <5 function points)
3	Maintenance (repairing customer defects for good will and pro bono)
4	Warranty repairs (repairing defects under formal contract of for a fee)
5	Customer support (responding to client phone calls or problem reports)
6	Error-prone module removal (eliminating very troublesome code segments)
7	Mandatory changes (required or statutory changes such as new tax laws)
8	Complexity or structural analysis (charting control flow plus complexity metrics)
9	Code restructuring (reducing cyclomatic and essential complexity)
10	Optimization (increasing performance or throughput)
11	Migration (moving software from one platform to another)
12	Conversion (changing the interface or file structure)
13	Reverse engineering (extracting latent design information from code)
14	Reengineering (transforming legacy application to modern forms)
15	Dead code removal (removing segments no longer utilized)
16	Dormant application elimination (archiving unused software)
17	Nationalization (modifying software for international use)
18	Mass updates such as Euro or Year 2000 Repairs
19	Refactoring, or reprogramming applications to improve clarity
20	Retirement (withdrawing an application from active service)
21	Field service (sending maintenance members to client locations)
22	Reporting bugs or defects to software vendors
23	Installing updates received from software vendors

Each of the 23 forms of modifying existing applications has a different reason for being carried out. However, it often happens that several kinds of modification take place concurrently. For example, enhancements and defect repairs are very common in the same release of an evolving application. There are also other sequences or patterns for these modification activities. For example, reverse engineering often precedes reengineering and the two occur so often together as to almost comprise a linked set. For releases of large applications and major systems, the author has observed from 6 to 10 forms of maintenance, all leading up to the same release.

Geriatric Problems of Aging Software

Once software is put into production, it continues to change in three important ways as follows:

1. Latent defects still present at release must be found and fixed after deployment.
2. Applications continue to grow and add new features at a rate of between 5%and 10% per calendar year, due either to changes in business needs or to new laws and regulations, or both.
3. The combination of defect repairs and enhancements tends to gradually degrade the structure and increase the complexity of the application. The term for this increase in complexity over time is called "entropy." The average rate at which software entropy increases is about 1% to 3% per calendar year.

Because software defect removal and quality control are imperfect, there will always be bugs or defects to repair in delivered software applications. The current U.S. average for defect removal efficiency is only about 90% of the bugs or defects introduced during development (3) and has only improved slowly over more than 20 years. The actual values are about 4.5 bugs per function point created during development. But the range is from <2.5 to >6.5 bugs per function point. If 90% of these are found before release, about 0.25–0.65 bugs per function point will be released to customers.

However, best-in-class organizations combine low defect potentials with defect removal efficiency (DRE) levels approaching and sometimes exceeding 99%. Clearly maintenance costs will be much lower for software with 99% DRE than for software that is below 90% DRE. Every company and government organization should measure defect potentials and defect removal efficiency levels.

Since defect potentials tend to rise with the overall size of the application, and since defect removal efficiency levels tend to decline with the overall size of the application, the overall volume of latent defects delivered with the application rises with size. This explains why super-large applications in the range of 100,000 function points, such as Microsoft Windows and many enterprise resource planning (ERP) applications, may require years to reach a point of relative stability. These large systems are delivered with thousands of latent bugs or defects.

Not only is software deployed with a significant volume of latent defects, but a phenomenon called "bad fix injection" has been observed for more than 50 years. Roughly 7% of all defect repairs will contain a new defect that was not there before. For very complex and poorly structured applications, these bad-fix injections have topped 20% (3).

Even more alarming, once a bad fix occurs it is very difficult to correct the situation. Although the U.S. average for initial bad-fix injection rates is about 7%, the secondary injection rate against previous bad fixes is about 15% for the initial repair and 30% for the second. A string of up to five consecutive bad fixes has been observed, with each attempted repair adding new problems and failing to correct the initial problem. Finally, the 6th repair attempt was successful.

In the 1970s, the IBM Corporation did a distribution analysis of customer-reported defects against their main commercial software applications. The IBM personnel involved in the study, including the author of the book, were surprised to find that defects were not randomly distributed through all of the modules of large applications (4).

In the case of IBM's main operating system, about 5% of the modules contained just over 50% of all reported defects. The most extreme example was a large data base application, where 31 modules out of 425 contained more than 60% of all customer-reported bugs. These troublesome areas were known as "error-prone modules (EPM)."

Similar studies by other corporations such as AT&T and ITT found that error-prone modules were endemic in the software domain. More than 90% of applications larger than 5,000 function points were found to contain error-prone modules in the 1980s and early 1990s. Summaries of the error-prone module data from a number of companies were published in the author's book *Software Quality: Analysis and Guidelines for Success* (3).

Fortunately, it is possible to surgically remove error-prone modules once they are identified. It is also possible to prevent them from occurring. A combination of defect measurements, static analysis of all legacy code, formal design inspections, formal code inspections, and formal testing and test-coverage analysis has been proven to be effective in preventing error-prone modules from coming into existence (5).

Today, error-prone modules are almost non-existent in organizations that are higher than level 3 on the capability maturity model integrated (CMMI) of the Software Engineering Institute. However, they remain common and troublesome for level 1 organizations, and for organizations that lack sophisticated quality measurements and quality control.

If the author's clients are representative of the U.S. as a whole, more than 50% of U.S. companies still do not utilize the CMMI at all. Of those who do use the CMMI, less than 15% are at level 3 or higher. This implies that error-prone modules may exist in more than half of all large corporations and in a majority of state government software applications as well.

Once deployed, most software applications continue to grow at annual rates of between 5% and 10% of their original functionality. Some applications, such as Microsoft Windows, have increased in size by several hundred percent over a 10-year period.

The combination of continuous growth of new features coupled with continuous defect repairs tends to drives up the complexity levels of aging software applications. Structural complexity can be measured via metrics such as cyclomatic and essential complexity using a number of commercial tools. If complexity is measured on an annual basis and there is no deliberate attempt to keep complexity low, the rate of increase is between 1% and 3% per calendar year.

However, and this is an important fact, the rate at which entropy or complexity increases is directly proportional to the initial complexity of the application. For example, if an application is released with an average cyclomatic complexity level of less than 10, it will tend to stay well structured for at least 5 years of normal maintenance and enhancement changes.

But if an application is released with an average cyclomatic complexity level of more than 20, its structure will degrade rapidly and its complexity levels might increase by more than 2% per year. The rate of entropy and complexity will even accelerate after a few years.

As it happens, both bad-fix injections and error-prone modules tend to correlate strongly (although not perfectly) with high levels of complexity. A majority of error-prone modules have cyclomatic complexity levels of 10 or higher. Bad-fix injection levels for modifying high-complexity applications are often higher than 20%.

In the late 1990s, a special kind of geriatric issue occurred which involved making simultaneous changes to thousands of software applications. The first of these "mass update" geriatric issues was the deployment of the Euro, which required changes to currency conversion routines in thousands of applications. The Euro was followed almost immediately by the dreaded year 2000 or Y2K problem (6), which also involved mass updates of thousands of applications. In March of 2007, another such issue occurred when the starting date of daylight savings time was changed.

Future mass updates will occur later in the century, when it may be necessary to add another digit to telephone numbers or area code. Yet another and very serious mass update will occur if it becomes necessary to add digits to social security numbers in the second half of the 21st century. There is also the potential problem of the Unix time clock expiration in 2038.

Metrics Problems with Small Maintenance Projects

There are several difficulties in exploring software maintenance costs with accuracy. One of these difficulties is the fact that maintenance tasks are often assigned to development personnel who interleave both development and maintenance as the need arises. This practice makes it difficult to distinguish maintenance costs from development costs because the programmers are often rather careless in recording how time is spent.

Another and very significant problem is that fact that a great deal of software maintenance consists of making very small changes to software applications. Quite a few bug repairs may involve fixing only a single line of code. Adding minor new features such as perhaps a new line-item on a screen may require less than 50 source code statements.

These small changes are below the effective lower limit for counting function point metrics. The function point metric includes weighting factors for complexity, and even if the complexity adjustments are set to the lowest possible point on the scale, it is still difficult to count function points below a level of perhaps 15 function points (7).

An experimental method called "micro function points" is in development for small maintenance changes and bug repairs. This method is similar to standard function points, but drops down to three decimal places of precision. Thus changes that involve only a fraction of a standard IFPUG function point can be measured. The micro function point method became available in 2016 and usage has expanded each year since then.

Of course the work of making a small change measured with micro function points may be only an hour or less. But if as many as 10,000 such changes are made in a year, the cumulative costs are not trivial. Micro function points are intended to eliminate the problem that small maintenance updates have not been subject to formal economic analysis.

Quite a few maintenance tasks involve changes that are either a fraction of a function point, or may at most be less than 10 function points or about 1000 COBOL source code statements. Although normal counting of function points is not feasible for small updates and micro function points are still experimental, it is possible to use the "backfiring" method or converting counts of logical source code statements in to equivalent function points. For example, suppose an update requires adding 100 COBOL statements to an existing application. Since it usually takes about 105 COBOL statements in the procedure and data divisions to encode 1 function point, it can be stated that this small maintenance project is "about 1 function point in size."

If the project takes one work day consisting of six hours, then at least the results can be expressed using common metrics. In this case, the results would be roughly "6 staff hours per function point." If the reciprocal metric "function points per staff month" is used and there are 20 working days in the month, then the results would be "20 function points per staff month."

Metrics Problems with ERP Maintenance

Many large corporations use enterprise resource planning (ERP) packages such as SAP, Oracle, PeopleSoft, J.D. Edwards, and many others. These packages are large and complex systems in the size range of 200,000 function points and up.

Worse, dozens or even hundreds of legacy applications need to be ported into ERP packages when they are deployed. Porting is a form software modification that is difficult to count via function points because no new features are added. Table 13.4 shows size of function points for porting software applications. The ports were needed for a total of 723 applications out of a portfolio total of 2,366 applications. ERP sizing and porting are features of Software Risk Master.

As can be seen, ERP and portfolio sizing and estimating are much more complicated than sizing and estimating individual applications.

Best and Worst Practices in Software Maintenance

Because maintenance of aging legacy software is very labor intensive, it is quite important to explore the best and most cost effective methods available for dealing with the millions of applications that currently exist. The sets of best and worst practices are not symmetrical. For example, the practice that has the most positive impact on maintenance productivity is the use of trained maintenance experts. However, the factor that has the greatest negative impact is the presence of "error-prone modules" in the application that is being maintained.

Table 13.4   ERP Portfolio Porting Measured with Function Points

	Corporate Functions Corporate Functions	ERP Port? 1 = yes; 0 = no	ERP Ports	App Size Funct. Pts.	ERP Port Size Funct. Pts.
1	Accounts payable	1	18	44,457	3,112
2	Accounts receivable	1	22	55,968	3,918
3	Advertising	0	–	–	
4	Advisory boards – technical	0	–	–	
5	Banking relationships	1	38	131,543	9,208
6	Board of directors	0	–	–	
7	Building maintenance	0	–	–	
8	Business intelligence	1	21	73,972	5,178
9	Business partnerships	1	18	44,457	3,112
10	Competitive analysis	0	–	–	
11	Consultant management	0	–	–	
12	Contract management	1	32	94,868	6,641
13	Customer resource management	1	56	140,585	9,841
14	Customer support	1	45	67,003	4,690
15	Divestitures	1	10	15,000	1,050
16	Education – customers	0	–	–	
17	Education – staff	0	–	–	
18	Embedded software	0	–	–	
19	Energy consumption monitoring	0	–	–	
20	Energy acquisition	0	–	–	
21	Engineering	0	–	–	
22	ERP – Corporate	1	63	252,982	17,709
23	Finances (corporate)	1	84	235,591	16,491
24	Finances (divisional)	1	63	170,358	11,925
25	Governance	1	10	25,000	1,750

(Continued)

Table 13.4 (Continued)

	Corporate Functions Corporate Functions	ERP Port? 1 = yes; 0 = no	ERP Ports	App Size Funct. Pts.	ERP Port Size Funct. Pts.
26	Government certification (if any)	0	–	–	
27	Government regulations (if any)	0	–	–	
28	Human resources	1	7	11,248	787
29	Insurance	1	6	8,935	625
30	Inventory management	1	45	67,003	4,690
31	Legal department	0	–	–	
32	Litigation	0	–	–	
33	Long-range planning	1	7	18,747	1,312
34	Maintenance – product	0	–	–	
35	Maintenance – buildings	0	–	–	
36	Manufacturing	1	178	311,199	21,784
37	Market research	0	–	–	
38	Marketing	1	27	39,911	2,794
39	Measures – customer satisfaction	0	–	–	
40	Measures – financial	1	24	35,571	2,490
41	Measures – market share	0	–	–	
42	Measures – performance	0	–	–	
43	Measures – quality	0	–	–	
44	Measures – ROI and profitability	1	32	47,434	3,320
45	Mergers and acquisitions	1	24	59,284	4,150
46	Office suites	0	–	–	
47	Open-source tools – general	0	–	–	
48	Order entry	1	27	39,911	2,794

Table 13.4 (Continued)

	Corporate Functions Corporate Functions	ERP Port? 1 = yes; 0 = no	ERP Ports	App Size Funct. Pts.	ERP Port Size Funct. Pts.
49	Outside services – manufacturing	0	–	–	
50	Outside services – legal	0	–	–	
51	Outside services – marketing	0	–	–	
52	Outside services – sales	0	–	–	
53	Outside services – terminations	0	–	–	
54	Outsource management	0	–	–	
55	Patents and inventions	0	–	–	
56	Payrolls	1	21	52,837	3,699
57	Planning – manufacturing	1	42	63,254	4,428
58	Planning – products	1	10	15,000	1,050
59	Process management	1	12	17,828	1,248
60	Product design	0	–	–	
61	Product nationalization	0	–	–	
62	Product testing	1	38	56,376	3,946
63	Project offices	0	–	–	
64	Project management	0	–	–	
65	Purchasing	1	30	44,781	3,135
66	Quality control	1	13	20,003	1,400
67	Real estate	0	–	–	
68	Research and development	0	–	–	
69	Sales	1	45	67,003	4,690
70	Sales support	1	15	22,444	1,571
71	Security – buildings	0	–	–	
72	Security – computing and software	0	–	–	

(Continued)

Table 13.4   (Continued)

	Corporate Functions Corporate Functions	ERP Port? 1 = yes; 0 = no	ERP Ports	App Size Funct. Pts.	ERP Port Size Funct. Pts.
73	Shareholder relationships	1	8	29,449	2,061
74	Shipping/receiving products	1	27	66,518	4,656
75	Software development	0	–	–	
76	Standards compliance	0	–	–	
77	Stocks and bonds	1	21	73,972	
78	Supply chain management	1	47	70,973	
79	Taxes	1	42	105,424	
80	Travel	0	–	–	
81	Unbudgeted costs – cyber-attacks	0	–	–	
82	Warranty support	1	7	10,025	
Portfolio Total		**38**	**723**	**1,768,917**	**123,824**

Table 13.5 illustrates a number of factors which have been found to exert a beneficial positive impact on the work of updating aging applications and shows the percentage of improvement compared to average results.

At the top of the list of maintenance "best practices" is the utilization of full-time, trained maintenance specialists rather than turning over maintenance tasks to untrained generalists. Trained maintenance specialists are found most often in two kinds of companies: (1) large systems software producers such as IBM; (2) large maintenance outsource vendors. The curricula for training maintenance personnel can include more than a dozen topics and the training periods range from 2 weeks to a maximum of about 4 weeks.

Since training of maintenance specialists is the top factor, Table 13.6 shows a modern maintenance curriculum such as those found in large maintenance outsource companies.

The positive impact from utilizing maintenance specialists is one of the reasons why maintenance outsourcing has been growing so rapidly. The maintenance productivity rate of some of the better maintenance outsource companies is roughly twice that of their clients prior to the

Table 13.5   Impact of Key Adjustment Factors on Maintenance

(Sorted in order of maximum positive impact)	
Maintenance Factors	Plus Range
Maintenance specialists	35%
High staff experience	34%
Table-driven variables and data	33%
Low complexity of base code	32%
Test coverage tools and analysis	30%
Static analysis of all legacy code	29%
Reengineering tools	27%
High level programming languages	25%
Reverse engineering tools	23%
Complexity analysis tools	20%
Defect tracking tools	20%
"Mass update" specialists	20%
Automated change control tools	18%
Unpaid overtime	18%
Quality measurements	16%
Formal base code inspections	15%
Regression test libraries	15%
Excellent response time	12%
Annual training of >10 days	12%
High management experience	12%
HELP desk automation	12%
No error prone modules	10%
On-line defect reporting	10%
Productivity measurements	8%
Excellent ease of use	7%
User satisfaction measurements	5%
High team morale	5%
Sum	**503%**

Table 13.6   Sample Maintenance Curricula for Companies Using Maintenance Specialists

Software Maintenance Courses	Days	Sequence
Error-prone module removal	2.00	1
Complexity analysis and reduction	1.00	2
Reducing bad-fix injections and error-prone modules (EPM)	1.00	3
Defect reporting and analysis	0.50	4
Change control	1.00	5
Configuration control	1.00	6
Software maintenance workflows	1.00	7
Mass updates to multiple applications	1.00	8
Maintenance of COTS packages	1.00	9
Maintenance of ERP applications	1.00	10
Regression testing, static analysis, and legacy defect removal	2.00	11
Test library control	2.00	12
Test case conflicts and errors	2.00	13
Dead code isolation	1.00	14
Function points for maintenance	0.50	15
Reverse engineering	1.00	16
Reengineering	1.00	17
Refactoring	0.50	18
Maintenance of reusable code	1.00	19
Object-oriented maintenance	1.00	20
Maintenance of agile and extreme code	1.00	21
Total	**23.50**	

completion of the outsource agreement. Thus even if the outsource vendor costs are somewhat higher, there can still be useful economic gains.

Let us now consider some of the factors which exert a negative impact on the work of updating or modifying existing software applications. Note that the top-ranked factor which reduces maintenance productivity, the presence of error-prone modules, is very asymmetrical.

The absence of error-prone modules does not speed up maintenance work, but their presence definitely slows down maintenance work.

In general, more than 80% of latent bugs found by users in software applications are reported against less than 20% of the modules. Once these modules are identified, then they can be inspected, analyzed, and restructured to reduce their error content down to safe levels.

Table 13.7 summarizes the major factors that degrade software maintenance performance. Not only are error-prone modules troublesome, but many other factors can degrade performance too. For example, very complex "spaghetti code" is quite difficult to maintain safely. It is also troublesome to have maintenance tasks assigned to generalists rather than to trained maintenance specialists.

A very common situation which often degrades performance is lack of suitable maintenance tools, such as defect tracking software, change management software, test library software, and so forth. In general, it is very easy to botch up maintenance and make it such a labor-intensive activity that few resources are left over for development work.

The last factor, or lack of unpaid overtime, deserves a comment. Unpaid overtime is very common among software maintenance and development personnel. In some companies, it amounts to about 15% of the total work time. Because it is unpaid it is usually unmeasured. That means side by side comparisons of productivity rates or costs between groups with unpaid overtime and groups without will favor the group with unpaid overtime because so much of their work is uncompensated and hence invisible. This is a benchmarking trap for the unwary. Because excessive overtime is psychologically harmful if continued over long periods, it is unfortunate that unpaid overtime tends to be ignored when benchmark studies are performed.

Given the enormous amount of effort that is now being applied to software maintenance, and which will be applied in the future, it is obvious that every corporation should attempt to adopt maintenance "best practices" and avoid maintenance "worst practices" as rapidly as possible.

Methodologies That Are Maintenance-Strong and Maintenance-Weak

There were about 60 named software development methodologies in 2018 as shown in the author's new book by CRC Press, *Software Methodologies: A Quantitative Guide*. The majority of these were developed mainly for new development or "Greenfield" applications and are "maintenance weak." However, some methodologies were envisioned as

Table 13.7 Impact of Key Adjustment Factors on Maintenance

(Sorted in order of maximum negative impact)	
Maintenance Factors	*Minus Range*
Error prone modules	−50%
Embedded variables and data	−45%
Staff inexperience	−40%
High complexity of base code	−30%
Lack of test coverage analysis	−28%
Manual change control methods	−27%
Low level programming languages	−25%
No defect tracking tools	−24%
No "mass update" specialists	−22%
No static analysis of legacy code	−18%
No quality measurements	−18%
No maintenance specialists	−18%
Poor response time	−16%
Management inexperience	−15%
No base code inspections	−15%
No regression test libraries	−15%
No help desk automation	−15%
No on-line defect reporting	−12%
No annual training	−10%
No code restructuring tools	−10%
No reengineering tools	−10%
No reverse engineering tools	−10%
No complexity analysis tools	−10%
No productivity measurements	−7%
Poor team morale	−6%
No user satisfaction measurements	−4%
No unpaid overtime	0%
Sum	**−500%**

providing lifetime support for software applications and therefore are "maintenance strong" or effective in "brownfield" projects.

Unfortunately, the world's most popular methodology, Agile, is in the "maintenance-weak" category. It was designed almost exclusively for new development and has no solid features for dealing with legacy applications. A majority of agile users revert to waterfall for their maintenance work.

Probably, the best of the older "standard" methodologies for maintenance and enhancements work are IBM's Rational Unified Process (RUP) and the pair of methods developed by Watts Humphrey and now endorsed by the Software Engineering Institute: Team Software Process (TSP) and Personal Software Process (PSP).

However, because maintenance is not as exciting as new development, it has become a major growth industry for outsource vendors. Quite a few of these have developed custom or proprietary maintenance methodologies of their own, such as the "managed maintenance" approach developed by Computer Aid Inc. (CAI). Other major outsource vendors with large maintenance contracts include IBM, Accenture, and CSC but there are many others.

Some of the tool suites used by these maintenance outsource companies include the following features:

1. Maintenance work benches.
2. Code restructuring tools.
3. Translators from old languages (i.e. COBOL) to modern languages (i.e. Java).
4. Data mining tools for extracting lost requirements and algorithms from old code.
5. Automatic function point counting of legacy applications.
6. Cyclomatic complexity analyzers.
7. Static analysis tools for locating hidden bugs in legacy code.
8. Test coverage tools.
9. Security analysis tools to guard against cyber-attacks.
10. Redocumentation tools to refresh obsolete requirements.
11. Estimating tools such as SRM that predict costs and feature growth.

There are also a number of off-shore outsource vendors who promise lower costs than U.S. vendors. While this may be true, off-shore work is quite a bit more complicated due to large time-zone differences and also to the fact that almost daily contact may be needed between the maintenance teams and the legacy software owners.

Among the author's clients in the Fortune 500 category, about 65% of maintenance work is farmed out to vendors and only 35% stays in house: mainly mission-critical applications or those that process classified or highly confidential data such as financial records or competitive information.

Customer Support: A Major Maintenance Weakness

Many readers of this chapter have probably tried to get customer support from software vendors. Some companies don't even provide contacts with customer support personnel; others depend upon user groups or forums. Very few companies are ranked "good" or "excellent" for customer support with Apple often heading the list and IBM usually cited.

The author's own experiences with contacting customer support are not good: the average wait for telephone contact with a live person was more than 12 minutes. About half of the support personnel did not speak English well enough to understand their comments; about 25% did not understand the problem and had no effective solutions.

Internal software is usually better than commercial software, but even so support is often an afterthought and assigned to development personnel rather than to dedicated support personnel.

The following are five factors that influence how many customer support personnel will be needed for any given application:

1. The size of the application in function points.
2. The number of customers or users ranging from 1 person to millions of users.
3. The number of latent bugs or defects in the application when released.
4. The legal liabilities of the software vendor in case of bugs or failures.
5. The prestige and public image sought by the vendor vs. competitors.

Obviously big and complicated applications with hundreds or even thousands of bugs will need more support personnel than small, simple software packages with few bugs.

Note: The author's Software Risk Master (SRM) tool predicts numbers of customer support personnel for a three-year period after release. It also predicts numbers of bugs, numbers of incidents, numbers of customer calls for help, and other topics that are of significance to those responsible for geriatric care of released software.

Software Entropy and Total Cost of Ownership

The word "entropy" means the tendency of systems to destabilize and become more chaotic over time. Entropy is a term from physics and is not a software-related word. However entropy is true of all complex systems, including software. All known compound objects decay and become more complex with the passage of time unless effort is exerted to keep them repaired and updated. Software is no exception. The accumulation of small updates over time tends to gradually degrade the initial structure of applications and makes changes grow more difficult over time.

Table 13.8 illustrates the impact of entropy over a 10-year period. Each year accumulated changes will degrade the application's structure and raise cyclomatic complexity. Also, the higher complexity will progressively lower testing defect removal efficiency (DRE).

Entropy can be stopped or reversed using methods such as refactoring or restructuring. Also frequent use of static analysis can help. Obviously, every software legacy application should have test coverage tools and also cyclomatic complexity tools available and used often.

For software applications, entropy has long been a fact of life. If applications are developed with marginal initial quality control, they will probably be poorly structured and contain error-prone modules. This means that every year, the accumulation of defect repairs and maintenance updates will degrade the original structure and make each change slightly more difficult. Over time, the application will destabilize and "bad fixes" will increase in number and severity. Unless the application is restructured or fully refurbished, eventually it will become so

Table 13.8   Complexity and Entropy Over Time

Year	Cyclomatic Complexity	Testing DRE
2015	15	92%
2016	16	92%
2017	17	91%
2018	19	90%
2019	20	90%
2020	22	88%
2021	24	87%
2022	26	86%
2023	28	85%
2024	30	84%

complex that maintenance can only be performed by a few experts who are more or less locked into the application.

By contrast, leading applications that are well structured initially can delay the onset of entropy. Indeed, well-structured applications can achieve declining maintenance costs over time. This is because updates do not degrade the original structure, as in the case of "spaghetti bowl" applications where the structure is almost unintelligible when maintenance begins.

The total cost of ownership of a software application is the sum of six major expense elements: (1) the initial cost of building an application; (2) the cost of enhancing the application with new features over its lifetime; (3) the cost of repairing defects and bugs over the application's lifetime; (4) the cost of customer support for fielding and responding to queries and customer-reported defects; (5) the cost of periodic restructuring or "refactoring" of aging applications to reduce entropy and thereby reduce bad-fix injection rates; (6) removal of error-prone modules via surgical removal and redevelopment. This last expense element will only occur for legacy applications that contain error-prone modules.

Similar phenomena can be observed outside of software. If you buy an automobile that has a high frequency of repair as shown in Consumer Reports and you skimp on lubrication and routine maintenance, you will fairly soon face some major repair problems – usually well before 50,000 miles.

By contrast, if you buy an automobile with a low frequency of repair as shown in Consumer Reports and you are scrupulous in maintenance, you should be able to drive the car more than 100,000 miles without major repair problems.

Summary and Conclusions

In every industry, maintenance tends to require more personnel than those building new products. For the software industry, the number of personnel required to perform maintenance is unusually large and may soon top 70% of all technical software workers. The main reasons for the high maintenance efforts in the software industry are the intrinsic difficulties of working with aging software. Special factors such as "mass updates" that began with the roll-out of the Euro and the year 2000 problem are also geriatric issues.

Given the enormous efforts and costs devoted to software maintenance, every company should evaluate and consider best practices for maintenance and should avoid worst practices if at all possible.

References and Books by Capers Jones That Discuss Software Maintenance

Jones, Capers; *Software Methodologies: A Quantitative Guide*; CRC Press; 2017a.

Jones, Capers; *Quantifying Software: Global and Industry Perspectives*; CRC Press; 2017b.

Jones, Capers; *A Guide to Software Measures and Metrics*; CRC Press; 2017c.

Jones, Capers; *The Technical and Social History of Software Engineering*; Addison Wesley; 2014.

Jones, Capers; and Bonsignour, Olivier; *The Economics of Software Quality*; Addison Wesley Longman, Boston, MA; 2011; ISBN: 10: 0-13-258220-1; 585 pages.

Jones, Capers; *Software Engineering Best Practices*; McGraw Hill, New York, NY; 2010; ISBN: 978-0-07-162161-8; 660 pages. (Being translated into Chinese by IBM China).

Jones, Capers; *Applied Software Measurement*; McGraw Hill, New York, NY; 2008; ISBN: 978-0-07-150244-3; 662 pages. (Available in English, Japanese, and Chinese editions)

Jones, Capers; *Estimating Software Costs*; McGraw Hill, New York, NY; 2007; ISBN: 13: 978-0-07-148300-1. (Available in English and Japanese editions).

Jones, Capers; *Software Assessments, Benchmarks, and Best Practices*; Addison Wesley Longman, Boston, MA; 2000; ISBN: 0-201-48542-7; 657 pages.

Books by Additional Authors

Boehm, Barry; *Software Engineering Economics*; Prentice Hall, Englewood Cliffs, NJ; 1981; 900 pages.

Booch, Grady; *Object Solutions: Managing the Object-Oriented Project*; Addison Wesley, Reading, MA; 1995.

Capability Maturity Model Integration; *Version 1.1; Software Engineering Institute*; Carnegie-Mellon Univ.; Pittsburgh, PA; March 2003; http://www.sei.cmu.edu/cmmi/.

Brooks, Fred: *The Mythical Man-Month*; Addison-Wesley, Reading, MA, 1974, rev.; 1995.

Charette, Bob; *Software Engineering Risk Analysis and Management*; McGraw Hill, New York, NY; 1989.

Charette, Bob; *Application Strategies for Risk Management*; McGraw Hill, New York, NY; 1990.

Cohn, Mike; *Agile Estimating and Planning*; Prentice Hall PTR, Englewood Cliffs, NJ; 2005; ISBN: 0131479415.

DeMarco, Tom; *Controlling Software Projects*; Yourdon Press, New York; 1982; ISBN: 0-917072-32-4; 284 pages.

Ewusi-Mensah, Kweku; *Software Development Failures*; MIT Press, Cambridge, MA; 2003; ISBN: 0-26205072-2; 276 pages.

Gack, Gary; *Managing the Black Hole – The Executives Guide to Project Risk*; The Business Expert Publisher, Thomson, GA; 2010; ISBN: 10: 1-935602-01-2.

Galorath, Dan; *Software Sizing, Estimating, and Risk Management: When Performance is Measured Performance Improves*; Auerbach Publishing, Philadelphia, PA; 2006; ISBN: 10: 0849335930; 576 pages.

Garmus, David; and Herron, David; *Measuring the Software Process: A Practical Guide to Functional Measurement*; Prentice Hall, Englewood Cliffs, NJ; 1995.

Garmus, David; and Herron, David; *Function Point Analysis – Measurement Practices for Successful Software Projects*; Addison Wesley Longman, Boston, MA; 2001; ISBN: 0-201-69944-3; 363 pages.

Glass, R.L.; *Software Runaways: Lessons Learned from Massive Software Project Failures*; Prentice Hall, Englewood Cliffs, NJ; 1998.

Hill, Peter R.; *Practical Software Project Estimation*; McGraw Hill; 2010.

Harris, Michaael; Herron, David; and Iwanicki, Stacia; *The Business Value of IT: Managing Risks, Optimizing Performance, and Measuring Results*; CRC Press (Auerbach), Boca Raton, FL; 2008; ISBN: 13: 978-1-4200-6474-2; 266 pages.

Humphrey, Watts; *Managing the Software Process*; Addison Wesley, Reading, MA; 1989.

International Function Point Users Group (IFPUG); *IFPUG Counting Practices Manual*; Release 4; International Function Point Users Group, Westerville, OH; April 1995; 83 pages.

International Function Point Users Group (IFPUG); *IT Measurement – Practical Advice from the Experts*; Addison Wesley Longman, Boston, MA; 2002; ISBN: 0-201-74158-X; 759 pages.

Park, Robert E. et al; *Software Cost and Schedule Estimating – A Process Improvement Initiative*; Technical Report CMU/SEI 94-SR-03; Software Engineering Institute, Pittsburgh, PA; May 1994.

Park, Robert E. et al; *Checklists and Criteria for Evaluating the Costs and Schedule Estimating Capabilities of Software Organizations*; Technical Report CMU/SEI 95-SR-005; Software Engineering Institute, Pittsburgh, PA; January 1995.

McConnell; *Software Estimating: Demystifying the Black Art*; Microsoft Press, Redmund, WA; 2006.

Roetzheim, William H.; and Beasley, Reyna A.; *Best Practices in Software Cost and Schedule Estimation*; Prentice Hall PTR, Upper Saddle River, NJ; 1998.

Strassmann, Paul; *Information Productivity*; Information Economics Press, Stamford, CT; 1999.

Strassmann, Paul; *Information Payoff*; Information Economics Press, Stamford, CT; 1985.

Strassmann, Paul; *Governance of Information Management: The Concept of an Information Constitution*, 2nd ed.; (eBook); Information Economics Press, Stamford, CT; 2004.

Strassmann, Paul; *The Squandered Computer*; Information Economics Press, Stamford, CT; 1997.

Stukes, Sherry; Deshoretz, Jason; Apgar, Henry; and Macias, Ilona; *Air Force Cost Analysis Agency Software Estimating Model Analysis*; TR-9545/008-2;

Contract F04701-95-D-0003, Task 008; Management Consulting & Research, Inc., Thousand Oaks, CA; September 30, 1996.

Wellman, Frank; *Software Costing: An Objective Approach to Estimating and Controlling the Cost of Computer Software*, Prentice Hall, Englewood Cliffs, NJ; 1992; ISBN: 0-138184364.

Whitehead, Richard; *Leading a Development Team*; Addison Wesley, Boston, MA; 2001; ISBN: 10: 0201675267; 368 pages.

Yourdon, Ed; *Death March – The Complete Software Developer's Guide to Surviving "Mission Impossible" Projects*; Prentice Hall PTR, Upper Saddle River, NJ; 1997; ISBN: 0-13-748310-4; 218 pages.

Yourdon, Ed; *Outsource: Competing in the Global Productivity Race*; Prentice Hall PTR, Upper Saddle River, NJ; 2005; ISBN: 0-13-147571-1; 251 pages.

Readings on Software Maintenance

Arnold, Robert S.; *Software Reengineering*; IEEE Computer Society Press, Los Alamitos, CA; 1993; ISBN: 0-8186-3272-0; 600 pages.

Arthur, Lowell Jay; *Software Evolution – The Software Maintenance Challenge*; John Wiley & Sons, New York; 1988; ISBN: 0-471-62871-9; 254 pages.

Gallagher, R.S.; *Effective Customer Support*; International Thomson Computer Press, Boston, MA; 1997; ISBN: 1-85032-209-0; 480 pages.

Grubb, Penny; and Takang, Armstrong; *Software Maintenance – Concepts and Practice*; World Scientific Pub. Co; 2003; ISBN: 981-238-425-1.

Kan, Stephen H.; *Metrics and Models in Software Quality Engineering*; Addison Wesley, Reading, MA; 2003; ISBN: 0-201-72915-6; 528 pages.

McCabe, Thomas J.; "A Complexity Measure"; *IEEE Transactions on Software Engineering*; December 1976; pp. 308–320.

Muller, Monika; and Abram, Alain (editors); *Metrics in Software Evolution*; R. Oldenbourg Vertag GmbH, Munich; 1995; ISBN: 3-486-23589-3.

Parikh, Girish; *Handbook of Software Maintenance*; John Wiley & Sons, New York; 1986; ISBN: 0-471-82813-0; 421 pages.

Pigoski, Thomas M.; *Practical Software Maintenance – Best Practices for Managing Your Software Investment*; IEEE Computer Society Press, Los Alamitos, CA; 1997; ISBN: 0-471-17001-1; 400 pages.

Polo, Macario et al; *Advances in Software Maintenance, Management, Technologies, and Solutions*; World Scientific Pub. Co.; 1996; ISBN: 981-022826-0.

Sharon, David; *Managing Systems in Transition – A Pragmatic View of Reengineering Methods*; International Thomson Computer Press, Boston, MA; 1996; ISBN: 1-85032-194-9; 300 pages.

Takang, Armstrong; and Grubh, Penny; *Software Maintenance Concepts and Practice*; International Thomson Computer Press, Boston, MA; 1997; ISBN: 1-85032-192-2; 256 pages.

Chapter 14

Function Points as a Universal Metric

Introduction

Function point metrics are the most accurate and effective metrics yet developed for software sizing and also for studying software productivity, quality, costs, risks, and economic value. The newer SNAP metric may also add value for the work effort of dealing with non-functional requirements.

In the future, function point metrics combined with SNAP can easily become universal metrics used for all software applications and for all software contracts in all countries. However, there are some logistical problems with function point metrics that need to be understood and overcome in order for function point metrics to become the primary metric for software economic analysis.

The ultimate goal of function point metrics should be to size and estimate all known types of software applications including but not limited to:

- New projects
- Enhancements to existing software
- Maintenance changes to existing software
- Internal software
- Commercial software
- Embedded and real time software
- Artificial Intelligence (AI) projects

DOI: 10.1201/9781003193128-16

- Data base, data analytics, and data warehouse projects
- Large systems >100,000 function points
- Small changes <1.00 function points
- Analysis of canceled and failed software projects
- Analysis of factors in software litigation

As of today, manual function point counting and SNAP counting are too slow and costly to be used on large software projects above 10,000 function points in size. Also, application size is not constant but grows at about 2% per calendar month during development and 8% or more per calendar year for as long as software is in active use so size needs continuous adjustments.

This chapter discusses a method of high-speed function point and SNAP counting that can size any application in less than two minutes, and which can predict application growth during development and for 10 years after release. This new method is based on pattern matching and was created by Namcook Analytics LLC for use in the Software Risk Master (SRM) estimation tool.

The main software cost drivers circa 2020 in descending order of magnitude are as follows:

1. Finding and fixing defects
2. Producing paper documents
3. Coding or programming
4. Dealing with software requirements changes
5. Dealing with non-functional requirements
6. Management
7. Meetings and communications

Function point metrics are the only available metric that can measure six of the seven cost drivers individually or together for economic analysis of total software projects. The newer SNAP metric measures non-functional requirements.

The older "lines of code" or LOC metric only measured coding and did not even measure coding accurately. LOC metrics penalize modern high-level programming languages as discussed later in topic 14 of this chapter.

CEOs and other C-level executives want to know much more than just the coding part of software applications. They want to know the full cost of applications and their complete schedules from requirements through delivery. They also want to know multi-year maintenance and enhancement costs plus total cost of ownership (TCO).

Function point metrics were invented by A.J. Albrecht and colleagues at IBM's White Plains development center circa 1975. Function point metrics were placed in the public domain by IBM in 1978. Responsibility for function point counting rules soon transferred to the International Function Point User's Group (IFPUG). Their web site is www.IFPUG.org.

Function point metrics were developed by IBM due to serious mathematical and economic problems associated with the older "lines of code" metric or LOC. The LOC metric penalizes high-level programming languages and also cannot be used to evaluate requirements, design, business analysis, user documentation, or any other non-coding activities.

In the current era circa 2018, function point metrics were the major metric for software economic and productivity studies. At least 60,000 software projects have been measured using IFPUG function point metrics, including more than 5,000 projects that are publically available from the International Software Benchmark Standards Group (ISBSG). Their web site is www.ISBSG.org. See also the author's blog or http://Namcookanalytics.com.

The Strengths of Function Point Metrics

1. IFPUG function point metrics have more measured projects than all other metrics combined.
2. IFPUG function point metrics are endorsed by ISO/IEC standard 20926:2009.
3. Formal training and certification examinations are available for IFPUG function point counting.
4. Hundreds of certified IFPUG function point counters are available in most countries.
5. Counts of function points by certified counters usually are within 5% of each other.
6. IFPUG function point metrics are standard features of most parametric estimating tools such as KnowledgePlan, SEER, and Software Risk Master.
7. Function points are increasingly used for software contracts. The government of Brazil requires function points for all software contracts.

The Weaknesses of Function Point Metrics

1. Function point analysis is slow. Counting speeds for function points average perhaps 500 function points per day.

2. Due to the slow speed of function point analysis, function points are almost never used on large systems >10,000 function points in size.

3. Function point analysis is expensive. Assuming a daily counting speed of 500 function points and a daily consulting fee of $1,500 counting, an application of 10,000 function points would require 20 days and cost $30,000. This is equal to a cost of $3.00 for every function point counted.

4. Application size is not constant. During development, applications grow at perhaps 2% per calendar month. After development, applications continue to grow at perhaps 8% per calendar year. Current counting rules do not include continuous growth.

5. More than a dozen function point, counting variations exist circa 2018 including COSMIC function points, NESMA function points, FISMA function points, fast function points, backfired function points, and a number of others. These variations produce function point totals that differ from IFPUG function points by perhaps + or –15%.

A New Method for High-Speed Function Point Analysis

In order to make function point metrics easier to use and more rapid, the author of this book developed a high-speed function point method that has been used on several hundred software applications.

The high-speed sizing method is embedded in the Software Risk Master™ (SRM) sizing and estimating tool under development by Namcook Analytics LLC. A working version is available on the Namcook Analytics web site, www.Namcook.com. The version requires a password from within the site.

The Namcook Analytics high-speed method includes the following features:

1. From more than 200 trials, sizing speed averages about 1.87 minutes per application. This speed is more or less constant between applications as small as 10 function points or as large as 300,000 function points.

2. The sizing method often comes within 5% of manual counts by certified counters. The closest match was an SRM predicted size of 1,802 function points for an application sized manually at 1,800 function points.

3. The sizing method can also be used prior to full requirements, which is the earliest of any known software sizing method.

4. The patent-pending method is based on external pattern matching rather than internal attributes. As long as an application can be placed on the SRM taxonomy, the application can be sized.

5. The method can size all types of software including operating systems, ERP packages, telephone switching systems, medical device software, web applications, smart-phone applications, and normal information systems applications.

6. The sizing method is metric neutral and predicts application size in a total of 15 metrics including IFPUG function points, the new SNAP metric for non-functional attributes, COSMIC function points, story points, use-case points, logical code statements, and many others.

7. The sizing method predicts application growth during development and for 5 years of post-release usage.

A Short Summary of Pattern Matching

Today, very few applications are truly new. Most are replacements for older legacy applications or enhancements to older legacy applications. Pattern matching uses the size, cost, schedules, and other factors from legacy applications to generate similar values for new applications.

Software pattern matching as described here is based on a proprietary taxonomy developed by the author, Capers Jones. The taxonomy uses multiple-choice questions to identify the key attributes of software projects. The taxonomy is used to collect historical benchmark data and also as basis for estimating future projects. The taxonomy is also used for sizing applications.

For sizing, the taxonomy includes project nature, scope, class, type, problem complexity, code complexity, and data complexity. For estimating, additional parameters such as CMMI level, methodology, and team experience are also used.

The proprietary Namcook taxonomy used for pattern matching contains 122 factors. With 122 total elements, the permutations of the full taxonomy total to 214,200,000 possible patterns. Needless to say more than half of these patterns have never occurred and will never occur.

In the software industry in 2018, the total number of patterns that occurred with relatively high frequency was much smaller: about 25,000.

The SRM tool uses the taxonomy to select similar projects from its knowledge base of around 26,000 projects. Mathematical algorithms are used to derive results for patterns that do not have a perfect match.

However, a great majority of software projects do have matches because they have been done many times. For example, all banks perform similar transactions for customers and therefore have similar software packages. Telephone switches also have been done many times and all have similar features.

Pattern matching with a good taxonomy to guide the search is a very cost-effective way for dealing with application size.

Pattern matching is new for software sizing but common elsewhere. Two examples of pattern matching are the Zillow data base of real-estate costs and the Kelley Blue Book of used automobile costs. Both use taxonomies to narrow down choices and then show clients the end results of those choices.

Increasing Executive Awareness of Function Points for Economic Studies

Because of the slow speed of function point analysis and the lack of data from large applications, function points are a niche metric below the interest level of most CEOs and especially CEOs of Fortune 500 companies with large portfolios and many large systems including ERP packages.

In order for function point metrics to become a priority for C level executives and a standard method for all software contracts, the following improvements are needed:

1. Function point size must be available in a few minutes for large systems; not after weeks of counting.
2. The cost per function point counted must be lower than $0.05 per function point rather than today's costs of more than $3.00 per function point counted.
3. Function point metrics must be able to size applications ranging from a low of 1 function point to a high of more than 300,000 function points.
4. Sizing of applications must also deal with the measured rates of requirements creep during development and the measured rates of post-release growth for perhaps 10 years after the initial release.
5. Function points must also be applied to maintenance, enhancements, and total costs of ownership (TCO).
6. Individual changes in requirements should be sized in real-time as they occur. If a client wants a new feature that may be 10 function points in size, this fact should be established within a few minutes.

7. Function points should be used for large-scale economic analysis of methods, industries, and even countries.
8. Function points should be used to measure consumption and usage of software as well as production of software.
9. Function points must be applied to portfolio analysis and system architecture.
10. Function points can and should be used to size and estimate collateral materials such as documentation, test case volumes, and reusable materials used for applications.

Topic 1: Sizing Application Growth during Development and After Release

Software application size is not a constant. Software projects grow continuously during development and also after release. Following are some examples of the features of the patent-pending sizing method embedded in Software Risk Master™. Table 14.1 shows an example of the way SRM predicts growth and post-release changes.

Note that calendar years 2, 4, and 8 show a phenomenon called "mid-life kickers" or major new features added about every four years to commercial software applications. Multi-year sizing is based on empirical data from a number of major companies such as IBM where applications have been in service for more than 10 years.

Software applications should be resized whenever there are major enhancements. Individual enhancements should be sized, and all data should be accumulated starting with the initial delivery. Formal sizing should also take place at the end of every calendar year or every fiscal year for applications that are deployed and in active use.

Topic 2: Predicting Application Size in Multiple Metrics

There are so many metrics in use in 2018 that as a professional courtesy to users and other metrics groups SRM predicts size in the metrics shown in Table 14.2. Assume that the application being sized is known to be 10,000 function points using IFPUG version 4.2 counting rules.

Because SRM is metric neutral, additional metrics could be added to the list of supported metrics if new metrics become available in the future.

Table 14.1 SRM Multi-Year Sizing Example

Patent application 61434091. February 2012				
Nominal application size in IFPUG function points	10,000			
SNAP points	1,389			
Language	C			
Language level	2.50			
Logical code statements	1,280,000			
	Function Points	SNAP Points	Logical Code	
Size at end of requirements	10,000	1,389	1,280,000	
Size of requirement creep	2,000	278	256,000	
Size of planned delivery	12,000	1,667	1,536,000	
Size of deferred features	−4,800	(667)	(614,400)	
Size of actual delivery	7,200	1,000	921,600	
Year 1 usage	12,000	1,667	1,536,000	Kicker
Year 2 usage	13,000	1,806	1,664,000	
Year 3 usage	14,000	1,945	1,792,000	
Year 4 usage	17,000	2,361	2,176,000	Kicker
Year 5 usage	18,000	2,500	2,304,000	
Year 6 usage	19,000	2,639	2,432,000	
Year 7 usage	20,000	2,778	2,560,000	
Year 8 usage	23,000	3,195	2,944,000	Kicker
Year 9 usage	24,000	3,334	3,072,000	
Year 10 usage	25,000	3,473	3,200,000	

SRM also predicts application size in terms of logical code statements or "LOC." However with more than 2,500 programming languages in existence and the majority of projects using several languages, code sizing requires that users inform the SRM tool as to which language(s) will be used. This is done by specifying a percentage of various languages from an SRM pull-down menu that lists the languages supported. Currently, SRM supports about 180 languages for sizing, but this is just an arbitrary number that can easily be expanded.

Table 14.2 Metrics Supported by SRM Pattern Matching

Alternate Metrics	Size	% of IFPUG
IFPUG 4.3	10,000	100.00%
Automated code based	10,700	107.00%
Automated UML based	10,300	103.00%
Backfired function points	10,000	100.00%
Cosmic function points	11,429	114.29%
Fast function points	9,700	97.00%
Feature points	10,000	100.00%
FISMA function points	10,200	102.00%
Full function points	11,700	117.00%
Function points light	9,650	96.50%
IntegraNova models	10,900	109.00%
Mark II function points	10,600	106.00%
NESMA function points	10,400	104.00%
RICE objects	47,143	471.43%
SCCQI function points	30,286	302.86%
Simple function points	9,750	97.50%
SNAP non-functional metrics	1,818	18.18%
SRM pattern matching	10,000	100.00%
Story points	5,556	55.56%
Unadjusted function points	8,900	89.00%
Use case points	3,333	33.33%

Topic 3: Sizing All Known Types of Software Application

One of the advantages of sizing by means of external pattern matching rather than sizing by internal attributes is that the any known application can be sized. Table 14.3 shows 40 samples of applications size by the SRM high-speed method.

This list of 40 applications was sized by the author in about 75 minutes, which is a rate of 1.875 minutes per application sized. The cost per function point sized is less than $0.001. As of 2013, SRM sizing was the

Table 14.3 Examples of Software Size via Pattern Matching

Using Software Risk Master™		
	Applications	*Size in IFPUG Function Points*
1	Oracle	229,434
2	Windows 7 (all features)	202,150
3	Microsoft Windows XP	66,238
4	Google docs	47,668
5	Microsoft Office 2003	33,736
6	F15 avionics/weapons	23,109
7	VA medical records	19,819
8	Apple I Phone	19,366
9	IBM IMS data base	18,558
10	Google search engine	18,640
11	Linux	17,505
12	ITT System 12 switching	17,002
13	Denver Airport luggage (original)	16,661
14	Child Support Payments (state)	12,546
15	Facebook	8,404
16	MapQuest	3,793
17	Microsoft Project	1,963
18	Android OS (original version)	1,858
19	Microsoft Excel	1,578
20	Garmin GPS navigation (hand held)	1,518
21	Microsoft Word	1,431
22	Mozilla Firefox	1,342
23	Laser printer driver (HP)	1,248
24	Sun Java compiler	1,185
25	Wikipedia	1,142
26	Cochlear implant (embedded)	1,041
27	Microsoft DOS circa 1998	1,022

Table 14.3   (Continued)

	Using Software Risk Master™	
	Applications	*Size in IFPUG Function Points*
28	Nintendo Gameboy DS	1,002
29	Casio atomic watch	933
30	Computer BIOS	857
31	SPR KnowledgePlan	883
32	Function Point Workbench	714
33	Norton anti-virus	700
34	SPR SPQR/20	699
35	Golf handicap analysis	662
36	Google Gmail	590
37	Twitter (original circa 2009)	541
38	Freecell computer solitaire	102
39	Software Risk Master™ prototype	38
40	ILOVEYOU computer worm	22

fastest and least expensive method of sizing yet developed. This makes SRM useful for Agile projects where normal function point analysis is seldom used.

Because sizing is based on external attributes rather than internal factors, SRM sizing can take place before full requirements are available; this is 3 to 6 months earlier than most other sizing methods. Early sizing leaves time for risk abatement for potentially hazardous projects.

Topic 4: Function Points for Early Analysis of Software Risks

Software projects are susceptible to more than 200 risks in all, of which about 50 can be analyzed using function point metrics. As application size goes up when measured with function point metrics, software risks also go up.

Table 14.4 shows the comparative risk profiles of four sample projects of 100, 1,000, 10,000, and 100,000 function points. All four are

Table 14.4 Average Risks for IT Projects by Size

(Predictions by Software Risk Master™)	
Risks for 100 function points	
Cancellation	8.36%
Negative ROI	10.59%
Cost overrun	9.19%
Schedule slip	11.14%
Unhappy customers	36.00%
Litigation	3.68%
Average Risks	**13.16%**
Financial Risks	**15.43%**
Risks for 1000 function points	
Cancellation	13.78%
Negative ROI	17.46%
Cost overrun	15.16%
Schedule slip	18.38%
Unhappy customers	36.00%
Litigation	6.06%
Average Risks	**17.81%**
Financial Risks	**25.44%**
Risks for 10,000 function points	
Cancellation	26.03%
Negative ROI	32.97%
Cost overrun	28.63%
Schedule slip	34.70%
Unhappy customers	36.00%
Litigation	11.45%
Average Risks	**28.29%**
Financial Risks	**48.04%**
Risks for 100,000 function points	
Cancellation	53.76%

Table 14.4 (Continued)

(Predictions by Software Risk Master™)	
Negative ROI	68.09%
Cost overrun	59.13%
Schedule slip	71.68%
Unhappy customers	36.00%
Litigation	23.65%
Average Risks	**52.05%**
Financial Risks	**99.24%**

"average" projects using iterative development. All four are assumed to be at CMMI level 1.

All of the data in Table 14.4 are standard risk predictions from SRM. Risks would go down with higher CMMI levels, more experienced teams, and robust methodologies such a RUP or TSP.

Small projects below 1,000 function points are usually completed without too much difficulty. But large systems above 10,000 function points are among the most hazardous of all manufactured objects in human history.

It is an interesting phenomenon that every software breach of contract lawsuit except one where the author of this book worked as an expert witness were for projects of 10,000 function points and higher.

Topic 5: Function Points for Activity-Based Sizing and Cost Estimating

In order to be useful for software economic analysis, function point metrics need to be applied to individual software development activities. Corporate executives at the CEO level want to know all cost elements, and not just "design, code, and unit test" or DCUT as it is commonly called.

SRM has a variable focus that allows it to show data ranging from full projects to 40 activities. Table 14.5 shows the complete set of 40 activities for an application of 10,000 function points in size.

SRM uses this level of detail for collecting benchmark data from large applications. In predictive mode prior to requirements, this much detail is not needed, so a smaller chart of accounts is used.

This chart of accounts works for methods such as waterfall. Other charts of accounts are used for iterative, agile, and other methods which segment development into sprints or separate work packages.

Table 14.5   Function Points for Activity-Based Cost Analysis

	Development Activities	*Work Hours per Function Point*	*Burdened Cost per Function Point*
1	Business analysis	0.02	$1.33
2	Risk analysis/sizing	0.00	$0.29
3	Risk solution planning	0.01	$0.67
4	Requirements	0.38	$28.57
5	Requirement inspection	0.22	$16.67
6	Prototyping	0.33	$25.00
7	Architecture	0.05	$4.00
8	Architecture inspection	0.04	$3.33
9	Project plans/estimates	0.03	$2.00
10	Initial design	0.75	$57.14
11	Detail design	0.75	$57.14
12	Design inspections	0.53	$40.00
13	Coding	4.00	$303.03
14	Code inspections	3.30	$250.00
15	Reuse acquisition	0.01	$1.00
16	Static analysis	0.02	$1.33
17	COTS package purchase	0.01	$1.00
18	Open-source acquisition	0.01	$1.00
19	Code security audit	0.04	$2.86
20	Ind. Verif. & Valid.	0.07	$5.00
21	Configuration control	0.04	$2.86
22	Integration	0.04	$2.86
23	User documentation	0.29	$22.22
24	Unit testing	0.88	$66.67
25	Function testing	0.75	$57.14
26	Regression testing	0.53	$40.00
27	Integration testing	0.44	$33.33

Table 14.4 (Continued)

	Development Activities	*Work Hours per Function Point*	*Burdened Cost per Function Point*
28	Performance testing	0.33	$25.00
29	Security testing	0.26	$20.00
30	Usability testing	0.22	$16.67
31	System testing	0.88	$66.67
32	Cloud testing	0.13	$10.00
33	Field (Beta) testing	0.18	$13.33
34	Acceptance testing	0.05	$4.00
35	Independent testing	0.07	$5.00
36	Quality assurance	0.18	$13.33
37	Installation/training	0.04	$2.86
38	Project measurement	0.01	$1.00
39	Project office	0.18	$13.33
40	Project management	4.40	$333.33
Cumulative Results		**20.44**	**$1,548.68**

Major applications that have separate components would use a chart of accounts for each component. All of these could be merged at the end of the project.

One advantage of activity-based costing with function point metrics is that it eliminates "leakage" from measurement studies. For too many studies cover only "design, code, and unit test" or DCUT. These partial activities are less than 30% of the effort on a large software application.

C-level executives want and should see 100% of the total set of activities that goes into software projects, not just partial data. From analysis of internal measurement programs, IT projects only collect data on about 37% of the total effort for software. Only contract software with charges on a time and material basis approach 100% cost collection, plus defense applications developed under contract.

A few major companies such as IBM collect data from internal applications that approach 100% in completeness, but this is fairly rare. The most common omissions are unpaid overtime, project management, and the work of part-time specialists such as business analysts, quality assurance, technical writers, function point counters, and the like.

Topic 6: Function Points and Methodology Analysis

One topic of considerable interest to both C level executives and also to academics and software engineers is how various methodologies compare. Software Risk Master™ includes empirical results from more than 30 different software development methodologies; more than any other benchmark or estimation tool.

Table 14.6 shows the approximate development schedules noted for 30 different software development methods. The rankings run from slowest at the top of the table to fastest at the bottom of the table.

Software Risk Master™ also predicts staffing, effort in months and hours, costs, quality, and 5-years of post-release maintenance and enhancement. Table 14.6 only shows schedules since that topic is of considerable interest to CEOs as well as other C level executives.

Note that Table 14.6 assumes close to a zero value for certified reusable components. Software reuse can shorten schedules compared those shown in Table 14.6.

Table 14.6 also assumes an average team and no use of the capability maturity model. Expert teams and projects in organizations at CMMI levels 3 or higher will have shorter schedules than those shown in Table 14.6.

SRM itself handles adjustments in team skills, CMMI levels, methodologies, programming languages, and volumes of reuse.

Topic 7: Function Points for Evaluating the Capability Maturity Model (CMMI®)

Civilian CEOs in many industries such as banking, insurance, commercial software, transportation, and many kinds of manufacturing care little or nothing about the Software Engineering Institute's (SEI) capability maturity model. In fact many have never even heard of either the SEI or the CMMI.

In the defense industry, on the other hand, the CMMI is a major topic because it is necessary to be at CMMI level 3 of higher in order to bid on some military and defense software contracts. The SEI was formed in 1984 and soon after started doing software process assessments, using a methodology developed by the late Watts Humphrey and his colleagues.

The original assessment method scored organizations on a 5-point scale ranging from 1 (very chaotic in software) through 5 (highly professional and disciplined). The author of this book had a contract with the U.S. Air Force to explore the value of ascending the various CMM and

Table 14.6 Application Schedules

	Application Size = (IFPUG 4.2)	10	100	1,000	10,000	100,000
	Methods	Schedule Months	Schedule Months	Schedule Months	Schedule Months	Schedule Months
1	Proofs	2.60	6.76	17.58	45.71	118.85
2	DoD	2.57	6.61	16.98	43.65	112.20
3	Cowboy	2.51	6.31	15.85	39.81	100.00
4	Waterfall	2.48	6.17	15.31	38.02	94.41
5	ISO/IEC	2.47	6.11	15.10	37.33	92.26
6	Pairs	2.45	6.03	14.79	36.31	89.13
7	Prince2	2.44	5.94	14.49	35.32	86.10
8	Merise	2.44	5.94	14.49	35.32	86.10
9	DSDM	2.43	5.92	14.39	34.99	85.11
10	Models	2.43	5.89	14.29	34.67	84.14
11	Clean rm.	2.42	5.86	14.19	34.36	83.18
12	T-VEC	2.42	5.86	14.19	34.36	83.18
13	V-Model	2.42	5.83	14.09	34.04	82.22
14	Iterative	2.41	5.81	14.00	33.73	81.28
15	SSADM	2.40	5.78	13.90	33.42	80.35

(Continued)

Table 14.6 (Continued)

	Application Size = (IFPUG 4.2)	10	100	1,000	10,000	100,000
	Methods	Schedule Months	Schedule Months	Schedule Months	Schedule Months	Schedule Months
16	Spiral	2.40	5.75	13.80	33.11	79.43
17	SADT	2.39	5.73	13.71	32.81	78.52
18	Jackson	2.39	5.73	13.71	32.81	78.52
19	EVO	2.39	5.70	13.61	32.51	77.62
20	IE	2.39	5.70	13.61	32.51	77.62
21	OO	2.38	5.68	13.52	32.21	76.74
22	DSD	2.38	5.65	13.43	31.92	75.86
23	RUP	2.37	5.62	13.34	31.62	74.99
24	PSP/TSP	2.36	5.56	13.11	30.90	72.86
25	FDD	2.36	5.55	13.06	30.76	72.44
26	RAD	2.35	5.52	12.97	30.48	71.61
27	Agile	2.34	5.50	12.88	30.20	70.79
28	XP	2.34	5.47	12.79	29.92	69.98
29	Hybrid	2.32	5.40	12.53	29.11	67.61
30	Mashup	2.24	5.01	11.22	25.12	56.23
	Average	**2.41**	**5.81**	**14.03**	**33.90**	**81.98**

CMMI levels to ascertain if there were tangible improvements in quality and productivity. Twenty companies were visited for the study.

There are tangible improvements in both quality and productivity gains at the higher CMMI levels from a statistical analysis. However, some companies that don't use the CMMI at all have results as good as companies assessed at CMMI level 5. Tables 14.7.1 through 14.7.4 show CMMI results for various sizes of projects.

The higher levels of the CMMI have better quality than similar civilian projects, but much lower productivity. This is due in part to the fact the DoD oversight leads to huge volumes of paper documents. Military projects create about three times as many pages of requirements, specifications, and other documents as do civilian projects of the same size. Software paperwork costs more than source code for military and defense applications regardless of CMMI levels. DoD projects also

Table 14.7.1   Quality Results of the Five Levels of the CMMI®

(Results for applications of 1000 function points in size)			
CMMI Level	*Defect Potential per FP*	*Defect Removal Efficiency*	*Delivered Defects per FP*
1	5.25	82.00%	0.95
2	5.00	85.00%	0.75
3	4.75	90.00%	0.48
4	4.50	94.00%	0.27
5	4.00	98.00%	0.08

Table 14.7.2   Quality Results of the Five Levels of the CMMI®

(Results for Applications of 10,000 Function Points in Size)			
CMMI Level	*Defect Potential per FP*	*Defect Removal Efficiency*	*Delivered Defects per FP*
1	6.50	75.00%	1.63
2	6.25	82.00%	1.13
3	5.50	87.00%	0.72
4	5.25	90.00%	0.53
5	4.50	94.00%	0.27

**Table 14.7.3   Productivity Rates for the
Five Levels of the CMMI®**

(Results for Applications of 1000 Function Points in Size)		
CMMI Level	*Function Points per Month*	*Work Hours per Function Point*
1	6.00	22.00
2	6.75	19.56
3	7.00	18.86
4	7.25	18.21
5	7.50	17.60

**Table 14.7.4   Productivity Rates for the
Five Levels of the CMMI®**

(Results for Applications of 10,000 Function Points in Size)		
CMMI Level	*Function Points per Month*	*Work Hours per Function Point*
1	2.50	52.80
2	2.75	48.00
3	3.50	37.71
4	4.25	31.06
5	5.50	24.00

use independent verification and validation (IV&V) and independent testing, which seldom occurs in the civilian sector.

Both Namcook Analytics and the SEI express their results using five-point scales but the significance of the scales runs in the opposite direction. The Namcook scale was published first in 1986 in Capers Jones' book *Programming Productivity* (McGraw Hill) and hence is several years older than the SEI scale. In fact the author of this book began doing assessments inside IBM at the same time Watts Humphrey was IBM's director of programming, and about 10 years before the SEI was even incorporated.

Namcook Excellence Scale			Meaning	Frequency of Occurrence
1	=	Excellent	State of the art	2.0%
2	=	Good	Superior to most companies	18.0%
3	=	Average	Normal in most factors	56.0%
4	=	Poor	Deficient in some factors	20.0%
5	=	Very Poor	Deficient in most factors	4.0%

The SEI maturity level scale was first published by Watts Humphrey in 1989 in his well-known book *Managing the Software Process* (Humphrey 1989).

SEI Maturity Level			Meaning	Frequency of Occurrence
1	=	Initial	Chaotic	75.0%
2	=	Repeatable	Marginal	15.0%
3	=	Defined	Adequate	8.0%
4	=	Managed	Good to excellent	1.5%
5	=	Optimizing	State of the art	0.5%

Simply inverting the Namcook excellence scale or the SEI maturity scale is not sufficient to convert the scores from one to another. This is because the SEI scale expresses its results in absolute form, while the Namcook scale expresses its results in relative form.

Large collections of Namcook data from an industry typically approximate a bell-shaped curve. A collection of SEI capability maturity data is skewed toward the Initial or chaotic end of the spectrum. However, it is possible to convert data from the Namcook scale to the equivalent SEI scale by a combination of inversion and compression of the Namcook results. Software Risk Master ™ includes bi-directional conversions between the SEI and Namcook scales.

The Namcook conversion algorithms use two decimal places, so that scores such as 3.25 or 3.75 are possible. In fact even scores below 1 such as 0.65 are possible. The SEI method itself uses integer values but the two-decimal precision of the Namcook conversion method is interesting to clients.

Topic 8: Function Points for Software Quality Analysis

Function points are the best metric for software quality analysis. The older metric "cost per defect" penalizes quality and also violates standard economic assumptions. Quality economics are much better analyzed using function point metrics than any other. A key advantage of function points for quality analysis is the ability to predict defects in requirements and design as well as code defects. Requirements and design defects often outnumber code defects. Table 14.8 shows a typical defect pattern for a waterfall project of 1,000 function points at CMMI level 1 coding in the C language.

Table 14.8.1 shows a sample of the full quality predictions from SRM for an application of 1,000 function points. The table shows a "best case" example for a project using TSP and being at CMMI level 5.

Function points are able to quantify requirements and design defects, which outnumber coding defects for large applications. This is not possible using LOC metrics. Function points are also superior to "cost per defect" for measuring technical debt and cost of quality (COQ). Both technical debt and COQ are standard SRM outputs.

Table 14.8.1 is only an example. SRM can also model various ISO standards, certification of test personnel, team experience levels, CMMI levels, and in fact a total of about 200 specific quality factors.

For many years, the software industry has used "cost per defect" as key metric for software quality. In fact, there is an urban legend that "it costs 100 times as much to fix a bug after release as early in development." Unfortunately, the whole concept of cost per defect is mathematically flawed and does match standard economics. The urban legend has values that resemble the following:

Defects found during requirements	=	$250
Defects found during design	=	$500
Defects found during coding and testing	=	$1,250
Defects found after release	=	$5,000

While such claims are often true mathematically, the following are three hidden problems with cost per defect that are usually not discussed in the software literature:

1. Cost per defect penalizes quality and is always cheapest where the greatest numbers of bugs are found.
2. Because more bugs are found at the beginning of development than at the end, the increase in cost per defect is artificial. Actual

Table 14.8 SRM Defect Prediction for Waterfall Development

1,000 function points; inexperienced team; CMMI level 1; Waterfall; C language

106,670 logical code statements; 106.7 KLOC

Defect Potentials	Defects	Per FP	Per KLOC	Pre-Test Removal	Test Removal	Defects Delivered	Cumul. Effic.
Requirements	1,065	1.07	9.99	70.00%	54.00%	147	86.20%
Design	1,426	1.43	13.37	76.00%	69.00%	106	92.56%
Code	1,515	1.52	14.20	77.00%	74.00%	91	94.02%
Documents	665	0.66	6.23	79.00%	19.00%	113	82.99%
Bad fixes	352	0.35	3.30	59.00%	61.00%	56	84.01%
Total	**5,023**	**5.02**	**47.09**	**74.24%**	**60.36%**	**513**	**89.79%**

Table 14.8.1   SRM Quality Estimate

	Output Results			
Requirements defect potential	134			
Design defect potential	561			
Code defect potential	887			
Document defect potential	135			
Total Defect Potential	1,717			
Per function point	1.72			
Per KLOC	32.20			
	Efficiency	Remainder	Bad Fixes	Costs
Defect Prevention				
JAD	27%	1,262	5	$28,052
QFD	30%	888	4	$39,633
Prototype	20%	713	2	$17,045
Models	68%	229	5	$42,684
Subtotal	**86%**	234	15	$127,415
Pre-Test Removal				
Desk check	27%	171	2	$13,225
Static analysis	55%	78	1	$7,823
Inspections	93%	5	0	$73,791
Subtotal	**98%**	6	3	$94,839
Test Removal				
Unit	32%	4	0	$22,390
Function	35%	2	0	$39,835
Regression	14%	2	0	$51,578
Component	32%	1	0	$57,704
Performance	14%	1	0	$33,366
System	36%	1	0	$63,747
Acceptance	17%	1	0	$15,225
Subtotal	**87%**	1	0	$283,845

Table 14.8.1 (Continued)

	Output Results		
Pre-Release Costs	1,734	3	$506,099
Post-Release Repairs (Technical Debt)	1	0	$658
Maintenance Overhead			$46,545
Cost of Quality (COQ)			$553,302
Defects delivered		1	
High severity		0	
Security flaws		0	
High severity %		11.58%	
Delivered Per FP		0.001	
High severity per FP		0.000	
Security flaws per FP		0.000	
Delivered per KLOC		0.014	
High severity per KLOC		0.002	
Security flaws per KLOC		0.001	
Cumulative Removal Efficiency		99.96%	

time and motion studies of defect repairs show little variance from end to end.

3. Even if calculated correctly, cost per defect does not measure the true economic value of improved software quality. Over and above the costs of finding and fixing bugs, high quality leads to shorter development schedules and overall reductions in development costs. These savings are not included in cost per defect calculations, so the metric understates the true value of quality by several hundred percent.

Let us consider the cost per defect problem areas using examples that illustrate the main points.

As quality improves, "cost per defect" rises sharply. The reason for this is that writing test cases and running them act like fixed costs. It is a well-known law of manufacturing economics that:

> *If a manufacturing cycle includes a high proportion of fixed costs and there is a reduction in the number of units produced, the cost per unit will go up.*

As an application moves through a full test cycle that includes unit test, function test, regression test, performance test, system test, and acceptance test the time required to write test cases and the time required to run test cases stays almost constant, but the number of defects found steadily decreases.

Table 14.8.2 shows the approximate costs for the three cost elements of preparation, execution, and repair for the test cycles just cited using the same rate of $75.75 per hour for all activities.

What is most interesting about Table 14.8.2 is that cost per defect rises steadily as defect volumes come down, even though Table 14.8.2 uses a constant value of 5 hours to repair defects for every single test stage. In other words, every defect identified throughout Table 14.1 had a constant cost of $378.25 when only repairs are considered.

In fact all three columns use constant values and the only true variable in the example is the number of defects found. In real life, of course, preparation, execution, and repairs would all be variables. But by making them constant, it is easier to illustrate the main point: *cost per defect rises as numbers of defects decline.*

Let us now consider cost per function point as an alternative metric for measuring the costs of defect removal.

An alternate way of showing the economics of defect removal is to switch from "cost per defect" and use "defect removal cost per function point." Table 14.8.3 uses the same basic information as Table 14.8.3, but expresses all costs in terms of cost per function point.

The advantage of defect removal cost per function point over cost per defect is that it actually matches the assumptions of standard economics. In other words, as quality improves and defect volumes decline, cost per function point tracks these benefits and also declines. High quality is shown to be cheaper than poor quality, while with cost per defect high quality is incorrectly shown as being more expensive.

Topic 9: Function Points and Software Maintenance, Enhancements, and Total Cost of Ownership (TCO)

Software costs do not end when the software is delivered. Nor does delivery put an end to the need to monitor both costs and quality. Some applications have useful lives that can span 20 years or more. These applications are not fixed, but add new features on an annual basis.

Table 14.8.2 Cost per Defect for Six Forms of Testing

(Assumes $75.75 per staff hour for costs)

	Writing Test Cases	Running Test Cases	Repairing Defects	TOTAL COSTS	Number of Defects	$ per Defect
Unit test	$1,250.00	$750.00	$18,937.50	$20,937.50	50	$418.75
Function test	$1,250.00	$750.00	$7,575.00	$9,575.00	20	$478.75
Regression test	$1,250.00	$750.00	$3,787.50	$5,787.50	10	$578.75
Performance test	$1,250.00	$750.00	$1,893.75	$3,893.75	5	$778.75
System test	$1,250.00	$750.00	$1,136.25	$3,136.25	3	$1,045.42
Acceptance test	$1,250.00	$750.00	$378.75	$2,378.75	1	$2,378.75

Table 14.8.3   Cost per Function Point for Six Forms of Testing

(Assumes $75.75 per staff hour for costs)					
(Assumes 100 function points in the application)					
	Writing Test Cases	Running Test Cases	Repairing Defects	Total $ per FP	Number of Defects
Unit test	$12.50	$7.50	$189.38	$209.38	50
Function test	$12.50	$7.50	$75.75	$95.75	20
Regression test	$12.50	$7.50	$37.88	$57.88	10
Performance test	$12.50	$7.50	$18.94	$38.94	5
System test	$12.50	$7.50	$11.36	$31.36	3
Acceptance test	$12.50	$7.50	$3.79	$23.79	1

Therefore, function point metrics need to continue to be applied to software projects after release.

Post-release costs are more complex than development costs because they need to integrate enhancements or adding new features, maintenance or fixing bugs, and customer support or helping clients when they call or contact a company about a specific application.

The need to keep records for applications that are constantly growing over time means that normalization of data will need to be cognizant of the current size of the application. The method used by SRM is to normalize results for both enhancements and maintenance at the end of every calendar year, i.e. the size of the application is based on the date of December 31. The pre-release size is based on the size of the application on the day it was first delivered to clients. The sizes of requirements creep during development are also recorded.

Table 14.9 shows the approximate rate of growth and the maintenance and enhancement effort for five years for an application of a nominal 1,000 function points when first delivered.

The original development cost for the application was $1,027,348. The costs for five years of maintenance and enhancements the cost were $2,081,700 or more than twice the original development cost. The TCO is the sum of development and the 5-year M&E period. In this example, the TCO is $3,109,048.

CEOs and other C level executives want to know the "total cost of ownership" (TCO) of software and not just the initial development costs.

Five-year maintenance and enhancement predictions are standard outputs from SRM.

Table 14.9 Five Years of Software Maintenance and Enhancement for 1000 Function Points

(Maintenance + Enhancement)

	Year 1	Year 2	Year 3	Year 4	Year 5	5-Year
	2018	*2019*	*2020*	*2021*	*2022*	*Total*
Annual enhancements in FP	80	86	93	101	109	**469**
Application Growth in FP	1,080	1,166	1,260	1,360	1,469	**1,469**
Application Growth in LOC	57,600	62,208	67,185	67,185	78,364	**78,364**
Cyclomatic complexity increase	11.09	11.54	12.00	12.48	12.98	**12.98**
Enhancement staff	0.81	0.88	0.96	1.05	1.15	0.97
Maintenance staff	5.68	5.72	5.85	6.36	7.28	6.18
Total staff	**6.49**	**6.61**	**6.81**	**7.41**	**8.43**	**7.15**
Enhancement effort (months)	9.72	10.61	11.58	12.64	13.80	58.34
Maintenance effort (months)	68.19	68.70	70.20	76.31	87.34	370.74
Total effort (months)	**77.91**	**79.30**	**81.78**	**88.95**	**101.14**	**429.08**
Total effort (hours)	**10,283.53**	**10,467.77**	**10,794.70**	**11,741.94**	**13,350.37**	**56,638.31**
Enhancement effort %	12.47%	13.37%	14.16%	14.21%	13.64%	13.60%

(Continued)

Table 14.9 (Continued)

(Maintenance + Enhancement)

	Year 1	Year 2	Year 3	Year 4	Year 5	5-Year
	2018	*2019*	*2020*	*2021*	*2022*	*Total*
Maintenance effort %	87.53%	86.63%	85.84%	85.79%	86.36%	86.40%
Total effort %	**100.00%**	**100.00%**	**100.00%**	**100.00%**	**100.00%**	**100.00%**
Enhancement cost	$77,733	$84,845	$92,617	$101,114	$110,403	$466,712
Maintenance cost	$331,052	$316,674	$304,368	$315,546	$347,348	$1,614,988
Total cost	**$408,785**	**$401,518**	**$396,985**	**$416,660**	**$457,751**	**$2,081,700**
Enhancement cost %	19.02%	21.13%	23.33%	24.27%	24.12%	22.42%
Maintenance cost %	80.98%	78.87%	76.67%	75.73%	75.88%	77.58%
Total cost	**100.00%**	**100.00%**	**100.00%**	**100.00%**	**100.00%**	**100.00%**

High quality can reduce development costs by about 15% but reduces maintenance costs by more than 45% per year. The cumulative economic value of quality methods such as inspections and static analysis is much better when demonstrated using TCO than when only using development.

The TCO of the "average" sample shown here was just over $3,000,000. The TCO of a high-quality version of the same application that used pretest inspections and static analysis would probably have been below $1,500,000 with the bulk of the saving accruing after release due to lower customer support and maintenance costs.

Topic 10: Function Points and Forensic Analysis of Canceled Projects

CEOs of Fortune 500 companies have less respect for their software organizations than for other technical groups. The main reason for this is that large software projects are more troublesome to CEOs and corporate boards than any other manufactured object in history.

Large software projects are canceled far too often and run late and miss budgets in a majority of cases. Until quality improves along with estimation and safe completion of large systems, software organizations will be viewed as a painful necessity rather than a valuable contributor to the bottom line.

About 35% of large systems >10,000 function points are canceled and never delivered to end users or clients. These canceled projects are seldom studied but forensic analysis of failures can lead to important insights.

The reason that CEOs care about forensic analysis is that many failed projects end up in litigation. Between the financial loss of the cancellation and possible legal fees for litigation, a failed project of 10,000 function points is about a $30,000,000 write off. A failure for a major system of 100,000 function points is about a $500,000,000 write off. This much wasted money is a top issue for CEO's.

Because they are terminated, the size of the project at termination and accumulated costs and resource data may not be available. But SRM can provide both values.

Note that terminated projects have no downstream "technical debt" because they are never released to customers. This is a serious omission from the technical debt metaphor and is one of the reasons why it is not completely valid for economic analysis (Tables 14.10.1, 14.10.2, and 14.10.3).

Table 14.10.1   Odds of Cancellation by Size and Quality Level

(Includes negative ROI, poor quality, and change in business need)			
Function Points	*Low Quality*	*Average Quality*	*High Quality*
10	2.00%	0.00%	0.00%
100	7.00%	3.00%	2.00%
1,000	20.00%	10.00%	5.00%
10,000	45.00%	15.00%	7.00%
100,000	65.00%	35.00%	12.00%
Average	**27.80%**	**12.60%**	**5.20%**

Table 14.10.2   Probable Month of Cancellation from Start of Project

(Elapsed Months from Start of Project)			
Function Points	*Low Quality*	*Average Quality*	*High Quality*
10	1.4	None	None
100	5.9	5.2	3.8
1,000	16.0	13.8	9.3
10,000	38.2	32.1	16.1
100,000	82.3	70.1	25.2
Average	**45.5**	**30.3**	**16.9**
Percent	**150.10%**	**100.00%**	**55.68%**

When high-quality projects are canceled, it is usually because of business reasons. For example, the author of this book was working on an application when his company bought a competitor that already had the same kind of application up and running. The company did not need two identical applications, so the version under development was canceled. This was a rational business decision and not due to poor quality or negative ROI.

When low-quality projects are canceled, it is usually because they are so late and so much over budget that their return on investment (ROI) turned from positive to strongly negative. The delays and cost overruns

Table 14.10.3   Probable Effort from Project Start to Point of Cancellation

(Effort in Terms of Person Months)			
Function Points	*Low Quality*	*Average Quality*	*High Quality*
10	0.8	None	None
100	10.0	7.9	5.4
1,000	120.5	92.0	57.0
10,000	2,866.5	2,110.1	913.2
100,000	61,194.7	45,545.5	13,745.5
Average	**21,393.9**	**15,915.9**	**4,905.2**
Percent	**134.42%**	**100.00%**	**30.82%**

explain why low-quality canceled projects are much more expensive than successful projects of the same size and type. Function point metrics are the best choice for forensic analysis of canceled projects.

Much of the forensic analysis of disastrous projects takes place in the discovery and deposition phases of software litigation. From working as an expert witness in many of these cases, the main reasons for canceled projects are as follows:

1. Optimistic estimates which predict shorter schedules and lower costs than reality.
2. Poor quality control which stretches out test schedules.
3. Poor change control in the face of requirements creep which tops 2% per calendar month.
4. Poor and seemingly fraudulent status tracking which conceals serious problems.

In general poor management practices are the chief culprit for canceled projects. Managers don't understand quality and try and bypass pre-test inspections or static analysis, which later doubles testing durations.

Then managers conceal problems from clients and higher management in the false hope that the problems will be solved or go away. The inevitable results are massive cost overruns, long schedule delays, and outright cancellation. It is no wonder CEOs have a low regard for the software groups in their companies.

Topic 11: Portfolio Analysis with Function Point Metrics

To be useful and interesting to CEOs and other C level executives, function points should be able to quantify not just individual projects but also large collections of related projects such as the full portfolio of a Fortune 500 company.

A full corporate software portfolio is an expensive asset that needs accurate financial data. In fact the author of this book has worked on several IRS tax cases involving the asset value of corporate portfolios. One of these tax cases involved the value of the EDS portfolio at the time it was acquired by General Motors. Another interesting tax case involved the asset value of the Charles Schwab software portfolio.

Since portfolios are taxable assets when companies are sold, it is obvious why they need full quantification. Function points are the best metric for portfolio quantification, although clearly faster methods are needed than manual function point analysis. Up until recently "backfiring" or mathematical conversion from source code to function points was the main method used for portfolio analysis.

Table 14.11 is an example of the special SRM predictions for corporate portfolios. This prediction shows the size in function points for the portfolio of a Fortune 500 manufacturing company with 100,000 total employees.

It is obvious that sizing a full portfolio with more than 2,300 applications and more than 5,000,000 function points cannot be accomplished by manual function point counting. At an average counting rate of 500 function points per day, counting this portfolio would take 10,385 days. At a cost of $1,500 per day, the expense would be $5,192,197.

This fact alone explains why faster and cheaper function point analysis is a critical step leading to interest in function points by chief executive officers (CEOs) and other C level executives.

Topic 12: Industry Studies Using Function Point Metrics

One of the high-interest levels of CEOs and other C level executives is in the area of how their companies compare to others in the same business sector, and how their business sectors compare to other business sectors. Function point metrics are the best choice for these industry studies.

Table 14.12 shows approximate productivity and quality results for 68 U.S. industries using function points as the basis of analysis.

Table 14.11   Portfolio Analysis of a Fortune 500 Manufacturing Company

	Corporate Functions	Number of Applications Used	Function Points	Lines of Code
1	Accounts payable	18	26,674	1,467,081
2	Accounts receivable	22	33,581	1,846,945
3	Advertising	32	47,434	2,134,537
4	Advisory boards – technical	6	8,435	463,932
5	Banking relationships	38	131,543	7,234,870
6	Board of directors	4	6,325	347,900
7	Building maintenance	2	3,557	195,638
8	Business intelligence	21	73,972	4,068,466
9	Business partnerships	18	44,457	2,445,134
10	Competitive analysis	30	74,635	4,104,901
11	Consultant management	3	4,609	253,486
12	Contract management	32	94,868	5,217,758
13	Customer resource management	56	140,585	7,732,193
14	Customer support	45	67,003	3,685,140
15	Divestitures	10	15,000	825,000
16	Education – customers	7	11,248	618,663
17	Education – staff	4	6,325	347,900
18	Embedded software	84	252,419	21,455,576
19	Energy consumption monitoring	4	6,325	347,900
20	Energy acquisition	5	7,097	390,350
21	Engineering	79	276,699	20,752,447
22	ERP – Corporate	63	252,982	17,708,755
23	Finances (corporate)	84	210,349	11,569,183
24	Finances (divisional)	63	157,739	8,675,663
25	Governance	10	25,000	1,375,000
26	Government certification (if any)	24	35,571	1,956,383
27	Government regulations (if any)	13	20,003	1,100,155
28	Human resources	7	11,248	618,663

(Continued)

Table 14.11   (Continued)

	Corporate Functions	Number of Applications Used	Function Points	Lines of Code
29	Insurance	6	8,935	491,421
30	Inventory management	45	67,003	3,685,140
31	Legal department	24	35,571	1,956,383
32	Litigation	32	47,434	2,608,879
33	Long-range planning	7	18,747	1,031,105
34	Maintenance – product	75	112,484	6,186,627
35	Maintenance – buildings	6	8,435	632,634
36	Manufacturing	178	311,199	23,339,917
37	Market research	38	56,376	3,100,659
38	Marketing	27	39,911	2,195,098
39	Measures – customer satisfaction	4	6,325	347,900
40	Measures – financial	24	35,571	1,956,383
41	Measures – market share	8	12,621	694,151
42	Measures – performance	9	14,161	778,850
43	Measures – quality	10	15,000	825,000
44	Measures – ROI and profitability	32	47,434	2,608,879
45	Mergers and acquisitions	24	59,284	3,260,639
46	Office suites	8	29,449	1,619,686
47	Open-source tools – general	67	100,252	5,513,837
48	Order entry	27	39,911	2,195,098
49	Outside services – manufacturing	24	35,571	1,956,383
50	Outside services – legal	27	66,518	3,658,497
51	Outside services – marketing	15	22,444	1,234,394
52	Outside services – sales	17	25,182	1,385,013
53	Outside services – terminations	9	11,141	612,735
54	Outsource management	32	47,434	2,608,879
55	Patents and inventions	19	28,255	1,554,010

Table 14.11 (Continued)

	Corporate Functions	Number of Applications Used	Function Points	Lines of Code
56	Payrolls	21	52,837	2,906,047
57	Planning – manufacturing	42	63,254	3,478,996
58	Planning – products	10	15,000	825,000
59	Process management	12	17,828	980,514
60	Product design	56	140,585	7,732,193
61	Product nationalization	13	30,004	1,650,233
62	Product testing	38	56,376	3,100,659
63	Project offices	32	55,340	3,043,692
64	Project management	10	27,500	1,512,500
65	Purchasing	30	44,781	2,462,941
66	Quality control	13	20,003	1,100,155
67	Real estate	8	12,621	694,151
68	Research and development	106	370,739	20,390,634
69	Sales	45	67,003	3,685,140
70	Sales support	15	22,444	1,234,394
71	Security – buildings	21	31,702	1,743,628
72	Security – computing and software	32	110,680	6,087,384
73	Shareholder relationships	8	29,449	1,619,686
74	Shipping/receiving products	27	66,518	3,658,497
75	Software development	79	238,298	13,106,416
76	Standards compliance	13	20,003	1,100,155
77	Stocks and bonds	21	73,972	4,068,466
78	Supply chain management	47	70,973	3,903,498
79	Taxes	42	84,339	4,638,662
80	Travel	10	25,000	1,375,000
81	Unbudgeted costs – cyber attacks	32	86,963	4,782,945
82	Warranty support	7	10,025	551,384
		2,366	**5,192,567**	**308,410,789**

Table 14.12 Approximate Industry Productivity and Quality Using Function Point Metrics

	Industry	Software Productivity 2020	Defect Potentials 2020	Removal Efficiency 2020	Delivered Defects 2020
1	Government – intelligence	7.20	5.95	99.50%	0.03
2	Manufacturing – medical devices	7.75	5.20	98.50%	0.08
3	Manufacturing – aircraft	7.25	5.75	98.00%	0.12
4	Telecommunications operations	9.75	5.00	97.50%	0.13
5	Manufacturing – electronics	8.25	5.25	97.00%	0.16
6	Manufacturing – telecommunications	9.75	5.50	96.50%	0.19
7	Manufacturing – defense	6.85	6.00	96.25%	0.23
8	Government – military	6.75	6.40	96.00%	0.26
9	Entertainment – films	13.00	4.00	96.00%	0.16
10	Manufacturing – pharmaceuticals	8.90	4.55	95.50%	0.20
11	Smartphone/tablet applications	15.25	3.30	95.00%	0.17
12	Transportation – airlines	8.75	5.00	94.50%	0.28
13	Software (commercial)	15.00	3.50	94.00%	0.21
14	Manufacturing – automotive	7.75	4.90	94.00%	0.29
15	Transportation – bus	8.00	5.10	94.00%	0.31
16	Manufacturing – chemicals	8.00	4.80	94.00%	0.29
17	Banks – investment	11.50	4.60	93.75%	0.29

	Industry	Software Productivity	Defect Potentials	Removal Efficiency	Delivered Defects
		2020	2020	2020	2020
18	Open source development	13.75	4.40	93.50%	0.29
19	Banks – commercial	11.50	4.50	93.50%	0.29
20	Credit unions	11.20	4.50	93.50%	0.29
21	Professional support – medicine	8.55	4.80	93.50%	0.31
22	Government – police	8.50	5.20	93.50%	0.34
23	Entertainment – television	12.25	4.60	93.00%	0.32
24	Manufacturing – appliances	7.60	4.30	93.00%	0.30
25	Software (outsourcing)	14.00	4.65	92.75%	0.34
26	Manufacturing – nautical	8.00	4.60	92.50%	0.35
27	Process control	9.00	4.90	92.50%	0.37
28	Stock/commodity brokerage	10.00	5.15	92.50%	0.39
29	Professional support – law	8.50	4.75	92.00%	0.38
30	Games – computer	15.75	3.00	91.00%	0.27
31	Social networks	14.90	4.90	91.00%	0.44
32	Insurance – life	10.00	5.00	91.00%	0.45
33	Insurance – medical	10.50	5.25	91.00%	0.47
34	Public utilities – electricity	7.00	4.80	90.50%	0.46

(Continued)

Table 14.12 (Continued)

	Industry	Software Productivity	Defect Potentials	Removal Efficiency	Delivered Defects
		2020	2020	2020	2020
35	Education – university	8.60	4.50	90.00%	0.45
36	Automotive sales	8.00	4.75	90.00%	0.48
37	Hospitals	8.00	4.80	90.00%	0.48
38	Insurance – property and casualty	9.80	5.00	90.00%	0.50
39	Oil extraction	8.75	5.00	90.00%	0.50
40	Consulting	12.70	4.00	89.00%	0.44
41	Public utilities – water	7.25	4.40	89.00%	0.48
42	Publishing (books/journals)	8.60	4.50	89.00%	0.50
43	Transportation – ship	8.00	4.90	88.00%	0.59
44	Natural gas generation	6.75	5.00	87.50%	0.63
45	Education – secondary	7.60	4.35	87.00%	0.57
46	Construction	7.10	4.70	87.00%	0.61
47	Real estate – commercial	7.25	5.00	87.00%	0.65
48	Agriculture	7.75	5.50	87.00%	0.72
49	Entertainment – music	11.00	4.00	86.50%	0.54
50	Education – primary	7.50	4.30	86.50%	0.58
51	Transportation – truck	8.00	5.00	86.50%	0.68

	Industry	Software Productivity 2020	Defect Potentials 2020	Removal Efficiency 2020	Delivered Defects 2020
52	Government – state	6.50	5.65	86.50%	0.76
53	Manufacturing – apparel	7.00	3.00	86.00%	0.42
54	Games – traditional	7.50	4.00	86.00%	0.56
55	Manufacturing – general	8.25	5.20	86.00%	0.73
56	Retail	8.00	5.40	85.50%	0.78
57	Hotels	8.75	4.40	85.00%	0.66
58	Real estate – residential	7.25	4.80	85.00%	0.72
59	Mining – metals	7.00	4.90	85.00%	0.74
60	Automotive repairs	7.50	5.00	85.00%	0.75
61	Wholesale	8.25	5.20	85.00%	0.78
62	Government – federal civilian	6.50	6.00	84.75%	0.92
63	Waste management	7.00	4.60	84.50%	0.71
64	Transportation – trains	8.00	4.70	84.50%	0.73
65	Food – restaurants	7.00	4.80	84.50%	0.74
66	Mining–coal	7.00	5.00	84.50%	0.78
67	Government – county	6.50	5.55	84.50%	0.86
68	Government – municipal	7.00	5.50	84.00%	0.88
	Total/Averages	**8.95**	**4.82**	**90.39%**	**0.46**

When looking at Table 14.12, the industries that built complex physical devices such as computers, airplanes, medical devices, and telephone switching systems have the best quality. This is because the physical devices won't work unless the software works well with almost zero defects.

For productivity, a different set of industries are at the top including computer games, social networks, entertainment, some commercial vendors (who work many hours of unpaid overtime) and small tablet and smartphone applications built by one or two developers.

Topic 13: Global Studies Using Function Point Analysis

In today's world, software development is a global business. About 60% of Indian companies and more than 80% of Indian outsource companies use function points in order to attract outsource business, with considerable success. As already mentioned, Brazil now requires function points for all government outsource contracts.

Clearly global competition is a topic of critical interest to all C level executives including CEOs, CFOs, CTOs, CIOs, CROs, and all others.

Function point metrics are the best (and only) metric that is effective for very large scale global studies of software productivity and quality. Table 14.13 shows approximate results for 68 countries.

Some of the data in Table 14.13 is provisional and included primarily to encourage more studies of productivity and quality in countries that lack effective benchmarks circa 2013. For example, China and Russia are major producers of software but seem to lag India, Brazil, the Netherlands, Finland, and the United States in adopting modern metrics and function points.

Topic 14: Function Points versus Lines of Code (LOC) for Software Economic Analysis

Normally, CEOs and other C level executives don't care and may not even know about which programming languages are used for software. However in 1970 within IBM, a crisis attracted not only the attention of IBM chairman Thomas J. Watson Jr. but also many other C level executives and vice presidents such as Bob Evans, Vin Learson, Ted Climis, and a number of others.

The crisis was due to the fact that more than half of the schedule and cost estimates in the Systems Development Division and other software groups were wrong and always wrong in the direction of excessive optimism. Worse, the estimates with the largest errors were for projects using the newest and best programming languages such as APL, PL/S, and several others. Only estimates for projects coded in assembly language were accurate.

This crisis was eventually solved and the solution created two useful new concepts: (1) the development of function point metrics by A.J. Albrecht and his colleagues at the IBM White Plains lab; (2) the development of IBM's first parametric estimation tool by the author of this book and Dr. Charles Turk at the IBM San Jose lab. Function points were created in order to provide a language-independent metric for software economic analysis. The IBM development planning system (DPS) was created to estimate projects in any programming language or combination of languages.

For a number of years, IBM had used ad hoc estimation ratios based on code development for predicting various non-coding tasks such as design, documentation, integration, testing, and the like. When modern languages such as PL/S began to supplant assembly language, it was quickly discovered that ratios no longer worked.

For example, the coding effort for PL/S was only half the coding effort for assembly language. The ratio used to predict user documentation had been 10% of coding effort. But for PL/S projects coding effort was cut in two and the manuals were as big as ever, so they were all 50% over budget.

In order to restore some kind of order and rationality to estimates IBM assigned a numeric level to every programming language. Basic assembly was "level 1" and other languages were assigned values based on how many assembly statements would be needed to be equivalent to 1 statement in the target language. Thus, Fortran was a level 3 language because it took 3 assembly statements to provide the functionality of 1 Fortran statement. This method used ratios from basic assembly for predicting non-coding work.

For several years after the discovery of LOC problems, IBM used LOC for coding in the true language for coding the application but used basic assembly language to derive ratios for non-coding work. This was an awkward method and explains why IBM invested several million dollars in developing both function point metrics and a formal parametric estimation tool that could handle estimates for applications in all programming languages.

IBM executives were not happy about having to use assembly to show the value of modern languages so they commissioned Al Albrecht and his colleagues to start work on a metric that would be language independent. As we all know, function points were the final result.

Table 14.13 Approximate Global Productivity and Quality in Function Points

		Approximate Software Productivity (FP per Month)	Approximate Defect Potentials in 2020 (Defects per FP)	Approximate Defect Removal Efficiency	Approximate Delivered Defects in 2020 (Defects per FP)
1	Japan	9.15	4.50	93.50%	0.29
2	India	11.30	4.90	93.00%	0.34
3	Denmark	9.45	4.80	92.00%	0.38
4	Canada	8.85	4.75	91.75%	0.39
5	South Korea	8.75	4.90	92.00%	0.39
6	Switzerland	9.35	5.00	92.00%	0.40
7	United Kingdom	8.85	4.75	91.50%	0.40
8	Israel	9.10	5.10	92.00%	0.41
9	Sweden	9.25	4.75	91.00%	0.43
10	Norway	9.15	4.75	91.00%	0.43
11	Netherlands	9.30	4.80	91.00%	0.43
12	Hungary	9.00	4.60	90.50%	0.44
13	Ireland	9.20	4.85	90.50%	0.46
14	United States	8.95	4.82	90.15%	0.47
15	Brazil	9.40	4.75	90.00%	0.48
16	France	8.60	4.85	90.00%	0.49

		Approximate Software Productivity (FP per Month)	Approximate Defect Potentials in 2020 (Defects per FP)	Approximate Defect Removal Efficiency	Approximate Delivered Defects in 2020 (Defects per FP)
17	Australia	8.88	4.85	90.00%	0.49
18	Austria	8.95	4.75	89.50%	0.50
19	Belgium	9.10	4.70	89.15%	0.51
20	Finland	9.00	4.70	89.00%	0.52
21	Hong Kong	9.50	4.75	89.00%	0.52
22	Mexico	8.65	4.85	88.00%	0.58
23	Germany	8.85	4.95	88.00%	0.59
24	Philippines	10.75	5.00	88.00%	0.60
25	New Zealand	9.05	4.85	87.50%	0.61
26	Taiwan	9.00	4.90	87.50%	0.61
27	Italy	8.60	4.95	87.50%	0.62
28	Jordan	7.85	5.00	87.50%	0.63
29	Malaysia	8.40	4.65	86.25%	0.64
30	Thailand	7.90	4.95	87.00%	0.64
31	Spain	8.50	4.90	86.50%	0.66
32	Portugal	8.45	4.85	86.20%	0.67
33	Singapore	9.40	4.80	86.00%	0.67

(Continued)

Table 14.13 (Continued)

		Approximate Software Productivity (FP per Month)	Approximate Defect Potentials in 2020 (Defects per FP)	Approximate Defect Removal Efficiency	Approximate Delivered Defects in 2020 (Defects per FP)
34	Russia	8.65	5.15	86.50%	0.70
35	Argentina	8.30	4.80	85.50%	0.70
36	China	9.15	5.20	86.50%	0.70
37	South Africa	8.35	4.90	85.50%	0.71
38	Iceland	8.70	4.75	85.00%	0.71
39	Poland	8.45	4.80	85.00%	0.72
40	Costa Rica	8.00	4.70	84.50%	0.73
41	Bahrain	7.85	4.75	84.50%	0.74
42	Ukraine	9.10	4.95	85.00%	0.74
43	Turkey	8.60	4.90	84.50%	0.76
44	Viet Nam	8.65	4.90	84.50%	0.76
45	Kuwait	8.80	4.80	84.00%	0.77
46	Colombia	8.00	4.75	83.50%	0.78
47	Peru	8.75	4.90	84.00%	0.78
48	Greece	7.85	4.80	83.50%	0.79
49	Syria	7.60	4.95	84.00%	0.79
50	Tunisia	8.20	4.75	83.00%	0.81

		Approximate Software Productivity (FP per Month)	Approximate Defect Potentials in 2020 (Defects per FP)	Approximate Defect Removal Efficiency	Approximate Delivered Defects in 2020 (Defects per FP)
51	Saudi Arabia	8.85	5.05	84.00%	0.81
52	Cuba	7.85	4.75	82.50%	0.83
53	Panama	7.95	4.75	82.50%	0.83
54	Egypt	8.55	4.90	82.75%	0.85
55	Libya	7.80	4.85	82.50%	0.85
56	Lebanon	7.75	4.75	82.00%	0.86
57	Iran	7.25	5.25	83.50%	0.87
58	Venezuela	7.50	4.70	81.50%	0.87
59	Iraq	7.95	5.05	82.50%	0.88
60	Pakistan	7.40	5.05	82.00%	0.91
61	Algeria	8.10	4.85	81.00%	0.92
62	Indonesia	8.90	4.90	80.50%	0.96
63	North Korea	7.65	5.10	81.00%	0.97
64	Nigeria	7.00	4.75	78.00%	1.05
65	Bangladesh	7.50	4.75	77.00%	1.09
66	Burma	7.40	4.80	77.00%	1.10
	Average/Total	**8.59**	**4.85**	**86.27%**	**0.67**

Table 14.14.1 shows the numeric levels for a variety of common programming languages. The table also shows the approximate number of logical source code statements per function point.

For some of the older languages such as COBOL and FORTRAN, the ratios of source code statements to function points were derived by Al Albrecht personally and then passed into wider usage outside of IBM.

The values for logical code statements per function point only reflect average, and the ranges due to individual programming styles can vary by more than 2 to 1 in both directions. This is why mathematical conversion between logical code and function points is not very accurate, in spite of being very easy.

At this point, we will discuss a hypothetical software application of 1,000 function points in size. We will also make two simplifying assumptions to illustrate the value of function point metrics and the economic problems of LOC metrics: (1) coding speed will be assumed to be a constant value of 1,000 LOC per staff month for every language; (2) the total effort for non-coding work such as requirements, design, documentation, management, etc. will be assumed to be an even 50 staffs months of effort. Table 14.14.2 shows the total effort for building the hypothetical application of 1,000 function points using these two assumptions.

Now that we know the total effort for the application of 1,000 function points in size, how do we measure economic productivity? The standard definition for economic productivity is *"goods or services produced per unit of labor or expense."* Let us consider the results for the sum of the coding and non-coding effort using both function points per staff month and LOC per staff month. Table 14.14.3 shows both values.

As can easily be seen, the LOC data does not match the assumptions of standard economics and indeed moves in the opposite direction from real economic productivity. It has been known for many hundreds of years that when manufacturing costs have a high proportion of fixed costs and there is a reduction in the number of units produced, the cost per unit will go up.

The same logic is true for software. When a "Line of Code" is defined as the unit of production, and there is a migration from low-level procedural languages to high-level and object-oriented languages, the number of "units" that must be constructed declines.

The costs of paper documents such as requirements and user manuals do not decline and tend to act like fixed costs. This inevitably leads to an increase in the "Cost per LOC" for high-level languages, and a reduction in "LOC per staff month" when the paper-related activities are included in the measurements.

On the other hand, the function point metric is a synthetic metric totally divorced from the amount of code needed by the application.

Table 14.14.1 Programming Language "Levels" from IBM

Language Levels	Languages	Logical Code Statements per Function Point
0.50	Machine language	640.00
1.00	Basic Assembly	320.00
1.45	JCL	220.69
1.50	Macro Assembly	213.33
2.00	HTML	160.00
2.50	C	128.00
3.00	Algol	106.67
3.00	Bliss	106.67
3.00	Chill	106.67
3.00	COBOL	106.67
3.00	Coral	106.67
3.00	Fortran	106.67
3.00	Jovial	106.67
3.25	GW Basic	98.46
3.50	Pascal	91.43
3.50	PL/S	91.43
4.00	ABAP	80.00
4.00	Modula	80.00
4.00	PL/I	80.00
4.50	ESPL/I	71.11
4.50	Javascript	71.11
5.00	Forth	64.00
5.00	Lisp	64.00
5.00	Prolog	64.00
5.00	Basic (interpreted)	64.00
5.25	Quick Basic	60.95
6.00	C++	53.33
6.00	Java	53.33

(*Continued*)

Table 14.14.1   (Continued)

Language Levels	Languages	Logical Code Statements per Function Point
6.00	PHP	53.33
6.00	Python	53.33
6.25	C#	51.20
6.50	Ada 95	49.23
6.75	RPG III	47.41
7.00	CICS	45.71
7.00	DTABL	45.71
7.00	Ruby	45.71
7.00	Simula	45.71
8.00	DB2	40.00
8.00	Oracle	40.00
8.50	Mixed Languages	37.65
8.50	Haskell	37.65
9.00	Pearl	35.56
9.00	Speakeasy	35.56
10.00	APL	32.00
11.00	Delphi	29.09
12.00	Objective C	26.67
12.00	Visual Basic	26.67
13.00	ASP NET	24.62
14.00	Eiffel	22.86
15.00	Smalltalk	21.33
16.00	IBM ADF	20.00
17.00	MUMPS	18.82
18.00	Forte	17.78
19.00	APS	16.84
20.00	TELON	16.00
25.00	QBE	12.80
25.00	SQL	12.80
50.00	Excel	6.40

Table 14.14.2 Development Effort for 1,000 Function Points

(Assumes a constant rate of 1000 lines of code per month)			
(Assumes a constant value of 50 months for non-code work)			
Languages	Coding Months	Non-code Months	Total Months
Machine language	640	50	690
Basic Assembly	320	50	370
JCL	221	50	271
Macro Assembly	213	50	263
HTML	160	50	210
C	128	50	178
Algol	107	50	157
Bliss	107	50	157
Chill	107	50	157
COBOL	107	50	157
Coral	107	50	157
Fortran	107	50	157
Jovial	107	50	157
GW Basic	98	50	148
Pascal	91	50	141
PL/S	91	50	141
ABAP	80	50	130
Modula	80	50	130
PL/I	80	50	130
ESPL/I	71	50	121
Javascript	71	50	121
Forth	64	50	114
Lisp	64	50	114
Prolog	64	50	114
Basic (interpreted)	64	50	114
Quick Basic	61	50	111
C++	53	50	103

(*Continued*)

Table 14.14.2   (Continued)

(Assumes a constant rate of 1000 lines of code per month)			
(Assumes a constant value of 50 months for non-code work)			
Languages	*Coding Months*	*Non-code Months*	*Total Months*
Java	53	50	103
PHP	53	50	103
Python	53	50	103
C#	51	50	101
Ada 95	49	50	99
RPG III	47	50	97
CICS	46	50	96
DTABL	46	50	96
Ruby	46	50	96
Simula	46	50	96
DB2	40	50	90
Oracle	40	50	90
Mixed Languages	38	50	88
Haskell	38	50	88
Pearl	36	50	86
Speakeasy	36	50	86
APL	32	50	82
Delphi	29	50	79
Objective C	27	50	77
Visual Basic	27	50	77
ASP NET	25	50	75
Eiffel	23	50	73
Smalltalk	21	50	71
IBM ADF	20	50	70
MUMPS	19	50	69
Forte	18	50	68
APS	17	50	67
TELON	16	50	66
QBE	13	50	63
SQL	13	50	63
Excel	6	50	56

Table 14.14.3   Function Points versus LOC per Month for Calculating Economic Productivity Rates

Languages	Function Pts. per Month	LOC per Month
Machine language	1.45	927.54
Basic Assembly	2.70	864.86
JCL	3.69	815.29
Macro Assembly	3.80	810.13
HTML	4.76	761.90
C	5.62	719.10
Algol	6.38	680.85
Bliss	6.38	680.85
Chill	6.38	680.85
COBOL	6.38	680.85
Coral	6.38	680.85
Fortran	6.38	680.85
Jovial	6.38	680.85
GW Basic	6.74	663.21
Pascal	7.07	646.46
PL/S	7.07	646.46
ABAP	7.69	615.38
Modula	7.69	615.38
PL/I	7.69	615.38
ESPL/I	8.26	587.16
Javascript	8.26	587.16
Forth	8.77	561.40
Lisp	8.77	561.40
Prolog	8.77	561.40
Basic (interpreted)	8.77	561.40
Quick Basic	9.01	549.36
C++	9.68	516.13
Java	9.68	516.13

(Continued)

Table 14.14.3   (Continued)

Languages	Function Pts. per Month	LOC per Month
PHP	9.68	516.13
Python	9.68	516.13
C#	9.88	505.93
Ada 95	10.08	496.12
RPG III	10.27	486.69
CICS	10.45	477.61
DTABL	10.45	477.61
Ruby	10.45	477.61
Simula	10.45	477.61
DB2	11.11	444.44
Oracle	11.11	444.44
Mixed Languages	11.41	429.53
Haskell	11.41	429.53
Pearl	11.69	415.58
Speakeasy	11.69	415.58
APL	12.20	390.24
Delphi	12.64	367.82
Objective C	13.04	347.83
Visual Basic	13.04	347.83
ASP NET	13.40	329.90
Eiffel	13.73	313.73
Smalltalk	14.02	299.07
IBM ADF	14.29	285.71
MUMPS	14.53	273.50
Forte	14.75	262.30
APS	14.96	251.97
TELON	15.15	242.42
QBE	15.92	203.82
SQL	15.92	203.82
Excel	17.73	113.48

Therefore, function point metrics can be used for economic studies involving multiple programming languages and object-oriented programming languages without bias or distorted results. The function point metric can also be applied to non-coding activities such as requirements, design, user documentation, integration, testing, and even project management.

When using the standard economic definition of productivity, which is *"goods or services produced per unit of labor or expense"* it can be seen that the function point ranking matches economic productivity assumptions.

The function point ranking matches economic assumptions because the versions with the lowest amounts of both effort and costs have the highest function point productivity rates and the lowest costs per function point rates.

The LOC rankings, on the other hand, are the exact reversal of real economic productivity rates. This is the key reason why usage of the LOC metric is viewed as "professional malpractice" when it is used for cross-language productivity or quality comparisons involving both high-level and low-level programming languages.

The phrase "professional malpractice" implies that a trained knowledge worker did something that was hazardous and unsafe and that the level of training and prudence required to join the profession should have been enough to avoid the unsafe practice.

Since it is obvious that the "lines of code" metric does not move in the same direction as economic productivity, and indeed moves in the opposite direction, it is a reasonable assertion that misuse of LOC metrics for cross-language comparisons should be viewed as professional malpractice if a book or published data caused some damage or harm.

One of the severe problems of the software industry has been the inability to perform economic analysis of the impact of various tools, methods, or programming languages. It can be stated that the "lines of code" or LOC metric has been a significant barrier that has slowed down the evolution of software engineering, since it has blinded researchers and prevented proper exploration of software engineering factors.

Function point metrics, on the other hand, have opened up many new forms of economic study that were impossible using distorted and inaccurate metrics such as "lines of code" and "cost per defect."

The ability of function point metrics to examine programming languages, methodologies, and other critical software topics is a long step in the right direction.

Topic 15: Function Points and Software Usage and Consumption

One of the newer uses of function point metrics is that of studying software usage and consumption as well as studying software development and maintenance. This field is so new that it has almost no literature except for a paper published by the author of this book.

It is interesting to start this topic with an overview of how much software an ordinary U.S. citizen uses and owns on a daily basis. Table 14.15.1 shows approximate software ownership for a fairly affluent person holding down a managerial or technical job.

Only about 50 years ago, the amount of software owned by anyone would have been close to zero. Today we use software every waking moment, and quite a few devices such a home alarm systems keep working for us while we are asleep, as do embedded medical devices.

The next set of topics where function points are adding insights are the amount of software used by the software engineering and management communities. Table 14.15.2 shows the approximate amount of software used by software project managers.

Table 14.15.1   U.S. Personal Ownership of Software Circa 2013

Products	Function Points	Hours Used per Day
Home computer	1,000,000	2.50
Tablet	800,000	3.00
Automobile	350,000	3.00
Smart phone	35,000	2.00
Televisions	35,000	4.00
Social networks	20,000	2.50
Medical devices	12,000	24.00
Audio equipment	10,000	1.50
Electronic books	7,500	1.50
Home alarm system	5,000	24.00
Digital camera	3,500	1.00
Hearing aids	3,000	12.00
Digital watches	2,500	12.00
Sum	**2,283,500**	

**Table 14.15.2   Numbers and Size Ranges of Software Project
Management Tools**

	(Tool sizes are expressed in terms of IFPUG function points, version 4.2)			
	Project Management Tools	*Lagging*	*Average*	*Leading*
1	Project planning	1,000	1,250	3,000
2	Project cost estimating			3,000
3	Statistical analysis			3,000
4	Methodology management		750	3,000
5	Reusable feature analysis			2,000
6	Quality estimation			2,000
7	Assessment support		500	2,000
8	Project office support		500	2,000
9	Project measurement			1,750
10	Portfolio analysis			1,500
11	Risk analysis			1,500
12	Resource tracking	300	750	1,500
13	Governance tools			1,500
14	Value analysis		350	1,250
15	Cost variance reporting	500	500	1,000
16	Personnel support	500	500	750
17	Milestone tracking		250	750
18	Budget support		250	750
19	Function point analysis		250	750
20	Backfiring: LOC to FP			300
21	Earned value analysis		250	300
22	Benchmark data collection			300
Subtotal		1,800	4,600	30,000
Tools		4	12	22

Project managers in leading or sophisticated companies such as IBM,
Google, Microsoft, and the like deploy and use more than 30,000 function points of project management tools.

The next topic of interest shows the volumes of software tools utilized by software engineers themselves. Because software engineering

has been highly automated for many years, there is not as large a difference in Table 14.15.3 as there was in Table 14.15.2.

If we went through the entire suites of tools used for development, maintenance, testing, quality assurance, technical manuals, and administration, we would find that leading software development organizations use about 90 tools that total to more than about 150,000 function points.

Lagging companies use only about 30 tools at a little more than 25,000 function points.

Average companies use about 50 different tools with a total size of perhaps 50,000 function points.

Table 14.15.3   Numbers and Size Ranges of Software Engineering Tools

	(Tool sizes are expressed in terms of IFPUG function points, version 4.2)			
	Software Engineering Tools	*Lagging*	*Average*	*Leading*
1	Compilers	3,500	3,500	3,500
2	Program generators		3,500	3,500
3	Design tools	1,000	1,500	3,000
4	Code editors	2,500	2,500	2,500
5	GUI design tools	1,500	1,500	2,500
6	Assemblers	2,000	2,000	2,000
7	Configuration control	750	1,000	2,000
8	Source code control	750	1,000	1,500
9	Static analysis (code)		1,500	3,000
10	Automated testing		1,000	1,500
11	Data modeling	750	1,000	1,500
12	Debugging tools	500	750	1,250
13	Data base design	750	750	1,250
14	Capture/playback	500	500	750
15	Library browsers	500	500	750
16	Reusable code analysis			750
Subtotal		**15,000**	**22,500**	**31,250**
Tools		**12**	**14**	**16**

These differences in tool usage patterns also correlate with software quality and productivity levels. However, other factors such as team experience, methodologies, and CMMI levels are also correlated with higher productivity and quality so it is not yet possible to isolate just the impacts of tools themselves.

From analysis of more than 28,000 software projects, various patterns have been noted of tools and methods that are used by successful projects. The definition of "success" includes productivity and quality results >25% better than average for the same size and class of software, combined with schedules about 15% shorter than average. The patterns of success are as follows:

Patterns of Tools Noted on Successful Software Projects

1. TSP, RUP, or hybrid as the development methods for large applications.
2. Agile, XP, iterative, Prince2, or defined methods for small applications.
3. Achieving > CMMI 3 for defense projects.
4. Early sizing of projects using automated tools.
5. Early risk analysis of projects before starting.
6. Early quality predictions using automated tools.
7. Early use of parametric estimation tools for cost and schedule predictions.
8. Use of automated project management tools for team assignments.
9. Use of automated project office support tools for large projects.
10. Use of automated requirements modeling tools for critical projects.
11. Use of certified collections of reusable materials (design, code, test cases, etc.).
12. Use of static analysis tools for code in all languages supported by static analysis.
13. Use of inspections and inspection support tools for requirements and design.
14. Use of certified test personnel for critical applications.
15. Use of cyclomatic complexity code analysis tools.
16. Use of test coverage tools that show requirements and path coverage.
17. Use of automated test tools for unit, function, regression, and other tests.
18. Use of formal mathematical test case design methods.

19. Use of formal change control and change control boards.
20. Accurate status reports that highlight potential problems.

Software projects at the leading edge usually range from about 12 to more than 25 function points per staff month in terms of productivity.

Defect potentials on leading projects are <3.00 per function point combined with defect removal efficiency (DRE) levels that average > 97% for all projects and 99% for mission-critical projects.

Excellence in quality control and change control leads to more than 95% of these projects being finished and delivered. Those that are not delivered are terminated for business reasons such as mergers, acquisitions, or divestitures. More than 90% of projects in this class are on time and within planned budgets, and about 15% are slightly faster and below planned budgets.

When you consider the other end of the spectrum or software projects that have worse than average results, this is what you find. We are now dealing with the opposite side of a bell-shaped curve, and considering projects that are <25% worse than average for the same size and class of software, combined with schedules about 15% longer than average. The following are the patterns of failing projects:

Patterns of Tools Noted on Unsuccessful Projects

1. Waterfall development methods for large applications.
2. Cowboy or undefined methods for small applications.
3. CMMI 1 for defense projects.
4. No early sizing of projects using automated tools.
5. No early risk analysis of projects before starting.
6. No early quality predictions using automated tools.
7. Manual and optimistic estimation methods for cost and schedule predictions.
8. No use of automated project management tools for team assignments.
9. No use of automated project office support tools for large projects.
10. No use of automated requirements modeling tools for critical projects.
11. No use of certified collections of reusable materials (design, code, test cases, etc.).
12. No use of static analysis tools for code in any language.
13. No use of inspections and inspection support tools for requirements and design.

14. No use of certified test personnel for critical applications.
15. No use of cyclomatic complexity code analysis tools.
16. No use of test coverage tools that show requirements and path coverage.
17. Little use of automated test tools for unit, function, regression, and other tests.
18. No use of formal mathematical test case design methods.
19. No use of formal change control and change control boards.
20. Inaccurate status reports that conceal potential problems.

Software projects at the trailing edge usually range from about 3 to perhaps10 function points per staff month in terms of productivity.

Poor quality is the main reason for schedule slips and cost overruns. Defect potentials are usually >5.00 per function point combined with DRE levels that almost always average < 85% for all projects and seldom top 90% even for mission-critical projects. In some cases, DRE on lagging projects drops below 80%. These dismal projects do not use either inspections or static analysis and terminate testing prematurely due to not understanding quality economics.

Exploration of software consumption and software tool usage should be a valuable new form of research for the software engineering and function point communities.

Topic 16: Function Points and Software Outsource Contracts

The government of Brazil already requires function point metrics for all contracts involving software. Both South Korea and Italy may soon do the same. Function point metrics are an excellent choice for software outsource agreements.

Some of the topics where function points should be used in contracts would include, but are not limited to:

- Cost per function point for fixed-price contracts.
- Work hours per function point for time and materials contracts.
- Delivered defect densities expressed in terms of defects per function point.
- Function points combined with DRE. Contracts should require that the vendor top a specific level of DRE such as 97%, measured by counting internal defects and comparing them to user-reported defects in the first 90 days of usage.

SRM includes estimates for both the odds of litigation occurring and also for the probable legal expenses for both the plaintiff and the defendant. For example if an outsource contract for an application of 10,000 function points goes to court for breach of contract, the probable costs to the plaintiff will be about $7,500,000 and the probable costs to the defendant will be about $9,000,000 if the case goes through trial (about 90% settle out of court). Of course whichever side loses will have much higher costs due to probable damages and perhaps paying court costs for both sides.

Software Risk Master predicts attorney fees, paralegal fees, and expert witness fees. It also predicts the lost time for executives and technical staff when they are involved with discovery and depositions. SRM also predicts the probable month the litigation will be filed, and the probable duration of the trial.

About 90% of lawsuits settle out of court. SRM cannot predict out of court settlements since many of these are sealed and data is not available.

In the modern era, an increasingly large number of organizations are moving toward outsourcing or the use of contractors for development or maintenance (or both) of their software applications. Although the general performance of outsourcing vendors and contract software development organizations is better than the performance of the clients they serve, it is not perfect.

When software is developed internally within a company and it runs late or exceeds its budget, there are often significant disputes between the development organization and the clients who commissioned the project and are funding it, as well as the top corporate executives. Although these internal disputes are unpleasant and divisive, they generally do not end up in court under litigation.

When software is developed by a contractor and runs late or exceeds the budget, or when it is delivered in less than perfect condition, the disputes have a very high probability of moving to litigation for breach of contract. From time to time, lawsuits may go beyond breach of contract and reach the point where clients charge fraud.

As international outsourcing becomes more common, some of these disputes involve organizations in different countries. When international laws are involved, the resolution of the disputes can be very expensive and protracted. For example, some contracts require that litigation be filed and use the laws of other countries such as Hong Kong or China.

The author of this book has often commissioned to perform independent assessments of software projects where there is an anticipation of some kind of delay, overrun, or quality problem. He has also been engaged to serve as expert witnesses in a dozen lawsuits involving breach of contract between clients and software contractors. He has also been engaged to work as an expert in software tax cases.

From participating in a number of such assessments and lawsuits, it is obvious that most cases are remarkably similar. The clients charge that the contractor breached the agreement by delivering the software late, by not delivering it at all, or by delivering the software in inoperable condition or with excessive errors.

The contractors, in turn, charge that the clients unilaterally changed the terms of the agreement by expanding the scope of the project far beyond the intent of the original agreement. The contractors also charge some kind of non-performance by the clients, such as failure to define requirements or failure to review delivered material in a timely manner.

The fundamental root causes of the disagreements between clients and contractors can be traced to the following two problems:

- Ambiguity and misunderstandings in the contract itself.
- The historical failure of the software industry to quantify the dimensions of software projects before beginning them.

Although litigation potentials vary from client to client and contractor to contractor, the overall results of outsourcing within the United States approximates the following distribution of results after about 24 months of operations, as derived from observations among the author's clients.

Table 14.16.2 shows all projects and all contracts. The odds of litigation rise steeply with application size.

As of today, the software industry does not really know how to build large software projects well. Far too many are terminated, don't work when delivered, or end up in court for breach of contract. The actual

Table 14.16.1 Approximate Distribution of U.S. Outsource Results after 24 Months

Results	Percent of Outsource
Arrangements	
Both parties generally satisfied	70%
Some dissatisfaction by client or vendor	15%
Dissolution of agreement planned	10%
Litigation between client and contractor probable	**4%**
Litigation between client and contractor in progress	**1%**

Table 14.16.2 Odds of Outsource Litigation by Application Size

10 function points	<0.5% chance of litigation
100 function points	<1% chance of litigation
1,000 function points	<3% chance of litigation
10,000 function points	+ or – 12% chance of litigation
100,000 function points	+ or – 25% chance of litigation

technologies for building large systems exist, but less than 5% of companies know them based on on-site discussions with executives and development teams. This is true of outsource companies as well as commercial developers, in-house IT systems, and even games.

From process assessments performed within several large outsource companies, and analysis of projects produced by outsource vendors, our data indicates better than average quality control approaches when compared to the companies and industries who engaged the outsource vendors.

Software estimating, contracting, and assessment methodologies have advanced enough so that the root causes of software outsource contracts can now be overcome. Software estimation is now sophisticated enough so that a formal estimate using one or more of the commercial parametric software estimation tools in conjunction with software project management tools can minimize or eliminate unpleasant surprises later due to schedule slippages or cost overruns.

Indeed, old-fashioned purely manual cost and schedule estimates for major software contracts should probably be considered an example of professional malpractice. Manual estimates are certainly inadequate for software contracts or outsource agreements whose value is larger than about $500,000.

A new form of software contract based on the use of function point metrics is clarifying the initial agreement and putting the agreement in quantitative, unambiguous terms. This new form of contract can also deal with the impact of creeping user requirements in a way that is agreeable to both parties. As mentioned earlier, the government of Brazil now requires function point metrics for all software contracts.

For major software contracts involving large systems in excess of 10,000 function points independent assessments of progress at key points may also be useful.

As stated, the author of this book has been an expert witness in a dozen breach of contract lawsuits.

The four most common reasons for breach of contract include the following:

1. Optimistic estimates by the vendor before starting.
2. Inadequate quality control and bypassing inspections and static analysis.
3. Inadequate change control in the face of >2% requirements creep per month.
4. Project managers concealing problems from both clients and their own executives.

Outsource contracts are often poorly formed and contain clauses that don't make sense. For example, a contract between a vendor and a State government included a clause that required the vendor to deliver "zero defect" software. This was technically impossible and should not have been in the contract. The vendor should never have agreed to this, and the vendor's lawyer was flirting with professional malpractice to allow such a clause to remain.

Other cases where function points have been useful in deciding the issues include the following:

A Canadian case involved 82 major changes which doubled the size of an application from 10,000 to 20,000 function points. The client refused to pay claiming that the changes were "elaborations" and not new features. The court decided that since function points measure features, the 82 changes were in fact new features and ordered the defendant to pay the vendor.

An arbitration in Hong Kong involved adding 13,000 function points to an application late in development. The contract was a fixed-price contract. Since it is a proven fact that late changes cost more than original work, the vendor was asking for additional fees to recover the higher costs. Following is the author's suggested format for a project status report.

Note that the first topic each month will be a discussion of "red flag" items that might throw off the schedule or costs of the project.

Suggested Format for Monthly Status Reports for Software Projects

1. **Status of last months "red flag" problems**.
2. **New "red flag" problems noted this month**.
3. Change requests processed this month versus change requests predicted.

4. Change requests predicted for next month.
5. Size in function points for this month's change requests.
6. Size in function points predicted for next month's change requests.
7. Schedule impacts of this month's change requests.
8. Cost impacts of this month's change requests.
9. Quality impacts of this month's change requests.
10. Defects found this month versus defects predicted.
11. Defects predicted for next month.
12. Costs expended this month versus costs predicted.
13. Costs predicted for next month.
14. Deliverables completed this month versus deliverables predicted.
15. Deliverables predicted for next month.

Although the suggested format somewhat resembles the items calculated using the earned value method, this format deals explicitly with the impact of change requests and also uses function point metrics for expressing costs and quality data.

An interesting question is the frequency with which milestone progress should be reported. The most common reporting frequency is monthly, although exception reports can be filed at any time that it is suspected that something has occurred that can cause perturbations. For example, serious illness of key project personnel or resignation of key personnel might very well affect project milestone completions and this kind of situation cannot be anticipated.

It might be thought that monthly reports are too far apart for small projects that only last six months or less in total. For small projects, weekly reports might be preferred. However, small projects usually do not get into serious trouble with cost and schedule overruns, whereas large projects almost always get in trouble with cost and schedule overruns. This chapter concentrates on the issues associated with large projects. In the litigation where the author of this book has been an expert witness, every project under litigation except one was larger than 10,000 function points in size.

Daily scrum sessions, while useful and interesting, have no legal standing in the case of litigation. Due to the absence of minutes or notes of what transpired, scrum sessions can make litigation complex.

For outsource projects under contract, a formal status report signed by project managers would be the best technical choice. The author of this book is not an attorney and this should not be construed as legal advice for outsource contracts seek the advice of an attorney on the need for formal written status reports. Table 14.16.3 shows potential costs for the plaintiff for an application of 10,000 function points in size that ends up in breach of contract litigation.

Table 14.16.3   Plaintiff Outsource Litigation Analysis

Project function points	10,000
Consequential damage	**$25,118,864**
Attorney hourly $	$400.00
Paralegal hourly $	$150.00
Expert hourly $	$450.00
Executive hourly $	$200.00
Staff hourly $	$75.00
Planned project duration	34
Probable month of filing	40
Probable trial duration	24
Odds of out of court settlement	**83.00%**
Plaintiff legal fees	$4,000,000
Plaintiff paralegal fees	$1,500,000
Plaintiff expert fees	$337,500
Plaintiff executive costs	$1,500,000
Plaintiff staff costs	$412,500
Total	$7,750,000
Consequential damages per FP	$2,511.89
Litigation $ per FP	$775.00

Table 14.16.4 shows the same 10,000 function point application, but the probable costs for the defendant are shown instead of the plaintiff.

The information in Tables 14.16.1 through 14.16.4 is generic and not based on any specific case. Defendant costs are often higher than those of the plaintiff because the downside of losing a major breach of contract lawsuit can be very expensive indeed.

Once again, the author of this book is not an attorney and is not providing any legal advice. Readers considering litigation for software projects in trouble should seek legal advice from attorneys. But having worked as an expert witness in a number of breach of contract cases, it seems much better to have a good contract before starting and to have

Table 14.16.4   Defendant Litigation Analysis

Project function points	10,000
Damages if suit is lost	**$57,987,729**
Attorney hourly $	$400.00
Paralegal hourly $	$150.00
Expert hourly $	$450.00
Executive hourly $	$200.00
Staff hourly $	$75.00
Planned project duration	34
Probable month of filing	40
Probable trial duration	24
Odds of out of court settlement	**83.00%**
Plaintiff legal fees	$4,800,000
Plaintiff paralegal fees	$1,650,000
Plaintiff expert fees	$495,000
Plaintiff executive costs	$1,700,000
Plaintiff staff costs	$487,500
Total	$9,132,500
Potential $ if suit is lost	**$74,870,228**
Litigation $ per FP	$913.25
$ per FP if suit is lost	$7,487

a successful project outcome. Litigation is costly and time consuming for both parties. The technologies of software are good enough so that almost all projects could be successful if the vendors actually know and use state of the art methods.

For example a way of minimizing the odds of litigation would be to include a clause in outsource contracts that require the outsource vendor to record development defects and a mandate that DRE should top 97% measured by comparing internal defects and customer-reported defects, i.e. the vendor should guarantee that at least 97 out of every 100 bugs were removed. This is technically possible, and high levels of

DRE speed schedules and lower both development and maintenance costs.

Topic 17: Function Points and Venture Funding of Software Startups

Every year there are hundreds of new software companies starting up. Many of these receive funding from venture capitalists. Some of these companies grow to become hugely successful such as Microsoft, Google, and Facebook. However, more than 90% of these software startup companies fail.

A common reason for failure is that the startup companies burn through several rounds of financing because they are late in developing and bringing their product to market. SRM has a standard feature that predicts the development costs and schedules for new software applications. If these applications are venture funded, SRM also has a standard feature for predicting the number of rounds of venture financing needed, as well as the equity dilution for the entrepreneurs.

As an example, the State of Rhode Island acted as a venture capitalist for Curt Schilling's game company, Studio 38. The state did not perform due diligence nor did it realize that more than one round of funding would be needed.

In the aftermath of the Studio 38 bankruptcy, SRM was used to carry out a retroactive post-mortem. SRM predicted an 88% chance of failure for Studio 38. It also predicted that the total amount of funding needed would not just be $75,000,000 for the first release, but instead $206,000,000 would be needed when post-release maintenance and quality control costs were included. These risk and cost predictions took only 7 minutes.

Tables 14.17.1 through 14.17.3 illustrate the risk predictions and venture funding feature for three software applications, all of 1,000 function points in size. Table 14.17.1 shows a best-case scenario with a top-gun team using state of the art methods. Table 14.17.2 shows an average team and average methods. Table 14.17.3 shows an unsophisticated team using unsafe methods. Note that 1,000 function points is fairly small, but not unusual for the first release of a new commercial software package.

The investment cost per function point for the best-case scenario is $919.58 which encompasses both software development and also support functions such as marketing, sales, administration, and management.

Table 14.17.2 shows exactly the same size and type of software application, but developed by an average team.

Table 14.17.1   Risks and Venture Funding for a Top Software Team

Risks		Venture Investment
Cancellation	6.73%	$574,718
Negative ROI	8.52%	**Rounds**
Cost overrun	7.63%	1
Schedule slip	8.97%	**Total Equity**
Unhappy clients	10.32%	$919,548
Litigation	3.14%	**Dilution**
Average Risks	**7.55%**	**41.50%**
Financial Risk	**14.05%**	**Ownership**
		58.50%

Table 14.17.2   Risks and Venture Funding for an Average Software Team

Risks		Venture Investment
Cancellation	11.73%	$1,656,443
Negative ROI	14.86%	**Rounds**
Cost overrun	13.30%	2
Schedule slip	15.64%	**Total Equity**
Unhappy clients	17.99%	$2,815,954
Litigation	5.48%	**Dilution**
Average Risks	**13.17%**	**55.50%**
Financial Risk	**24.50%**	**Ownership**
		44.50%

The investment cost per function point for the average case is $2,815.95. This is the investment needed for the total company including software, marketing, sales, administration, and management. In other words, function points can be applied to software corporate startups if software is the main and only product. The CEOs in this case would be the actual entrepreneurs.

Table 14.17.3 Risks and Venture Funding for a Marginal Software Team

Risks		Venture Investment
Cancellation	17.84%	$6,206,913
Negative ROI	22.60%	**Rounds**
Cost overrun	20.22%	3
Schedule slip	23.79%	**Total Equity**
Unhappy clients	27.36%	$10,551,752
Litigation	8.33%	**Dilution**
Average Risks	**20.02%**	78.00%
Financial Risk	**37.25%**	**Ownership**
		22.00%

Table 14.17.3 shows the risks and venture funding for the same size and type of software project, but with an inexperienced team using marginal methods.

The investment for the worst-case scenario is shocking $10,551.72. It is unlikely that professional venture capitalists would put so much money into such a poorly staffed and organized group. Almost certainly, the funds would stop before the third round and the company would go bankrupt without making their initial delivery.

The early failure of venture-backed software companies is harmful to both the entrepreneurs and to the venture capitalists. Software Risk Master (SRM) can be used prior to any actual investment and show both parties the probable schedules, costs, team size, and quality to bring the first release to market. SRM can also predict post-release enhancements and maintenance of 5 years. It also predicts numbers of bugs that might be released and the customer support costs needed to deal with them.

Topic 18: Function Points for Analysis of Software Occupation Groups

Several years ago, the author of this book was commissioned by AT&T to perform a study on the various kinds of occupation groups employed by large organizations that produced software. Some of the participants in the study included AT&T itself, IBM, Ford Motors, Texas Instruments, the U.S. Navy, and a dozen other somewhat smaller organizations.

The study found a total of 116 different occupations associated with software. No individual project employs all 116, but several large systems in large companies have employed 50 different occupations. In fact for large systems, pure programming may be less than 25% of the total effort.

The study also encountered the following interesting sociological phenomena:

- Not a single Human Resource organization in either corporations or government agencies actually knew how many software personnel were employed. It was necessary to interview unit management to find out.
- A surprising number of engineers building embedded software refused to be called "software engineers" and insisted on their academic titles such as electrical engineer, automotive engineer, aeronautical engineer or whatever it was. The reason for this is because "software engineering" does not have the same professional respect among C level executives as the other forms of engineering.
- Due to the fact that some software personnel refused to be identified as software engineers and no HR group knew software employment, we can assume that the Department of Commerce statistics on U.S. software employment are probably wrong, and wrong by undercounting the engineers who refuse to accept software engineering job descriptions.

One of the many problems with the older "lines of code" or LOC metric is that it cannot be used to measure the performance of business analysts, quality assurance, technical writers, project managers, or any of the 116 occupation groups other than pure programmers.

Function point metrics, on the other hand, can be used to measure the performance of all 116 occupations. There are two key methods for doing this. The first is to use function points to measure the "assignment scope" or the amount of work assigned to one person in a specific occupation. The second is to use function points to measure the "production rate" or the amount of work one person can perform in a given time period such as a calendar month.

Here is a small example just to illustrate the points. Assume the project under development is 1,000 function points in size.

To measure the work of software quality assurance specialists (SQA), assume that the assignment scope is 500 function points. This means that two SQA personnel will be needed for the total application of 1,000 function points.

Assume that the production rate of the two SQA personnel is each 250 function points per calendar month. That means that each SQA person will need two calendar months to complete their analysis of the quality of their portion of the application.

Putting both sets of measures together, the application of 1,000 function points needed 2 SQA personnel who together worked for a total of 4 months. The net productivity for SQA in this case would be 1,000 function points divided by 4 months of effort or 250 function points per staff month. Using the reciprocal measure of work hours per function point, the SQA effort would be 1.89 work hours per function point. Note that these are merely examples to illustrate the math and should not be used for actual estimates.

The main point is that function point metrics are the only available metric that can analyze the contributions of all 116 different occupation groups. Table 14.18 lists the 116 occupations in alphabetical order.

Software engineering is following a similar path as did the older forms of engineering, and for that matter of medicine and law. The path includes more and more granular forms of specialization.

As more different kinds of specialists appear and begin to work on large and complex software applications, pure coding is no longer the major activity. In fact many large applications create more English words by far than they do code, and the costs of the words are much higher. Some military software projects have been measured at creating about 400 English words for every Ada statement!

Function point metrics are useful in analyzing the overall performance of the occupation groups employed on large and complex software systems.

As an example of the diversity of occupations on large software applications, Table 14.19.1 shows the pattern of occupation groups for a very large system of 100,000 function points. Table 14.19 is a standard output from SRM.

Although programmers are the largest occupation group with an average size of 290 personnel, that is only 25.92% of the total personnel employed. Large systems use many occupations.

Topic 19: Data Used by Fortune 500 C-Level Executives

Large corporations in the Fortune 500 class spend between about $1,000,000 and $6,000,000 per year for various kinds of benchmarks.

Table 14.18   Software Specialization Circa 2020

1	Accounting/Financial Specialists
2	Agile coaches
3	Architects (Software)
4	Architects (Systems)
5	Architects (Enterprise)
6	Assessment Specialists
7	Audit Specialists
8	Baldrige Award Specialists
9	Baselining Specialists
10	Benchmarking Specialists
11	Business analysts (BA)
12	Business Process Reengineering (BPR) Specialists
13	Capability Maturity Model Integrated (CMMI) Specialists
14	CASE and tool Specialists
15	Client–Server Specialists
16	CMMI Assessors
17	Complexity Specialists
18	Component Development Specialists
19	Configuration Control Specialists
20	Cost Estimating Specialists
21	Consulting Specialists
22	Curriculum Planning Specialists
23	Customer Liaison Specialists
24	Customer Support Specialists
25	Data Base Administration Specialists
26	Data Center Support Specialists
27	Data quality Specialists
28	Data Warehouse Specialists
29	Decision Support Specialists
30	Development specialists
31	Distributed Systems Specialists

Table 14.18 (Continued)

32	Domain Specialists
33	Earned Value Specialists
34	Education Specialists
35	E-Learning Specialists
36	Embedded Systems Specialists
37	Enterprise Resource Planning (ERP) Specialists
38	Executive Assistants
39	Frame Specialists
40	Expert-System Specialists
41	Function Point Specialists (certified)
42	Generalists (who perform a variety of software-related tasks)
43	Globalization and Nationalization Specialists
44	Graphics Production Specialists
45	Graphical User Interface (GUI) Specialists
46	Human Factors Specialists
47	Information Engineering (IE) Specialists
48	Instructors (Management Topics)
49	Instructors (Software Topics)
50	Integration Specialists
51	Intellectual Property (IP) Specialists
52	Internet specialists
53	ISO Certification Specialists
54	Joint Application Design (JAD) Specialists
55	Kanban Specialists
56	Kaizen Specialists
57	Knowledge specialists
58	Key Process Indicators (KPI) specialists
59	Library Specialists (for project libraries)
60	Litigation support Specialists
61	Maintenance Specialists
62	Marketing Specialists

(Continued)

Table 14.18 (Continued)

63	Member of the Technical Staff (multiple specialties)
64	Measurement Specialists
65	Metric Specialists
66	Microcode Specialists
67	Model Specialists
68	Multi-Media Specialists
69	Network maintenance Specialists
70	Network Specialists (LAN)
71	Network Specialists (WAN)
72	Network Specialists (Wireless)
73	Neural Net Specialists
74	Object-Oriented Specialists
75	Outsource Evaluation Specialists
76	Package Evaluation Specialists
77	Pattern Specialists
78	Performance Specialists
79	Programming Language Specialists (Java, C#, Ruby, PHP, SQL, etc.)
80	Project Cost Analysis Specialists
81	Project managers
82	Project Office Specialists
83	Project Planning Specialists
84	Process Improvement Specialists
85	Productivity Specialists
86	Quality Assurance Specialists
87	Quality function deployment (QFD) Specialists
88	Quality Measurement Specialists
89	Rapid Application Development (RAD) Specialists
90	Research Fellow Specialists
91	Reliability Specialists
92	Repository Specialists
93	Reengineering Specialists

Table 14.18 (Continued)

94	Requirements engineer
95	Reverse engineering Specialists
96	Reusability Specialists
97	Reverse Engineering Specialists
98	Risk Management Specialists
99	Sales Specialists
100	Sales Support Specialists
101	Scrum masters
102	Security Specialists
103	Standards Specialists
104	Systems Analysis Specialists
105	Systems Support Specialists
106	Technical Translation Specialists
107	Technical Writing Specialists
108	Test Case Design Specialists
109	Testing Specialists (Automated)
110	Testing Specialists (Manual)
111	Testing Specialists (Model Driven)
112	Total Quality Management (TQM) Specialists
113	Virtual Reality Specialists
114	Web Development Specialists
115	Web Page Design Specialists
116	Web Masters

Most companies don't actually know their benchmark costs because they are scattered across all operating units. There is no central reporting or consolidation of benchmark cost data. Only consultants who visit a number of business units realize how many different kinds of benchmarks are used in large companies.

- Human resource groups use benchmarks on compensation levels. They also perform internal benchmark studies on morale.
- Legal groups use benchmarks on patent and other forms of litigation.

Table 14.19 Occupation Groups and Part-Time Specialists

(Application size = 100,000 function points)		
	Normal Staff	*Peak Staff*
Programmers	290	434
Testers	256	384
Designers	138	228
Business analysts	138	214
Technical writers	60	84
Quality assurance	51	82
1st line managers	45	63
Data base administration	26	34
Project Office staff	23	31
Administrative support	26	33
Configuration control	15	21
Project librarians	12	17
2nd line managers	9	13
Estimating specialists	9	12
Architects	6	9
Security specialists	3	5
Performance specialists	3	5
Function point counters	3	5
Human factors	3	5
3rd line managers	2	3
Total Staff	**1,119**	**1,680**

- Marketing and sales groups use benchmarks on competitive products and market shares. They also carry out proprietary benchmark studies of customer satisfaction.
- Manufacturing groups use benchmarks on cost per unit and manufacturing speed.
- Computer operation groups use data center benchmarks.
- Engineers use many different kinds of hardware benchmarks.
- Purchasing groups use benchmarks on pricing ranges for standard parts and devices.

- Software groups use benchmarks on productivity, quality, maintenance, and other topics.

Table 14.19.1 summarizes the interest levels in 70 different kinds of benchmarks by a sample of C-level executives (CEO and CFO) from several Fortune 500 companies studied by the author.

This set of corporate benchmark uses many different metrics. However, function point metrics are used for 33 benchmarks out of the total of 70 shown. As of 2013, there was no other metric that was more widely used for software than function point metrics. There is no metric that is more reliable or more accurate for software economic analysis than function point metrics. With more than 50,000 software projects measured using function points, the volume of function point benchmark data is larger than all other metrics combined.

- LOC metrics are useless for requirements and design analysis and they also penalize high-level languages. They are harmful for economic studies covering multiple programming languages.
- Cost per defect penalizes quality and does not measure the value of quality.
- Story points are not standardized and have no major collections of benchmark data.
- Use-case points are useful for applications that use the UML and use-cases, but worthless for other kinds of software.

Function point metrics are the best metric yet developed for understanding software productivity, software quality, and software economics.

Topic 20: Combining Function Points with Other Metrics

Although function point metrics are powerful and have many uses, they are not the only useful metric for software projects. This topic illustrates how function points can be combined with other metrics to improve overall understanding of software quality and software economics.

Function Points and Defect Removal Efficiency (DRE)

Software quality is the weak link of software engineering. In general about 50 cents out of every dollar spent on software goes to finding and fixing bugs. Metrics for evaluating software quality such as "cost

Table 14.19.1 Software Benchmarks Used by Fortune 500 C-Level Executives

	Software Benchmarks	CEO Interest	CFO Interest	Best Metrics Used for Benchmarks
1	Competitive practices within industry	10	10	**$ per function point**
2	Project failure rates (size, methods)	10	10	**Function points**
3	Risks: Software	10	10	**Function points + DRE**
4	Patent litigation and results	10	10	Cases won, lost; specific issues
5	Outsource contract success/failure	10	10	Function points, defect removal
6	Risks: corporate/financial	10	10	Dollars/litigation/competition
7	Risks: Legal	10	10	**Function points, defect removal**
8	Cyber Security attacks (number, type)	10	10	Vulnerabilities; defense
9	Return on investment (ROI)	10	10	**Function points, ROI**
10	Total cost of ownership (TCO)	10	10	**Function points, ROI**
11	Customer satisfaction	10	10	Percentage of satisfied clients
12	Data quality	10	10	Data points (hypothetical)
13	Cost of Quality (COQ)/technical debt	10	10	**Function points, defect removal**
14	Development costs: major projects	10	10	**Function points**
15	Litigation – canceled projects/poor quality	10	10	No standard metrics
16	Litigation – intellectual property	10	10	No standard metrics
17	Portfolio size, maintenance costs	10	10	**Function points**
18	Litigation – breach of contract	10	10	No standard metrics

	Software Benchmarks	CEO Interest	CFO Interest	Best Metrics Used for Benchmarks
19	Software development Benchmarks	9	10	**Function points**
20	Occupation group compensation	9	10	Average $ per occupation
21	ERP installation/customization	9	10	**Function points/data points**
22	Data center benchmarks	9	10	$ per transaction; transactions speed
23	Occupation groups by industry, size	9	10	Occupations by industry
24	Employee morale	10	9	Percentage of satisfied workers
25	Team compensation level	10	9	Compensation by occupation
26	Attrition by occupation, size, industry	10	9	Attrition % by job title
27	CMMI assessments within organization	9	9	Key process indicators (KPI)
28	Customer support benchmarks	9	9	Customers served per time unit
29	Enhancement costs	8	10	**Function points**
30	Skills inventories by occupation	8	9	Skill list
31	Best Practices – maintenance	8	9	**Function points**
32	Maintenance costs (annual)	8	9	**Function points, defect removal**
33	Data base size	9	8	Data points (hypothetical_
34	Industry productivity	10	7	**Function points**
35	Team morale	9	8	Percentage by occupation group
36	ISO standards certification	9	7	No standard metrics

(Continued)

Table 14.19.1 (Continued)

	Software Benchmarks	CEO Interest	CFO Interest	Best Metrics Used for Benchmarks
37	Productivity – project	8	8	Function points
38	Technical debt	8	8	Function points, defect removal
39	Application sizes by type	8	8	Function points
40	Best Practices – requirements	6	9	Function points
41	Team attrition rates	7	8	Percentage by job title
42	Best Practices – test efficiency	8	7	Function points, defect removal
43	Coding speed in LOC	7	8	Lines of code (LOC)
44	Litigation – employment contracts	7	8	No standard metrics
45	Code quality (only code – nothing else)	7	7	Lines of code (LOC)
46	Application types	7	7	Taxonomy
47	Cost per defect (caution: unreliable)	6	7	Cost per defect; cost per FP
48	Software maintenance/serviceability	6	7	Function points/complexity
49	Hardware performance benchmarks	6	7	MIPS
50	Country productivity	8	5	Function points
51	Best Practices – pre-test defects	6	6	Function points, defect removal
52	Earned value (EVA)	5	7	Function points
53	Best Practices – defect prevention	5	6	Function points, defect prevention
54	Methodologies: Agile, RUP, TSP, etc.	5	6	Function points

	Software Benchmarks	CEO Interest	CFO Interest	Best Metrics Used for Benchmarks
55	Methodology comparisons	5	6	**Function points**
56	CMMI levels within industries	6	5	Percentage by CMMI levels
57	Test coverage benchmarks	5	6	Requirements, control flow coverage
58	Best Practices - design	5	5	**Function points**
59	Productivity - activity	4	6	**Function points/activities**
60	Standards benchmarks	5	5	**Function points, defect removal**
61	DCUT benchmarks: function points	3	7	**Function points**
62	Application class by taxonomy	4	5	Taxonomy
63	Serviceability benchmarks	4	5	Maintenance assignment scope
64	Tool suites used	4	4	**Function points by tool types**
65	SNAP non- functional size metrics	3	4	**SNAP plus normal function points**
66	Metrics used by company	3	3	Percentage by metric
67	Programming Languages used	3	3	Language levels
68	Certification benchmarks	3	3	**Function points, defect removal**
69	DCUT benchmarks: LOC	1	2	Logical code statements
70	Cyclomatic complexity benchmarks	1	1	Cyclomatic complexity

per defect" have been inaccurate and fail to show true quality economics. Quality metrics such as "defects per KLOC" ignore requirements and design defects, which outnumber code defects for large software systems.

Function point metrics combined with DRE provide the strongest and most accurate set of quality metrics yet developed. DRE is combined with a function-point value called "defect potential" or the total numbers of bugs that are likely to be found. Here too this metric originated in IBM in the early 1970's. In fact the author of this book was on one of the original IBM teams that created this metric and collected data from internal projects.

The DRE metric was developed in IBM in the early 1970s at the same time IBM was developing formal inspections. In fact this metric was used to prove the efficiency of formal inspections compared to testing by itself.

The concept of DRE is to keep track of all bugs found by the development teams and then compare those bugs to post-release bugs reported by customers in a fixed time period of 90 days after the initial release.

If the development team found 900 bugs prior to release and customer reported 100 bugs in the first 3 months, then the total volume of bugs was an even 1,000 so DRE is 90%. This combination is simple in concept and powerful in impact.

The U.S. average for DRE is just a bit over 85%. Testing alone is not sufficient to raise DRE much above 90%. To approach or exceed 99% in DRE, it is necessary to use a synergistic combination of pre-test static analysis and inspections combined with formal testing using mathematically designed test cases, ideally created by certified test personnel. DRE can also be applied to defects found in other materials such as requirements and design. Table 14.20 illustrates current ranges for defect potentials and DRE levels in the United States for applications in the 1,000 function point size range.

Predictions of defect potentials and DRE levels are standard features of SRM. In fact not only are they standard, but they are also patent-pending features.

Function Points and Natural Metrics such as "Document Pages"

A function point is a synthetic metric comprised of five elements that are essentially invisible to the human eye or at least hard to see without close examination: inputs, outputs, inquiries, logical files, and interfaces.

Table 14.20   Function Points and Defect Removal Efficiency (DRE)

Defect Origins	Defects per Function Point	Defect Removal Efficiency (DRE)	Delivered Defects per Function Point
Best Case			
Requirements	0.50	98.00%	0.01
Design	0.60	98.00%	0.01
Code	0.80	99.50%	0.00
User documents	0.40	99.00%	0.00
Bad Fixes	0.20	98.00%	0.00
Total	**2.50**	**98.64%**	**0.03**
Average Case			
Requirements	1.00	75.00%	0.25
Design	1.25	87.00%	0.16
Code	1.75	95.50%	0.08
User documents	0.60	91.00%	0.05
Bad Fixes	0.40	78.00%	0.09
Total	**5.00**	**87.34%**	**0.63**
Worst Case			
Requirements	1.50	70.00%	0.45
Design	2.00	80.00%	0.40
Code	2.50	92.00%	0.20
User documents	1.00	85.00%	0.15
Bad Fixes	0.75	68.00%	0.24
Total	**7.75**	**81.42%**	**1.44**

A natural metric is a count of visible objects that are easy to see and in many cases can even be touched and examined using many senses. A prime example of a natural metric for software applications is "pages of documentation."

Software applications are highly paper driven. In fact some defense software projects create more than 100 document types containing more than 1,400 English words for every Ada statement. The cost of the words is greater than the costs of the code itself.

One of the interesting attributes of agile software development is a sharp reduction in paperwork volumes for requirements and design, due to having embedded users. Of course even agile cannot reduce paperwork for FDA or FAA certification, or for large defense contracts where production of various paper documents are contractually mandated.

Documentation is often produced in multiple languages. For example, in Canada both French and English are required. For commercial products marketed globally, user documents may need to be translated into 20 languages or more. Translation used to be a major cost element but automatic translation tools such as Google translate have lowered the cost.

Software documents are also major sources of error. Software requirements average about 1.0 defects per function point and design about 1.25 defects per function point. Summed together requirements and design defects often outnumber code defects, which average about 1.75 per function point.

Function point metrics are very useful for quantifying both the sizes of the various documents and also their costs for creation and updates. Document sizing using function point metrics is a standard feature of SRM. This feature might have been patented when it was first developed, but the mathematics for sizing documents using function points was created by the author of this book in the 1970s and hence is considered to be prior art. Table 14.20.1 illustrates a subset of total documentation for a major system of 10,000 function points in size.

Table 14.20.1 only illustrates a sample of major document types. The full set of documents is too large for this chapter. Over and above the normal documentation shown in Table 14.20.1, quite a few special kinds of documents are needed for software projects that require FDA or FAA certification. Paperwork is a major software cost driver and function points are the best metric for quantifying both paperwork volumes and paperwork costs.

When you narrow the focus to a specific type of document, such as requirements, function point normalization reveals some important issues that could not easily be studied. Table 14.20.2 shows requirements for applications ranging in size from 10 to 100,000 function points.

As projects grow in size, requirements soon become too big for one person to read and understand. For a major system of 100,000 function points, it would take 600 work days to read the requirements, and nobody could understand more than about 2% of them. This is why segmentation into smaller components is needed for major systems.

Table 14.20.1 Function Points for Document Prediction

(Application of 10,000 function points in size)					
Document Sizes	*Pages*	*Pages per Funct. Pt.*	*English Words*	*English Words per Funct. Pt.*	*Percent Complete*
Requirements	2,126	0.21	850,306	85.03	73.68%
Architecture	376	0.04	150,475	15.05	78.63%
Initial design	2,625	0.26	1,049,819	104.98	68.71%
Detail design	5,118	0.51	2,047,383	204.74	75.15%
Test plans	1,158	0.12	463,396	46.34	68.93%
Development Plans	550	0.06	220,000	22.00	76.63%
Cost estimates	376	0.04	150,475	15.05	79.63%
User manuals	2,111	0.21	844,500	84.45	85.40%
HELP text	1,964	0.20	785,413	78.54	86.09%
Courses	1,450	0.15	580,000	58.00	85.05%
Status reports	996	0.10	398,205	39.82	78.63%
Change requests	2,067	0.21	826,769	82.68	78.68%
Bug reports	11,467	1.15	4,586,978	458.70	81.93%
Total	**32,384**	**3.24**	**12,953,720**	**1,295.37**	**78.24%**

Table 14.20.2 Initial Requirements Size and Completeness

Function Points	*Require Pages*	*Pages per Funct. Pt.*	*Complete Percent*	*Days to Read*	*Amount Understood*	*Require Defects*
10	6	0.60	100.00%	0.10	100%	4
100	40	0.40	99.00%	0.68	100%	26
1,000	275	0.28	91.34%	5.02	93%	171
10,000	2,126	0.21	73.68%	48.09	13%	1,146
100,000	19,500	0.20	31.79%	600.00	2%	7,657

There are three key points for large software projects: (1) paperwork is often the most expensive item produced on large software projects; (2) some paper documents such as requirements and design contain many errors or defects that need to be included in quality studies; (3) function point metrics are the most effective metric for sizing documents and studying document creation costs, as well as defects or bugs found in various documents.

For a 10,000 function point software application, the U.S. average is about 10.43 pages per function points; 2,607 English words per function point. Total documentation costs are $783.86 per function point which comprises 24.30% of the total application development costs. Defects in requirements and design would top 2.25 per function point which is larger than code defects of about 1.75 defects per function point.

Function Points and Goal Question Metrics (GQM)

The goal, question, metric approach was developed by Dr. Victor Basili of the University of Maryland. It has become a useful and popular approach. The essential concept is to start with defining a business goal, then develop questions about how the goal might be approached, and then develop metrics that can measure the approach to the goal.

In its original form, the GQM approach was highly individual and each company or application might have its own set of goals. However since software projects have been studied for more than 50 years, they have a known set of major problems that would allow a standard set of goals and questions to be developed. Function point metrics are congruent with and can be used with many of these standard software goals. A few examples of common problems and related goals are as follows:

- Reduce requirements creep >0.5% per calendar month from today's rate of >2.0% per calendar month.
- Reduce software defect potentials from >5.00 defects per function point to <2.50 defects per function point.
- Raise software DRE up >99% from today's value of <86%.
- Improve customer satisfaction for released software to >97% "satisfied" from today's value of <80% satisfied.
- Reduce software development costs to < $400 per function point from today's average value of > $1,000 per function point.
- Reduce annual maintenance costs to < $50 per function point from today's average value of > $125 per function point.

- Reduce cancellation rates for applications >10,000 function points to <1% from today's rate of >15%.

These are general goals that deal with common software problems that occur with high frequency. There may also be unique and specific goals for individual projects, but all of the goals shown above probably need to be addressed for every major software project.

Function Points and Earned Value Analysis (EVA)

The earned-value method originated in the 1960s and has become a popular approach with its own professional association. EVA is used on many government and defense projects including both software and hardware. EVA is a large and complex topic, and this chapter only shows how function points can be congruent with other EVA measures.

The essence of EVA is that prior to starting a major project, a development plan is created that shows progress of specific deliverables on a timeline. This is called Planned Value or PV. As the project gets under way costs and results are tracked. Successful completion is called Earned Value of EV. If the project is running late or spending more than anticipated, the curves for PV and EV will draw apart, indicating that corrective actions are needed.

For software EVA is not a perfect tool because it omits quality, which is both a major cost driver for software and the #1 reason for schedule delays. A modified form of EVA for software would combine standard EVA tracking with an additional set of quality reports that compared planned defect removal efficiency (PDRE) with actual defect removal efficiency (ADRE). For example if the defect estimate for function test predicted 100 bugs and only 50 were found, it was due to the fact that quality was better than expected or due to the fact that DRE was lower than expected?

Companies such as IBM with good defect prediction tools and sophisticated defect removal methods can easily modify EVA to include quality cost drivers. The current versions of SRM predict defects found by every form of removal activity including requirements and design inspections, static analysis, code inspections, and 18 different forms of testing. Independent verification and validation (IV&V) is also predicted for defense projects that require it.

Another use of function points in an EVA context would be to divide applications into discrete components. For example, an application of 1,000 function points in size might be segmented into 10 components of

100 function points. Each component would be an EVA unit that could be inserted into standard EVA calculations.

Function Points, Story Points, and Velocity on Agile Projects

Function point metrics are not widely used on Agile projects, in part because manual counting of function points is too slow and expensive to fit the Agile philosophy. Many agile projects use story points as an alternate metric, and they use velocity as a tool for predicting completion of stories in a specific time period such as a week or a month.

The high-speed sizing method of SRM which sizes applications in about 1.8 minutes is a good match to the agile philosophy. To facilitate use by agile projects, SRM can also do bi-directional conversion between story points and use-case points. It can also predict velocity.

As a small example, assume an application of 1,000 function points is being built using the agile methodology. That is roughly equivalent to 556 story points, assuming each user story encompasses about 2 function points. SRM predicts a total of 6 sprints for this project, each of which would last about 2.38 months. In total, there would probably be about 71 scrum meetings. Each sprint would develop about 92 stories. Velocity would be about 39 stories per month.

Since SRM also has a very precise measurement mode, these predictions could be measured and changed by examining many agile projects. This is needed since unlike function points there is no certification for counting user stories and no ISO standard for what story points encompass. Among the author's clients, story points vary by about 3 to 1 in contents. The bottom line is that function points can easily be added to the set of methods used by agile projects now that they can be calculated in only a few minutes. They would not replace story points but they would allow agile projects to be compared against large data bases such as those maintained by the International Software Benchmark Standards Group (ISBSG).

Function Points and Return on Investment (ROI)

For CEOs and other kinds of C-level executives, return on investment or ROI is the top concern for every form of product development including software projects. The oldest methods of calculating ROI include accounting rates of return and internal rates of return. Newer methods include economic value added (EVA), return on assets (ROA), return on infrastructure employed (ROIE), and real options valuation (ROV). An interesting book that discusses these topics in a software context is *The Business Value of IT* by Michael Harris, David Herron, and Stasia Iwanicki. An older book that also contains useful value data is *Software Project Management, A Unified Framework*, by Walker Royce.

In general, software applications provide value in one of the following three distinct fashions:

1. The software lowers operational costs and improves worker performance.
2. The software is marketed and generates both direct and indirect revenue streams.
3. The software provides intangible value such as aiding medical science or improving national security against external attack.

Since this chapter is concerned with using function point metrics to demonstrate software economic value, only the first two methods will be discussed; operational efficiency and revenue generation.

Case 1: Software Improves Operational Performance

Let us assume that an insurance company is building a claims management system that will improve claims handling by 20% compared to current methods.

Assume that the software is 10,000 function points in size and was developed at a cost of $1,000 per function point or $10,000,000 in total.

Assume the insurance company employees 1,000 claims agents, and their compensation is $60,000 per year or a total of $60,000,000 per year.

A 20% improvement in agent performance will generate cost savings of $12,000,000 per year. If you assume that the internal time horizon for calculating ROI is 5 years, then the application would save $60,000,000 for a cost of $10,000,000. The simple ROI of the project would be $6.00 for every $1.00.

This is not necessarily an exciting ROI but it is good enough for the company to fund the project. Using function point metrics, the development cost of the application was $1,000 per function point, and the value of the application over a 5-year period was $6,000 per function point.

This is a simple case to illustrate that function points are useful in value analysis. In real life maintenance, inflation, changes in numbers of workers, and many other factors would need to be included.

For example after the 20% annual increase in performance, the company might decide to downsize claims agents and lay off 10% of the staff or 100 agents. This would change the long-range value calculations. Alternatively, the company's business might increase by 20% so the full current staff is still needed.

Case 2: Software Generates Direct and Indirect Revenues Streams

In this case, let us assume that a new commercial software vendor funded by venture capital plans to bring out a new application that they expect will be used by many consumers or customers. Let us assume that the application is 1,000 function points in size and will be built at a cost of $1,000 per function point or $1,000,000 in total.

However since the company is new and venture funded, an additional $1,000,000 will be needed to fund marketing, sales, and management. A third $1,000,000 will be needed to fund the advertising rollout for the application, i.e. the venture investment is $3,000,000 or $3,000 per function point.

The company assumes that this application will be acquired by 1,000,000 customers per year at a cost of $100 per copy or $100,000,000 per year in direct revenues.

The company also assumes that 50% of the customers will request training in the application, which will be offered for $200 per client. Here too the annual revenues will be $100,000,000.

IF the project is delivered on time and meets expectations, annual revenues will be $200,000,000.

This case has the following caveats that need to be considered carefully:

- If the application is delivered one month early, it might generate additional revenues of more than $16,000,000 for that month.
- If the application is delivered one month late, it might lose revenues of more than $16,000,000 for the month.
- If the quality of the application is poor and DRE is below 90%, then potential sales will be reduced by 75%.
- If the quality of the application is high and DRE is above 97%, then potential sales will be increased by 25%.
- If the product is initially successful within a year, "fast followers" will be offering similar products. The time line for zero competition is a very narrow band.

Venture capital horizons are normally only three years so let us consider what might occur in terms of value over a three-year period.

The **best-case scenario** is that by means of effective development utilizing inspections, static analysis, and formal testing, the application is delivered 1 month early and has a measured DRE level of 98%. Post-release maintenance will cost $500,000 per year.

In this case, annual revenues will be $250,000,000 per year plus the extra $16,000,000 for being early. The three-year revenue stream would total to $786,000,000 which is $786,000 per function point.

When the initial venture investment is $3,000 per function point plus three years of maintenance total to $4,500,000. When this is compared to the three-year revenue stream, the ROI is $175 for every $1.00 invested. This kind of ROI is the hope of every entrepreneur and every venture capitalist.

For the best-case scenario, the total venture investment was $4,500 per function point and the revenue stream amounted to $786,000 per function point. The entrepreneurs are on their way to billionaire status. Patents and aggressive patent litigation keep fast followers at bay.

The **worst-case scenario** is that the company is inept in software development and tries to deliver early by bypassing pre-test static analysis and inspections to save time. Instead of saving time, the application is so buggy when test begins that the testing cycle stretches out for an extra 6 months so the application lost $96,000,000 in first year revenues.

Cumulative DRE is a dismal 83%. Not only that but another round of venture funding is needed bringing the total investment to $6,000,000. Post-release maintenance on all of the delivered bugs cost $5,000,000 per year.

Due to shipping late and having poor quality, the total revenues for three years are only $125,000,000. Between the initial investment of $6,000,000 and annual maintenance costs of $5,000,000 per year, the three-year costs for this case are $21,000,000.

If you divide the revenues of $125,000,000 by the costs of $21,000,000, the ROI for the project is positive but only $5.95 for every dollar invested. This low ROI is actually below the level that most venture funds would invest in.

The three-year costs totaled to an alarming $21,000 per function point. The revenue stream was only $125,000 per function point. While the company managed to stay in business for three years, which is rare for venture-funded software companies, it is obvious that poor quality is reducing market share and raising maintenance costs to unacceptable levels.

Worse, the basic idea of the product attracted the attention of "fast followers" who bring out similar products with extra features at lower cost and better quality. As a result, revenues erode and market share plummets.

Within two years, the initial product generated only $10,000,000 per year in revenues with expenses of $10,000,000 due to poor quality. The company goes bankrupt in year 5 while the leading fast follower establishes a strong new market for the basic idea and soon becomes a billion-dollar company.

The essential point is that function point metrics are useful in value analysis, but in order to optimize value and make software appealing to CEOs, other C-level executives, and to the venture capital community, the software organization needs to understand effective development practices and also software economics.

Partial measures such as "design, code, and unit test" or DCUT have no place in economic value analysis, nor do inaccurate measures such as "lines of code" (LOC), and "cost per defect." Leakage or failing to measure 100% of development costs should also be avoided.

The recent "technical debt" metric is an interesting and useful metaphor, but woefully incomplete. As currently defined by a majority of users, "technical debt" only covers about 17% of the total cost of poor quality.

Technical debt omits the costs of software projects whose quality is so bad they are canceled and never released. Even more serious, technical debt omits the costs of litigation and damages against vendors who are sued for poor quality and lose the lawsuits. The costs of litigation and damage can be larger than normal "technical debt" costs by more than 1,000 to 1.

For that matter, expensive and ineffective development methods such as pair programming should be avoided. Pair programming more than doubles software costs at no tangible improvement in schedules, quality, or application value.

Function point metrics can be applied to software size, software development, software documentation, software quality, software maintenance, software outsource contracts, and software venture capital investment. No other software metric has such a wide range of usefulness.

Summary and Conclusions

Function point metrics are the most powerful metrics yet developed for studies of software economics, productivity, risks, and quality. They are much better than older metrics such as "lines of code" and "cost per defect." They are also much better than alternate metrics such as "story points" and "use-case points."

However, the slow speed and high costs of manual function point analysis has caused function points to be viewed by top-executives such as CEOs as a minor niche metric. In order to be useful to C level executives, function point metrics need the following:

1. Faster counting by more than an order of magnitude from today's averages.
2. Lower costs down below $0.05 per function point counted.
3. Methodology benchmarks for all known methods.
4. Quality benchmarks for defect prevention, pre-test removal, and testing.
5. Maintenance, enhancement, and TCO benchmarks.
6. Portfolio benchmarks for many companies and government groups.
7. Industry benchmarks for all software-intensive industries.
8. Global benchmarks for all countries that produce software in large volumes.

This chapter discusses a patent-pending method of sizing software projects in less than 2 minutes, with function points as one of the default metrics produced. SRM produces development estimates in about 3 minutes; quality estimates in 4 minutes; and maintenance estimates in 4 minutes.

The SRM tool can do more than size. The SRM tool can also predict the results and risks of any methodology, any level of team experience, any CMMI level, and programming language (or combination), and any volume of reusable materials.

Function point metrics might well become the global standard for software economic analysis once they can be applied to large systems >10,000 function points; use full activity-based costs instead of partial project data; are applied to portfolios which might contain thousands of applications and millions of function points; and to industry and national software comparisons. There are no other metrics that are as effective as function points for software economic analysis.

References and Readings

Jones, Capers; "A Short History of Lines of Code Metrics"; Namcook Analytics Technical Report; Narragansett, RI; 2012a.

This report provides a mathematical proof that "lines of code" metrics violate standard economic assumptions. LOC metrics make requirements and design invisible. Worse, LOC metrics penalize high-level languages. The report asserts that LOC should be deemed professional malpractice if used to compare results between different programming languages. There are other legitimate purposes for LOC, such as merely measuring coding speed.

Jones, Capers; "A Short History of the Cost Per Defect Metrics"; Namcook Analytics Technical Report; Narragansett, RI; 2012b.

This report provides a mathematical proof that "cost per defect" penalizes quality and achieves its lowest values for the buggiest software applications. It also points out that the urban legend that "cost per defect after release is 100 times larger than early elimination" is not true. The reason for expansion of cost per defect for down-stream defect repairs is due to ignoring fixed costs. The cost per defect metric also ignores many economic topics such as the fact that high quality leads to shorter schedules.

Jones, Capers: "Sizing Up Software"; *Scientific American Magazine*; Vol. 279, No. 6, December 1998; pp. 104–111.

Jones, Capers; "Early Sizing and Early Risk Analysis"; Capers Jones & Associates LLC; Narragansett, RI; July 2011.

Jones, Capers; and Bonsignour, Olivier; *The Economics of Software Quality*; Addison Wesley Longman, Boston, MA; 2011; ISBN: 10-0-13-258220-1; 585 pages.

Jones, Capers; *Software Engineering Best Practices*; McGraw Hill, New York, NY; 2010; ISBN: 978-0-07-162161-8; 660 pages.

Jones, Capers; *Applied Software Measurement*; McGraw Hill, New York, NY; 2008; ISBN: 978-0-07-150244-3; 662 pages.

Jones, Capers; *Estimating Software Costs*; McGraw Hill, New York, NY; 2007a; ISBN: 13: 978-0-07-148300-1.

Jones, Capers; *Software Assessments, Benchmarks, and Best Practices*; Addison Wesley Longman, Boston, MA; 2000; ISBN: 0-201-48542-7; 657 pages.

Jones, Capers; *Conflict and Litigation Between Software Clients and Developers*; Software Productivity Research, Inc., Burlington, MA; September 2007b; 53 pages; (SPR technical report).

Additional Literature

The literature on function point metrics is quite extensive. Following are some of the more useful books:

Abran, Alain; *Software Estimating Models*; Wiley-IEEE Computer Society; 2015.

Abran, Alain; *Software Metrics and Metrology*; Wiley-IEEE Computer Society; 2010.

Abran, Alain; *Software Maintenance Management: Evolution and Continuous Improvement*; Wiley-IEEE Computer Society; 2008.

Abran, Alain; and Dumke, Reiner R; *Innovations in Software Measurement*; Shaker-Verlag, Aachen, DE; 2005; ISBN: 3-8322-4405-0; 456 pages.

Abran, Alain; Bundschuh, Manfred; Dumke, Reiner; Ebert, Christof; and Zuse, Horst; *Software Measurement News*; Vol. 13, No. 2; October 2008 (periodical).

Bundschuh, Manfred; and Dekkers, Carol; *The IT Measurement Compendium*; Springer-Verlag, Berlin, DE; 2008; ISBN: 978-3-540-68187-8; 642 pages.

Chidamber, S.R.; and Kemerer, C.F.; "A Metrics Suite for Object-Oriented Design"; *IEEE Transactions on Software Engineering*; Vol. SE20, No. 6; June 1994; pp. 476–493.

Dumke, Reiner; Braungarten, Rene; Büren, Günter; Abran, Alain; and Cuadrado-Gallego, Juan J. (editors); *Software Process and Product Measurement*; Springer-Verlag, Berlin; 2008; ISBN: 10-3-540-89402-0; 361 pages.

Ebert, Christof; and Dumke, Reiner; *Software Measurement: Establish, Extract, Evaluate, Execute*; Springer-Verlag, Berlin, DE; 2007; ISBN: 978-3-540-71648-8; 561 pages.

Gack, Gary; *Managing the Black Hole: The Executives Guide to Software Project Risk*; Business Expert Publishing, Thomson, GA; 2010; ISBN: 10: 1-935602-01-9.

Gack, Gary; *Applying Six Sigma to Software Implementation Projects*; http://software.isixsigma.com/library/content/c040915b.asp.

Galorath, Dan; and Evans, Michael; *Software Sizing, Estimation, and Risk Management*; Auerbach Publications, Boca Raton, FL; 2006.

Garmus, David; and Herron, David; *Measuring the Software Process: A Practical Guide to Functional Measurement*; Prentice Hall, Englewood Cliffs, NJ; 1995.

Garmus, David; and Herron, David; *Function Point Analysis – Measurement Practices for Successful Software Projects*; Addison Wesley Longman, Boston, MA; 2001; ISBN: 0-201-69944-3; 363 pages.

Gilb, Tom; and Graham, Dorothy; *Software Inspections*; Addison Wesley, Reading, MA; 1993; ISBN: 10-0201631814.

Harris, Michael D.S., Herron, David; and Iwanicki, Stasia; *The Business Value of IT*; CRC Press, Auerbach, Boca Raton, FL; 2008; ISBN: 978-14200-6474-2.

International Function Point Users Group (IFPUG); *IT Measurement – Practical Advice from the Experts*; Addison Wesley Longman, Boston, MA; 2002; ISBN: 0-201-74158-X; 759 pages.

Kemerer, C.F.; "Reliability of Function Point Measurement – A Field Experiment"; *Communications of the ACM*; Vol. 36; 1993; pp. 85–97.

Parthasarathy, M.A.; *Practical Software Estimation – Function Point Metrics for Insourced and Outsourced Projects*; Infosys Press, Addison Wesley, Upper Saddle River, NJ; 2007; ISBN: 0-321-43910-4.

Putnam, Lawrence H.; *Measures for Excellence – Reliable Software on Time, Within Budget*; Yourdon Press—Prentice Hall, Englewood Cliffs, NJ; 1992; ISBN: 0-13-567694-0; 336 pages.

Putnam, Lawrence H.; and Myers, Ware; *Industrial Strength Software - Effective Management Using Measurement*; IEEE Press, Los Alamitos, CA; 1997; ISBN: 0-8186-7532-2; 320 pages.

Royce, Walker; *Software Project Management – Unified Framework*; Addison Wesley, Boston, MA; 1999.

Stein, Timothy R.; *The Computer System Risk Management Book and Validation Life Cycle*; Paton Press, Chico, CA; 2006; ISBN: 10-1-9328-09-5; 576 pages.

Stutzke, Richard D.; *Estimating Software-Intensive Systems*; Addison Wesley, Upper Saddle River, NJ; 2005; ISBN: 0-201-70312-2; 918 pages.

Index

Page numbers in **bold** refer to table; page numbers followed by 'n' refer to notes number.

Printed in the United States
by Baker & Taylor Publisher Services